THE RIVER POLLUTION DILEMMA
IN VICTORIAN ENGLAND

Modern Economic and Social History Series

General Editor: Derek H. Aldcroft

Titles in this series include:

The River Pollution Dilemma in Victorian England

Nuisance Law versus Economic Efficiency

LESLIE ROSENTHAL
Keele University, UK

Routledge
Taylor & Francis Group

LONDON AND NEW YORK

First published 2014 by Ashgate Publishing

2 Park Square, Milton Park, Abingdon, Oxon OX14 4RN
711 Third Avenue, New York, NY 10017, USA

Routledge is an imprint of the Taylor & Francis Group, an informa business

First issued in paperback 2016

British Library Cataloguing in Publication Data
A catalogue record for this book is available from the British Library

The Library of Congress has cataloged the printed edition as follows:
Rosenthal, Leslie, Dr.
   The River Pollution Dilemma in Victorian England: Nuisance Law Versus Economic Efficiency / by Leslie Rosenthal.
      pages   cm. – (Modern Economic and Social History)
   Includes bibliographical references and index.
   1. Water – Pollution – Law and legislation – Great Britain. 2. Environmental policy – Great Britain – Cases. 3. Environmental policy – Great Britain – History. I. Title.
   KD3375.R67 2014
   344.4104'6343–dc23   2013031422

ISBN 978-1-4094-4182-3 (hbk)
ISBN 978-1-138-24618-8 (pbk)

To Harriet

Contents

Contents

List of Maps

List of Maps

Modern Economic and Social History Series
General Editor's Preface

Economic and social history has been a flourishing subject of scholarly study during recent decades. Not only has the volume of literature increased enormously but the range of interest in time, space and subject matter has broadened considerably so that today there are many sub-branches of the subject which have developed considerable status in their own right.

One of the aims of this series is to encourage the publication of scholarly monographs on any aspect of modern economic and social history. The geographical coverage is world-wide and contributions on the non-British themes will be especially welcome. While emphasis will be placed on works embodying original research, it is also intended that the series should provide the opportunity to publish studies of a more general thematic nature which offer a reappraisal or critical analysis of major issues of debate.

Derek H. Aldcroft
University of Leicester

Preface and Acknowledgements

For stimulating and generating the initial interest and ideas which led to this book, I am indebted to the happy accident of being asked at short notice to teach an academic course in 'law and economics'. As a result, I became increasingly curious about the actual post-litigation course of events which would have followed the court hearings of the individual civil law cases put forward as examples, but empirical detail on these outcomes seemed elusive. I was especially interested by the circumstances of a Victorian sewage pollution dispute in England, at Birmingham, where it seemed a real dilemma had been posed by the conflicting sanitary needs of the rapidly changing urban society of the time and the existing requirements of the English civil law concerning nuisance. For Birmingham, and then for other similar cases, it became increasingly intriguing to discover the empirical detail about 'what happened next.' The results of pursuing this enquiry into the history, context and outcomes of these river pollution cases, at Birmingham and elsewhere, you will find in the pages that follow. I greatly enjoyed the searching out and gathering of the evidence, and discovering the (unexpected) presence among it of Victorian luminaries like Charles Dickens, Michael Faraday and William Ewart Gladstone.

My research for this book has fundamentally depended upon the availability of original documentation held in public archives. I am grateful for the assistance offered by staff at the National Archives at Kew; Oxfordshire Record Office at Oxford; Barnsley Archive and Local Studies Centre at Barnsley Library; Birmingham City Archives at the Central Library, Birmingham; Staffordshire Record Office at Stafford; Warwickshire County Record Office at Warwick; Harrogate Library; Greater Manchester County Record Office; the West Yorkshire Archive Service at Leeds and Wakefield; Northamptonshire Record Office at Northampton; the Tunbridge Wells Archives at the Royal Tunbridge Wells Museum and Art Gallery; and Wolverhampton City Archives at Wolverhampton. For their responses to specific queries I would like to thank: Ian Beavis and Anne Harris at Tunbridge Wells, Diane Huntingford at Tonbridge, Lyndon Cave at Leamington Spa, Geoff Deighton of the Bilton Historical Society, Pam Clarke of the Westhoughton Local History Group, and Joan Topping of the Hindley and District History Society. Thanks are also extended to the British Academy for a grant (under SG51126) that provided for visits to consult local and national archives and to Keele University for access to important informational sources.

I am grateful for the ideas, help and encouragement provided by friends and colleagues: I thank Elisabeth Carter, Ray Cocks, Alison Cornes, Richard Cornes, Brian Doherty, Jenny Hartley, Roger Hartley, Gauthier Lanot, Peter Lawrence, Frank Stephen, Julie Thompson, Jay Weiser and Tim Worrell. Special thanks go to Phil Catney who insisted the research deserved a formal framework and to

Rosemary O'Kane who read and encouraged me through various versions. Any remaining errors are entirely my own responsibility. Most of all, I am ever thankful to my family, Rosemary and Harriet Rosenthal, for their love and their tolerant listening to my 'tales of the sewers.'

Leslie Rosenthal
Alsager, Spring 2013.

Chapter 1

Introduction: The River Pollution Dilemma

The river pollution dilemma was a seemingly intractable problem involving towns and civil courts in England during the nineteenth century. It arose as the industrial revolution in Britain brought new circumstances, generating new difficulties regarding town sewage and the increased levels of sewage effluent appearing in Britain's rivers. Both the background to the dilemma and the dilemma itself can be described quite simply. In the Victorian era, increasing urbanisation was bringing larger and larger populations together into bigger and bigger towns. New ideas and approaches for improving health and sanitation for these urban populations were emerging based on the provision and facilities of a water carriage system: new improved engineering would first bring clean fresh water supplies to urban homes and industry, and then would circulate through sewer networks to carry away the domestic excreta, waste and effluvia that were viewed as direct causes of disease and fever. For non-coastal towns, however, most often wastewater from the sewers was simply discharged or spilled into the rivers and streams of the countryside and often overwhelmed the natural processes of the waterways to noxious and nauseous effect. The sanitation of the towns, it seemed, required the despoiling of the countryside. No available treatment could be relied upon to treat the sewage effectively enough to avoid gross pollution of the rivers and the environs through which the rivers passed: a technological solution would not begin to become available before the twentieth century began.

But rural landowners were not helpless against the actions of town authorities in such matters. Precedent and tradition within English law held, and continue to hold, that landholders have legal rights to enjoy their property and associated running waters free from interference from others: absolutely protected by civil law rules relating to *nuisance*. The highest courts of the land might be approached in defence of these landowner rights and powerful judicial orders, backed by all the forces of the court, are available to successful complainants. In particular, these rights are not challengeable by appeals that greater good, for example concerning the sanitation and health of large numbers in the towns, may arise from violating property rights held by, for example, small numbers of rural gentry. The Court of Chancery is the traditional resort of such complaints and, during the Victorian era, proved fully capable of both finding the responsible towns liable for the nuisance resultant from the sewage in the rivers and issuing remedial orders to protect landowners from the towns' polluting activities. These powers included the ability to order the closing of the sewer wastewater outlets into rivers.

Herein lay the river pollution dilemma. Stopping or closing down newly opened and developed sewage networks and sanitation schemes in large towns would create impossible social problems: how could a town cope with the court denying it its only available means of discharging its sewage? Could the courts, actually, in the event, bring down such a calamity upon the town? And would the courts, actually, in the event, bring down such a calamity upon the town?

This dilemma was by no means a purely academic or philosophical puzzle to be mulled over. There were a sizeable number of instances, at the Court of Chancery and elsewhere, where Victorian town sanitary and sewage authorities were indeed sued for nuisance over their sewage disposal methods by individuals and groups of neighbouring landholders. Invariably, the outcome was for the town to be found unequivocally liable for the nuisance. In such circumstances injunctions requiring the halting of the town's sewage pollution of the rivers concerned would come to be expected. However, although the sanitary activities and practices of the affected towns were usually undeniably, and often deeply, affected, it transpires that in no instance can it be found that the sewage network of any town was actually stopped on the order of the court. How the river sewage pollution dilemma played out, in practice, for a number of individual towns so affected is the core subject of this book.

The analytical method used to explore the dilemma is to examine the history and context of a number of Victorian-era civil disputes over river pollution where nuisance suits were brought. The history and context of ten disputes are described in detail, along with less detailed reference to others, and these histories have been collected together into chapters to illustrate the major common themes and routes by which the nuisance disputes and the associated dilemmas played out. The towns involved in the sewage pollution disputes include both large industrialising centres, such as Birmingham, Leeds and Wolverhampton, as well as much smaller communities, including Tunbridge Wells and Harrogate. Included also are two instances of river pollution nuisance cases which, while not directly sewage-related, further illustrate the ways that disputes under nuisance law can end. As many of the disputes stretched over extended time periods and involved numerous court hearings and appearances, some of the case studies illustrate more than just one of the pathways by which the dilemma played out.

Given the major objective of the study is to follow through the history and context of the disputes and detail how they evolved in practice, this is not a study in legal history as normally understood. Legal research, even in a historical context, is usually concerned with aspects of the establishment of liability, legal argument, leading cases and, perhaps, the establishment of new precedent, and in such pursuit the record of the court judgment and proceedings themselves are of most immediate interest. The leading figure advocating consideration of law cases in their wider setting as required here is A.W. Brian Simpson, and he laments that legal scholarship is rarely if ever interested in the empirical and historic context in which a case takes place.[1] But in pursuit of the wider post-litigation course and outcomes of these

---

[1]   A.W. Brian Simpson, *Leading Cases in the Common Law* (Oxford: Oxford University Press, 1995), 7–12.

river pollution disputes, more is required than can be provided by just the collected detail of pre-trial depositions, courtroom argument and final judgment on liability, and so reports of court hearings are of less central importance to the study here than they would be in a purely legal examination of, for example, the evolution of the law on environmental protection. What is required here is information on how the towns reacted to their adverse judgment: whether injunctions and orders were obeyed or later violated; whether sequestrations resulted and with what effect; how any abatements of the nuisance were effected; and, in the end, how town sanitary authorities went about avoiding the potentially catastrophic closing down of their sewer discharges. In essence – what happened next?

Sources which usually inform legal treatises will seldom suffice for investigations of post-litigation outcomes. Fortunately, information and evidence on the consequent post-litigation histories of these river nuisance disputes is often (but not always) available from a number of other sources. As the defendants in most of the cases examined are local governing bodies with authority over town sewage affairs – town councils, local boards of health and boards of improvement commissioners – varied sources of information can be available. Formal minutes of meetings and submitted reports for these public bodies and their sub-committees are usually still in existence as sources; though the level of detail provided, their completeness and the amount of self-protective censoring does vary considerably among the examples. Similarly, as the affairs of these public bodies are properly of concern and interest to the general local populace, the local newspapers of the town will often provide priceless details of debates and controversies among the members of the ruling authorities, detail the actual progress on the sanitation of the town and provide general colour and reflect local opinion that could not otherwise be accessed. (The digitalisation of local and provincial newspapers in the UK will surely have revolutionary effects on the study of local history.)

Where public bodies are not involved, the situation is very different. Evidence from sources for private persons and organisations is much more elusive. Had the concern of the study required the investigation of Victorian nuisance disputes between purely private individuals and commercial enterprises, rather than those involving public authorities, finding documentary evidence on the post-litigation outcomes would have proved much more troublesome. Nevertheless, the plaintiff or complainant side of the disputes covered were indeed private individuals or groups of individuals, and one might normally expect this side of the disputes to have left little documentary trace after a century and a half. Unfortunately, for most of these plaintiffs – millers (at Northampton and Banbury), small landowners (along the Dearne at Barnsley), and middle-class professionals and businessmen (at Leamington Spa and Harrogate) – this is the case. But, in the narratives set out here, there appear a surprising number of historically important and celebrated individuals and, for some of these more eminent and aristocratic complainants, including Charles Adderley (Lord Norton) at Birmingham and the Giffard family at Wolverhampton, useful archives of relevant materials exist. Indeed, for one of the cases examined, material from the plaintiff side, from the Legh family archive, provided the *only* source for any detailed information on the dispute, and without this source no information at all would have been available from which to construct the relevant detail of the dispute.

It will already be clear that the very nature of the phenomenon being investigated here precludes the use of classic methodological approaches to the investigation. There exists no prospect, for example, of double-blind experiments or the use of formal statistical analysis on an unbiased sample of cases. It is difficult enough to assemble any sample of Victorian civil court cases on river pollution nuisance, let alone a valid randomly selected one. Even the full set of such disputes that reached the court system remains uncertain, and will have to await full digitisation of archive records. In any case, as will become clear, the nature of the problem is such that out-of-court settlement of disputes is possible, before any formal court record is made, so a full list of these nuisance disputes is not only unavailable but could never be assembled.

The method being applied here is that of a comparative case study, a less formal approach to analysis but one that remains common in many disciplines, including history, politics, medicine and psychology.[2] To find the examples included in this book, use was made, perforce, of information contained in law reports, local authority reports and newspaper accounts for known cases, from whence reference to further contemporary cases and disputes were found that could also be followed up. After initial review, detailed post-litigation histories were constructed for the cases reported in detail here – cases which could most clearly illustrate both the river pollution dilemma itself and the different means that were actually adopted or emerged to tackle the dilemma. Hence the bulk of the chapters below present the historical narrative of these case studies. The histories have, however, been grouped together as examples to illustrate a particular means, strategy or path taken, by court or defendant or both, that allowed the dispute to come to an end. In order to do so, the cases have been compared historically, using guiding hypotheses[3] from the sub-field of 'law and economics' to search out and interpret patterns in the ways in which the river sewage dilemma was evaded.

Establishing the presence and significance of patterns of response to the river pollution dilemma is one objective of this study, but there remain others. The case studies, considered in their historical context, also stand as absorbing histories of disputes that often stood at the centre of important episodes in the urban development of major Victorian British towns and can cast light on the urban, civic and social histories of the towns concerned. In the main, these episodes have been little explored and undeservedly under-researched.

---

    [2]   Arend Lijphart, 'Comparative Politics and the Comparative Method', *The American Political Science Review*, 65 (1971): 682–93; Theda Skocpol, 'Emerging Agendas and Recurrent Strategies in Historical Sociology', in *Visions and Method in Historical Sociology*, (ed.) Theda Skocpol (Cambridge: Cambridge University Press, 1984), 368–74.

    [3]   Rosemary H.T. O'Kane, *Paths to Democracy: Revolution and Totalitarianism* (London: Routledge, 2004), 20–1.

Chapter 2
Victorian Britain I: Public Health and Local Government

... the twentieth century looks back upon the 1840s with a puzzled wonder of an Alice stepping into the world behind the looking-glass.[1]

It is difficult, perhaps impossible, to conjure up the look and feel of societies of the past. The Britain of a century-and-a-half ago was different not only in terms of material prosperity, technological skills and knowledge: it was also crucially different in terms of the era's own expectations of what an ordered society could look like or was capable of looking like. Twenty-first-century citizens have conscious and unconscious awareness of (if not always access to) possibilities and potentialities for individuals and society that were unavailable to even to the most far-seeing and speculative of the dreamers, philosophers and social reformers of the nineteenth century.

Much of the content of this book concerns the consequences of the necessary management of the growing quantities of human and industrial waste resultant from the concentrations of humanity and human industry in and around urban communities over that period. Britain, at the forefront of the industrial revolution, was also the pioneer in having to deal with the problems of waste and sewage disposal that resulted. To better understand the background against which the events of the river pollution dilemma disputes developed, this chapter presents a brief review of the relevant urban public health developments over the span of the Victorian period in Britain between 1830 and 1900. This will serve as a common background and a setting against which the river pollution case studies that follow may be seen.

Edwin Chadwick and the Water Carriage System

Many aspects of his life make Edwin Chadwick a formidable historical figure. Here, of primary interest is his role in the development and popularisation of the water carriage idea for the modern city. Chadwick was the major mover promoting the water carriage system and his work push-started the sanitary reform movement in Britain from the late 1830s. It was Chadwick who, forcefully and confidently,

---

[1]   Samuel Edward Finer, *The Life and Times of Sir Edwin Chadwick* (London: Methuen, 1952), 216.

but without many influential prior examples to guide him, and no practical contemporary ones, developed a plan and put forward a model for the urban environment for the modern era that has become so ubiquitous that alternatives seem almost unthinkable.

The water carriage system[2] refers to the integrated system by which water having been carried into the urban area, usually for a variety of primary purposes, is then used in a secondary manner as a means of collecting, through a sewer network, the waste products of the industrial and domestic sectors (typically using water closets) and is the medium used to carry off these waste products away from the town, often to rivers or the sea. None of the individual pieces of the jigsaw can be viewed as novel to the nineteenth century: water had commonly been piped even into Romano-British settlements to be used for sophisticated, albeit mostly public, latrines and baths, and there was nothing new about flushing toilets and using drains, sewers and rivers to carry away waste from urban communities.[3] But to envisage for the modern urban area an integrated, 'arterial' water carriage system and network serving diffused private households as a central element to improve urban health, as presented by Chadwick, was novel and was by no means 'in the air' as the Victorian era opens. With a water carriage system urban waste, with its unpleasantness and unwholesomeness, could be quickly removed while it was still fresh and before its disease-causing properties could become, as then believed, increasingly dangerous as it accumulated. The practical implications of the actual institution of such an integrated and interdependent system and the support required for its maintenance have proved to be extraordinarily far-reaching.

For the establishment of a water carriage waste system in a sizeable urban centre, there would first need to be a substantial water supply available both to carry the waste away and to flush the system. The water supply would ideally have to be continuous and under enough pressure to do its waste-carrying job as well as clearing blockages and scouring the sewers. Early in the nineteenth century, most water was supplied to towns by public and private water providers from a rag-bag of wells, rivers and streams, mostly via communal sources and often of questionable quality. Queues of people collecting water at wells, pools and springs were features of poor areas in Victorian towns and often commented upon. Furthermore, any piped supply of water to the public was also almost invariably intermittent. It was normally available for only a few hours each day: the absence of provision of a

---

2   To avoid confusion, it should be noted that in other contexts, the term 'water carriage' is sometimes used to describe water-borne transportation on rivers and canals; and in others to describe just individual parts of the sanitary network, like use of WCs, rather than the whole integrated system.

3   Examples exist in Roman towns and in Han dynasty China: even the palace of Minos at Knossos on Crete in 1500 BC, it is claimed, had piped water, flush toilets and drains, see W.J. Corrigan, 'Sanitation under the Ancient Minoan Civilisation', *Canadian Medical Association Journal*, 27 (1932), 77–8.

reliable and available water source for fire services to fight fires on Sundays, for example, proved to be a worry in many provincial towns.[4] For a continuous water supply to feed any proposed water carriage system, new, extensive and expensive water supplies and delivery systems for towns would have to be provided. In the event, such supplies did appear, often piped many miles from new sources, and using dams and reservoirs built through huge civic investment by local authority-owned and managed facilities. When water quality became an issue, this was often assured by public acquisition of the private water companies.

In addition, for the speedy removal of urban waste, a modern sewer system was needed which would cover the entirety of the urban area, and this would need to be built to high standards to cope with the problems and pressures the water carriage system would bring. The old haphazardly-provided sewers and culverts and ditches that served for waste disposal, with their right-angle turns, unreliable connections, unpaved bottoms and inconsistent gradients would not suffice. Most existing facilities would have to be replaced. Newly developing water-engineering expertise and Victorian 'can-do' approaches would have to provide all the new innovations required here for self-cleaning, self-scouring and continuous blockage-removal. Finally, the sewers would be carrying off sewage in the form of organic waste product which was considered to be of high value to agriculture, and it would be wasteful not to return this to the land through application as agricultural fertiliser in liquid or processed solid manure form. At the opening of the Victorian era, little of the required infrastructure for the application of the water carriage system was in place, not in Britain and not anywhere else in the world.

In order for a water carriage system to function effectively, compatible standards would require management and supervision that could ensure the separate parts would be coordinated and consistent. There would need to be sources for large-scale and long-term investment, finance and control, local, hands-on, day-to-day administrative oversight and the enforcing of payment of charges for the service. Local public authorities and municipalities, if such existed and were so empowered, would be a logical means by which the facilities of the water carriage system could be provided and standards assured. The water carriage system needed local government to exist, and local government found the water carriage system justified its existence. And both would have to be encouraged along, at the very least, via boosts, nudges and encouragement from central government. As the nineteenth century progressed, both local government and the water carriage system began to be able to provide what the other required; and through the century they evolved together so that by the end of the century both had become close to what we see today. The development of the water carriage system shaped, to a major extent, British local government and administration.[5]

---

[4]   The residue of this history has contributed to such anachronistic anomalies as the retention of cold-water tanks in modern domestic British dwellings.

[5]   For the (parallel) US experience, see Stanley K. Schultz and Clay McShane, 'To Engineer the Metropolis: Sewers, Sanitation, and City Planning in Late-Nineteenth-Century

Edwin Chadwick (1800–90) was born in Longsight, Manchester, but the family soon moved to London where Chadwick was to train as a lawyer, though he never practiced as such. In 1829, Chadwick became secretary and friend to Jeremy Bentham, who, at the end of his life, acted as mentor and benefactor to the young man. The utilitarianism of Bentham and John Stuart Mill has been seen as giving Chadwick a philosophical and moral basis and a belief in the role, even the duty, of the state to intervene in pursuit of the general benefit of society.

Chadwick is always viewed by historians as a man with outstanding abilities, who was highly intelligent, obsessively hard-working and dedicated.[6] Finer, his biographer, describes a man with formidable intellectual powers but who, once he had formulated an opinion from the facts and figures he accumulated, turned into a ferocious advocate, 'positive and dogmatic to a degree'.[7] Chadwick, Finer reports, while lacking both patience and humour, was touchy, intolerant, churlish and unwilling to admit to error, with no tact or diplomatic skill: he was angry, indignant and seems to have been notably charmless. Nevertheless, the traditional views of Chadwick hold that he was an 'ardent crusader' with a 'powerful belief in the struggle for social amelioration':[8] and that he supported interventionist communal and state action in order to enhance individual happiness.[9] But even those with more ambivalent views about Chadwick and the sanitary reform movement[10] can acknowledge how revolutionary and unexpected was Chadwick's placing of the water carriage system at the centre of the movement for public health and express 'awe' at the achievements of the sanitary movement he provoked.[11]

Chadwick rose to public prominence with his influence on and connection to the reform of the English Poor Law[12] and the work after 1834 of the Poor Law Commission, to which he was appointed Secretary. It was only after 1838, when Chadwick's clear personal ambitions were thwarted within the offices

---

America', *The Journal of American History*, 65 (1978): 389–411.

[6]   Many fine accounts of Chadwick and his work exist: Finer, *Life and Times*; Richard A. Lewis, *Edwin Chadwick and the Public Health Movement* (London: Longmans, 1952); Anthony Brundage, *England's Prussian Minister: Edwin Chadwick and the Politics of Government Growth, 1832–1854* (Pennsylvania: Pennsylvania State University Press, 1988); Christopher Hamlin, *Public Health and Social Justice in the Age of Chadwick: Britain 1800–1854* (Cambridge: Cambridge University Press, 1988).

[7]   Finer, *Life and Times*, 2.

[8]   Tristram Hunt, *Building Jerusalem: The Rise and Fall of the Victorian City* (London: Phoenix, 2005), 34.

[9]   Anthony S. Wohl, *Endangered Lives: Public Health in Victorian Britain* (London: J.M. Dent, 1983), 143.

[10]   Some see him as a technocratic social administrator responding to pressure to cut the costs of welfare, see Christopher Hamlin and Sally Sheard, 'Revolutions in public health: 1848, and 1998?', *British Medical Journal*, 317 (1998): 587–91.

[11]   Hamlin, *Public Health*, 14.

[12]   For which he was widely reviled.

administrating the Poor Law that he turned to the investigation of what is now referred to as the 'public health' aspects of the condition of the poor in Britain. This led to the publication of Chadwick's *Sanitary Report* in 1842 and it was here that proposals for modern town water carriage waste-disposal systems first prominently appear.[13] The *Sanitary Report*, with its many recommendations, is now seen as providing an initialising general framework for reform which provided the basis around which elements of the sanitary movement of the Victorian era could form.

Formally, the *Sanitary Report* was the response of the Poor Law Commission to a request in 1839 for an enquiry into the cause of disease among the labouring classes in Britain.[14] Chadwick was released from his secretarial duties to pursue the request. He proceeded by requesting evidence and reports and collecting open-ended questionnaire responses from sources, formal and informal, nationally and internationally. He then fashioned the wealth of returned written and statistical evidence, responses and data into a general report.

It is the content of the first two substantive chapters of the main section of Chadwick's *Sanitary Report*[15] that most directly concern sanitation, as it is now understood, and discuss the public health aspects of the state of towns, sewers and the water carriage system. These chapters present a picture of Britain, often through direct quotations from his respondents, of a sordid and squalid urban scene, and one which the case studies will make increasing familiar. For Chadwick, this is where he is able to present evidence to establish a chain of causation from want of sanitation, poor drainage, waste and inadequate water supply to the prevalence of disease among the poor.[16] Chadwick argues that the proximate causes of fever lie

---

[13]   Edwin Chadwick, *Sanitary Report: Report on an Inquiry into the Sanitary Condition of the Labouring Population of Great Britain*, Report Of Poor Law Commissioners, Nos. 006, 007, 008, 1842.

[14]   This was to expand two earlier reports to the Poor Law Commission in 1838 on the causes of disease (fever) in London (Poor Law Commissioners, *Fourth Annual Report*, 1837–38, No. 147; and Poor Law Commissioners, *Fifth Annual Report*, 1839, No. 239). The whole scheme originated with Chadwick, who had both encouraged the original London fever reports and also encouraged Charles Blomfield, Bishop of London, to make the request to extend these London enquiries to cover the whole country. See Finer, *Life and Times*, 155–63; and M.W. Flinn, 'Introduction' in *Report on the Sanitary Conditions of the Labouring Population of Great Britain by Edwin Chadwick, 1842*, (ed.) M.W. Flinn (Edinburgh: Edinburgh University Press, 1965), 45.

[15]   It is legitimate to ascribe the authorship of the *Sanitary Report* to Chadwick alone, as only his name appears on the title page of the substantive portion of the report. Formally, however, his authored report forms only part of the 'Report to Parliament ... from the Poor Law Commissioners' and a ten-page letter of introduction, signed by the three Commissioners precedes Chadwick's title page.

[16]   For Hamlin, *Public Health*, the line of causation proposed is by no means neutral and reveals Chadwick's concern to avoid the implications that would flow from allowing other factors (especially poverty and working conditions) to be introduced as elements of 'public health'. Pursuing public health in these restrained Chadwickian terms, designedly

with 'decomposing animal and vegetable substances, by damp and filth, and close and overcrowded dwelling' and that:

> ... where these circumstances are removed by drainage, proper cleansing, better ventilation and other means of diminishing atmospheric impurity, the frequency and intensity of such disease is abated; and where the removal of the noxious agencies appears to be complete, such disease almost entirely disappears.[17]

Chadwick hardly considers any but the prevailing miasmic theory of public disease and fever. He ascribes contagious disease and fevers, like cholera and typhoid, to the poisoned air and smells arising from the fermentation of organic waste materials (human, animal and vegetable) of which there was little shortage in Britain's towns.[18] Hence at the top of Chadwick's recommendations was that provision be made for:

> ... the removal of all refuse of habitations, streets, and roads, and the improvement of the supplies of water [and the] immediate removal of decomposing refuse ... by use of water and self-acting means of removal by improved and cheaper sewers and drains.[19]

The more plentiful and available is the supply of water to flush and clean the cities, so the more quickly and effectively can the waste be carried off by the drains and sewers, then the less disease there would be. For the virtuous circle justifying the water carriage system to be complete, all that is further required is that the carried-off sewage effluent be kept from the rivers and returned to the soil as fertiliser for farms.[20] However wrong the theory that disease is created anew as infective material in decomposing and festering organic filth, emphasis on deposited waste as a source of disease was, it turned out, a good place to start. Later in his report, Chadwick gingerly reviewed the (radical) changes to the existing archaic administrative and legal structure for town government that might be required to provide and manage the urban infrastructure of the new town drainage systems, and suggests the establishment of permanent local boards of

---

or not, allowed indignant support from many strands of society to come together to animate an influential Victorian lobby for sanitary reform.

[17]   Chadwick, *Sanitary Report*, 368–72.

[18]   Chadwick's famous dictum was: '... all smell is, if it be intense, immediate acute disease; and eventually we may say that, by depressing the system and rendering it susceptible to the action of other causes, all smell is disease', Select Committee on Metropolitan Sewage Manure, *Report*, No. 474, 1846, 109.

[19]   Chadwick, *Sanitary Report*, 370.

[20]   Flinn, 'Introduction', 59, clearly misses the point here in believing 'one of the more curious bees in Chadwick's bonnet is his enthusiasm for the use of untreated sewage as a field manure'.

health for each provincial locality, employing professional engineers, the whole to be overseen from London.

Chadwick's report set out an innovative, even revolutionary programme for the sanitation of towns: the realisation of the originality of the vision is only dimmed by its being the everyday, workaday model upon which modern towns and cities rely. But the *Sanitary Report* remains imperfect: it was by no means complete. For the critic, there are numerous analytic and practical holes in Chadwick's analysis and flaws in his arguments and recommendations. The miasmic theory of fever upon which his schemes rested was incorrect, and big returns could have accrued from closer attention to the improvement of water *quality*.[21] The *Sanitary Report* failed to tackle a long list of unresolved technical issues concerning whether a large-scale untested water carriage system based on a constant, pressured water supply was even technically everywhere feasible. It is easy to ignore how casual and underdeveloped was civil engineering at this time: even the best basic shape and material for sewers became controversial issues.[22] The calculation of the likely cost of the new interconnected sanitary networks was also vague and less than realistic, and it left unresolved whether these innovations would prove too costly, both for the poor, at whom such policies were most obviously aimed, and for the rich, who would pay most.

Central to the argument of this book, a major flaw arose concerning the fate of the sewage outflows of the water carriage system. No demand from agriculture emerged for the liquefied effluent, and no reliable treatment was available. In the event, sewage was mostly just allowed to flow into the rivers and streams. As Finer comments:

> The disposal of the sewage was the loose end of the arterial system; the use of sewage as manure was so neat a solution from the point of view of both economy and engineering that Chadwick refused to believe it was not – one way or another – a practical one.[23]

In retrospect, constructing new local government administrative structures and retro-fitting the drainage systems of cities in what was already the most urbanised nation in the world required such a vast outlay of effort, and financial and physical

---

[21] The confusions between the basic filth-poison/miasmic *cause* of fever and the undoubted roles of 'contagion' and predisposing factors (like urban over-crowding) made agreement difficult between medical authorities. The later statistical analyses of public health fever records by John Snow and William Farr, which, even before the definitive establishment of the germ theory pointed to polluted water rather than air as the fever carrier, would have to wait until the 1850s and 1860s.

[22] Christopher Hamlin, 'Edwin Chadwick and the Engineers, 1842–1854: Systems and Antisystems in the Pipe-and-Brick Sewers War', *Technology and Culture*, 33 (1992): 680–709.

[23] Finer, *Life and Times*, 300.

investment that it is a surprise the very idea of Chadwick's new integrated sanitary water carriage system survived.[24]

The central authorities of the time required a second opinion, and a new commission, the Royal Commission on the Health of Towns and Populous Places, was established in 1843, only months after the *Sanitary Report* was issued. In the event, the *Reports* of the Health of Towns Commission,[25] based on surveys of social conditions in fifty large British towns, vindicated Chadwick's recommendations, and together Chadwick's *Sanitary Report* and the Health of Towns Commission's *Reports* primed a first wave of public opinion in favour of reform and improvement of urban sanitation ('public health') in Britain. The findings and recommendations of these public reports would provide the required backing and evidence for the Public Health Act of 1848 and lay a path for the many other interventions and further legislation concerning public health and sanitation that continued to be enacted through the nineteenth century.

The Public Health Act (1848) and Local Government

The governing authorities of provincial towns responsible for the provision and disposal of the town's sewage provide most of the defendants in our river pollution case studies. These authorities appear in a variety of forms, sometimes as familiar town councils but sometimes in less familiar form as a Board of Improvement Commissioners or Local Board of Health. As will become clear, which institution was involved depends on the particular history of the town and the stage reached of British local government reform and development.

At the start of the nineteenth century, for towns in England and Wales, what minor local government that existed was an unfamiliar and confusing patchwork consisting of the remains of a medieval, even Anglo-Saxon, system modernised by an overlay of institutions which localities had established by obtaining specific, private Acts of Parliament applicable only to themselves. Any individual provincial town and its local governing bodies might have inherited a history from earlier times giving them a unique mix of governing institutions, constitution and powers. Ecclesiastically-based parishes within the town might still administer the Poor Laws and ancient Courts Leet might still retain policing duties and other responsibilities left over from manorial times. Many towns, but not all, would have acquired Royal Charters, so becoming Boroughs by 'incorporation', but with

---

24   The overall cost of public investment in new water supply, sewers and sewerage treatment under Victoria is unavailable, but likely dwarfs infrastructural canal and/or railway investment in nineteenth century Britain.

25   Royal Commission on Health of Towns: *First Report*, No. 572, 1844; *Second Report*, Nos. 602, 610, 1845. Chadwick himself, though formally not part of the new inquiry, exercised substantial influence on it, see Hamlin, *Public Health*, 217–24; Finer, *Life and Times*, 234; and Brundage, *England's Prussian Minister*, 92–6.

differing privileges, which might have conferred specific rights and duties. When new or wider powers not included in their existing set were desired, the town could approach Parliament and attempt through the passing of a new private Act of Parliament to acquire this new power. As the importance and populations of towns grew in the eighteenth century, it was commonplace for towns to use this method to pass new laws, often termed Improvement Acts, to raise finance and create new bodies to manage new projects and duties covering activities such as providing street lighting and sewerage and drainage. Hence, towns might acquire Boards of Improvement Commissioners or Street or Sewage or Paving Commissioners and these can be seen up to the 1870s, still supervising local government activities independently of town councils in many towns.[26]

The first major attempt to reform and standardise the local government constitutions of English and Welsh towns came with the 1835 Municipal Corporations Act. The majority of existing incorporated boroughs with town charters (as in the cases of Leeds and Banbury) would now become municipal boroughs governed by a town council subject to election by ratepayers, with permanent town clerks and financial officers to provide legal expertise and open, audited financial accounts. These town councils were required by the act to take on responsibility for local policing, but only optionally authorised to take responsibility for local improvements, sewers and drainage. Unincorporated towns could apply to become incorporated municipal boroughs, and many of the larger new industrial towns (including Birmingham) did so over the following years.

Such was the confused situation of provincial English town government administration before 1848 when the Public Health Act passed into law. A central plank of the new act included one of the recommendations of both the Health of Towns Commission and of Chadwick: that Local Boards of Health be established to manage local public health facilities under the general supervision of a General Board of Health in London.[27] Setting up local boards remained optional rather than compulsory for local authorities, but these boards would have powers to oversee local water supplies and sewers and related public health activities. If an existing incorporated town or municipal borough took on the powers of a local board, then the town council selected and appointed its members: otherwise, the local board membership was to be elected from and by local property-holders and ratepayers.

---

[26] There existed no general law concerning the numbers, constitution or membership of these boards. Locally differing rules might allow perpetual self-selection by appointment, privately restricted nomination and self-election, or election by more general or more restricted sections of the local ratepayers or populace. The opportunities for conspiratorial and less-than-public-spirited activities among such semi-secretive bodies must have been ever-present.

[27] Edwin Chadwick became one of the three members of the General Board of Health. It only survived until 1858, when central supervision over local public health activities was split between the Privy Council, the Local Government Act Office (under the Home Office) and the Poor Law Board, until 1871.

Typically, and take-up was initially slow,[28] the existing local authority would itself simply take on the powers of a Local Board of Health under the act. In 1858, the Local Boards of Health became just Local Boards and the ability to take up the powers of the 1848 act was extended to other local institutions, especially Improvement Commissioners.

The timing of the disputes for our case studies involves sanitary authorities at around this stage of the development of local government, so a diversity of form of the sanitary body will appear. Indeed, even for contemporary commentators[29] local government for provincial towns at this time in England, and their public health and sanitary provision, still appears thoroughly confused and piecemeal; even bumbling.[30] The existing legislation was essentially permissive rather than compulsory, so take-up was variable and this resulted in lack of uniformity in application between even contiguous sections of towns. Local desires for independence from centralised fiat and for freedom to enjoy traditional modes of local autonomy often made interference from London unwelcome and provoked resistance. Even where the new local administrative structures were established, membership and practical control of such bodies was likely not to have altered much from what had previously existed in the town, so, in consequence, use and application of the newly acquired powers might simply not happen. Added to this, there always existed genuine difficulties and real practical challenges in improving sanitation facilities. In any event, as Wohl has it: '... corruption, lethargy, innate conservatism and especially parsimony of local government officials have become almost a *cliché* of Victorian public health reforms'.[31]

There was a 'second wave' of public health regulation and legislation in the 1870s, which followed the findings of the Royal Sanitary Commission of 1869–71.[32] The Commission found: '... many places with very defective sanitary government and still more with practically none at all, owing to the defective exercise of the powers which the law confers'.[33] New legislative reforms followed, which extended the powers available to local administrative bodies and, in the main, moved away from more permissive authorisation of public health activity and more towards requiring and compelling the same.[34] This second wave of reform was to culminate with the Public Health Act of 1875.

---

[28]   Wohl, *Endangered Lives*, 154.

[29]   Henry Aubrey Husband, *Sanitary Law: A Digest of the Sanitary Acts of England and Wales* (Edinburgh: Livingstone, 1883), 2.

[30]   Christopher Hamlin, 'Muddling in Bumbledom: On the Enormity of Large Sanitary Improvements in Four British Towns, 1855–1885', *Victorian Studies*, 32 (1988): 55–83.

[31]   Wohl, *Endangered Lives*, 169.

[32]   Royal Sanitary Commission, *First Report*, No. 4218, 1868–9; *Second Report*, C.281, C.281–I, C.281–II, 1871.

[33]   Royal Sanitary Commission, *Second Report*, C.281, 11.

[34]   In 1871, the Local Government Board Act re-established a single unified Local Government Board to supervise, from London, local government sanitary activities.

By this point in the 1870s, the need for a simplification of the laws and administration of public health had become acute. Michael, in 1874, counted 81 relevant acts on the administration of sanitary law, 700 or so local bodies, and a 'jumble of statutes' comprising a 'disgrace to our statute book'.[35] He provides a Proustian description of the confused pattern of local responsibilities:

> ... in 1872, there existed Local Boards and Local Boards of Health in districts constituted under the Acts of 1848 and 1858, sewer authorities and nuisance authorities under the Sanitary Acts, and Improvement Commissioners under Local Acts; and, owing to the anomalous provisions of the so-called Sanitary Acts, there were some places where Local Improvement Acts were in force in boroughs, Local Commissioners to provide sewers and drains, and a Municipal Corporation constituted a sewer authority to do the same work; local boards with full powers over roads, lighting, water-supply, and drainage; and sewer authorities having no power over roads, or over the drains which had been constructed in them by highway authorities acting under the Nuisances Acts; towns which had become surrounded by great outlying populations, chiefly formed for the express purpose of avoiding sanitary restrictions, and who had expressly located themselves outside sanitary control, and beyond the reach of sanitary taxation; districts which, sometimes to the number of four, met in the centre of the most densely populated portion of a town, subject to different authorities with different powers, carrying out different Acts, and with widely diverse views as to the obligations of sanitary law; streets in which one side, and even in some cases where parts of houses, were within the district of a Local Board, and the other without the district, and also without supervision or control; whole parishes so surrounded with other districts or parishes, and so situated, as to make drainage impossible, except through the subjacent parish or district, and others where efficient drainage was alone possible by judicious combination and united action; rivers and streams passing through carefully kept districts, carrying on with them in their course the poisonous filth accumulated in other towns or villages through which the stream had previously passed, where it was used as the common carrier to get rid of troublesome and dangerous accumulations.[36]

Then the Public Health Act (1872) imposed on England (outside London) urban and rural sanitary authorities covering the country, so for urban areas, the existing corporation, board of improvement commissioners or the local board of health became the relevant urban sanitary authority.

[35]   William H. Michael, 'The Public Health Act, 1872: Its Defects and Suggested Amendments', *The British Medical Journal*, 1 (692) (1874): 443–6. William Henry Michael (1822–92) had been a surgeon and had been mayor of Swansea in 1857, before turning to the law, becoming a QC in 1878.

[36]   Ibid.

The Public Health Act of 1875, with its eleven parts and 343 sections, consolidated the previous statutes over sanitation and simplified the English local government structure concerning the provision of public health activities. The powers and duties, permissive and compulsory, of the urban sanitary authority over a broad range of sanitary functions were specified, including over water supply and sewage, and wide powers were awarded for the management of sewerage and for the raising of rates and loans for these purposes. In addition, duties were imposed to ensure all dwellings had appropriate drainage and access to WCs, privies, ashpits and the like.

Although the sanitary functions of local government were much more settled after 1875, the form of local governance was not yet everywhere uniform. It took later legislation, especially the Local Government Act of 1888, to rationalise the overall structure of local government in England and Wales, finally separating civic local administration from its ecclesiastical and manorial roots, and provide the framework of elected County Councils, Borough Councils, and urban and rural District Councils which were to become familiar features into the twentieth century.

Summary

The public bodies who were to become the defendants in the river pollution disputes of our case studies will be seen to be a collection of diversely-named local administrative bodies whose common responsibilities were for sewage and drainage provision within the towns concerned. Some are familiar Town Councils and Corporations, but others carry designations – Local Boards of Health, Boards of Improvement Commissioners and Boards of Streets Commissioners – that are now unfamiliar. During the Victorian period, the administrative structure of the local government of towns in Britain was ponderously evolving as unplanned and unprecedented growth in the towns required new duties and responsibilities to be taken up. Many of these changing responsibilities concerned public health and the water carriage system: matters of sanitation, water supply and sewerage were becoming central concerns for local government.

Chapter 3

Victorian Britain II: River Pollution and Sanitary Engineering

The disposal of the sewage proved to be a major flaw in Chadwick's vision for the water carriage system. For the sewage waste that was to be collected and dispersed out of the towns so quickly and efficiently by the new copious water supplies, Chadwick foresaw the liquefied sludge being efficiently piped to farms and its manurial value recovered by agriculture. The soil and farm would receive back the returned nutrients, revenues gained by sales of effluent by sewage authorities would contribute to the costs of the system and an efficient circle of virtue would be completed.

But whatever the initial hopes and over-ambitious estimates concerning such a solution for the disposal of the sewage, little profit was ever to arise from long-running attempts to achieve such an end. The distribution of liquefied sewage and effluent around local farms by pipe proved costly and greatly problematic, and the end product required careful and skillful handling: suspicions about disease were never allayed. Farms anyway neither wanted nor required such manure at all times and over all seasons of the year and more convenient sources of cheap and easily managed fertilizer were, throughout this period from 1840–80, becoming widely available to British agriculture, in particular in the form of nitrates and guano from South America.

Rivers and River Pollution

Much easier for towns than distributing its sewage effluent around the local farming community would be simply to lead the contents of their drains and sewers to a nearby body of water and allow the effluent to flow away downstream or downtide. Most convenient was the open sea and tidal waters for coastal towns, and most troublesome were minor river systems for the inland towns. But so long as the content of the drainage of towns was dominated by rainwater run-off, then small amounts of domestic sewage and industrial waste would tend to be diluted and degraded quickly and naturally and would be little noticed in the nation's rivers. As towns grew and sewage networks developed, and as WCs replaced the increasingly unacceptable cesspits and middens, however, the increasing sewage pollution of Britain's rivers became a growing concern.

From the 1850s, river pollution had become impossible to ignore and a series of official investigations and enquiries began to be reported.[1] Around the time of the 1858 Great Stink on the Thames in London[2] the Royal Commission on the Sewage of Towns[3] was describing the condition of Britain's rivers as 'poisonous'[4] and by 1864 delegations were petitioning the government for legislation on sewage disposal and the prevention of river pollution.[5] Although the government of the day was willing to legislate to extend local authorities' power for projects to dispose of sewage on the land,[6] any new legislation aimed directly at river pollution prevention would, perhaps, step on the toes of too many industrial (and other) interests.

In response to increasing pressure to act on river pollution from vocal elements in Parliament,[7] in 1865, the Royal Commission on Rivers Pollution Prevention (Rivers Pollution Commission of 1865) was established with three commissioners asked to inquire into and gather evidence on the best means of remedying pollution and rescuing the rivers, and to make recommendations for keeping sewage and other pollutants out of rivers without 'risk to public health or serious injury to … manufactures'.[8]

The three commissioners originally appointed were Robert Rawlinson (as chairman), John Thornhill Harrison and John Thomas Way.[9] By 1868, the Rivers

---

[1]   Wohl, *Endangered Lives*, 233–56.

[2]   Exacerbated by summer temperatures, low rainfall, sewage back-up and tidal circumstances, the resulting Great Stink on the Thames in 1858 has become the stuff of legend. The history of London's Victorian river pollution, its sewers and Joseph Bazalgette's work there is well-documented, see Stephen Halliday, *The Great Stink of London* (Stroud: Sutton Publishing, 1999) and Stephen Halliday, *Making the Metropolis* (Derby: Breedon Books, 2003).

[3]   Royal Commission on Sewage of Towns: *First Report*, No. 2262, 1857; *Second Report*, No. 2882, 1861; *Third Report*, No. 3472, 1865.

[4]   Royal Commission on Sewage of Towns, *Second Report*, 8.

[5]   *Times*, 12 December 1864.

[6]   One example is the Utilization of Sewage Act of 1865.

[7]   For example, Lord Robert Montagu's doomed River Waters Protection Bill in February 1865 (*Hansard*, 9 February 1865).

[8]   See Lawrence E. Breeze, *The British Experience with River Pollution, 1865–1876* (New York: Peter Lang, 1993).

[9]   Robert Rawlinson (1810–98) was to become a very well-known water and sanitary engineer, ubiquitous as a consultant on sanitary matters. He became Chief Inspector to the Local Government Board and was knighted in 1888 ('Robert Rawlinson', *ICE Minutes*, 134, 1 January (1898): 386–91). John Thornhill Harrison (1815–91) was a civil engineer and farmer and later an inspector with the Local Government Board ('John Thornhill Harrison', *ICE Minutes*, 109, 1 January (1892): 405–7). John Thomas Way (1820?–83) had been Professor at the Royal Agricultural College at Cirencester and was then Consulting Chemist to the Royal Agricultural Society: he was to acquire the sobriquet 'father of soil chemistry' for his pioneering work on the subject in the 1850s.

Pollution Commission of 1865 had submitted three reports, the first on the Thames, the second on the River Lee (or Lea, which ran through London's industrial heartland) and the third on the Yorkshire rivers, Aire and Calder.[10] However, among these original 1865 commissioners, Harrison fell out with Rawlinson and Way, and in 1868 the three commissioners resigned and so a new board of three new members was appointed. The new commissioners for the Rivers Pollution Commission of 1868 were William Thomas Denison[11] as chairman, Edward Frankland[12] and John Chalmers Morton.[13] Denison died in 1871, while investigations were still in progress and he was not replaced, leaving the formidable Frankland to dominate the commission as chair. Confusingly, the 1868 commissioners, rather than continuing the report numbering of their predecessors, started their investigations again with a second 'First Report'. The new commissioners were able to submit four more reports on river environments *per se,* covering waterways in Lancashire (Mersey and Ribble); rivers of the woollen manufacturing areas; rivers of Scotland; and rivers of mining and manufacturing areas. They also produced a damning report on the commercial ABC sewage treatment system and a final one on the domestic water supply of towns.[14] By 1874, the Rivers Pollution Commission in its two manifestations had issued, over a nine-volume series of reports, a huge amount of information covering the condition of Britain's rivers and waterways. Much of their evidence came from publicly-held local enquiries around the country with interested parties invited to participate (Edwin Chadwick, as a riverside resident of Richmond, appears as a witness), but much else came from their own enterprise. For just their own four river reports, the 1868 Commission held enquiries in

---

[10] Royal Commission on Rivers Pollution Prevention of 1865 (Rivers Pollution Commission of 1865), *First Report* (River Thames), No. 3634, 1866; *Second Report* (River Lee), No. 3835, 1867; *Third Report* (Rivers Aire and Calder), No. 3850, 1867.

[11] William Thomas Denison (1804–71) had a career in the Royal Engineers and in Australia and India as a colonial administrator at the highest levels and he was knighted in 1846, see *Times*, 20 January 1871.

[12] Edward Frankland (1825–99) was a world-class chemist, credited with formulating the law of valence for chemical bonding, contributing to the theory of spectral analysis and originating investigations of the calorific value of food and the science of sewage. In 1863 he was appointed as Professor of Chemistry at the Royal Institution and he was knighted in 1895. His obituary cited him as having 'secured a place in the history of science from which no changes of fashion can oust him' ('Edward Frankland', *ICE Minutes*, 139, 1 January (1900): 343–9; Christopher Hamlin, *A Science of Impurity: Water Analysis in Nineteenth Century Britain* (Berkeley: University of California Press, 1990).

[13] John Chalmers Morton (1821–88) was an agriculturalist and editor of the Agricultural Gazette.

[14] Royal Commission on Rivers Pollution Prevention of 1868 (Rivers Pollution Commission of 1868), *First Report* (Rivers Mersey and Ribble), C.37, 1870; *Second Report*, (The ABC process), C.181, 1870; *Third Report* (Woollen Manufactures Rivers), C.347, 1871; *Fourth Report* (Scottish Rivers), C.603, 1872; *Fifth Report* (Mining and Metal Manufactures Rivers), C.951, 1874; *Sixth Report* (Water Supply), C.1112, 1874.

around 98 towns, and the commissioners personally examined dozens of sites, toured rivers, lakes, factories and sewage works, analysed thousands of water samples and carried out hundreds of experiments on water and sewage.[15]

That the commissioners found evidence of the appalling condition of the rivers systems they were inspecting will surprise no-one: after all, that was what they were appointed to investigate, and some eye-opening evidence appears. Perhaps a single verbal snapshot of a river scene from one report might stand as an example. Describing the River Worth in Yorkshire, a worker in the wool industry soberly reported:

> Opposite my works the bed of the river has silted up very considerably: forty years ago the bed was five or six feet deeper than it is at present, and the silting up to this great depth has been caused by ashes and rubbish thrown in by manufacturers and others. Formerly trout were very plentiful in the stream, but now no living thing can exist except rats, which feed on the dead carcases of animals thrown in. The river for more than half a mile above my works is very seriously polluted by town sewage and refuse from manufactories and works and in the summer the stench is so bad that the smell is perceptible for more than half a mile off.[16]

The commissioners became increasingly sceptical about the ability of the existing legal restrictions under civil nuisance law to be effective in improving the observed conditions:

> The law, as it at present exists, is only applicable to local and individual cases. There is no power of general application. One town or one manufacturer may be proceeded against, but there is no authority having the means and the power to deal with nuisances throughout an entire drainage area ... We found the law relative to the pollution of these rivers to be the subject of general and well-grounded dissatisfaction. Theoretically, the law recognizes that protection is due to public and private rights in running water. It prohibits all public nuisance, and imposes upon each riparian proprietor the obligation of allowing running water to pass on its course without obstruction or pollution. But a person, judging from the appearance of the streams in the West Riding, would infer the contrary to be the law, and would conclude that there existed a general license to commit every kind of river abuse.[17]

And the report later continues:

---

[15]   Rivers Pollution Commission of 1868, *Fifth Report*, 1874, 51.
[16]   Rivers Pollution Commission of 1868, *Third Report*, 1871, 14.
[17]   Rivers Pollution Commission of 1865, *Third Report*, 1867, 52.

[T]he principal offenders are the governing bodies of large towns. They are rarely prosecuted by private persons because few are willing to bear the expense and odium of acting as public prosecutors. To instigate legal proceedings against a large town with a view to compel it to adopt a different mode of disposing of its sewage, at a cost of many thousands of pounds, is to provoke a wealthy adversary to a conflict in which every step will be contested. ... Accordingly, whatever the convenience to the public, the nuisance continues unabated. Rich and poor submit to it as a sort of destiny.[18]

As to the generally deplorable condition of the rivers of Britain, the major cause was consistently argued, by both sets of commissioners, to be untreated town sewage. Still, the commissioners were of the opinion that the effects of industrial waste and town sewage in the rivers could be largely mitigated with existing technology at an acceptably low cost. In this they were certainly over-optimistic. For industrial waste, the commissioners offered practical advice for the particular problems they saw, such as encouraging manufacturers to allow liquid waste to settle out in standing lagoons before discharge, and they firmly supported the total banning of solid matter being allowed into rivers. As for town sewage, improvements were available, it was argued, in the form of prior treatment through application to the land in 'irrigation and intermittent filtration' (described below) before discharge. But the major obstacle for progress on improving the general state of the rivers, the commissioners believed, was that the level of contamination was now so great that there was little incentive for individual polluting firms or sewage-spilling towns to reduce their own discharges when any individual contribution would have such negligible effect. As such, the situation constitutes what is now called a 'tragedy of the commons.'[19] The solution necessary to deliver improvements, the commissioners believed, would be to constitute river conservancy boards and authorities acting across the entirety of a river-basin system, which would be equipped with strong powers to intervene.

The final set of the Commission's recommendations for controlling river pollution at the policy level appears in the Fifth Report in 1874.[20] In a preliminary portion, based upon Frankland's experimental work, a series of specific standards for the purity of liquids were established, failing which, it was recommended, the liquid should be considered inadmissible to pass into streams. As an example, one of the standards set was 'any liquid which contains, in 100,000 parts by weight, more than one part of sulphur, in the condition either of sulphuretted hydrogen or of a soluble sulphuret'. The standards were considered as starting points for pollution control, to be tightened as better purification treatments emerged. The major recommendations for new statutory regulations were then simply: a) enact the forgoing standards of purity, with penalties for discharging into watercourses

---

[18]   Rivers Pollution Commission of 1865, *Third Report*, 1867, 118.
[19]   Garrett Hardin, 'The Tragedy of the Commons', *Science*, 162 (1968): 1243–8.
[20]   Rivers Pollution Commission of 1868, *Fifth Report*, 1874, 48–50.

liquids failing the purity standards; and b) forbid with penalties the casting of solid material into watercourses. The administrative framework to manage the new rules would require new local institutions in the form of river-basin-wide conservancy boards, employing independent inspectors and empowered to enforce the quality standards.

Rivers Pollution Prevention Act 1876

Following the end of the Rivers Pollution Commission in 1874, had the recommendations of the commission been translated faithfully into statute law, Britain would have had a river protection framework many decades ahead of its time. But industrial and local government interests began to be mobilised in opposition as fears grew concerning the costs and potential effects on industry of such regulation.[21] When Parliament again considered what should be done about river pollution control, the measures that finally made it into statute law in 1876 were far from those recommended by the Royal Commission.

The Rivers Pollution Prevention Act of 1876 has six parts and twenty-two clauses. Part I straightforwardly forbids any solid matter being deposited in streams or rivers that alters the flow or pollutes the water. Part II concerned sewage, and, whether in solid or liquid form, the discharge of such matter into a stream, river, lake or watercourse is forbidden, but now with some qualification. Prohibition would only apply to newly discharging systems and a complete defence would be available if the offending authority could show they had used 'the best practical and available means to render harmless the sewage matter so falling or flowing or carried into the stream.'[22] Part III concerned industrial waste and it became an offence to permit draining into a stream any 'poisonous, noxious or polluting' matter from factory or mine which degrades any water used by the process: and a similar qualifying statement applied that a defence would be that the enterprise had used 'the best practical and *reasonably* available means to render harmless' this waste matter. The remaining parts of the act set up the administrative background and applied the act, with appropriate modifications, to Scotland and Ireland. For our purposes, it is necessary to point out explicitly that one clause (Clause 16) stipulates that 'nothing in the Act shall legalise any act or default which would but for this Act be deemed to be a nuisance or otherwise contrary to law', so that common law nuisance and duties with regard to riparian property rights remained wholly intact, unaffected by the passage of the new measure.

The flaws in the 1876 Act become apparent when compared with the recommendations of the Royal Commission. The meaning of the words 'poisonous', 'noxious' and 'polluting', for example, were never defined, nor

---

[21]   Breeze, *British Experience*, 175–88.

[22]   A similar form of words ('best practical means') had previously been used as part of the Alkali Acts.

was the meaning of 'best practical and available means' for waste treatment explained. The far-sighted possibility of defining water quality standards in terms of chemical analysis failed entirely to be included. No new powerful river-basin-wide conservancy boards would be established. The enforcement of the new law would be through the county courts, where judges would have the responsibility for restraining miscreants and applying fines for misdeeds. In bringing cases to the attention of the court, for sewage pollution, an individual (or body) could initiate an action in the court against a sanitary authority and a sanitary authority could act against another sanitary authority with regard to a local stream. For industrial pollution, only the local sanitary authority could institute an action under the act and this required consent from the Local Government Board in London, whose inspectors would validate whether 'best practical and reasonably available' means were being employed.

The absence of defined standards of water quality, the policing role assigned to the sanitary authorities (after all, major offenders) and the failure to establish river-basin-wide authorities with enforcement powers, all contributed to disable the 1876 Act in dealing with the pollution problems faced by the rivers. Its failures in this respect were widely acknowledged. In 1899, the act was described as:

> ... so full of technicalities, and so much encumbered by restrictions, that it has proved inoperative in practice. The pollution of our rivers still continues to such an extent that it is a disgrace, in my judgment, to the civilisation of this country.[23]

The Royal Commission on Sewage Disposal in 1901 summed it up as follows: '... we are satisfied that the Rivers Pollution Prevention Act, 1876, has not resulted in the general purification of our rivers. This is largely due to the reluctance of the authorities to put the Act in force.'[24] Failure to establish enforcement agencies at the river basin level proved to be a missed opportunity, as when *ad hoc* river conservancy boards were established with some teeth (for example, the West Riding of Yorkshire Rivers Board from 1894) these boards made noticeable inroads into clearing up their rivers.

In general, the 1876 Rivers Pollution Prevention Act remained little used over our period[25] even though it remained Britain's only statutory river protection

---

[23] Sir Francis Sharp Powell (*Hansard*, 8 March 1899).

[24] Royal Commission on Sewage Disposal, *Interim Report*, Cd. 685, 1901, xi.

[25] As indicated by the paucity of references in the annual reports of the Local Government Board during the 1880s: for example, for 1885–6, the Local Government Board issued a single consent for a prosecution of industrial pollution under the act (Local Government Board, *Fifteenth Report*, C.4844, 1886, 308). Wohl reports only nine prosecutions in total each year (Wohl, *Endangered Lives*, 249) and Hassan reports only twenty-six successful actions initiated under the act up to 1886 (John Hassan, *A History of Water in Modern England and Wales* (Manchester: Manchester University Press, 1998), 33).

legislation.[26] Provincial town authorities, as we shall see, were to be far more wary and nervous of prosecution for nuisance under civil law than they ever were to be fearful of prosecutions under the statutory law of 1876. Under the civil law of nuisance, a claim that sanitary authorities were using the 'best available means' for sewage treatment was not a sufficient defence.

As will become clear, even the 'best available means' offered by the sewage engineering of the day was hardly admirably effective: it was the absence of engineering technology that would reliably and effectively treat their sewage that placed local sanitary authorities in such a difficult position when faced with nuisance suits.

Sewage Treatment Engineering

Under the arterial water carriage system, the fate of the sewage waste being transported through the sewers out of the urban area was a critical factor for the rivers. The temptation for the members of any sanitary authority, eager as ever not to expend their funds and tax themselves unnecessarily, was always simply to outfall the effluent into a nearby watercourse and forget it. But if the sanitary authority was to consider treating its sewage, what treatment processes might be available for them to apply? Were it cheap and easy to abate sewage pollution nuisance, then no real dilemma would arise with regard to sewage in rivers. Just as Britain's Victorian towns were among the first to embrace the modern concept of water carriage waste systems, so they were forced to be among the first to attempt to tackle the new science of sewage treatment and sanitary engineering.[27]

In earlier times, consideration of sewage waste must have been concerned with how best to use such organic waste for its manurial benefits rather than to discard it or treat or purify it. And for small unwanted quantities, disposal of the offending material directly onto nearby land or into water would be the normal course: there, natural biological action, decomposition and dilution would follow. But where land or water disposal becomes less available, as in towns, then large amounts of unwanted sewage matter is likely to become a more serious problem.

Within the urban areas of early Victorian Britain, in the absence of sewers the fate of the human and domestic waste product of household, backyard and courtyard privies would vary. For rich and poor, cesspits were ubiquitous. For the richer areas, there might be regular clearances and collection by night-soil men and carts, and WCs and sewerage were increasingly available. In the poorer areas,

---

[26]   This was to remain Britain's sole general statutory measure for protection of its rivers for nearly eighty years, until replaced by the Rivers Pollution Prevention Act (1951).

[27]   The definitive source on sewage treatment in Britain up to 1974 is the epic multi-part, twelve-volume work: Henry Herbert Stanbridge, *History of Sewage Treatment in Britain* (Maidstone: Institute of Water Pollution Control, 1976–1977). Henry Herbert Stanbridge (1906–1986) was general manager of the Hogsmill Valley Joint Sewage Board.

however, privy content would typically be led off to cesspits (cesspools, privy middens, ashpits), which were often open to the skies. Here, the liquid constituents would seep away through the land and the more solid content and excreta would accumulate, often for months, sometimes indefinitely, until intermittently dug out manually and carted away. Until such processes were better regulated by public intervention or regulation, tales of the under-provision of facilities, the irregularity of clearances, overflowing cesspools and the resultant unspeakable insanitary conditions are the stuff of the Victorian sanitary enquires. Under such conditions, the fate of the liquid portions of the effluent would be to filter from the cesspools into the ground, often into watercourses and water supplies; and the fate of the solid matter would be to be forgotten or moved on by the night-soil industry to local agriculture or into dumps or river systems.

As the provision of sewers and sewerage services became more regular, sanitary authorities began to consider the alternative techniques open to them to deal with or treat the effluent of their citizenry, other than crudely directing it into rivers. But there existed only a limited selection of techniques available:

Privy Pan Systems

Surprisingly, night-soil collection systems, albeit in a more sophisticated and better regulated form, were to be retained in urban settings by a number of important provincial British towns until well into the modern period. Stanbridge reports that in 1894, numbers of towns, especially outside the south, were still using variations of this system, and use continued well into the twentieth century.[28] Here, rather than household waste being directed to sewers or cesspits, 'privy pans' (containers, pails, tubs or buckets) were placed individually under privies to collect the household's excreta. The privy pans themselves would usually be collected and replaced, serviced almost invariably by the local authority, usually weekly, as in the Rochdale Pail system and by the Goux system used at Halifax.[29] The privy pans would be lined with removable and degradable absorbent material such as straw or cotton waste for the Goux method, and dry earth or ash would be added to the pans by the household on use in the Rochdale system. The contents of the pans, once collected at municipal facilities, were typically mixed with household waste, ash and cinders, then dried and processed, and then sold on as fertiliser or otherwise disposed of. Such systems serving large portions of some urban areas proved very long-lasting. In 1895, Wolverhampton still had 13,500 pan-privies being serviced by the council;[30] Birmingham was still operating a privy pan collection for part of the town in 1913; and Halifax's system was retained until 1939.

[28]   Stanbridge, *History*, 1: 34–5.

[29]   Pierre Nicholas Goux (d. 1879) of The Goux Manure and Sanitary Company, held a patent for the invention of 'improvements in collecting and in disinfecting human excreta and converting the same into manure'.

[30]   *Birmingham Daily Post*, 24 October 1895.

Sewage Farm Treatments

The earliest attempts to cleanse or treat sewage waste by application to the land developed from the age-old desire to utilise the nutrients in sewage by returning them to the soil. As explained earlier, returning sewage to the land was Chadwick's preferred means of dealing with water carriage effluent in the *Sanitary Report*. Two land irrigation approaches, often grouped together as 'sewage farming', existed in the second half of the nineteenth century, known as Broad Irrigation and Intermittent Downwards Filtration.

a) Broad Irrigation

This was the original form of land application for sewage treatment and this approach grew naturally out of intensifying the familiar and widespread agricultural practice of using organic manure as a crop fertiliser. The only large-scale example of deliberate agricultural application of town sewage that Chadwick was able to cite was at the Craigentinny meadows, where four crops of grass were irrigated with part of Edinburgh's sewage annually.[31]

Broad irrigation as a sewage treatment method is straightforward to describe. Typically, the sewage farm land is first divided into a number of areas with each section prepared similarly and usage is then rotated over the sections. For a given area, gutters or furrows ('carriers') are cut into the land so that liquid sewage can flow along the rows, following the land contours. Temporary earth dams or plates or sluices encourage the sewage to spread and flow over and through the top surface of the farm before being allowed to enter the watercourse. An appropriate crop, often quick-growing rye grass, can use the enriched land, and the method would be repeated after harvesting. Treatment, it was believed, would be achieved as the more noxious and offensive potions of the sewage would be beneficially taken up by the crops or detained in the soil by mechanical filtration to decompose and oxidise: the remaining liquid would then run off as a pure stream.[32]

Broad irrigation, using town sewage as liquid manure, held great advantage in its utilizing familiar agricultural processes and so was widely understood and taken up by a number of authorities.[33] Of course, in practice, schemes employed would differ according to the local circumstances of sewage composition and local geology and soil condition; and with local knowledge and opinion. The advice given indicated that, in general, an acre of land would be required by broad irrigation to

---

[31]   At the Craigentinny meadows, about 200 acres were irrigated with the waters of the 'Foul Burn' which carried about half of Edinburgh's drainage. Pumps were used to spread the slurry, with the fields rotated for use every three weeks; and sewage irrigation was continued all year round except for Sundays (General Board of Health (Henry Austin), *Report on the Means of Deodorizing and Utilizing the Sewage of Towns*, No. 2262, 1857, 44).

[32]   Royal Commission on Metropolitan Sewage Discharge, *Second Report*, C.4253, 1884–85, 28.

[33]   Stanbridge, *History*, 6: 13–24.

treat the sewage of somewhere between 50–100 persons per annum.[34] Also, it was recommended that some preliminary settlement and screening of the sewage was required to remove the more solid content and detritus before any application to the land. Sometimes the method proved trickier than expected: often it was found that such farms needed careful handling or the land would become unusably saturated and 'sewage-sick'. Ideally, the method required extensive, nearby and expensive amounts of land with suitably friable and porous soil conditions[35] and such broad irrigation farms always carried a (justifiable) suspicion of being, themselves, a likely source of local nuisance and, possibly, water-borne disease.

b) Intermittent Downwards Filtration

This alternative sewage farm method utilised the land to treat the sewage (literally) at greater depth. The key was to under-drain a section of land using land drainage pipes, at a depth of around six feet, with the surface land levelled enough to form a shallow lagoon to contain the sewage for long enough for it to be absorbed into the ground. The liquid sewage is repeatedly introduced to the section and is cleansed, it was believed, through being filtered by the soil, until the liquid is collected and carried away to the watercourse by the under-draining pipework.

The method was mooted and developed by Edward Frankland in 1870, in his work for the Rivers Pollution Commission of 1868. Broad irrigation used the top surface of the land (and any vegetation) to treat the sewage but Frankland saw that a greater depth of land and soil used, as he believed, as a chemical filter, would increase the cleansing power of any land treatment. He backed his theory with a series of laboratory experiments where sewage effluent was allowed to filter through tubes of various soil types and he concluded that the sewage of 2,000–3,000 persons could be effectively cleansed by each deep-drained sewage farm acre. Prepare an area of only five acres with drainage pipes at a depth of six feet, split the area into four sections so that each section received six hours of effluent in rotation, and the sewage of a watercloset town of 10,000 could be treated.[36] Frankland also realised that it must be a similar effect that was effectively cleansing the fluid effluent escaping from urban cesspools. It was only later that it became known that it was biological effects rather than mechanical filtration that provided the more important process. Despite its promise, Frankland thought it unlikely that his experimentally-based method could be used as an acceptable treatment for town sewage. The repeated flooding of the land sections precluded its use to cultivate crops, so the manurial content of the sewage would be unexploited. Also, he thought that as the method, in practice, would leave solid matter on the surface, this would probably cause 'formidable nuisance' locally.

---

[34] Local Government Board, *Sewage Disposal Report*, C.1410, 1876, 30–5.

[35] Doubly difficult for such as London, to find 150,000 acres within the clayey Thames valley.

[36] Rivers Pollution Commission of 1868, *First Report*, 1870 [C.37], 69–70.

But Frankland's scheme was immediately improved, and largely popularised as a practical process, by John Bailey Denton.[37] Denton was a land-drainage engineer and he would have been well aware how water in drainage pipes normally ran clear, and he also knew that crops flourished when under-draining kept roots unsaturated, no matter how wet the soil surface might be. To accommodate crop cultivation, Denton proposed laying out the surface of the deep-drained land in a series of ridges and furrows with crops growing on the ridges and the sewage flowing and pooling along the furrows, allowing the land to be usefully cultivated. In his practical applications for sewage farms, Denton's plans usually rested the sections of intermittent filtration land for two years out of three to avoid sewage-sickness, and he normally included broad irrigation areas and settling tanks along with areas of intermittent filtration. Denton successfully demonstrated the practicality of his improved schema at Merthyr Tydfil and thereafter, with practised self-promotion, he became one of the best known sewage farm engineers, providing treatment schemes for a number of British towns.

Sewage farming, in the form of either broad irrigation or intermittent downwards filtration, could not provide fully effective sewage treatment to solve the problems of sewage pollution in the rivers, though it surely helped. Stanbridge ascribes the failures of sewage farming as due to confusion over the role of the farms, especially over whether the purpose was primarily to provide a profit or to prevent the pollution of rivers, but also cites the use of unsuitable land, industrial waste poisoning the processes and incompetent management.[38] Sewage farming was slow to be accepted in Britain, with few farms using either broad irrigation or intermittent filtering during the 1870s. No doubt take-up was retarded by the cost of the land required for the initial investment as well as difficulties finding the careful management required.

As we shall see, however, the setting up of sewage farms to treat their sewage outflows was often the response by local sanitary authorities to the demands of the courts for prompt and appropriate reaction to river pollution nuisance suits. And though the court might have been mollified by the establishment of sewage farms, much evidence remains that the poor state of the rivers themselves was often far from abated by the use of sewage farming. From the evidence of the examples below, for small towns with limited sewage flows, where spacious, well-suited land was available at close quarters and where profit was not demanded from the enterprise, sewage farming did improve the state of the sewage-affected streams

---

[37]   John Bailey Denton (1814–93), agricultural surveyor and land and sewage engineer, consulted and contracted for a number of towns. He appears again in the chapters below at Barnsley, Tunbridge Wells, Harrogate and Northampton. Anthony D.M. Phillips, 'Denton, John Bailey', *Oxford Dictionary of National Biography* (Oxford: Oxford University Press, 2004): doi:10.1093/ref:odnb/50168.

[38]   Stanbridge, *History*, 6: 18–24.

(Leamington, Banbury, Tunbridge Wells). For large towns however, sewage farms provided at best only marginal relief (Birmingham, Wolverhampton).

Chemical Precipitation

The major alternative to sewage farming for treatment of urban waste and sewage involved the fully 'scientific' application of various chemicals added to the initial mix, with the intention of a) hastening settlement and precipitation of the sewage in tanks; and/or b) deodorizing and disinfecting the effluent. On the settling and precipitation side, chemicals would encourage the organic matter contained in the sewage flow to precipitate out while standing in vast tanks at the treatment plant. Indeed the formation of a rich organic sludge to be exploited commercially was a primary objective for many sanitary authorities.[39] Once the more solid faecal matter had dropped out to form the sludge at the bottom of the tank, the more liquid parts of the sewage would be moved on, possibly to new tanks to repeat the process and produce more sludge: eventually the remaining liquid would pass, without much further ado, into the river or stream. In addition to aiding sludge-precipitation, the chemicals that were added would also deodorize and disinfect the liquid effluent flowing into the river.[40] The sludge itself would be periodically removed (dug out) from the tanks, dried and processed and eventually carted away. The hope that the nutrients contained in the sewage sludge could be transformed into profitable fertiliser was an incentive that from the 1840s motivated the production of a large number of patented chemical precipitation processes to exploit this idea.[41] But neither profitable output of valuable agricultural manure, nor treatment that allowed liquid sewage effluent to re-enter the local streams harmlessly, was ever fully realised.

The typical town sewage works using such a system would be positioned next to the out-fall river downstream and at the end of the town's sewer network. At the plant, first the sewage would be screened to catch the grossest of the mixed-in rubbish and detritus, and then the chemical of choice, often lime and lime-based mixtures, would be added. Next, the now liquid sewage would be led through the heart of the plant where there would be two parallel sets of, perhaps, four-to-six huge settling tanks, with each set being used alternately. The sewage would enter and then be allowed to stand in the first of the series of settling tanks so that suspended solids held in solution in the liquid could precipitate out over a (short) period of time. The liquid portion of the separated solution would then be led off to the next tank in line to drop more of its suspended solids; and the process was repeated down the line of tanks until the remaining ('clarified') liquid was allowed to escape into the river. After some length of time, or when the sludge capacity of

---

39   Stanbridge, *History*, 3: 8–20.

40   Stanbridge, *History*, 3: 4–7.

41   Stanbridge, *History*, 3: 9–11 reports hundreds of patents sought and describes twelve.

the set of tanks was exhausted, the sludge could be removed from the tanks while the flow of sewage was switched to the parallel set of tanks. As the sludge removed would be too wet to allow easy handling, drying would need to be applied, perhaps by heating, pressing or by evaporation from air-drying in lagoons (for months). Eventually, the solidified sludge could be carted away. Living close to one of these plants was definitely not to be recommended.

Chemical treatment of sewage is not wholly ineffective. For example, adding lime (calcium oxide), it is now understood, has a two-fold effect. Firstly, lime neutralises the electrical charges carried by particles of organic matter partly dissolved or suspended in water which causes the particles to mutually repulse each other; the addition of the chemical causes the suspended particles more quickly to clump together and settle out so the sludge solidifies at a faster rate.[42] Secondly, there is a deodorising and disinfectant effect on the effluent which comes from the acidity (calcium hydroxide) produced by the lime treatment. Although this disinfectant effect is normally not powerful enough to fully sterilise the liquid, it can be enough to retard the putrefaction of the organic matter retained in the liquid. So the liquid passing from the plant to the river is clarified, disinfected and deodorized and this may make the liquid appear to be cleansed enough to be safely discharged. There are a number of instances of mayors and councilmen bravely demonstrating the efficacy of the process at such plants by drinking glasses of the water at the outflow. However, it was widely known that chemically-treated and precipitated sewage effluent still contained large amounts of organic matter which would again, and quite quickly, begin to putrefy in the rivers and streams: cynics believed the most effective result of the process was to cleanse the sewage temporarily, and for long enough to allow it to pass down the river to become someone else's problem. In any event, manure produced from the sludge made the fertiliser a specialist product with little commercial appeal: promises of profit from such schemes proved totally unreliable.

Successive commissions on sewage utilisation and disposal held that chemical precipitation processes were defective and most believed that the only useful place for such schemes was as a preliminary to land treatment on sewage farms. A typical view was that:

> By no known mechanical or chemical means can such [sewage] water be more than partially cleansed: it is always liable to putrefy again. Processes of filtering and deodorization cannot, therefore, be relied upon to do more than mitigate the evil. ... If the sewage of towns is no longer to flow into rivers the only alternative which remains is to dispose of it on the land.[43]

---

[42]   Leonard B. Escritt and Sidney F. Rich, *The Work of the Sanitary Engineer* (Macdonald and Evans, London, 1949), 142–3.

[43]   Select Committee on Sewage (Metropolis), *Report*, No. 487, 1864, vi.

Frankland's Rivers Pollution Commission of 1868 had a particular dislike of these chemical methods for sewage treatment. It reported analyses of effluents from chemical treatment plants '... still so highly charged with putrescible animal matters as to be utterly unfit for admission into running water'[44] and that: 'We are compelled to admit that the present resources of [chemistry] held out no hope that the foul matters dissolved in sewage will be precipitated and got rid of by the application of chemicals to the offensive liquid'.[45] Indeed, the Commission was so unhappy with the Native Guano Company's ABC (alum, blood and clay) method for chemical precipitation, that they devoted the whole of one of their 1870 reports to a righteous demolition of its claims for efficacy in treating sewage.[46]

Notwithstanding the opinions of the official reports on the matter, applying chemical precipitation and relying on settlement in tanks remained a popular recourse for sewage authorities. Stanbridge reports surveys showing 174 towns were still using chemical methods in 1894 to process their sewage; and there were still 45 doing so in 1938.[47] Of the cases below, Leeds persisted over the entire Victorian period with chemical precipitation approaches, despite poor results, and Leamington Spa clung to the method until forced to switch to broad irrigation sewage farming.

For Victorian inland towns, choice over treatment regime was confined to these limited techniques as described, and the potential for success in sewage nuisance abatement using the techniques was, at best, less than assured. Indeed, many towns sensibly attempted to combine some or all of the available treatments to attempt to gain control over the quality of their effluent. Birmingham, for example, by the 1890s was simultaneously employing a privy pan interception system while subjecting its sewer contents to chemical treatment and settlement before application to sewage farms designed to use both broad irrigation and deep-drained filtration.

After the Event: Improved Sewage Treatments (Percolating Filters and Activated Sludge)

Happily for present-day public hygiene and sanitation, as well as for our rivers, the treatment of household sewage was fundamentally improved following new innovations unavailable to the Victorian sanitary authorities responsible for our nuisance cases. These important innovations in sewage treatment began to appear in Britain, and also in France, the US and Germany, twenty to thirty years beyond the time we consider, and well into the twentieth century. One key to the cleansing

---

44   Rivers Pollution Commission of 1868, *First Report*, 1870, 96.
45   Rivers Pollution Commission of 1868, *Second Report*, 1870, 20.
46   Rivers Pollution Commission of 1868, *Second Report*, 1870. The Native Guano Company was providing services to both Leeds and Leamington in two of the chapters below.
47   Stanbridge, *History*, 3: 14–15.

of sewage was to oxidise the constituent organic matter, and by the end of the nineteenth century it had become increasingly clear that successful land treatment was a biological rather than a mechanical filtering or chemical process and that aerobic bacterial action plays a central role in the oxidisation process.[48] Two successful oxidisation treatment approaches emerged: first *percolating filter* beds and then the now-dominant *activated sludge* method.

The use of percolating filter beds was the first of the biological treatment methods to become widely favoured in Britain: it was successfully developed around 1900.[49] The activated sludge process was first described, in an experimental setting, in 1913 by two Manchester engineers[50] and technical-scale activated sludge plants first appear in the UK and US after 1920. It is this technique nowadays that provides the basis of most industrial-scale wastewater treatment systems in widespread use.[51]

These new innovative and effective, biologically-based sewage treatment regimes were unavailable, however, to the local authorities of the British towns facing sanction from the courts over sewage nuisance in the late nineteenth century.

Summary

For Victorian Britain, expectations of increasing sanitary hygiene, backed by the influential notions of Chadwick's ideal water carriage system, placed demands on local authorities to provide full and proper drainage and sewerage at appropriate standards to the growing numbers of people (and WCs) in towns. But the prospects of providing adequate treatment to the increasing volumes of sewage effluent emerging from the new sewer networks were poor. The rudimentary treatment

---

[48]   Anaerobic bacteria are the basis for septic tank sewage treatments and require the reduction or exclusion of oxygen.

[49]   See Stanbridge, *History*, 6: 22–32 and Royal Commission on Sewage Disposal, *Final Report*, Cd. 7821, 1914–1916. The percolating filter bed is not a mechanical filtering process but a bed of loose material medium with a large rough surface area (of clinker or broken stones) which acts as a habitat for organisms and over which screened and settled liquid sewage is allowed to trickle and be treated until collected by under-drains to pass on for disposal.

[50]   Edward Ardern and William T. Lockett, 'Experiments on the oxidation of sewage without the aid of filters', *Journal of the Society of Chemical Industry*, 33 (1914): 523–39.

[51]   The method first develops from the waste a 'floc' of biologically active organic material (including bacteria, protozoa, moulds and yeasts) and for sewage treatment, this floc is mixed with the screened raw sewage and the mixture thoroughly aerated so the organic content of the sewage is quickly oxidised. The material is then drawn off to allow settlement of the solid sludge, with the now-treated clear liquid effluent flowing off and some of the activated sludge used to re-seed the floc for new application. The sludge residue is removed to agriculture, land-fill or the like.

techniques available could not be relied upon to give satisfactory results and were often considered impossibly and unacceptably expensive.

But allowing improperly treated sewage effluent to flow into rivers ran up against the age-old rights to protection against nuisance held by the land-owners of the countryside, and the river pollution dilemma arose from the jealous protection of riparian rights under civil law, and often applied by the august Court of Chancery.

Chapter 4
Nuisance Law and Nuisance Economics

Quarrelling neighbours and common lawyers, engaged in the process of dispute resolution at the margins of a largely traditional system of property law, inhabit one world, which is real and very untidy. Economists inhabit another world. Between them a gulf seems to be fixed.[1]

It was the clash between the requirements for an improved sanitary infrastructure and the long-established tenets of civil law in Britain that formed the setting for the river pollution dilemma that arose in the civil law courts. The received civil law on nuisance in England, inherited from the evolution of court-made rules and precedents, regards harmful water pollution as a violation of the property rights of others. After 1850, the position of English civil law had become quite clear regarding water use and river pollution that might violate riparian rights. Prior to the passing of the Rivers Pollution Prevention Act in 1876, laws under nuisance were the only legal protection for Britain's rivers and as the new statute was explicit in not overriding or superseding the existing common law rules, the common laws of nuisance retained whatever effectiveness they had. Indeed, for none of the cases to be considered below, did legal arguments, *per se*, successfully provide bases upon which the defendants were able to defend their actions, though this was by no means for want of trying. That the river pollution cases considered do not provide deeply important legal precedents may offer partial explanation for why the historical aspects of these cases have largely escaped prior investigation.

Most of the litigation of the river pollution nuisance cases, in line with tradition for such disputes, takes place in the venerable Court of Chancery, and Chancery has a special place in the history of the development and structure of English civil law.[2] Historically, Chancery's origin lies in its role as the royal secretariat and marks of these roots still persist. The Lord Chancellor, as head of the Chancery, long remained a political appointment and a minister of the Crown, and the title of Master of the Rolls, now an immensely important judicial post, harks back to the office's original role as keeper of royal records. Indeed, historically, Chancery's source of influence in civil disputes arose from its being granted, and retaining,

---

[1]   Simpson, *Leading Cases*, 179.

[2]   Duncan M. Kerly, *An Historical Sketch of the Equitable Jurisdiction of the Court of Chancery* (Cambridge: Cambridge University Press, 1890); Albert Kenneth Roland Kiralfy, *Potter's Historical Introduction to English Law* (London: Sweet & Maxwell, 1958); Stroud F.C. Milson, *Historical Foundations of the Common Law* (London: Butterworths, 1981); John Hamilton Baker, *An Introduction to English Legal History* (London: Butterworths, 1990).

the residual power of the monarch to intervene in specific areas and overturn prior decisions where, for example, existing legal rules were seen as inadequate or unjust, as 'Keeper of the King's Conscience'. Over time, the formally constituted Court of Chancery emerged, but the more discretionary nature of its origin enabled Chancery to play a looser and more flexible role in legal decisions than was allowed by the parallel 'common' law system which was considered more rigidly bound by existing rules and precedent. The legal principles practised in the Court of Chancery are known as 'equity'.

Until the mid-nineteenth century, there was a division of the central jurisdiction of civil law in England: the common law courts such as King's (Queen's) Bench, Common Pleas and Exchequer used the rules of common law (or just 'law'); the Court of Chancery used the rules of equity. Over time, differences in the systems gradually diminished so that by Victorian times when the court cases to be discussed below were being held, the principles of equity had become so fixed and process in Chancery had moved so close to the common law that Pettit is able to conclude that rather than there being two differing legal systems: 'By the early nineteenth century, equity had become simply that part of the law enforced in the Court of Chancery.'[3] Chancery had also acquired a reputation for bureaucratic tardiness in process, and also for waste and expense and bore the brunt, for example, of Dickens's informed critique of the English legal process in the opening sections of *Bleak House*. But important changes to the formal structure of the English legal system were introduced after mid-century, in particular by the Common Law Procedure Act (1854), the Chancery Amendment Act (Lord Cairns' Act, 1858) and the Judicature Acts (1873, 1875). These reforms brought together the two systems of common law and equity in a 'fusion' under which the rules of the two sections became, effectively, merged.

Nuisance Law

Within case law, nuisance covers disputes where one party's actions, unreasonably and in a continuing way, interfere with or harm another party's rights to use their property or enjoy their lifestyle. Nuisance embraces, as its stereotypical example, pollution in its various guises, including water pollution.

The early nineteenth century up to mid-century, but not thereafter, was a time when the legal context as regards the rights to water for property holders in England was still not fully clarified. Up to the 1850s, the background system of tort and nuisance law of the industrial revolution has been described as 'haphazard'[4] and as regards the law on riparian rights and water flow, it is argued there existed a

---

    [3] Phillip H. Pettit, *Equity & the Law of Trusts* (Oxford: Oxford University Press, 2009), 5.

    [4] Michael Lobban, *The Common Law and English Jurisprudence 1760–1850* (London: Clarendon Press, 1991), 285.

'diversity of views among the judges ... on almost every aspect of water law.'[5] This diversity of views within English civil law is usually presented as the result of a conflict between two competing underlying standards or rules for the use of flowing surface water: one known as *prior appropriation* and the other as *natural flow/riparianism*.[6]

On one side, *prior appropriation* theory maintains, at basis, that the first agent to exercise rights to use an amount of flowing surface water thereby establishes full rights to use the resource, with no regard at all to subsequent owners or users. Here the 'first come, first served' rights to use an amount of water are independent of land ownership and are appropriated under a system whereby past continued and beneficial use conveys a right to current use of the same amount of water. As developed in the western states of the US, if you are the first to use the river, say, to irrigate your ten acres of crops, as the 'senior appropriator' you acquire a right to that amount of water under continuous beneficial use, for perpetuity. Users who later acquire similar but 'junior appropriator' access may only exercise their rights over water usage once the prior rights of the series of more senior appropriators have been exercised, and may, indeed, find no actual water remaining. Water rights under this system, once acquired, are treated similarly to rights to other real property, most notably in that they may be traded and sold on, independently of the land on which the water originates, or through which it passes, or on which it is used.

By contrast, *natural flow* theory, or *riparianism,* maintains that owners of riparian rights can make ordinary or reasonable use of a water flow, up to a level that does not reduce the quantity or quality of the water flow available to other rights holders. Here, rights over water utilisation are normally attached to the land itself, and a landholder will usually be allowed reasonable use of water and river passing over or alongside property held. Hence, a new user will be allowed to take an amount of water for industrial use or to irrigate crops so long as such use does not interfere with other landholders' reasonable usage of the river. Riparianism would naturally preclude an upstream user polluting the stream to an extent that seriously and materially interfered with how downstream users might reasonably wish to use the stream or its water.

---

[5] Michael Taggart, *Private Property and Abuse of Rights in Victorian England: The Story of Edward Pickles and the Bradford Water Supply* (Oxford: Oxford University Press, 2002), 144.

[6] This only applies for common-law-based legal systems. For many jurisdictions, water rights may not be privately owned at all, but are vested in the public: water extraction is then permitted and administered by the state through the issue of licences defining the conditions, quantity and purpose allowed for use. Increasing statutory regulation over water usage is a common trend for all jurisdictions. See David H. Getches, *Water Law in a Nutshell* (St Paul, Minnesota: West Publishing Co, 1997); Roberto Cavallo Perin and Dario Casalini, 'Water Property Models as Sovereignty Prerogatives: European Legal Perspectives in Comparison', *Water*, 2 (2010): 429–38.

Up to the mid-nineteenth century, despite considerable case law and commentary,[7] grave uncertainties were evident as to whether prior appropriation or riparianism rules governed the English situation. However, in 1851, influenced by US experience, the leading English case Embrey v Owen established the Embrey doctrine and the ascendancy of the natural flow/riparianism rule for English law,[8] at least with respect to surface water flowing in natural streams and in proscribed channels. The decision in the case established:

> The right to have a stream of water flow in its natural state, without diminution or alteration, is an incident to the property in the land through which it passes; but this is not an absolute and exclusive right to the flow of all the water, but only subject to the right of other riparian proprietors to the reasonable enjoyment of it; and consequently it is only for an unreasonable and unauthorised use of this common benefit that any action will lie.[9]

Following Embrey, holders of riparian rights were cleared in law to use the flowing surface water within the riparian tract in any way required, but only so long as no material damage was done to others with riparian rights to the stream, and for any ordinary or reasonable means: interference by others with natural water rights becomes actionable and makes water pollution liable under nuisance law. As clarified by further case law,[10] this has remained the basic tenet of English water rights and water usage ever since: reasonable or ordinary use of water on your land is allowable, but further use may not interfere with other rights-holders' reasonable or ordinary use.[11]

The most common defence offered by towns accused of nuisance in the cases considered here is that their actions are in the public interest and that any harm caused by their activities is more than offset by the benefits available from, say, the establishing of a water carriage sewage disposal system for their town. This

---

[7]   The special nature of water and water flow allows much scope for complexity and clarification in water rights considerations and in the evolution of water law: Joel F. Brenner, 'Nuisance Law and the Industrial Revolution', *Journal of Legal Studies*, 3 (1974): 403–33; Raymond Cocks, 'Victorian Foundations?' in *Environmental Protection and the Common Law*, (eds) John Lowry and Rod Edmunds (Oxford: Hart Publishing, 2000), 1–25; Joshua Getzler, *A History of Water Rights at Common Law* (Oxford: Oxford University Press, 2004); William Howarth, *Wisdom's Law of Watercourses* (Crayford: Shaw & Sons, 1992); John P. McLaren, 'Nuisance Law and the Industrial Revolution – Some Lessons from Social History', *Oxford Journal of Legal Studies*, 3 (1983): 155–221.

[8]   Embrey v Owen (1851) 6 Ex 353.

[9]   Ibid.

[10]   McLaren, 'Nuisance Law', 176–80.

[11]   The opposing prior appropriation rule has commonly applied in more arid areas under common law where water tends to be annually more variable in quantity, typically the western states of the US.

'social utility' defence is a variant of the economic efficiency argument discussed at length below and lies at the base of what makes the sewage river pollution dilemma a dilemma. A common expression of this position is the (rather overstated) sentiment from a Northampton commissioner:

> ... is it not better that one family should suffer a nuisance [from sewage pollution] than that half Northampton should be poisoned?[12]

Within nuisance law this argument is called 'the balance of convenience', and if it were to be an allowable defence within English civil law no dilemma would arise: it will then come as no surprise that such a defence is not allowable in law. For five hundred years, following Aldred's Case in 1610,[13] the established general rule for nuisance in England has been that the existence of off-setting benefit from the actions causing the nuisance could not be taken as a defence, and this is well documented and well-understood: '... if an activity amounted to a nuisance, it would be actionable regardless of its utility: and this is the present law';[14] '[t]he common law rejected the idea of permitting what has come to be called the economically efficient level of pollution';[15] and '... it was no defence that ... his activity was of public utility and benefit'.[16] The Embrey doctrine and the riparian water law rules certainly allow little room for a social utility defence. Although often repeated and re-tested by the river pollution cases below, including, dramatically, in Attorney-General v Birmingham (1858), the English courts continued to reaffirm that any overall general welfare improvements deriving from the actions of the defendants would not provide relevant grounds for a defence of nuisance, at least so long as the nuisance can be shown to be sensible and material.[17] Hence, except where the injury is trivial, the English court allows the defence no balance of convenience or 'relative' arguments, weighing social benefits and costs, to justify nuisance actions.[18]

---

[12] *Northampton Mercury*, 4 September 1869.

[13] Aldred's Case (1610) 77 ER 816.

[14] Baker, *English Legal History*, 488.

[15] A.W. Brian Simpson, 'Coase v Pigou re-examined', *Journal of Legal Studies*, 25 (1996): 91.

[16] McLaren, 'Nuisance Law', 169.

[17] Getzler, *History of Water Rights*, 245–51; McLaren, 'Nuisance Law,' 169–80; Anthony I. Ogus, and Genevra M. Richardson, 'Economics and the Environment: A Study of Private Nuisance', *Cambridge Law Journal*, 26 (1977): 295–301; Simpson, *Leading Cases*, 170–90; Frank H. Stephen, *The Economics of the Law* (Hemel Hempstead: Wheatsheaf, 1988), 79–84; Stephen Tromans, 'Nuisance – Prevention or Payment', *Cambridge Law Journal*, 41 (1982): 87–109.

[18] An influential alternative view was aired by Lord Denning as Master of the Rolls, who set out a celebrated dissenting view in *Miller v Jackson* including '... nowadays it is a matter of balancing the conflicting interests of the two neighbours ... There is a contest

Another notable feature that established itself over the Victorian period is the coming to primacy in English law of the use of the injunction in the choice between injunctions and damages as the remedy for nuisance liability imposed by the court. It comes as a shock to learn that in practice, up to the mid-nineteenth century, injunctions were an uncommon remedy for nuisance. Up to that time, following a court decision that an offending party was liable for a nuisance, the usual outcome was the award of compensatory damages to be paid by the offender to the offended party. Injunctions were the preserve of the Court of Chancery under equity rules; in the common law courts, such as the Court of Queen's Bench, the award of damages was the only means available for the court to enforce its decisions. It was only after the reforms of the legal process after the mid-nineteenth century that the common law courts could apply injunctions and Chancery apply damages. Before this time it might require suits to be won both in the common law courts and then under equity, in the Court of Chancery, to obtain an injunction.[19] Little wonder reforms were required.

The popularity of injunctions as a remedy has grown ever since, despite injunctions remaining only a discretionary remedy. Damages only mitigate past offence and repeated offences require repeat visits to court: injunctions restrain future offences as repetition of the offence can lead to contempt of court and subsequent sequestration orders. The use of injunctions is now such that the English courts 'would almost invariably grant an injunction to restrain a continuing nuisance'[20] and the courts became, and so remain, reluctant to use remedial measures other than injunctions in nuisance cases.[21] Indeed, so routine has become the use of injunctive relief that commentators have pointedly characterised English nuisance law as offering 'absolute protection to plaintiffs: either the nuisance existed and an injunction was granted or courts avoided granting an injunction by deciding that no nuisance existed'.[22]

As English 'judge-made' civil law has been evolving historically, it has left eddies and creases in its fabric that have taken time to be overruled or smoothed

---

here between the interest of the public at large; and the interest of a private individual. As between their conflicting interests, I am of the opinion that the public interest should prevail over the private interest' (1977 3 QB 966 at 981). Denning's argument was subsequently criticised and rejected (*Kennaway v Thompson* 1981 QB 88, 1980 All ER 329), and Denning's intervention seems destined to remain a footnote.

[19]   Baker, *English Legal History*, 131. In the celebrated air pollution dispute of the 1860s between Tipping and the St Helens Smelting Company, the complainant, Tipping, first fought the case through the Queen's Bench, and up to the House of Lords and then went to Chancery and another appeal to obtain an injunction (Simpson, *Leading Cases*, 183–91).

[20]   Tromans, 'Nuisance', 88.

[21]   Ibid., 88–93.

[22]   Timothy Swanson and Andreas Kontoleon, 'Nuisance', in *Encyclopedia of Law and Economics*, (eds) Boudewijn Bouckaert and Gerrit de Geest (Cheltenham: Edward Elgar, 2000), 381.

or ironed out by new precedent or statutory adjustments. One of these is very noticeable in the progress of the Victorian nuisance case studies below: it concerns the role of the Attorney-General and the divergence between private nuisance and public nuisance. At basis, a public or common nuisance is characterised as an act which, by its nature, is a single nuisance which annoys or obstructs a number of (not necessarily landholding) individuals or is common over an entire vicinity. Private nuisance protects the property rights of a single individual landholder to enjoy the use of the land held, for example for crop-growing and the like. This enjoyment can include immaterial amenities like peace and quiet, but only non-trivial and material damage (like poisoned fishing grounds) confers *strict* liability: otherwise, concerning discomforting amenity loss, the reasonable expectations of the neighbourhood are taken into account. The effects of river pollution can fall under either public or private nuisance.

For public nuisance, in order to save the putative wrongdoer from being subject to a series of suits from those affected, the proper form of court action has generally been, since the sixteenth century, for the presumed offender to be sued only once, and in the name of the public. But a fundamental principle of English law maintains that the rights of the public are vested in the Crown, so that individuals are unable to assert public rights in their own name. The tradition, therefore, is for the Attorney-General to bring a 'relator action' on the 'relation' or 'information' of an individual in order to assert a public right. The Attorney-General, as an officer and legal representative of the Crown who has special privileges with regard to appearing before the courts, is able to assert these public rights on behalf of the wronged public. Still, beyond the Attorney-General's decision to lend the title to institute the proceedings, the actual conduct of any relator case under nuisance, including instigating the suit and paying, instructing and hiring counsel, remains entirely the responsibility of the relator. Hence, for example, the public nuisance action, discussed below, brought by Charles Bowyer Adderley against Birmingham's sewage pollution of the Tame, was disputed as a relator action under the name of Attorney-General v Birmingham (1858). Here, as with other relator cases described below, the role of the Attorney-General remained purely nominal and the relator role was generally indistinguishable from that of an individual plaintiff in a purely private action. In a further complication, however, actions with regard to river pollution (which will usually confer general annoyance) nevertheless continued to be sought under private nuisance law, and this is also allowed with the argument that the plaintiff was suffering *special* damage compared to the commonality.[23]

---

[23] John R. Spencer, 'Public Nuisance – a Critical Examination', *Cambridge Law Journal*, 48 (1989): 55–84; Baker, *English Legal History*, 492–4.

Nuisance Economics

The structure and influence of law and the legal system has always been a continuing topic for consideration among economists, but over the last half-century there has been huge growth in the area of discourse involving the analysis of the law using economic approaches and the tools of modern economics. The growth has been such that the disciplinary sub-group called 'law and economics' has arisen in both law and economic studies. Aspects and considerations from within this vast field of study provide useful context for the better understanding of the river sewage pollution dilemma of Victorian England: it provides guiding hypotheses for the cases under consideration.

Economic Efficiency

Within mainstream modern economic discourse, the ultimate aim and objective of policy-making and social activity is variously and nobly viewed as attempting to enhance the economic welfare of society. Economic welfare or 'efficiency' is often portrayed as referring to the total of goods and services produced by a society from its available resources for the benefit of its members (the *size* of the pie that society is able to produce) but 'efficiency' as used in economics is rather more subtle and complex than this might seem to imply: it requires more than just maximal material output from the material input in an crude engineering sense. To employ a basic illustration, the welfare of society as a whole can be increased, it is maintained, were a cheese-loving individual who holds some tomatoes and a tomato-lover who holds cheese, to swap some or all of their holdings: the two individuals will be more content, so society's welfare is improved, even though the total of material goods within the society has not changed. The pursuit of maximised economic welfare must therefore include considerations concerning improvements in social welfare resultant from such allocative adjustments. The ultimate goal would be achieved in an economy where, given the fixed resources (including knowledge and technologies available) the way that the economy was operating and organised was such that no potential adjustment[24] remains to be achieved that could improve any one individual agent's welfare without causing a decrease to the welfare of some other agent. This interpretation of the highest attainable level of welfare, given the constraints, is called *Pareto optimality* or *Pareto efficiency*.[25] This efficiency is also, often and equivalently, if more succinctly, characterised as a state of economic organisation of society where resources are placed where they are most highly *valued* by its members.

In these terms, if a society were considering the introduction of a proposed change to the way it was organised, the central question would be whether the new

---

24   This includes possible changes to the mix of what is being produced, or how it is being produced or to the allocation of goods and services to individuals.

25   Named for Vilfredo Pareto (1848–1923).

organisation of the resources would improve society's welfare, and the critical test would be whether the change would make at least one individual feel better off while no other individual felt they would be harmed by the change – deemed a *Pareto-superior* change for society. Those new to such concepts often scoff that there must be few such changes that harm no-one: 'it's a good wind that blows nobody ill.' But this is a mistake. Each of the myriad trades and exchanges that make up daily life in the markets, stores and workplaces of an economy constitute, so long as they remain voluntary and potentially rejectable, Pareto-superior changes for society. And where some are benefited and none lose out, changes are likely to occur without too much fuss, and without too much notice. But voluntary trade is one action where both sides feel themselves improved by the exchange; the trade would not otherwise proceed. Hence such trades thereby improve societal welfare.[26] A Pareto optimum would be where no more Pareto-superior changes remain to be completed, so no unexploited but possible mutually beneficial contracts between parties persist.

It may be accepted that proposals like private, mutually-advantageous trades, where some gain and none lose, can be viewed as invoking an increase in overall social welfare, but what of proposed changes where there will be both winners *and* losers? This will be the case with the river pollution episodes described below. A further test is required to judge such situations, and this is provided by the Kaldor-Hicks potential compensation criterion.[27] This test asks whether, after the proposed change has been instituted, it is possible for those who have gained from the change, potentially but adequately, to compensate those who have lost, yet after the potential compensation still regard themselves as improved. If, then, those who gain from the change gain more than the loss of those who lose, then the change is deemed to be welfare improving (even though no potential compensation is *actually* to be paid, so some *actually* lose). Whatever the possible philosophical and even logical criticisms that can be levelled at such a formulation for judging welfare improvements,[28] the Kaldor-Hicks criterion lies at the heart of formal (and informal) techniques for social policy evaluation, such as cost-benefit analysis. And any reader whose immediate reaction to the river sewage dilemma was to leap

---

[26]   This powerful argument lies at the heart of why economic commentators seem so wedded to 'free trade' and are so often seen as hostile to policies that would reduce or restrict the extent of voluntary trade. But this is not to ignore, perhaps, the controversial nature of some of the concepts involved. Some might contend, for example, that were all the gains from a proposed change to accrue, say, only to those already rich, increased relative inequality of distribution of welfare might be viewed as a worsening of social welfare, even if no one individual suffers a welfare decline.

[27]   Sometimes 'Hicks-Kaldor'. John Hicks (1904–89) and Nicholas Kaldor (1908–86) independently proposed this test.

[28]   For example, it may be shown that it is possible for a proposed change from state A to state B to pass the Kaldor-Hicks test whilst a subsequent proposal to move back from B to A may also pass the test (the Scitovsky paradox).

to the conclusion that, of course a populous town's sewage needs should override the rights of a single landowner, would probably justify this stance with recourse to some variant of the Kaldor-Hicks criterion.

Indeed this idea was clearly anticipated in a legal context in a comment from Baron George Bramwell in the Court of Exchequer,[29] as early as 1862:

> The public consists of all the individuals of it, and a thing is only for the public benefit when it is productive of good to those individuals on the balance of loss and gain to all. So that if all the loss and all the gain were borne and received by one individual, he on the whole would be a gainer. But whenever this is the case – whenever a thing is for the public benefit, properly understood, – the loss to the individuals of the public who lose will bear compensation out of the gains of those who gain. ... It is for the public benefit that trains should run, but not unless they pay their expenses. If one of those expenses is the burning down of a wood of such value that the railway owners would not run the train and burn down the wood if it were their own, neither is it for the public benefit they should if the wood is not their own.[30]

Of course, the Kaldor-Hicks criterion contains obvious parallels to the 'balance of convenience' argument presented by defendants within nuisance disputes before English courtroom judges and traditionally always formally rejected. Again, if balance of convenience arguments were to be an allowable defence in law, the reasonable presumption that the needs of extensive urban populations outweigh the inconveniences of sparse rural landowners would dismiss the nuisance suits brought by riparian complainants. Were this the case, no river sewage pollution dilemma would have arisen.

Beyond the formalisation of the economic efficiency background to the river sewage pollution dilemma, the arguments of welfare economics and the 'new institutional economics' provide other guiding hypotheses which may be usefully cited in exploring the histories and experiences of the legal case studies below. Hypotheses that may be found especially helpful may be summarised as: the Coase theorem, Demsetz's thesis and Posner's conjecture.[31]

---

[29]   Patrick S. Atiyah, 'Liability for Railway Nuisance in the English Common Law: A Historical Footnote', *Journal of Law and Economics*, 23 (1980): 191–6.

[30]   Bamford v Turnley (1862) 122 ER 27.

[31]   Demsetz's argument is a 'thesis' in Thomas W. Merrill, 'Introduction: the Demsetz Thesis and the Evolution of Property Rights', *Journal of Legal Studies*, 31(2002): 331–8; and Posner's argument is a 'conjecture' in David D. Friedman, *Law's Order: What Economics Has to Do with Law and Why It Matters* (Princeton: Princeton University Press, 2001), 110.

The Coase Theorem

The modern surge in interest in the application of economic principles and approaches to matters of law followed the celebrated contribution of Ronald Coase in an article published in 1960.[32] Coase highlighted a number of issues that indicated the centrality and importance of matters of property rights and transactions costs and initiated a debate and discussion leading to the argument now known as the Coase theorem.[33]

Within the economic analysis of the phenomenon, nuisance is typically viewed as an example of an external effect, or externality, arising out of the existence of conflicting or poorly delineated ownership of property rights. Discussion of externalities often arises in the important debate on the efficiency of a competitive market organisation of the economy.[34] Where externalities exist, as in the example of pollution, the effects of the actions of one agent (Mr A) spill-over directly on the welfare of other economic agents who are themselves not partners to the decision regarding Mr A's action itself. Calculations based on his own purely private costs and benefits can lead to levels of activity by Mr A that while optimal from the (polluting) Mr A's private point of view, would not be socially optimal were the costs (or benefits) of the external effect on the others affected to be taken into consideration. In the shorthand phrase, 'social and private costs diverge'. The result may be that an inefficient amount of the activity takes place and the market economy might consequently fail to provide socially efficient outcomes.

The ideas arising from the Coase theorem[35] play an important role in the discussion of externalities and their role in causing markets to fail to provide optimal outcomes and these ideas are therefore central to considerations of nuisance and pollution. The arguments of the Coase theorem are based on the proposition that a potential (unexploited) benefit exists in the presence of an external effect and this may or may not be capturable by the parties involved, depending on the presence

---

[32] Ronald H. Coase, 'The Problem of Social Cost', *Journal of Law and Economics*, 3 (1960): 1–44.

[33] Sometimes known as such under protest: see Michael R. Butler, and Robert F. Garnett, 'Teaching the Coase Theorem: Are we getting it Right?', *Atlantic Economic Journal*, 31 (2003): 133–45; Dee N. McCloskey, 'The So-called Coase Theorem', *Eastern Economic Journal*, 24 (1998): 367–71; Altug Yalcintas, *The 'Coase Theorem' vs. Coase Theorem Proper: How an error emerged and why it remained uncorrected so long* (SSRN, 2010), http://dx.doi.org/10.2139/ssrn.1628163.

[34] Francis M. Bator, 'The Anatomy of Market Failure', *Quarterly Journal of Economics*, 72 (1958): 351–79; Francis M. Bator, 'The Simple Analytics of Welfare Maximization', *American Economic Review*, 47 (1957): 22–59; Nicholas Mercuro and Steven G. Medema, *Economics and the Law* (Princeton: Princeton University Press, 1997); Stephen, *Economics of the Law*, 27–39.

[35] And from interpretations of the arguments of Coase, especially George Stigler, *The Theory of Price*, 3rd edn (New York: Macmillan, 1966).

and magnitude of 'transactions costs'. Transactions costs in practical terms can be viewed as referring to the costs of time and effort and legal, court and policing fees involved in negotiating, bargaining and contracting between parties. When unresolved external effects exist and the transactions costs of negotiation between the parties are sufficiently small, the potential net benefit from resolving the externality can be realised and shared and this provides an incentive for bargaining between the parties.

In a simple illustration, say Farmer Y's fertiliser run-off affects the waters used by Fishery Z and inflicts a negative external effect on this fishing enterprise. Attempts at bargaining can ensure the most valued use of the stream is nevertheless achieved. If Farmer Y values the stream as a run-off more highly than Fishery Z values a clean stream for its purposes, then the fishery will not be willing to offer a payment level that will induce Farmer Y to halt the run-off. In this case, the property right to use the river remains (efficiently) with Farmer Y, the party valuing it most highly. Unless the fishery's valuation of the resource at least matches Farmer Y's, it will be unable to acquire the resource. On the other hand, if the Fishery Z values a clean stream as a resource more highly than does Farmer Y for run-off purposes, some level of payment will allow the fishery to contract with Farmer Y to halt the run-off: the property right transfers (efficiently) to the party valuing it most highly, to the benefit of both parties. So, rational negotiation, through ensuring an allocation of resources that is the more highly valued, provides just what is required for enhanced economic efficiency. And note, both parties are improved after the side-payment is made. Under either end result, river usage (a property right) rests where it is more highly valued.

Legal disputes about whether towns may be allowed to continue to outflow their sewage into river systems, when viewed in a similar way as disputes about ownership of property rights, leads to the surprising conclusion that, so far as efficiency is concerned, the court's decision on which party owns the disputed property right is irrelevant, so long as such rights are clearly assigned and transactions costs are negligibly small. Rational bargaining will ensure that the contested property right will, in the end, be acquired by the party who values the right most highly, regardless of judicial decisions with regard to liability and property rights ownership and independently of which party wins the judicial decision.

The Coase theorem, whether grossly interpreted as arguing that bargaining will induce the efficient allocation of resources even in the presence of externalities or as arguing that the court's decisions on liability and entitlement is irrelevant to the final destination of the resource under dispute, relies upon transactions costs being negligible enough not to disrupt the trading or bargaining process. It is easy to see that where there are gross enough impediments to the bargaining process ('transactions costs are high') these powerful arguments will no longer hold. Negotiation between the parties may fail or prove infeasible because, perhaps, there are a large number of possible complainants who cannot organise themselves or coordinate, or because strategic stances involving bluff and holding-out are being poorly employed. Where bargaining is infeasible, the recommendation emerges that, in pursuit of efficiency, the courts 'should' in the first place decide liability and assign resources according to where they are most highly valued. This recommendation, a corollary to the Coase theorem, has gained a name as the normative Hobbes theorem.[36] But the recommendation that courts might, in any case, follow economic principles and act by assigning rights and deciding cases directly on economic efficiency grounds remains a controversial contention.[37]

No-one familiar with the legal process, in practice, could deny that direct negotiation and bargaining between the parties involved in disputes does often occur, before, during and after court hearings, necessarily where such bargaining is feasible, in line with the arguments of the Coase theorem. However, it is similarly clear that bargaining is not always feasible.

Aspects of the Coase theorem provide guiding hypotheses which have the potential to help us better understand the process of the case studies below. A blanket strict liability legal rule about nuisance that protects landholders and riparian rights holders under all circumstances from sewage nuisance from upstream towns is not efficient in the terms discussed above. Indeed, it may lead to the river pollution dilemma. But pre- or post-litigation bargaining can transform this rule into efficient outcomes, albeit requiring, at the limit, a frictionless negotiating process. If inefficient outcomes apparently persist, it may be illuminating to seek information on whether obstacles and inflexibilities in the institutional or social framework exist that may obstruct possible negotiated solutions. For example, for the sanitary authority defendants considered below, obtaining authorisation for action and access to funds was sometimes difficult, often requiring public mandate or an enabling act of parliament; and problems of group decision-making in committees are evident. Nevertheless, we will see that some (but certainly not all) of the nuisance disputes below end with negotiation and side-payments being made.

But the argument about settlement of disputes through bargaining also provides, at the very outset, a warning about case studies. A comparative case study approach can only investigate river pollution dilemma disputes for which evidence persists. But if negotiation were to be a viable means of settling a dispute and a settlement actually results, the case involving the dispute may be withdrawn from the court calendar before being formally adjudicated or even recorded, so that the cases that are seen as recorded or being heard by the court may be *special* and the sample of observed case studies may be unrepresentative of the generality of river

---

[36] Robert Cooter and Thomas Ulen, *Law and Economics*, (Addison-Wesley, 2000), 94.

[37] See Ronald H. Coase, 'Law and Economics and AW Brian Simpson', *Journal of Legal Studies*, 25 (1996): 103–19; Simpson, 'Coase v Pigou re-examined'; A.W. Brian Simpson, 'An Addendum', *Journal of Legal Studies*, 25 (1996): 99–101; A.W. Brian Simpson, 'The Story of *Sturges v Bridgman*: the Resolution of Land Use Disputes Between Neighbors', in *Property Stories*, (eds) Gerald Korngold and Andrew P. Morriss (New York: Foundation Press, 2004), 9–40.

pollution or other nuisance disputes. This problem constitutes a form of sample selection bias and no matter how careful or admirable the study, this argument remains a difficult hurdle for those investigating the empirical importance of the Coase theorem.[38]

Demsetz's Thesis

Demsetz's thesis, attributed to Harold Demsetz,[39] concerns the structure of the legal and institutional regime within which economic behaviour and activity takes place. Such an institutional regime concerns a wide range of societal rules, wider than merely those related to land tenure, and might include the rules concerning such matters as negligence and the enforceability of contacts. Normally for economic discourse, the underlying legal regime and structure of property rights is taken as fixed, but Demsetz's thesis argues that these rules not only affect behaviour and economic activity, but are likely to be themselves both subject to and affected by economic factors.

Within this context, property is traditionally viewed as a bundle of rights delineating control over its different attributes, and, for example, Henry Smith argues the case for differentiating these rights between those concerning what use may be made of the property (governance rules) and those concerning which individuals are to have access to the property (exclusion rules).[40] The argument around Demsetz's thesis was initially concerned with the way in which these property rights over land can change with regard to rights to hunt or collect resources over the land. These rights may allow 'open access' for all, with no restrictions on who might use the land; alternatively the land might be a 'commons' such that only members of the commons were allowed access, with all others excluded; or perhaps the land may be held under 'private property' with only designated owners allowed to decide upon who might use and have access to the land. Demsetz's thesis maintains that changes in the framework of property rights will be dependent upon changes in the costs and benefits and technologies associated with each framework. For example, excluding non-members of a commons or trespassers on private property requires resources to be used to enforce new exclusion rules, perhaps requiring fencing and guarding the areas concerned. To move to a property regime requiring such exclusion will only become sensible if

---

[38] See for example, Ward Farnsworth, 'Do Parties to Nuisance Cases Bargain after Judgment? A Glimpse inside the Cathedral', *University of Chicago Law Review*, 66 (1999): 373–436.

[39] Harold Demsetz, 'Toward a Theory of Property Rights', *American Economic Review*, 57 (1967): 347–59; Armen A. Alchian, 'Some Economics of Property Rights', *Il Politico*, 30 (1965): 816–29; Thomas W. Merrill, 'Introduction: the Demsetz Thesis and the Evolution of Property Rights', *Journal of Legal Studies*, 31 (2002): 331–8.

[40] Henry E. Smith, 'Exclusion Versus Governance: Two Strategies For Delineating Property Rights', *Journal of Legal Studies*, 31(2002): 453–87.

the benefits therefrom outweigh the costs. Hence, changes in the technologies of exclusion or the costs and benefits to be derived, it is argued, will therefore affect the structure of the legal and institutional framework of property rights. In this way, for example, new availability of cheap barbed wire might be associated with changes in the way land tenure rules were to be applied on the American prairies.

To illustrate the endogeneity of property rights regimes, Demsetz's employed an example concerning access to the Montagnais Indian beaver hunting ranges following the opening up by the Hudson Bay Company of trading in beaver furs in Quebec. Following the resultant increases in the value of beaver fur, it became worthwhile for the local tribes to devise and enforce new institutions to reduce overhunting; and so new exclusion rules emerged to restrict access and hunting in the areas concerned.[41]

The changing technologies and innovations of the Victorian industrial revolution certainly provided changes in costs and benefits enough to provide incentives for changes in the structure of property rights and duties. Were the new technological innovations of, say, the introduction of Chadwick's water carriage system or wastewater disposal in rivers to result in a changed cost-benefit balance and lead to variation in property rights or their enforcement, possibly in the form of a revision or relaxation of nuisance laws and their application, then Demsetz's thesis would be of clear applicability. In one of the cases below, it will be shown, an explicit new statutory law allowing the town to be exempted from river sewage nuisance suits was passed by Parliament. In a number of other cases, judges are clearly seen as unwilling to apply, unreservedly, traditional injunctive remedies and seem to be seeking devices whereby unwanted consequences might be mitigated. In these ways, Demsetz's thesis provides a further guiding hypothesis for the following analyses.

Posner's Conjecture

The new institutional economics provides a further guiding hypothesis in Posner's conjecture,[42] which maintains that the evolution of judge-made common law tends towards the development of rules which support or encourage economic efficiency.[43] Richard Posner is quite explicit about the proposition: '... the common law is best understood not merely as a pricing mechanism, but as a

---

[41] For other applications, see David D. Haddock and Lynne Kiesling, 'The Black Death and Property Rights', *Journal of Legal Studies*, 31 (2002): 545–87; Terry L. Anderson and Peter J. Hill, 'Cowboys and Contracts', *Journal of Legal Studies*, 31 (2002): 489–514; Dean Lueck, 'The Extermination and Conservation of the American Bison', *Journal of Legal Studies*, 31 (2002): 609–52.

[42] Richard A. Posner, *Economic Analysis of Law*, 1st edn (Boston: Little Brown, 1972).

[43] '... the economic analysis of law, as it has actually developed, had been heavily influenced by Judge Posner's conjecture that common law, but not statutory law, tends to be economically efficient'. Friedman, *Law's Order*, 110.

pricing mechanism designed to bring about an efficient allocation of resources, in the Kaldor-Hicks sense'.[44]

The conjecture arose from the comparative analysis of legal rules and the observation that common law process has often chosen, from the range of possible rules that might have become standard, rules that encourage economically efficient outcomes. One illustrative example considers the possible rule that might be applied by the common law as remedy for a breach of contract (to be applied where that contract fails to specify such sanction). Perhaps Company P fails to deliver to Mrs Q an artefact promised by a contract. One possible remedy that the law might apply would be, perforce, to *require* Company P to perform the duty specified by the contract ('specific performance') and, therefore, supply the artefact. An alternative remedy might be that Company P be required to compensate Mrs Q so that Mrs Q is no worse off than she would have been if the contract had been fulfilled ('compensatory damages'). On moral grounds, some might favour specific performance on the basis that promises freely made ought to be kept, but under either rule Mrs Q is no worse off. But if the contact had been breached because a third party, Mr R, had offered a higher price to Company P for the artefact involved, this implies he had a higher valuation of this than Mrs Q, and it follows that the breaking of the contract led to a more efficient outcome. Here, requiring specific performance, and insisting the original contract with Mrs Q be fulfilled, would be economically inefficient: with Mrs Q rather than Mr R, the artefact would be allocated where it is less highly valued. Allowing the contract to continue to be breached, but compensating Mrs Q with damages, provides an efficient solution and outcome.[45] Under common law, it emerged, compensatory damages rather than specific performance was, indeed, normally the remedy for breach of contract, whereas under some non-common-law legal frameworks specific performance is the extant remedy.

This, and other examples of the evolution and emergence of rules and remedies within the common law as it has developed which may be shown to lead to efficient outcomes, have given the Posner conjecture both plausibility and influence. Some have been able to argue that 'From its inception, a foundational claim of law and economics is that the common law tends to the promotion of economic efficiency.'[46] Whether the conjecture holds or does not hold remains, however, another matter.

---

[44]   Richard A. Posner, 'The Law and Economics Movement', *American Economic Review*, 77 (1987), 1–13.

[45]   The reader will already have noted that in the absence of transaction costs, rational bargaining would ensure the efficient solution emerged even under specific performance. Only where excessive transactions costs obstruct negotiation would the argument have force.

[46]   Todd J. Zywicki and Edward Peter Stringham, 'Common Law and Economic Efficiency', *George Mason Law & Economics Research Paper*, No. 10–43 (2010), 1.

Some are less than convinced[47] and Friedman, while allowing that 'The Posner thesis, whether true or false, has clearly been useful', also maintains:

> My own conclusion is that the jury is still out on the Posner thesis. Some features of the common law make sense as what we would expect in an efficient legal system, some do not, and in many cases we simply do not know with any confidence what the efficient rule would be.[48]

For our purposes, it seems on first viewing that the law of nuisance with regard to river pollution cannot be one whose form has evolved such that, in England by Victorian times, it was supporting efficient outcomes. Chancery's sewage nuisance dilemma only arises, *per se*, because inefficient liability decisions were resulting from the application of the legal process: the dilemma exists *because* the legal outcome is inefficient. Nevertheless, it will also soon become clear from the reports on the proceedings in our case studies that in the cases below, the Lord Chancellors, Vice-Chancellors and Masters of the Rolls of the Court of Chancery were often unwilling slavishly to apply remedies that would enforce these inefficient outcomes. Few Victorian judges would have known what an 'economically inefficient outcome' might be,[49] and most would have scoffed at the thought they might be applying economic principles to legal decisions, but the comments from the bench and their issued orders show they simply did not want to close down the sewers of these provincial towns and neither did they wish to harm their inhabitants or penalise by sequestration the members of their sanitary authorities. And that was what they were being asked to do.

Posner initially proposed that the tendency of the common law to move towards efficient rules arose simply from common law judges having a preference for rules that promoted efficient outcomes. So far as the river pollution cases below are concerned, there are clear signs that judges made every effort to avoid outcomes that would have arisen from applying remedies strictly in line with the letter of the nuisance laws. But no important new formal precedents on liability for nuisance over sewage pollution in the period were set and no new judge-made law arose concerning, for example, consideration of balances of convenience. However, among the variety of ways this dilemma played out, in a number of cases, was by judges applying the existing law *formally* to liability decisions while allowing contingencies, postponements and lengthy delays to the remedial process of the law which resulted *effectively* in the town proceeding, for extended periods, to continue their nuisance-producing pollution activities. Barnsley and Leeds provide such examples. Some might argue that, in face of a legal rule (river pollution nuisance) which, in the presence of transaction costs, would invoke inefficient

---

[47]   Steven Shavell, *Foundations of Economic Analysis of the Law* (Cambridge: Harvard University Press, 2004), 666–72.

[48]   Friedman, *Law's Order*, 306.

[49]   But see Atiyah, 'Liability for Railway Nuisance'.

outcomes (closure of town sewage networks) judges, unwilling to change formal precedent over liability, proved able to find less formal *ad hoc* means to mitigate remedies to promote more efficient outcomes. Posner's conjecture provides a further guiding hypothesis helping understanding of the history and context of the court cases presented.

Nuisance Management

A common view of the working of the court is to identify its role in cases of tort and nuisance as, at least, twofold.[50] Firstly the court must decide on liability concerning who holds the rights or entitlements in dispute. Secondly, the court must decide upon the choice of remedy by which these entitlements should be enforced, and among the enforcement remedies open to the court are injunction orders prohibiting (or requiring) certain actions by one party and orders for the payment of compensatory damages for any past or continuing harm. For this model, in short, a plaintiff and defendant appear at the civil court; facts, agreed or not, are presented; legal and other arguments are dispensed by the disputants; the judge then considers the arguments and, given the law as understood, makes liability or entitlement decisions about the property rights at dispute, and then decides what remedies should be applied to enforce the decision. In this model of the workings of the legal adjudication system, generally known as the 'traditional' or adversarial litigation system, and familiar to the Anglo-American scene, the court is seen as acting as a detached as well as an independent referee, and the dispute between the parties is settled by recourse to a combination of the presented facts pertinent to the case and the existing law and rules as understood and applicable given the circumstances. However, in the disputes in the river sewage nuisance case studies presented below, in practice the functional role taken by the civil legal system may be viewed rather differently. Especially noticeable is how, explicitly in some of our nuisance examples and implicitly in others, the court, rather than just making a judicial decision on a disputed property right and applying a remedy, is seen to be taking on a post-trial managerial or supervisory function.

Contingent Injunctions, Judicial Supervision and Consent Orders

Some commentators have emphasised that the remedies that courts can call on in nuisance disputes are wider than a choice merely between the awarding of snap-shot compensatory damages and the imposition of abatement injunctions immediately applied. Including in their orders a delay prior to implementation of the remedy introduces further options that the court can turn to in practice. Cooter

---

[50]   For elaboration and generalisation of such an approach, see, for example, Guido Calabresi and A. Douglas Melamed, 'Property Rules, Liability Rules and Inalienability: One View of the Cathedral', *Harvard Law Review*, 85 (1972): 1089–1128.

and Ulen commend serial damages to be continued over time for nuisance, rather than a one-off, final settlement, arguing that while serial damages require costly intermittent returns to court they also impose incentives for offenders continuously to adopt technical improvements to reduce the harm they impose.[51] Similarly, Tromans and Ogus and Richardson put cases for delayed or suspended injunctions (with or without interim damages), arguing that suspension is appropriate if time is required to achieve abatement of the nuisance and immediate abatement is problematic.[52] But the implication is that such suspensions are to be once-only and not for extended periods.[53] Injunctions suspended like this may be deemed *delayed* injunctions and are of the form: 'The order to stop doing (this action) comes into force on this future date (dd/mm/yy).'

What we will often see in the case studies below is the court applying *contingent* injunctions taking a form rather different from this. The court, after finding the offender liable for perpetrating a nuisance, then specifies some conditions to be fulfilled by the defendant which will require general or specific actions, in a manner quite different from a simple injunction/damages framework of enforcement remedies. In general, the form of the contingent injunctions ordered is: '... *if* (a specified condition) exists at this future date (dd/mm/yy), *then* this court will issue an order against you' and for the river sewage pollution cases, the initial order issued by the court is often in the form of: '... *if* polluting sewage outfalls into the river still continue at this future date (dd/mm/yy) *then* this court will issue an order against you'. As the future date arrives, the complainant then has the opportunity to test whether the local authority has fulfilled the conditions set, by returning to the court for a new hearing. If satisfied the set conditions have not been met, at this point, an injunction can be issued or a further contingent order made allowing the passage of further time before a new hearing at a future date. We will see long series of such contingent orders issued for some of the river pollution disputes (Birmingham, Leeds, Barnsley).

Where contingent orders are issued by the court, the court is acting in just the same way as would a supervisory agent or administrative overseer, rather than acting as exercising judicial authority in the traditional manner. The court is checking whether the local authority has done what it was required to do to alleviate the problem causing the dispute. Sometimes, the series of contingent orders only ends and a traditional injunction actually issued when circumstances have changed such that it is believed the terms of the injunction to be issued are under no danger of being violated (Leeds). In some cases documented below, the supervisory nature of the court's role is made even clearer because the court (or its agent) provides an explicit list of what the local authority needs to do to

---

[51]   Cooter and Ulen, *Law and Economics*, 170.

[52]   Tromans, 'Nuisance', 93–4; Ogus and Richardson, 'Economics and the Environment', 311.

[53]   Halsey v Esso Petroleum Ltd, (1961) 2 All ER 145, is a typical case cited in these circumstances but here the suspension of the order was for just six weeks.

improve its facilities to avoid the imposition of the injunction. For example, at Wolverhampton, these requirements included instructions as detailed as requiring the addition of a two-foot high waterproof bank at the treatment works, and at Leamington included requiring the doubling of the length of the settling canals and the adding of additional ventilators at their sewage works.

That the Court of Chancery might have been comfortable with such supervisory or administrative tasks is no surprise given the other legal functions it was performing. Chancery and equity have always had important functions in overseeing trusts and company liquidations and bankruptcies. In these areas, the court would be required to establish and empower executive officers and offices to run estates and assets; and after establishment, the court would be called upon to revise and supervise the actions of the executors or receivers and ensure compliance with legal and other requirements. Undertaking similar tasks to ensure Victorian sanitary authorities acted in accordance with existing instructions would be parallel functions.

Where, in civil disputes, future conduct is voluntarily agreed between the disputant parties, with or without the participation of the court, but where the written agreement arrived at is to be policed by the court, this becomes equivalent to a consent order or consent decree. Consent orders are now ubiquitous in all areas of civil dispute, and especially in family law, with their form itself now regulated by extensive statute law. Modern legal process could not function without them. The origins of consent orders must go deep into legal precedent, but their history is under-researched. Little formal acknowledgement of 'consent orders' as a legal device can be found much before 1850, and for river pollution nuisance not much before 1885.[54]

The traditional/adversarial model of the Anglo-American civil law process where judges merely preside rather than take an active role has been questioned by commentators discussing what is seen as a recent phenomenon in seeing supervisory functions taken on in civil courts by the 'managerial judge'.[55] This has been highlighted by discussion in the US on the place of 'public law litigation' and 'institutional reform litigation'.[56] This refers to litigation instituted in the courts based on claims that local government action or inaction violates a required legal provision, often concerning civil rights but also including local government provision of environmental services. The court then issues a consent decree, which is a compromise settlement agreed between plaintiff and defendant specifying in

---

[54]   Chuck v Cremer (1846) 47 ER 884; *Times*, 2 December 1846. An early example concerning river pollution nuisance is Attorney-General v Burslem Local Board, (1884), see *Times*, 16 February 1884.

[55]   Judith Resnick, 'Managerial Judges', *Harvard Law Review*, 96 (1982): 374–448; Elizabeth G. Thornburg, 'The Managerial Judge goes to Trial', *University of Richmond Law Review*, 44 (2010): 1261–1325.

[56]   Abram Chayes, 'The Role of the Judge in Public Law Litigation', *Harvard Law Review*, 89 (1976): 1281–1316.

detail the future actions the local authority is required to take. As supervised and enforced by the court, failure to comply with the specified requirements becomes a contempt of court. Examples of the application of such processes in the US have lasted decades. Some observers, with more faith in the competence and reliability of the courts than that of the executive powers of local authorities, view such process as admirable. But the agreed consent decrees may be so wide as to require specific actions which are not part of any existing federal, state or local legislation and may, therefore, constitute regulation of public institutions that amounts to new executive power affecting many not concerned with the original lawsuit. Critical commentators view this as 'democracy by decree' and suspect that this process undermines the conventional political process by which new laws and regulations are introduced.[57]

What does not seem to be at issue is the court's post-trial role in such matters as a supervisory or administrative agent, and the judge as post-trial 'manager'. Resnick notes that 'many techniques of post-trial management ... are not novel',[58] and as a number of the case studies below will demonstrate, the Court of Chancery can be observed taking a 'managerial' role, effectively supervising the post-trial activities of parties to nuisance disputes under Victoria, well before the modern era.

River Pollution Dilemma and the Role of the Courts

The history and context of the case studies that follow show how the social institutions of Victorian Britain managed the perplexing dilemma of the clash between the needs of the towns and industry to dispose of their waste and effluent and the rights of landholders to enjoy their land and water resources without nuisance from the same sources. Of special note, despite the absence of an effective means of treating large quantities and flows of sewage, in no instance did it transpire that the river sewage outflows were actually and decisively stopped on the order of the courts. Similarly, no new judge-made precedents had to be established by the courts to deal with the situations presented to them, and indeed, no new general statutory framework was established that would override the existing common law rules on nuisance.

The differing means by which this accommodation between what appears to be incompatible requirements was accomplished are contained in the case studies described in the following chapters. What is apparent, over all cases, is how eager and concerned is the court to *settle the dispute* and it is this aim, rather than the application of principle or precedent in the law, that may be seen to be paramount

---

[57] Ross Sandler and David Schoenbrod, *Democracy by Decree: what happens when courts run government* (New Haven and London: Yale University Press, 2003); Ross Sandler and David Schoenbrod, 'The Supreme Court, Democracy and Institutional Reform Litigation', *New York Law School Law Review*, 49 (2004–2005): 915–42.

[58] Resnick, 'Managerial Judges', 414.

in how the case progresses. And, surprisingly, the court is, in the end, mostly indifferent as to the means by which the dispute is settled. In a number of cases, the complainants will only require that the defendants sincerely take on the best available, if imperfectly effective, abatement schemes and the dispute ends with partial abatement but continuing physical nuisance at a seemingly actionable level (Birmingham). Sometimes the solution may arise from the independent actions of the disputants themselves, and a settlement comes about through a negotiated settlement without too much input from the court (Harrogate). The court will sometimes send away the disputants and instruct them, implicitly or explicitly, to come to an agreement, and this sometimes works. Sometimes, the defendant finds a solution that will satisfy the complainant by diverting the polluting material away from the complainant and directing the otherwise unchanged effluent towards another location (Northampton). In one case (Wolverhampton), new statutory law was passed to exempt the town from the consequences within nuisance law of their poor sewage treatment regime.

What many observers will be surprised to see is how often the High Court, in these case studies, is seen to be acting in a supervisory and overseeing role rather than in the pure judicial refereeing role that is traditionally assigned to it. Sometimes a voluntary contractual agreement between the parties about future conduct will be policed by the court, like a consent order. Sometimes the court itself will appoint experts to report on and institute inquiries into the best ways individual towns might proceed with their sanitary processes, and then issue contingent injunctions that will become operative only if some conditions have not been met. Multiple and lengthy suspensions and delays to orders issued against towns often result, but the courts are in effect acting to manage the way the defendants must respond.

For the majority of the cases studied, the court is seen to act, with repeated suspensions of injunctions, repeated contingent injunctions, threats of sequestration, delayed and suspended and quickly lifted sequestrations, in ways that show the unwillingness of the courts to *actually* halt the sewerage systems and networks of the towns. Nevertheless, the English courts remained steadfastly vehement in their avowal of the protection of the ancient rights of landholders in defence of encroachment via sewage nuisance. Hence, in *formal terms* involving entitlement and liability, nuisance law was upheld. In *effective terms*, taking into account remedies and the process of enforcement, however, the outcome was different.

With the guiding hypotheses in mind, we can now move on to consider the historical context and aftermath and longer-term outcomes of how the Victorian river pollution dilemma played out and was resolved, in detail, over several individual river pollution cases arising within the English court system.

Chapter 5
Birmingham, Adderley and the River Tame

Birmingham's dispute with Charles Adderley (Lord Norton) over Birmingham's pollution of the River Tame is, in many ways, preeminent among river pollution actions and central to the Victorian river sewage pollution dilemma.[1] The 1858 hearing of Attorney-General v Birmingham put Birmingham among the very first of the lengthy roll-call of English towns to be arraigned before the Court of Chancery charged with sewage nuisance[2] and the case is widely cited within the law of nuisance where it is often presented, over-simply, as a quickly-settled, straightforward action in nuisance law.[3] In fact, the dispute was extraordinarily protracted, taking close to forty years, from 1858 until 1895, to come to a final settlement. As will be seen, the court records also contain the most telling quotes summing up both the dilemma and the received stance of civil law on the topic. Over the decades the dispute persisted, Birmingham's unsuccessful attempts to abate the nuisance put its civil engineers at the forefront of Victorian sanitary engineering and its attempts to settle with or assuage the complainant would touch on many of the available solutions that were also to emerge in other cases and circumstances.

The hard-to-credit duration of the dispute indicates the intractability of the problem. As the defendant, the large town[4] of Birmingham was simply unable to deal adequately with its sewage effluent and wastewater tainting the local River Tame system. Behind the name of the Attorney-General was the relator Charles Bowyer Adderley, later Baron Norton, who was a notable and wealthy local landowner and a nationally prominent politician. Adderley's residence was at grand Hams Hall, next to the River Tame, and the property was subjected to gross and damaging nuisance from Birmingham's sewage outflows. The Court of Chancery, in line with established legal precedents, found the Birmingham local authority liable for the nuisance. In such simple terms lies the Victorian river pollution dilemma and raises the simple question: what actually did happen next?

---

[1] An earlier account is in Leslie Rosenthal, 'Economic Efficiency, Nuisance, and Sewage: New Lessons from Attorney-General v. Council of the Borough of Birmingham, 1858–95', *Journal of Legal Studies*, 36 (2007): 27–62.

[2] Earlier cases of river sewage nuisance suits in England have yet to emerge.

[3] Attorney-General v Birmingham, (1858) 4 K&J 528; 70 ER 220.

[4] Birmingham did not formally become a city until 1889.

Background

Of the numerous English urban agglomerations that grew from mere market towns to major urban centres during Britain's industrial revolution, the rise of none was more striking than that of Birmingham. From under 60,000 in 1800, by 1850, Birmingham's population had grown to around a quarter of a million, and the town was becoming the second most populous in England. It had become a manufacturing centre of global importance, producing a vast range of Victorian wares and staples: engines, machines and machine tools, guns, toys, jewellery and other hardware and metal-based industrial and household products, manufactured by mostly small enterprises and workshops, in a highly enterprising and competitive local economic environment.

It comes, again, as a surprise, to realise just how little local government there was in provincial towns like Birmingham when Victoria ascended the throne. Although by the 1830s Birmingham was a populous town, up to 1838 it did not have a charter to make it an incorporated borough, so it had no elected town council or corporation. Most local governance remained with a collection of uncoordinated and separate institutions, including the church parishes of the area, the manorial Courts Leet and the Boards of Guardians. For environmental and public health services, following the first Birmingham Improvement Act of 1769, civic duties lay with the Board of Street Commissioners whose major functions were originally based on cleaning, maintaining and lighting the roads and regulating Birmingham's markets;[5] funded by the power to raise a small local rate. Over time, new powers accrued to the board and in 1812 the fifty-man strong Street Commissioners became required to ensure that the public roads of the area were also well-drained.

Humble though it might sound, requiring the draining of highways often marks the unheralded beginnings of the creation of a new sanitary infrastructure and the beginnings of a water carriage system for towns. Well-drained streets require effective systems of gutters and culverts to carry off excess water into the local rivers and a working drainage system will attract, willy-nilly, all sorts of other industrial and general detritus and, especially, domestic effluvia. In the 1840s, Birmingham's commissioners took on sewerage duties more formally as sewerage began to replace cesspools and middens, which were becoming suspected as sources of contamination.[6] From 1845 the Surveyor to the Street Commissioners, John Pigott Smith,[7] began to organise sewers and a system of lesser drains to carry off the mix of run-off, wastewater and sewage to the River Tame and River Rea.

---

[5] Five Birmingham Improvement Acts expanded the powers of Birmingham's Board of Street Commissioners, in 1769, 1773, 1801, 1812 and 1828, see Conrad Gill, 'Birmingham under the Street Commissioners, 1769–1851', *University of Birmingham Historical Journal*, 1 (1948): 255–87.

[6] Conrad Gill, *History of Birmingham, Manor and Borough to 1865*, vol. 1 (London: Oxford University Press, 1952), 330.

[7] John Pigott Smith (1798–1861) was Surveyor to the Street Commissioners (1835–51) and then Birmingham Borough Surveyor (1851–57); 'Smith, John Pigott, 1798–1861', *ICE*

Following the Municipal Corporation Act of 1835, the town became an incorporated municipal borough with a more familiar local government structure of elected town council, mayor and aldermen,[8] and it became increasingly evident that local administrative power would increasingly rest with the town council. In 1851, the Street Commissioners wound themselves up, passing their duties and responsibilities to the Birmingham Corporation and its Public Works Committee.[9]

From the Street Commissioners, the Corporation inherited Pigott Smith's beginnings of an installed sewerage network,[10] including a main sewer which had been laid to the River Rea in 1846 and another main sewer which terminated at Saltley, where the Rea and the Tame converged. Sewer outlets into the rivers at Saltley opened in 1852 and 1853.[11] Investment in sanitary improvement was hardly premature. The foul living conditions and sanitation of Birmingham in the 1840s and 1850s, especially for the poor, are well-documented and disturbing contemporary narratives exist of the social conditions of its inhabitants.[12] Chadwick's *Sanitary Report* of 1842 estimated that around 50,000 people inhabited about 2,000 courts in the Birmingham parish. For a typical court, a single narrow entrance would lead from the street into a communal yard onto which ten or so small family dwellings opened. The courts were designed to be built side-by-side and back-to-back with adjacent courts and the conditions were sordid and overcrowded:

> The old courts are for the most part narrow, filthy, ill-ventilated and badly drained [with] a wash-house, an ash pit and a privy at the end or on one side of the court and not infrequently one or more pigsties and heaps of manure. Generally speaking the privies are in a most filthy condition.[13]

Minutes of Proceedings, 21 (1862): 594–5.

[8]   The town council would have forty-eight councillors representing the local wards of the town, one third elected annually, and sixteen aldermen each serving a six-year period. See Ernest Peter Hennock, *Fit and Proper Persons* (London: Edward Arnold, 1973), 22–3; 'The City of Birmingham', in Victoria History of the County of Warwick, 7, (ed.) W.B. Stephens (Oxford: OUP, 1964), 318–53.

[9]   Enabled by the 1851 Birmingham Improvement Act, which also transferred control over the urban infrastructure for a wider local neighbourhood to the Corporation. A number of clauses of this act were extracted from the Towns Improvement Clauses Act (1847).

[10]   Pigott Smith's sewerage plans fell foul of the miserly Birmingham Town Council of the time and he was controversially dismissed in 1857. Gill, *History of Birmingham*, 419; James L. Macmorran, *Municipal Public Works and Planning in Birmingham 1852–1972*, (Birmingham: City of Birmingham Public Works Committee, 1973), 29–32.

[11]   John Thackray Bunce, *History of the Corporation of Birmingham II*, (Birmingham: Birmingham Corporation, 1885), 126; Macmorran, *Municipal Public Works*, 7.

[12]   'Report on the State of the Public Health in the Borough of Birmingham', in Chadwick, *Sanitary Report*, 192–217; Robert A. Slaney, 'Report on Birmingham', in Royal Commission on Health of Towns, *Second Report*, No. 602 (1845): 1–120.

[13]   Chadwick, *Sanitary Report*, 195.

For Birmingham's general environment, drainage was haphazard: there was no separation of human waste, industrial effluent, general and abattoir detritus and rainwater run-off; and thousands of horses provided both local transport and copious street sweepings. With only rudimentary effluent disposal through ditches and drains into open cesspools and seldom-emptied middens and ashpits, and with infrequent and intermittent removal of night soil by hand and cart, Birmingham was, to contemporary sensibilities, let alone those of the present day, an extremely unpleasant, malodorous and unhealthy place in which to live and work. For Hunt, 'it was a disgusting city':[14] it would be hard to disagree.

With regard to the local rivers, the existing drainage of the town had long seeped and flowed gradually into the Rea and the Tame via the ditches and watercourses and the natural flow. But with increasing population and industry, the local river system was becoming overwhelmed. Even in the 1840s there were reports that the Rea was 'very offensive and ... covered with a thick scum of decomposing matter'[15] and presented, for about a mile 'a pestiferous surface of white scum, from which a noxious effluvia is exhaled.'[16]

So the situation in the 1850s saw Birmingham's nascent sewer network delivering its sewage through two main sewers directly, and completely untreated, into the Rea[17] and Tame at Saltley. And at this point, even before much of Birmingham was served by sewers, the rather minor local river system could not cope. As Gill says, 'the sanitation of a town meant the pollution of a countryside.'[18] In October 1854, Birmingham town council received complaints about the pollution of the Tame from Charles Bowyer Adderley, along with a group of other distinguished local landholders, including Sir Robert Peel, Lord Bradford and Lord Leigh.[19] This is the first recorded complaint from Adderley to Birmingham about sewage pollution, but from this moment he doggedly and persistently pursued his grievances over the spoiling of the Tame.

---

[14]   Tristram Hunt, *Building Jerusalem, The Rise and Fall of the Victorian City* (London: Phoenix, 2005), 324.

[15]   Chadwick, *Sanitary Report*, 191.

[16]   Slaney, 'Report on Birmingham', 4.

[17]   The Rea was the subject of a poignantly out-dated eighteenth-century rhyme: 'Grey willows whisper by the Rea, Where lovers dream and children play, In clean fields on a summer's day' (John Morris Jones, *The Waters of Birmingham* (Birmingham: Birmingham Public Libraries, 1979), 25); and an unlikely epithet: 'lively tripping Rea' (Gill, *History of Birmingham*, 124).

[18]   Gill, *History of Birmingham*, 427.

[19]   *Birmingham Gazette*, 9 October 1854. Sir Robert Peel (1822–95), MP for Tamworth and eldest son of the late prime minister, was resident at Drayton Manor, near Tamworth, on the Tame just north of Adderley's Hams Hall. George Bridgeman, 2nd Earl of Bradford (1789–1865) owned Castle Bromwich Hall, two miles along the Tame Valley from Saltley. William Henry Leigh, 2nd Baron Leigh (1824–1905), owned estates in Stoneleigh: his sister, Julia Anne (1820–87) was married to Charles Bowyer Adderley.

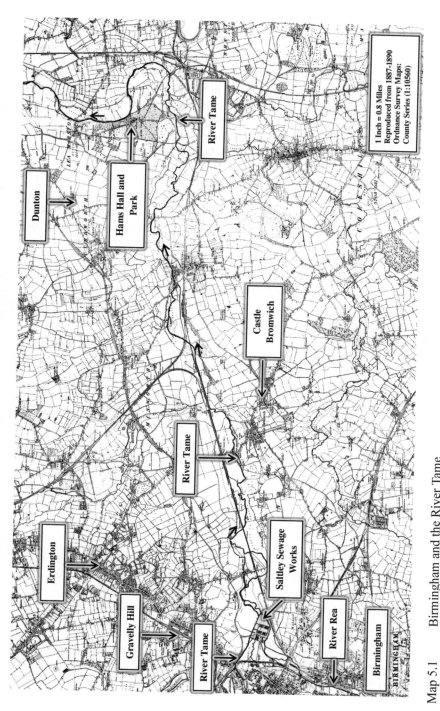

1 Inch = 0.8 Miles
Reproduced from 1887-1890
Ordnance Survey Maps:
County Series (1:10560)

Dunton

Hams Hall and Park

River Tame

Castle Bromwich

River Tame

Erdington

Gravelly Hill

River Tame

Saltley Sewage Works

River Rea

Birmingham

BIRMINGHAM

Map 5.1   Birmingham and the River Tame

Charles Bowyer Adderley, Lord Norton (1814–1905)

Charles Bowyer Adderley inherited Hams Hall with its park and estate in 1826. The hall itself was situated next to a sharp bend of the river Tame about seven miles downstream of Birmingham's sewer outlets at Saltley. Although Adderley himself is now largely forgotten, he was a leading public figure in his day, rich, influential and politically well-connected. A brief biography would note that he was (Tory) Member of Parliament for North Staffordshire over the course of no less than eight parliaments from 1841 until 1878, including spells as Under-Secretary for the Colonies (1866–8) and President of the Board of Trade (1874–8) and he acted as chairman of the Sanitary Commission whose report in 1871 preceded the Public Health Acts of 1872 and 1875.[20] At the grandest level, his most important lasting achievements probably concern his influential and sympathetic attitude towards colonial self-government, including, it is claimed, the construction of a first constitution for New Zealand, said to have been concocted on the terrace of Hams Hall during 1850.[21] Adderley even claimed credit, and precedent over Plimsoll himself, for the introduction of the celebrated Plimsoll line for the regulation of ship-loading limits.[22] Awarded a baronetcy to become Sir Charles Adderley in 1859, he was then created first Baron Norton of Norton-on-the-Moors in 1878, after which he served a further twenty-seven years in the House of Lords until his death, at ninety, in 1905.

Adderley had no reputation as a public speaker, but he was hard-working, tenacious and devout, and, given his social status, his views were even, in places, progressive.[23] He claimed deep commitment to the improvement of the social conditions of the local labouring classes and invested heavily, albeit profitably, in the general development of Saltley township where he held extensive property. But Adderley was also generously philanthropic, providing Birmingham, in 1855, with its first public park, still named Adderley Park. He also patronised (in many senses) the local music scene and the arts, and founded and funded a number of churches and charitable institutions, including a training college, library and museum. Adderley was, without doubt, a formidable opponent for Birmingham to confront in this dispute.

---

[20]   J.E.G. de Montmorency, 'Adderley, Charles Bowyer, First Baron Norton (1814–1905)', *Oxford Dictionary of National Biography*, (Oxford University Press, 2004): doi:10.1093/ref:odnb/3034; *Times*, 29 March 1905.

[21]   William S. Childe-Pemberton, *The Life of Lord Norton* (London: John Murray, 1909), 91.

[22]   Ibid., 215–18.

[23]   On the other hand, a case against him would not be impossible to construct: Adderley appears as a rather bumbling and obstructive figure in Jones's history of the campaign to introduce ship-loading limits (Nicolette Jones, *The Plimsoll Sensation*, (London: Abacus, 2006)).

Attorney-General v Birmingham (1858)

The means by which Charles Adderley sought to pursue his complaint about the harm imposed by Birmingham on his estate from the sewage pollution of the River Tame was through the relator action[24] of Attorney-General v Council of the Borough of Birmingham, held on 22–23 July 1858,[25] in the Court of Chancery[26] before Vice-Chancellor Sir William Page Wood.[27]

The hearing opened with establishing Adderley as the owner of rights to use the River Tame as it flowed past his estate at Hams Hall, followed by a description of the deterioration of the state of the river consequent to the opening of the new sewer outlets at Saltley earlier in the 1850s. The claim, repeatedly echoed in these sewage nuisance cases (to demonstrate material and non-trivial damage being caused) was that the water had deteriorated so that, 'fish had all died, cattle would no longer drink.'[28] Medical evidence on the harmful miasma from the river was also presented. Adderley had originally requested an injunction restraining Birmingham from causing the main sewer outflow to pollute and damage the Tame. In the event, however, he backed away from this and, instead, asked for two orders from the court: (i) an injunction to prevent Birmingham from attaching additional sewers into the existing main sewer leading to the Tame; and, (ii) a definite and effectual, guaranteed, *undertaking* from Birmingham that they would immediately resort to the most effectual means available to abate the nuisance being caused to the river. So Adderley, formally at this point, did not seek an injunction to prevent continuance of the sewage nuisance, but only sought to require that Birmingham not add to the problem and seek out and urgently apply the most effective available means of alleviating the current nuisance. He did, however, threaten that if *bona fide* attempts at alleviation were not undertaken immediately, he would ask to have the nuisance abated 'at any cost', presumably by seeking a straightforward restraint against causing nuisance.

For the defence, Birmingham's case did not deny the existence of the offences complained of, but raised a number of arguments, all of which the Vice-Chancellor rejected. One defence proposed was the balance of convenience or social utility argument and the relevant question posed by the defence was most directly reported in the *Times* as:

> [Are] the lives of 250,000 of her majesty's subjects in Birmingham to be imperilled for the convenience of an individual? Better that the legal rights of

---

[24] For explanation of 'relator action' see Chapter 4.

[25] This is the same year that brought, in June, 'The Great Stink' on the Thames in London.

[26] Court of Chancery Records: Pleadings, C15/446/A76, UK National Archives.

[27] William Page Wood (1801–81) later First Baron Hatherley.

[28] *Times*, 24 July 1858.

a few should suffer some interference than that a large and important town be delivered up to pestilence.[29]

In Kay and Johnson's report, the defence argument was the equally theatrical:

> ... the evil that must ensue if the Court should [find for Adderley] would be incalculable. If the drains are stopped, the entire sewage of the town will overflow. Birmingham will be converted into one vast cesspool ... The deluge of filth will cause a plague, which will not be confined to the 250,000 inhabitants of Birmingham, but will spread over the entire valley and become a national calamity. ... the progress of a nation in industry and wealth, is attended of necessity by inconvenience to individuals, against which it is in vain to struggle. In such cases private interests must bend to those of the country at large. The safety of the public is the highest law.[30]

This all became too much for the Vice-Chancellor, who intervened:

> We cannot talk of that in this Court. Here the safety of the public is that which the Legislature has said is for the safety of the public, and no more.

Vice-Chancellor Page Wood later expanded his view as follows, and an irritable tone still shows:

> ... it appears to me that, so far as this Court is concerned, it is a matter of almost absolute indifference whether the decision will affect a population of 25,000 [sic], or a single individual carrying on a manufactory for his own benefit. The rights of the Plaintiff [Adderley] must be measured precisely as they have been left by the Legislature. I am not sitting here as a committee for public safety, armed with arbitrary power to prevent what, it is said, will be a great injury not to Birmingham only, but to the whole of England; that is not my function. My function is only to interpret what the Legislature (the proper body to which all such arguments should be addressed) has considered necessary for the town of Birmingham. The town of Birmingham is to have neither more nor less than the Legislature has thought necessary for its protection. The Plaintiff's rights are neither more nor less than the Legislature has thought to leave him. [Nothing] has given the Defendants any right so to interfere with the river as to produce the nuisance of which the Plaintiff complains ... He has a clear right to enjoy the river. How the town is to be thoroughly drained without causing a nuisance is the business of the Defendants to discover.[31]

---

[29]   Ibid.

[30]   Attorney-General v Birmingham, (1858) 4 K&J 528.

[31]   Ibid.

A more definitive and unambiguous statement of the rejection of the social cost-benefit calculation that underlies any economic efficiency approach to legal process would be difficult to find. Hence, the argument from the social utility balance of convenience was decisively rejected.

Another failed defence proposed by Birmingham was that as the construction of Birmingham's sewers had statutory authority from the Birmingham Improvement Act (1851) which had incorporated clauses taken from the Towns Improvement Clauses Act (1847), statutory power had been therefore awarded Birmingham and this overrode any legal nuisance. This argument was rejected by the Vice-Chancellor who noted that one clause of the Towns Improvement Clauses Act explicitly required that 'nothing in the Act contained shall be construed to render lawful any act ... deemed to be a nuisance at common law' and that utilising the Act therefore carried this restriction also.[32]

In the event, two orders were made in Chancery in line with Adderley's requests.[33] Firstly, an immediate injunction was imposed to disallow Birmingham opening or adding or connecting any additional sewers into the existing sewer system unless and until a further order of the court was made. Secondly, it was ordered that:

> ... in the event of the Defendants not proceeding forthwith to take such steps as may be necessary and proper and due time being allowed for that purpose ... to prevent the pollution of the Tame ... the informant [Adderley] to be at liberty to apply on the first day of Michaelmas term for an extension of the injunction.

Michaelmas term would begin in November, 1858, and the threat is to extend by disallowing the nuisance entirely. Some have interpreted the second part of this order as suspending the injunction for a short period,[34] but, rather, it is the means of supplying judicial backing to the guarantee, required by Adderley, that Birmingham make good its promises to tackle the pollution nuisance. It constitutes a *contingent* threat by Chancery. If Birmingham's authorities do not take steps to prevent the pollution of the Tame before the period of grace expired in November, Chancery will listen to a request for a permanent injunction from Adderley.

---

[32]   Other rejected arguments were: a) that the inhabitants of Birmingham had had, and had exercised since time immemorial, a right to drain their houses into the Rea and Tame; b) that too long a period had elapsed between the onset of the nuisance and the legal complaint; c) that any such nuisance, if it existed, constituted nuisance at common law and should be dealt with by damages rather than by equitable injunctions; d) that Birmingham could not afford the necessary works required; and e) that it was not possible for the Court to frame an order to require, as requested, the Defendants to 'endeavour to remedy that evil' of the nuisance.

[33]   Court of Chancery Records: Orders, C/33/1052 1437.

[34]   For example, Tromans, 'Nuisance', 93, and Howarth, *Wisdom's Law*, 96.

In the event, Birmingham did add some treatment works at the Saltley site and Adderley did not return to up-grade his restraining order in November; but the order would eventually, in 1871, be converted to become more conventionally worded in restraining Birmingham from causing a nuisance in the river with its sewage.

History of the Dispute, 1858 to 1870

Birmingham Council's problems with its sewage effluent after 1858, both as a continuing legal difficulty and with regard to practical sanitary engineering, were not trivial. With proximity neither to large rivers nor to the open sea, which offer easier and cheaper disposal solutions, Birmingham had to deal with its sewage in an innovative manner. Still, although Adderley's action of 1858 was a problem, the court orders obtained were minor compared to the crisis of Chancery litigation and injunctions that was to hit Birmingham in 1871–2. As it stood after 1858, the orders required only that new sewer connections not be installed and that appropriate treatment be put in place at Saltley. There was only the threat, not the actuality, of an injunction requiring the river pollution nuisance to be removed or restrained.

At this point in its civic history, Birmingham was passing through a stage of penny-pinching torpor. It was under the control of a governing group who had 'a miserable record of narrowness and false economy'[35] and who did 'next to nothing for the improvement of the town',[36] over a period when 'parsimony ... gripped Council affairs in the 1850s and 1860s.'[37] The opportunity for refraining from infrastructure investment on new sewer construction and connection may not have been wholly unwelcome to this group. Nevertheless, no matter how begrudgingly, treatment of part of the sewage flow began after 1858 at the tiny Saltley sewage outlet site. In October 1859, a single filtration tank was put in place there, and in 1860 heavy pumping equipment and two larger filtration tanks were installed. At this time the site was also extended with the purchase, from Adderley himself, of a small amount of further land.[38] The treatment method being employed, which was always designated as an experiment, used the tanks to filter out of the flow the most solid portions of the sewage. The settled-out sludge was removed daily and was left to dry out over several months in heaps and lagoons around the seven acres of land at the site, before being moved on or disposed of as agricultural manure. The liquid wastewater portion flowed on directly into the river, to rely purely on natural processes for further cleansing. Unconvincingly, in 1864, the

---

[35]   Gill, *History of Birmingham*, 286.

[36]   Ernest Varvill Hiley, 'Birmingham City Government', in *Birmingham Institutions*, (ed.) John Henry Muirhead (Birmingham: Cornish, 1911), 102.

[37]   Derek Fraser, *Power and Authority in the Victorian City* (Oxford: Blackwell, 1979), 95.

[38]   Macmorran, *Municipal Public Works*, 10–11.

town council had claimed it had constructed 'on the most approved principles of modern science a complete and efficient system',[39] but for 1866 the report was more realistic, if gloomy, that:

> ... trials for effecting the purification of sewage before pouring it into the river have signally failed to give any hope of thereby dealing successfully with the increasing quantity of sewage.[40]

As the 1870s opened, Saltley was dealing with 50,000 tons of solid matter annually and 18 million gallons of liquid daily, but its treatment method had changed little, using the two settling tanks, with the remaining effluent flowing on into the Tame. What was begun as an experimental trial of sewage treatment had now become a permanent method. Macmorran sums up the situation for that time:

> Inadequate finance, inadequate legislation and, above all, virtually no available sewage treatment technique, must have made life very difficult for those charged with maintaining sanitary conditions in the rapidly growing industrial towns. Events had overtaken science.[41]

Over the 1860s, Adderley, too, must have been far from satisfied, as shown by the complaints he directed at the town council. In June 1865 he complains of the 'unhealthy and offensive state of the river';[42] in July 1865 the Tame is 'pestilential';[43] and in August 1865 it is 'dangerous'.[44] In September, 1866 his lawyers threatened 'the forbearance of Sir Charles must end.'[45] Finally, in 1870, Adderley's agents gave notice of an application to Chancery for a review of the 1858 orders which would now be altered to require Birmingham to refrain from actions causing a nuisance by polluting the Tame with its sewage.

The Gravelly Hill Relators, 1870 to 1871

Although, as we shall see, Adderley's case remained the most persistent and pressing for Birmingham, Adderley was not alone in going to law over Birmingham's sanitary arrangements around this time. In January 1860, Abel Rollason (1797–1872) and his son Abel Rollason (1822–93) sought an injunction at Chancery restraining Birmingham from discharging sewage to damage the

[39] 'Public Works Report' in Birmingham Town Council Minutes, 24 March 1871, Birmingham Corporation Archives, BCC, Birmingham Central Library, Birmingham.

[40] Ibid.

[41] Macmorran, *Municipal Public Works*, 11.

[42] Letter, 13 June 1865, Birmingham Town Council Minutes, 282.

[43] Letter, 16 July 1865, Birmingham Town Council Minutes, 295.

[44] *Birmingham Daily Post*, 2 August 1865.

[45] Letter, 17 Sept 1866, Birmingham Town Council Minutes, 374.

Rollasons' wire-drawing mill at Bromford Mill on the Tame, for which Birmingham agreed to pay a settlement and to clean the mill sluices, laying out £1,800 to cover the costs.[46] Also, in 1863, Zachariah Twamley, land agent to Lord Bradford at the Mill, Castle Bromwich, complained that Birmingham's sewage had filled the mill-dam, and Birmingham paid compensation.[47]

But by far the most important of these other suits was brought by a group known as the *Gravelly Hill relators,* who also pursued Birmingham in a public nuisance suit behind the name of the Attorney-General.[48] In May 1870, these complainants, residents of the Gravelly Hill area just north of the Saltley sewage works, applied at Chancery seeking an injunction restraining Birmingham from continuing a nuisance deriving from the Saltley sewage treatment works itself: this was not connected with any river pollution nuisance. This new action was instigated at almost the same time that Adderley re-applied to Chancery and some cooperation is evident.

The source of the Gravelly Hill complaints was the state of the acres at the Saltley works where Birmingham's parsimonious sewage treatment was being applied. The two large settling tanks, open to the sky, huge sludge lagoons and piles of solid matter (50,000 tons per year) being extracted from the sewage and stored there to dry must have provided a dominating scene and atmosphere. The Gravelly Hill relators occupied some rather grand villas on Gravelly Hill, Erdington, an otherwise pleasant suburban spot to the north of Aston and Birmingham, but too close to the heaps and lagoons of fermenting sewage faecal matter at Saltley.[49]

The four Gravelly Hill relators were comfortable, professional men: Edwin Wright, William Fowler, Edward Davenport, and William Loveridge. Although there remains little information on the internal history and dynamics of the group, strong social and geographical connections between them are evident. Edwin Wright (1818–89) was a retired solicitor and legal clerk to the local Justices of the Peace and to the Birmingham Board of Guardians: 'no lawyer was better known in the town.'[50] William Fowler (1818–87) was a prominent local land surveyor and land agent who had been consultant surveyor to Aston Corporation, a Warwickshire JP and chairman of the Aston Board of Guardians. Fowler would be appointed in 1874 by the Court of Exchequer to arbitrate the sewage pollution dispute at

---

46   The Rollasons' lawyer was Edwin Wright, later one of the Gravelly Hill relators. Court of Chancery Records: Pleadings: C15/780/R2; *Birmingham Daily Post,* 27 January 1860; Birmingham Town Council Minutes, 17 January 1860, 1 May 1860, 7 August 1860.

47   *Birmingham Daily Post,* 23 October 1863.

48   Attorney-General v Birmingham (Davenport).

49   Gravelly Hill, Erdington, in the 1870s still boasted a number of gravel pits from which its name derived. Administratively, Erdington and Aston were not absorbed into Birmingham until 1911. Nowadays the area is dominated by the imposing Gravelly Hill Interchange ('Spaghetti Junction') connecting major roads into Aston and Birmingham with the M6 motorway.

50   *Birmingham Daily Post,* 13 March 1889.

Wolverhampton in another of this book's studies (see Chapter 10). Edward Davenport (1818–77) was a corn and hop merchant, also an Aston Guardian, and William Loveridge (1814–92) was a jeweller and merchant in precious stones and also a member and one-time chairman of the Aston Board of Guardians. Strikingly, all four lived in a small area around Kingsbury Road on Gravelly Hill, Erdington, and three were long-term members of the Aston Board of Guardians.[51]

On 10 March 1871, the Gravelly Hill relators case (Attorney-General v Birmingham (Davenport)) was held at the Court of Chancery before Vice-Chancellor Sir James Bacon, with the relators asking for an injunction to restrain the Council from 'causing or permitting the sewage of the borough from being deposited at their sewage works in such a manner as to be a nuisance to the relators.'[52] For the relators, a careful case had been constructed, which first established the obligations of Birmingham under the Birmingham Improvement Act of 1851 that their sewage works 'be so made as to in no way become a nuisance'. This was backed by an imposing array of affidavits on the deterioration of the sanitary condition of the area since the opening of the sewage works at Saltley and was accompanied by a number of medical and other statements testifying to the 'foul offensive and obnoxious effluvia' and the 'injurious effect' of the 'fearful stenches', perceivable for miles around. The populace was reported to have had to close their windows and doors when the wind was in the wrong direction and some doctors had advised their clients to leave the area as soon as possible.[53]

For the defence, Birmingham feebly attempted to counter this case with affidavits from council employees saying they had never experienced ill-health and presented a demonstrably false claim that no complaints about the works had ever been received. Vice-Chancellor Bacon then told Birmingham severely that they had failed in a duty of trust in the matter: the situation at Saltley was such as to be 'dangerous to life and health ... destructive of the ordinary comforts and enjoyment of life ... and an unquestionable nuisance'. He told the corporation that their response to the problem had been 'supine' and continued with:

> Whether it has been, as suggested, from a reluctance on their part to spend money or whether the difficulty of curing the nuisance has actuated them or not I do not know ... They have not, in my opinion, discharged the duty incumbent upon them with the diligence and earnestness the public and the relators have a right to expect from them.

The injunction granted to the Gravelly Hill relators restrained Birmingham from:

---

[51] The Rollasons (see above) are also closely associated with this Gravelly Hill group: Edwin Wright was the Rollasons' lawyer and lived next-door to Abel Rollason (Jnr) on Kingsbury Road in 1881. Davenport, Loveridge, Fowler and Rollason are recorded on the census as close neighbours in 1871.

[52] Court of Chancery Records: Pleadings: C16/615/A62.

[53] *Birmingham Daily Post*, 13 March 1871.

... causing or permitting the sewage of the said borough, or any part thereof, to be deposited and exposed in tanks and reservoirs, and from otherwise dealing with or disposing of the said sewage, or any part thereof, in such a manner as to be a nuisance. [54]

A period of grace was allowed for the corporation to come into compliance with the order, which was thereupon suspended until November 1871.

Attorney-General v Birmingham (1871)

In parallel with the Gravelly Hill action, and at the same time, in March 1871, Adderley's own motion[55] to extend and update his Chancery order from 1858 came before Vice-Chancellor Bacon. Adderley asked that: firstly, his 1858 injunction stopping Birmingham connecting up more sewers to the existing main sewer outlet at Saltley be continued; and secondly that the wording on the second part of that order be changed so that Birmingham Council '... be restrained from permitting the sewage of the Borough to pass into the river Tame so as to cause a nuisance'. This extension was, of course, that threatened at the 1858 hearing. Birmingham declined to put any defence before Vice-Chancellor Bacon beyond asking for time to be allowed, in line with the Gravelly Hill order. The order was duly awarded and suspended to come into effect on 10 November 1871. It is now that Adderley's order formally becomes a delayed or suspended nuisance injunction, restraining the council from any sewage discharge that would cause a nuisance along the Tame.

The citizens of Birmingham were rightly apprehensive about the possible effects of the loss of their only means of treating and disposing of their sewage waste, were the injunctions to be rigorously enforced. The *Birmingham Daily Post* sounded a weary and pessimistic note:

Nothing is clearer than that the law forbids communities as much as individuals to create nuisances injurious to health or detrimental to property. It must also be allowed that the sewage works at Saltley do constitute a nuisance and a severe one ... But the issue of an injunction by no means lessens the real difficulty. The question is: What is to be done? It is very well to tell a hungry man that if he wants a dinner the London Tavern is open to him. But if he is destitute of the means to pay for the dinner, the London Tavern may just as well be non-existent. So with the proceedings in Chancery. It is the easiest thing possible to issue an injunction and to tell the Corporation of Birmingham that they must remove the sewage nuisance. But if there are no practical means of doing so the injunction to

---

54   Ibid.

55   Court of Chancery Records: Orders, C/33/1172 901; *Times*, 17 March 1871; *Birmingham Daily Post*, 17 March 1871.

perform an impossibility or next to one is not specially comforting to those upon whom such an obligation is laid. ... We sympathise with the landowners and with the people of Birmingham. We confess we are not hopeful of a satisfactory result whatever may be done or whoever may do it.[56]

The suspension of the two orders from the Gravelly Hill relators and Adderley until November 1871 was to give Birmingham time to clean up its sewage processes. So, as 1871 progressed, Birmingham's civic authorities were faced with two well-directed and comprehensive nuisance actions over their sanitary and sewerage policies.[57] It did not escape ironic notice that, in effect, this double-barrelled threat was such that Adderley's injunction aimed at stopping Birmingham directing its sewage into the river and, conversely, the Gravelly Hill injunction aimed at stopping Birmingham keeping its sewage at Saltley and out of the river.

The Civic Gospel, Joseph Chamberlain and Sewage

In the decades of the 1850s and 1860s, Birmingham's local governmental response to the challenges posed by want of civic amenity could be characterised by uncaring inaction and parsimony. This was true not only in matters of sanitation, but also for most activities that are nowadays expected of local government. However, the political background in the city was about to change following the acquisition of power on the town council by a group of energetic and enthusiastic reformers. These reformers, part of a movement evident in a number of British towns, were pursuing a radical vision that saw local civic action as the means by which the social and moral reconstruction of Victorian society might be achieved, no less. In Birmingham, this movement had its roots in dissenting and non-conformist religious interests, educational reform groups, trade unions, and a radical heritage;

---

[56]   *Birmingham Daily Post*, 14 March 1871.

[57]   Birmingham barely escaped a third action at this point when, in June 1871, complaints came in from a group including George Cecil Orlando Bridgeman (1845–1915), 4th Earl of Bradford, then MP for North Shropshire, over Birmingham's undoubted sewage pollution of the River Cole, another tributary of the Tame. The town council responded by resolving to build a new connecting sewer to divert the problematic sewage flow (*Birmingham Daily Post*, 21 June 1871).

and is closely and famously associated with the career of Joseph Chamberlain.[58] This new vision has gained the epithet: the Civic Gospel.[59]

With like-minded associates in Birmingham,[60] Joseph Chamberlain was part of a reforming political bloc which included Liberals, radicals and some Conservatives, whose members wrestled control of the town from the established 'old guard' over the period 1868–72. The rising power of this movement was fundamentally fuelled by the 1867 Reform Act, which had extended the vote and enfranchised a new and more reformist electorate of adult urban (working class) males.[61] The high point of the Civic Gospel movement in Birmingham was to come after Chamberlain was elected mayor for the first of his three successive terms (1873–5), declaring: 'In twelve months, by God's help, the town shall not know itself.'[62] Indeed, the town was transformed as the novel notion blossomed and became permanent that local government had a prime role to play in the reform of urban social conditions and in furthering the welfare and well-being of its local citizenry.

Birmingham's sewage crisis, 1870–2, plays an important but largely uncelebrated part in the general takeover of the Birmingham town council at that time by the reforming faction around Chamberlain. Originally, the Public Works Committee was the part of the council responsible for infrastructure functions, including sewerage, taken over from the old Street Commissioners. In 1870 this committee constituted a major power base within the council, long under the

---

[58]   Joseph Chamberlain (1836–1914) was an immensely influential British politician and statesman. After his spectacular rise to local prominence in Birmingham, in 1876 he became one of their MPs and moved on to high national office. Never prime minister, he was nevertheless a towering figure and one of the most important British politicians of the period. A brilliant speaker, he managed to provoke fundamental splits in both main contemporary British political parties and fathered a future prime minister and a political dynasty. J. Enoch Powell, *Joseph Chamberlain* (London: Thames and Hudson Ltd., 1977); Denis Judd, *Radical Joe: A Life of Joseph Chamberlain* (London: Faber and Faber Ltd., 2010).

[59]   Asa Briggs, *Victorian Cities* (Harmondsworth: Penguin Books, 1975). Hunt, *Building Jerusalem*, prefers the term: 'Municipal Gospel'.

[60]   Staunchly supported by, among others, John Thackray Bunce (1828–99), editor of the *Birmingham Daily Post* ('Chamberlain's organ') from 1862–98, and author of *History of the Corporation of Birmingham, II*.

[61]   A well-organised Liberal Party machine emerged in Birmingham, the Liberal Caucus, controlled by those around Chamberlain. The 1867 Reform Act made Birmingham a constituency returning three MPs while each voter was given only two votes, so the Caucus was created to direct voters in how to vote effectively to ensure three Liberal candidates were returned.

[62]   David Dilks, *Neville Chamberlain* (Cambridge: Cambridge University Press, 1984), 12.

control of the established powers with its membership jealously defended from the new reform elements by the committee's chairman, Ambrose Biggs.[63]

The two sewage pollution actions, by Adderley and the Gravelly Hill relators, about to be heard in March 1871, had panicked the Public Works Committee into commissioning a new enquiry into future sewage treatment policy that might deflect the wrath of Chancery. The resultant Public Works Committee report recognised sewage farm irrigation as the only viable mode for treating the town's sewage and recommended the acquisition of the necessary parliamentary powers to buy a huge area of 2,500–4,000 acres of Tame valley farmland.[64] This land would be used to apply broad irrigation treatment to the sewage which would be pumped and piped to the fields. The total cost was estimated at a colossal £275,000 and wide powers to acquire loans and compulsorily purchase the land would be required from Parliament. The ambition of the plan is testimony to the apprehension felt on the town council generated by the two Court of Chancery actions. The debate that ensued within Birmingham's town council on the Public Works Committee report proved epic, extending over six long adjourned special sessions, over June and July of 1871.[65]

The old guard of the Public Works Committee, in defending their report and its recommendations, made several tactical mistakes during the course of this debate. Not least, they had few answers to the criticisms that quickly emerged that the report was ill-directed at the deflection of the injunctions that were the reason for its production. It might take three years for the proposed scheme to start, which Chancery might be unwilling to sanction, and, anyway, the plan's success was not guaranteed: it would use treatment methods untried at the scale required at Birmingham. Further, the opposition to be expected in Parliament and among the farmers and landowners along the Tame valley, as well as the costs, were argued to be grossly underestimated. One critic observed that the scheme 'looked as though they were going to oblige Sir Charles Adderley by surrounding his property [with sewage] and stinking him out.'[66] Rather than long-term considerations, what was required, argued the opposition, was immediate action to satisfy Vice-Chancellor Bacon and address the injunctions. Along with winning the substantive arguments, Chamberlain's group also triumphed in the oratorical duel played out in the council chamber. Chamberlain himself delivered a joyful, tricolon-laden and mockingly critical speech showing his brilliant speech-making. For example, responding to the report's claim that the Saltley wastewater run-off was drinkable, he retorted:

[63]   Ambrose Biggs (1821–1909) was mayor of Birmingham in 1872.

[64]   Birmingham Corporation Public Works Committee of Enquiry, *The Sanitary Condition of Birmingham*, 24 March 1871 (reissued 6 June 1871), Birmingham Corporation Archive, Birmingham.

[65]   The reports in the *Birmingham Daily Post* on the debates total about 30,000 words.

[66]   From Henry Hawkes's opening for the reformers. *Birmingham Daily Post*, 21 June 1871.

[I have] seen the sewage water. It was not bright, it was not clear, and it was not potable ... if it was potable water, such as could be supplied to the town, the teetotal interest would fall off very considerably. The report was perfectly absurd, it was ridiculous, it was unworthy ...

and later:

Some people imagined that occasional smells were no matter, but they frequently brought in their train occasional fevers, occasional death and occasional injunction.[67]

Little wonder the speech was often interrupted by applause and laughter. In face of the attacks on their report, the Public Works Committee group fatally introduced a sarcastic and hubristic 'see-if-you-can-do-better' motion proposing that a further enquiry committee be engaged to solve the sewage question, which should consist only of Chamberlain with his dissenting group of reformers, including the formidable pairing of Henry Hawkes and Thomas Avery.[68] At the end of the debate this proposal was passed, which opened the way for the highly competent Thomas Avery to head the new Sewage Inquiry and, very quickly thereafter, to take the sanitary duties of Birmingham away from the Public Works Committee entirely.

The new Sewage Inquiry Committee under Avery quickly and enthusiastically gathered new engineering consultants and directed themselves much more closely to the question of how the specific and immediate problems raised by the Chancery actions could be tackled. They aimed for cheap and proven methods, costed and evaluated, and a huge new 300-page report was presented to the town council in October 1871.[69] Its most important recommendations were that: a) a domestic privy-pail system be introduced with weekly collection to allow the overdue abolition of the town's middens, while excluding such material from the sewers to spare the rivers; b) 1,000 acres of land down the Tame valley at Dunton, away from Saltley, be purchased for sewage works to treat the privy-pail contents and purify the sewage flow, using deep-drained irrigation methods; and c) that a new joint drainage commission with representation from all parishes draining into the Tame and Rea be created to supervise the river environment and any new treatment works. The new Sewage Inquiry Committee report was debated through October 1871 and the town council was asked, in effect, to choose between this alternative scheme and the original scheme of the Public Works Committee. In the

---

[67]   *Birmingham Daily Post*, 7 July 1871.

[68]   Henry Hawkes (1813–91) had been a member of the town council since 1844 and had been mayor in 1852. Thomas Avery (1812–94) of the family of scale and balance manufacturers was later three times mayor of Birmingham. Chamberlain excused himself from the new inquiry, citing over-commitment elsewhere.

[69]   Birmingham Corporation Sewage Inquiry Committee, *Report*, 3 October 1871, Birmingham Corporation Archive, Birmingham.

event, the reformers triumphed to the extent that the Sewage Inquiry Committee became Birmingham's permanent Sewage Committee, responsible for the sewerage of the borough and the works at Saltley. The new committee was also charged with preparing the Birmingham Sewerage Bill, which would authorise the necessary powers for the new scheme, to be presented to Parliament in 1872.

All these new investments would, however, take time, which Birmingham did not have. In November 1871, the injunctions against Birmingham were due to come into force, and with the injunctions in place, actions for contempt and sequestration would certainly follow. As things stood, Birmingham would deservedly lose.

Birmingham's Legal and Parliamentary Crises, 1872

The year 1872 proved difficult for the town of Birmingham, and Thomas Avery and his colleagues on Birmingham Town Council's new Sewage Committee must have rued their success in wresting control of Birmingham's sanitary affairs.

The two Chancery injunctions which had originally been suspended until November 1871 were further extended for a few weeks, and, in January 1872, Birmingham made application for a longer extension of the period of suspension, hoping to put off the injunctions to the middle of 1872.[70] But this time the Gravelly Hill relators opposed the motion and at the hearing, before Vice-Chancellor Bacon at Chancery, the written evidence included compelling testimony that rather than a diminution of the nuisance at Saltley, it had got rather worse. Birmingham's case for a further extension rested entirely on the work they had put into applying to Parliament for powers to put into effect their new sewage treatment plans, but Birmingham had little in the way of concrete action at Saltley to show. Vice-Chancellor Bacon requested: 'Don't speak of the number of meetings held; tell me what has been done'. To this, the reported interjection from the relators' counsel was: 'Nothing'. Bacon then proceeded to reemphasise that he could not, over the period of extension of now nearly twelve months, '... find a trace of their having discharged their duty towards their neighbours or having done at any time anything for the purpose of abating the nuisances ... Have they done an earthly thing?' Birmingham's applications for further extensions to the periods of delay for both injunctions were rejected and both the Gravelly Hill and Adderley injunctions thereby came into effect from 2 February 1872.

From this point, if the Gravelly Hill relators or Adderley could muster evidence of sewage nuisance from Birmingham in violation of the Chancery orders, a sequestration order could be issued, threatening to remove all the town council's assets and revenues into the hands of bailiffs and court-approved administrators. But despite his hard decision and harsh tone, Bacon still asked that the respondents 'do not press the Corporation too hard' and hoped that 'some arrangement can be

---

[70] *Birmingham Daily Post*, 31 January, 2 February 1872.

made satisfactory to both parties',[71] which indicated sentiments other than a purely judicial stance on the part of Chancery.

Birmingham's hopes for the permanent solution to their sewage nuisance problems lay in their plans for new works down the Tame valley. The threat from the injunctions would be countered by putting the treatment works at the end of a new seven-and-a-half-mile pipeline leading from the present sewer terminus at Saltley to a new site at Dunton, near Lea Marston, just beyond Adderley's Hams Hall. Initially the site would have 1,000 acres (but plans allowed for 900 acres more) to which the piped effluent would be transported. Huge covered settlement tanks combined with chemical applications would extract the sludge and the liquid would go to broad and deep-drained irrigation areas before any treated, cleansed and disinfected effluent water would be allowed into the Tame. That the new Dunton site was well away from Saltley would satisfy the Gravelly Hill complainants and that its outlet into the Tame lay beyond Adderley's estate at Hams Hall would, it was thought, satisfy Adderley. Thus, the nuisances behind both current injunctions would disappear. But to implement this plan, Birmingham needed powers only available from a parliamentary act to raise loans, to (compulsorily) purchase the land and to assure rights of passage for the pipes and conduits.

So, the Birmingham Sewerage Bill was prepared and introduced in the Commons in early 1872, which cruised past its Commons Second Reading at the end of February and moved before a Select Committee for detailed clause-by-clause scrutiny in April 1872.[72] About 300 acres of Adderley's land were earmarked for part of the Dunton scheme as were nearly 300 acres of Drayton Manor, owned by Sir Robert Peel, MP for nearby Tamworth. Although the two MPs were eager to torpedo the bill, they awaited its return to the floor of the Commons before striking. When the bill came back to the Commons for the debate on its Third Reading, a number of MPs spoke to oppose it, orchestrated and led by Peel and Adderley. Opposition arguments included that 'the many should not injure the few'; that 'the minority had a right to protection'; and that it would bring a 'leviathan nuisance ... a curse to the entire district' at Dunton. But doubts were also raised that the Dunton scheme was over-expensive, uncertain and experimental, and that revisions to the plans since the bill's introduction had fatally undermined the project. When the House divided, Adderley and Peel did not formally register No votes in the division on the bill, but they did act as tellers for the No lobby, which amounted to the same thing. The bill was defeated, by just three votes (145 votes to 148), a result greeted with loud cheers.[73]

There were no loud cheers back in Birmingham. The *Birmingham Daily Post* declared that the bill had fallen because of 'the interests of a class which happens to be paramount in Parliament' and continued:

---

71   *Times*, 1 February 1872.
72   The Select Committee sat from 20 April to 19 June 1872.
73   *Times*, 18 June 1872; *Birmingham Daily Post*, 18 June 1872.

What are large towns to do? ... The towns are ordered so to deal with their sewage as to prevent it from becoming a nuisance, the only means of so dealing with it being at the same time denied to them. Chancery forbids them to put sewage into rivers, or to accumulate it upon land. Parliament refuses to give the power of cleansing sewage in the only effectual way ... It is a renewal of Egyptian tyranny and mockery; they insist that we shall make the tale of bricks, and they will not give us straw.[74]

On Birmingham town council, the result was greeted angrily as 'a calamity, equally deplorable and unexpected'.[75] There was also great resentment about the roles played by Peel and Adderley, especially after details were revealed of failed negotiations concerning these two individuals.

Failed Negotiations 1872

That there were failed negotiations preceding the defeat of the ill-fated Birmingham Sewerage Bill illustrates the potential role of private arrangements within nuisance disputes. Both Adderley and Peel, it was revealed after the bill's defeat, had had talks with Birmingham with regard to the proposed sewerage scheme and these talks had progressed as far as haggling over prices for the voluntary sale of their land included in the scheme, which might otherwise be compulsorily purchased. The side conditions had also settled details concerning Adderley withdrawing his Chancery suit, and touched on agreements for both MPs dropping their parliamentary opposition.

Thomas Avery disclosed all this to Birmingham's town council during the post-mortem on the defeat of the bill in July 1872.[76] Avery first described a meeting with Sir Robert Peel's agent at Peel's Drayton Manor in January 1872. Here a suggestion was made that a sum of £100,000 for the 297 acres (at £333 per acre) of Drayton Manor required for the sewage scheme 'might be sufficient to remove Sir Robert's opposition'. Birmingham would only offer £150 per acre and no agreement emerged.[77]

Thomas Avery also revealed details of formal negotiations which had taken place with Adderley's representatives and this proved deeply embarrassing for Adderley, who had specified that these talks should remain strictly private.[78] In March 1872, with the Sewerage Bill passing its Second Reading at Westminster, Adderley had agreed a settlement and had (literally) signed a preliminary written agreement that 356 acres of the Hams Hall estate would be taken by Birmingham for the Dunton sewage irrigation scheme on a 100-year lease. In return, Birmingham

74   *Birmingham Daily Post*, 19 June 1872.
75   Ibid.
76   *Birmingham Daily Post*, 3 July 1872.
77   *Birmingham Daily Post*, 19 July 1872.
78   *Birmingham Daily Post*, 3 July 1872.

would pay an annual rent of £2,640, build a parsonage and settle all Adderley's parliamentary and Chancery costs. Nothing damaging so far, but, in addition, a central passage of the agreement reads:

> On agreement being signed and clauses settled, Sir Charles Adderley to withdraw all opposition to the bill. When bill passed and works executed, Sir C B Adderley bill and information in Chancery to be dismissed at expense of defendants.[79]

Avery was explicit that on a successful pecuniary agreement '... these two members of Parliament would have withdrawn their opposition to the Sewerage Bill and Sir Charles Adderley would have also consented to the dismissal of the suits in Chancery.'[80] This preliminary agreement was rejected by Birmingham because, they said, they wished to buy the land outright, and another meeting to discuss the outright sale of the land took place at the end of March 1872. The second round of negotiations is described by Adderley's solicitors in a letter to the town council.[81] After arguing that a 'fairer' purchase valuation of Adderley's 350 or so acres of land involved would have been for more than £70,000, the letter continues:

> Informal negotiations were ... based on the sale of the fee-simple [freehold] for a lump sum of £50,000. This was far below [advice received on] the very lowest sum he ought to accept; yet the Corporation, thinking he might be beaten down lower, offered through their advisers, at first £42,000, and then at the last moment £46,000, and so ended all chance of a compromise ...[82]

Birmingham rejected this second deal on the basis that the price was deemed extravagantly above the going market rates for the land.[83] It was reported that this rebuff had deeply offended Adderley and had stiffened his opposition to the Birmingham Sewerage Bill.[84]

Adderley's position here is very questionable. His coming to a private agreement to drop his nuisance suit at Chancery would have been a matter appropriate for himself. But real issues of probity and even corrupt practice were raised by his self-interested willingness to use his vote and position as an MP in order to secure private pecuniary terms to drop opposition to Birmingham's

---

[79]   Ibid.

[80]   *Birmingham Daily Post*, 12 July 1872.

[81]   Letter from Messrs Paines and Layton, Birmingham Town Council Minutes, 6 August 1872.

[82]   Ibid.

[83]   The £145 per acre is well in line with the £140–£160 per acre price for land quoted elsewhere and Birmingham paid £300 per acre for Mr Essington's acres near the Saltley site in 1875.

[84]   Letter from Hawksley to Hayes, Birmingham Sewage Committee Minutes, 3 April 1872.

Sewerage Bill; and Adderley must have known this. But it takes two partners to dance to such music, so some might maintain that Birmingham's willingness to be complicit raises similar issues.

There were furious exchanges about these matters in Birmingham's council chambers and between Avery, Hawkes, Adderley and Peel in the correspondence columns of the local press.[85] The MPs were accused of 'huckstering', 'misrepresentation', being 'activated by base and sordid motives' and 'defiling the Temple at Westminster' and Adderley complained of receiving abuse and 'imputations of corrupt motives' at an actionable level. The matter of the probity of the two MPs' pursuit of personal self-interest was even raised in Westminster, and led to the Speaker's peremptory judgment that the MPs had 'no pecuniary interest of a character which make it impossible for them to vote upon the question: and [it] appeared to me that their pecuniary interest seemed rather to be that this bill should pass than otherwise.'[86]

From the point of view of the river sewage pollution dilemma, the interest here is less with the morality of the negotiations and more with why Birmingham's negotiation with Adderley that could have ended this dispute failed. Arguments underlying the Coase theorem should have rendered negotiating the transfer of the land involved a viable option. Clearly, transactions costs were not so high as to preclude negotiations, and both sides indicate they were willing to trade in principle. The differences between the positions of the parties do not look unbridgeable: in Adderley's account, only a few thousand pounds separate the parties' positions. Given the court action was to last another twenty-plus years, the failure of the negotiations remains puzzling. Formally, it can be argued that alternative possibilities must have been perceived at the time, for example involving compulsory purchase under the Dunton scheme, to have been a lower cost method available to Birmingham. There may also have arisen difficulties in raising the finance involved if, indeed, extravagantly above-market prices had to have been paid or corrupt practice suspected. It is also possible that group decision-making within the concerned committees proved problematic. And, of course, even rational bargainers are allowed to make strategic mistakes under uncertainty. But some might think it curious and even naïve of Birmingham to choose to spurn this (tarnished) golden opportunity to buy-off Adderley directly.

Chancery and Sequestration, July 1872, and After

Birmingham had, in optimistic mood, made no interim attempt to tackle, physically, any part of the nuisances at Saltley or in the Tame while awaiting Parliament's approval of the Dunton plan in the Birmingham Sewerage Bill. With the failure of the bill and with no negotiated settlement with either of the complainants, Birmingham was now, simply, at the mercy of the two sets of relators. Either

---

85 *Birmingham Daily Post*, 12 July, 15 July, 16 July, 17 July 1872.
86 212 Parl. Deb. (3rd ser.) 15 July 1872, 1137.

would only have to turn up at Chancery to get a sequestration decision if requested. Such duly came to pass.

Just two weeks after the failure of the bill, on 1 July 1872, Adderley served notice of his intention to move for a writ of sequestration at Chancery and a similar notification from the Gravelly Hill relators followed two weeks later. Vice-Chancellor Bacon arranged to hear both suits together and at the end of July 1872, the motions for writs of sequestration from the two parties were heard.[87] The Gravelly Hill relators were able to marshal ample evidence that since the injunction had been issued in March 1871, the nuisance at Saltley had not in the least degree diminished but had continued in full force and even increased. Affidavits maintained that families had had to abandon property near Saltley because of the 'abominable nuisance' and that new bad smells never before experienced were arising from areas where sewage sludge was now being spread. The relators' counsel contended that Birmingham Corporation was treating the earlier orders of the court with the utmost contumely, and declaimed that 'judgments had been in vain, decree had been in vain, all in vain'.[88]

Birmingham responded by arguing that they would now, without their Sewerage Bill, deal with the nuisances with spanking new schemes provided by their appointed experts: Thomas Hawksley and William Hope.[89] Hawksley maintained that the river pollution could be tackled successfully by chemical means, in particular by the addition of sulphate of alumina and milk of lime to the liquid outflow at Saltley to deodorise and disinfect the effluent outflow. And Hope planned the end of the problems at Saltley: starting with improving, draining and under-draining the Saltley site; then the existing settlement tanks would be covered; and the accumulated sludge lagoons and mountains of solid sludge-matter, along with new deposits, would be removed elsewhere or laced with deodorising chemicals and dug into the land. But to put the plans into action, Birmingham argued, they would need more time, as much as eighteen months.

Vice-Chancellor Bacon sagely noted that according to Birmingham's own experts, even in the absence of new powers from Parliament, Birmingham had had it in their existing power to abate 'the most abominable nuisance destroying the health and, perhaps, the lives of many persons and you have done nothing ...',

---

[87]   Court of Chancery Records: Orders, C/33/1188 1437; *Birmingham Daily Post*, 27 July, 28 July 1872; *Times*, 29 July 1872.

[88]   A classic *tricolon diminuens*.

[89]   Thomas Hawksley (1807–93) was a well-known Victorian sewage and water engineer, President of the Institute of Civil Engineers 1872–3, and often consulted as an expert in sewage disputes (Geoffrey Morse Binnie, *Early Victorian water engineers* (London: Thomas Telford Ltd, 1981); 'Hawksley, Thomas, 1807–93', ICE Minutes of Proceedings, 117, 1894, 364–76). William Hope VC (1834–1909) had won the VC in the Crimea, aged 21, and became a notable advocate for sewage farming in the 1870s as proprietor of Bretons sewage farm at Romford (*York Herald*, 20 August 1874; *Times*, 18 December 1909; *London Gazette*, 22 February 1910).

and this made Birmingham even more culpable. By not doing their duty in these matters, Bacon continued, it was 'proved that there was persistent determination on the part of the Corporation of Birmingham not to do those things which the law has said it is incumbent upon them to do'. His decision was therefore that 'I must grant the sequestration.'[90]

Up to this point the proceedings at Chancery follow a traditional process and, given the case for the relators proven and Birmingham's culpability and poor record in dealing with the problems, the legal justification seems unarguable for the simple sequestration of Birmingham's assets and for the transfer of control over its sewage disposal to pass into more trustworthy hands. But Bacon chooses otherwise. He says 'I feel a difficulty in granting the sequestration' and after declaring that Hope's plans give 'a clear and simple mode of effectively preventing the [Gravelly Hill] nuisance' and that Hawksley's plans promise that the 'water becomes perfectly clear', Bacon explicitly calls for Birmingham 'to make an offer'. Birmingham's representatives jumped at this and immediately agreed to apply, at once, the sanitary and engineering methods suggested by their experts. But the relators objected and raised the question of Birmingham's proven untrustworthiness in carrying out the court's orders. Vice-Chancellor Bacon's solution was to allow the issuing of the sequestration orders but to enforce a six-month delay in their application, 'as a matter of indulgence', even while acknowledging that this was 'against the strict letter of the law.'[91]

This decision shows one of Chancery's flexibly practical solutions when faced with the river pollution dilemma. In allowing the sequestration order to lie for four or five months, until November 1872, Bacon is ordering Birmingham to do these engineering proposals, then come back and the court will check what has been agreed to be done is being done. This is not a suspended order but a contingent threat: Chancery would be supervising and monitoring the promised actions. What is clear here is that Bacon is not making a simple legal judgement but issuing an administrative decision and order.

Following the hearing, this time Birmingham did not hesitate and over the new period of grace threw battalions of workers, wagons, barges and money at the problems at the Saltley works. On 1 November 1872, a briefing by the Birmingham Sewage Committee, prepared for the upcoming visit back to Chancery, was released to detail the progress made to tackle each of the two sewage nuisances.[92] For the Gravelly Hill nuisance, they had pursued Hope's plans. The previously boggy acreage at Saltley had been deep-drained and embanked to save it from flooding, so making more of the area useable. The existing five acres of accumulated sewage sludge and mounds of faecal matter had been totally removed and distributed by boat and wagon to farmers and buried in deep trenches; and fresh accumulations of sludge were now treated with lime and quickly diverted to

---

[90]   *Birmingham Daily Post*, 28 July 1872.

[91]   Ibid.

[92]   *Birmingham Daily Post*, 1 November 1872.

local farmers or ploughed into the land. To deal with Adderley's complaints along the river, Hawksley was applying milk of lime and additional settling tanks to encourage increased precipitation from, and deodorisation of, the liquid effluent outflow. Although it was admitted that the results were not as perfect as might result from full passage through land irrigation, the outflow into the Tame was claimed to have attained a much higher level of clarity.

When the next hearing at Chancery before Vice-Chancellor Bacon came around on the 14 November, Avery was able to present this evidence of Birmingham's new good conduct, and add detail that up to 200 men had been employed to clean up 60,000 tons of sludge matter at the Saltley site, with the total 52 acres now cleared and some even planted with cabbages. There were no more offensive smells and the water outflow from the works was as clear, it was said, as the water already flowing in the river. Birmingham's counsel was able to claim that Birmingham had fulfilled the duties that the Vice-Chancellor had earlier required of them, and though the relators were able to find some points at issue, little cause remained to stop Vice-Chancellor Bacon granting further suspensions of the sequestration orders, until April 1873.[93] No objection to these new suspensions emerged: the *Birmingham Daily Post* noted that 'it was obvious from his tone that the Vice-Chancellor would have ordered the postponement with or without [the relators'] consent', and wryly congratulated Avery's Sewage Committee for delivering Birmingham from '… the shadow of "sequestration" – which is all the more alarming because even the lawyers do not quite know what it means.'[94]

Soon, as the clear-up and investments at Saltley progressed under the contingent threat from Chancery, Birmingham's sanitary authorities were able to eliminate one, at least, of the complaints. For the Gravelly Hill relators, the situation started to improve markedly. In June 1873 they allowed a further extension to their sequestration order up to December 1873, and then allowed another further long extension for another twelve months.[95] Finally, on 12 November 1874, Vice-Chancellor Bacon agreed to discharge the Gravelly Hill sequestration order, now two-and-a-half years old, awarded but never issued.[96] The Gravelly Hill relators consented to the discharge, but required that their nuisance injunction remain because, they said, it was only 'under the pressure of that order that the Corporation had at last become active'. It had taken four years for their complaints to be dealt with, but now at Saltley the faecal mountains were gone, the settling tanks were covered and any sewage sludge was being quickly dosed with lime and deep-ploughed into the ground. In 1876, one of the Gravelly Hill relators, William Fowler, was able to report that 'so far as the inhabitants of Gravelly Hill were concerned the nuisance of which they complained from Birmingham's

---

93   Court of Chancery Records: Orders, C/33/1188 2840; *Times*, 15 November 1872.
94   *Birmingham Daily Post*, 15 November 1872.
95   *Birmingham Daily Post*, 21 June 1873, Dec 3 1873.
96   Court of Chancery Records: Orders, C/33/1207 106.

sewage had entirely disappeared.'[97] For the Gravelly Hill nuisance, Chancery's supervisory role had initiated, organised and overseen a successful abatement of a major sewage pollution nuisance, albeit not the one in the river.

Adderley's Continuing Action

Adderley's nuisance problems proved not so easy to deal with: no treatment process existed to cleanse adequately the sewage effluent water outflowing at such volumes from the sewage-settlement tanks and works into the river. As the Gravelly Hill suit wound down, Adderley continued his action alone, objecting to Birmingham's applications in Chancery for relaxation of his Chancery orders and rejecting possible agreements.[98] But relations began to thaw.

Adderley still held, it is to be recalled, another injunction, dating back to 1858, restraining Birmingham from connecting up new sewers to the existing network.[99] In November 1874, Avery on the Sewage Committee tried to normalise the position by coming clean that 'he was perfectly aware that for many years the injunction [restraining new sewer connections] was disregarded and that many public sewers were constructed in defiance of it. It was a most lamentable thing to do ... ' and that it was time to 'do justice to their neighbours.'[100] So, just a week after the Gravelly Hill sequestration order was ended, Birmingham (with Adderley's agreement) went back to Chancery to revise the order so as to now allow the Corporation to connect up further sections of the town to the sewer network 'so long as their construction would not cause any pollution of the river Tame.'[101] This was part of a wider agreement.

By 1875, Adderley's writ of sequestration, not a mere injunction, had been awarded but suspended for a period approaching three years. Now a suspension of the whole dispute was agreed. In February 1875, Birmingham's Sewage Committee reported on new negotiations and temporary truce terms with Adderley. Birmingham was to pay Adderley £6,000 in damages and costs in exchange for: a) the unconditional ending of the injunction against connecting up new town sewers; b) the discharge of Adderley's (suspended) writ of sequestration; and c) a five-year stay of proceedings on the Tame pollution action. In return, Adderley required a new injunction against the sewage pollution of the Tame to be issued,

---

[97]   *Birmingham Daily Post*, 16 June 1876.

[98]   *Birmingham Daily Post*, 24 June 1874; Bunce, *History of the Corporation of Birmingham*, 138.

[99]   Adderley's puzzling reluctance to enforce this secondary injunction may owe something to his requiring a sewer network to underlie his own on-going profitable commercial property development of the Saltley township.

[100]   *Birmingham Daily Post*, 11 November 1874.

[101]   *Times*, 20 November 1874; *Birmingham Daily Post*, 20 November 1874.

however, and assurances that Birmingham 'proceed diligently with necessary work.'[102] The Council reported:

> The effect of this decree is to discharge not only the order for sequestration, but also the two injunctions granted in 1858 and 1871 respectively; and in lieu thereof a fresh injunction in the terms agreed upon is granted. The difficulties about sewering the town will thus be got rid of, and there will, in addition, be five years' peace.[103]

On the termination of the five years' peace in 1880, however, Adderley (now raised to Lord Norton) immediately renewed the action, complaining that the pollution of the Tame persisted and that 'nothing had been done.'[104] His legal advisors lent him great encouragement in continuing the complaint: their revealing advice included the following:

> It is absolutely essential for the preservation of your rights and those who come after you that you should keep the suit on foot. You need not be at all afraid of the expense, nor is it fruitless. Let me remind you that you have been a good deal more than recouped all expense that you have been put to already, and it seems beyond doubt that unless we throw away our cards we have something approaching a moral certainty of similar success in the future. Of course you will have a certain amount of opprobrium to face among the Birmingham people, but you are not thin skinned enough to mind this, and it cannot be more hereafter than it has been already ... [T]he case may go on a few years longer but you have the means in your hands of compelling an arrangement if you do not make us throw them away.[105]

Following this, in November 1881, Adderley again applied to Chancery requesting a sequestration order against Birmingham, alleging a breach of the injunction restraining them from permitting sewage into the River Tame so as to create a nuisance. This time, on payment of £600 'in full satisfaction of all costs incurred by him to the present time' Adderley agreed to allow his motion to stand over until March 1884.[106]

From this point on, for more than another decade, further motions for writs of sequestration were ordered to stand over at roughly two-yearly intervals, with Birmingham paying the legal expenses. All the while, Adderley's lawyers

---

102   Court of Chancery Records: Orders, C/33/1220 412.

103   Birmingham Town Council Minutes, 30 March 1875.

104   Letter from Paines, Layton, Cooper, and Pollock to Adderley, 9 April 1880, Norton Archive, 2393/41, Birmingham Central Library, Birmingham.

105   Letter from Paines to Adderley, 13 April 1880, Norton Archive, 2393/42.

106   Bunce, *History of the Corporation of Birmingham*, 139; *Birmingham Daily Post*, 12 November 1881.

continued to complain to Birmingham about the pollution: for example in 1890 being 'compelled to call the attention of the Corporation to the state of the river [Tame], which is repeatedly and disgustingly odorous'.[107] The last of these postponements was granted in April, 1890, to continue until 1892.

Birmingham's Sanitary Developments after 1872

As we have seen, the defeat in 1872 of the Birmingham Sewerage Bill had necessitated a desperate revision of Birmingham's plans for dealing with its sewage treatment and a three-fold strategy was followed thereafter to try to keep the pollution of the Tame under control and to fend off Adderley's legal suit.

The first step involved Birmingham intercepting a large amount of faecal matter at source, so to speak, through the introduction of a domestic privy-pan system. Although this looks to have been a retrograde step, there are a number of reasons why a privy-pan system was advantageous and Birmingham was one of a number of large towns adopting privy-pan systems at this time.[108] In 1874, Birmingham still had 20,000 cesspools, middens and ashpits in use, often intermittently cleared, open to the sky and estimated to cover thirteen acres of the town, 'poisoning the air with their exhalations and fouling the adjoining wells by their drainage.'[109] These needed to be phased out, but a quick switch to WCs and a wide-spread water carriage system serving the town could not happen until an adequate water supply was available.[110] Conversion from disposal through cesspools and middens to privy pans for (the mostly poorer) parts of the town began in 1874 and was no minor project. Privy-pan systems required pans or tubs capable of holding the product of the closet for seven days to be placed under each privy closet seat and portable ashtubs were also provided to each court for the copious ash produced by households. Replaced each week, the privy pans and ashtubs were collected and carried by custom night-soil carts to depots (the biggest at Montague Street Wharf). There, after screening and mixing, facilities existed for the contents to be burned, turned into clinker, manufactured into agricultural manure, transformed into dry-powder 'poudrette' manure and/or, by the cartload or boatload, taken off to farms or to be dumped into canal-side tips away from the town. The privy pan system, primly called 'interception', was run from 1876 by Birmingham's Health Department and actually grew steadily: the number of privy-pan closets in the scheme increased from 3,845 in 1874 at its inception to 38,865 in 1884, as compared to around 10,000 WCs.[111] In 1886 and 1887, the town council resolved that all new dwellings should utilise WCs and discontinued the expansion of the

---

[107] Letter from Paines to Birmingham Town Clerk, 5 September 1890, Norton Archive, 2343A/7.

[108] Including Rochdale, Manchester and Halifax.

[109] Bunce, *History of the Corporation of Birmingham*, 141.

[110] Welsh water sources were exploited after 1900.

[111] Bunce, *History of the Corporation of Birmingham*, 147.

interception system; but phasing out pans entirely had to await the new water supplies and an expanded sewer network. The policy replacing the last of the pan closets took ten years and continued up to 1913.[112]

The second part of Birmingham's strategy to deal with its river pollution involved the institutional changes that formed the Birmingham, Tame and Rea District Drainage Board, in 1877. Attempting to clean up the Tame required coordinated action from all the sanitary authorities of the area and this board took on responsibility for managing the rivers and sewage for the united area, alongside policing the industrial nuisances of the area under the 1876 Rivers Pollution Prevention Act. The board, with representation from six other local boards and three rural areas, was completely dominated by Birmingham itself, with Thomas Avery its first chairman.[113] Drainage boards like this proved a common requirement for successful river pollution control in Britain.

The third part of Birmingham's strategy concerned the treatment of the sewage. The major treatment works remained at Saltley after the failure of the Birmingham Sewerage Bill in 1872, and there was heavy investment there to abate the nuisances behind the Gravelly Hill suit. The Saltley site had grown to around 160 acres in 1877 (when the new drainage board first met) but two large extensions (1884 and 1896) and other land additions and consolidations resulted in Birmingham being responsible for a huge series of sewage irrigation farms along the Tame valley. The area taken amounted to over 2,000 acres by 1900, stretching over six miles down the north bank of the Tame, from Saltley all but to the gates of Hams Hall itself.[114]

The treatment being applied to Birmingham's sewage used the full range of tank-settlement and chemical application alongside deep-drained and broad irrigation, and little was to change between the 1870s and the 1910s. At the Saltley works, lime was mixed with the sewage flow and the mixture led through settling tanks to extract the sludge, which was run into beds, briefly allowed to dry in lagoons, and then ploughed into the land (with the land rotated in use every three years).[115] The remaining liquid effluent was led off to irrigate land for commercial crop growing around the rest of the sewage farmland, where the wastewater percolated

---

[112] Charles Anthony Vince, *History of the Corporation of Birmingham IV*, (Birmingham: Birmingham Corporation, 1923), 176–7. Thirty per cent of Birmingham's population were still using the privy pans in 1905 (Royal Commission on Sewage Disposal, *Fifth Report*, Cd. 4279, 1908, 620).

[113] Despite the state of the Tame then being the responsibility of the Drainage Board, Adderley's dispute continued to be with Birmingham Corporation.

[114] According to Vince, *History of the Corporation of Birmingham IV*, 167, it was the third largest sewage farm in Europe.

[115] In 1885, 135,000 cubic yards of sludge was being extracted and dug into 40 acres of land per year, and in 1899, over 300,000 cubic yards of sludge was being ploughed into 150 acres per year. (*The British Architect*, 'Birmingham New Sewage Works', 6 October 1899, 249).

over and through the land and drainage pipes and eventually emptied into the Tame. In the end, however, the best that could be claimed for the nineteenth-century irrigation methods applied along the Tame, was that the results were 'satisfactory': even the Tame Drainage Board's engineer allowed that by 1900 only 90 per cent of 'impurities' were being removed by the process.[116] Water from the lagoons periodically entered the Tame untreated and storm water and rainwater surges remained a problem. Despite the undoubtedly conscientious, serious and strenuous effort Birmingham was to put into their endeavours, the state of the river Tame remained foul.

The definitive word that acceptable standards had not been achieved even by the end of the nineteenth century may be left to be gloriously illustrated by ex-Prime Minister William Gladstone, whose visit to Adderley at Hams Hall in 1895 provoked his splendid comment that: 'The visit to Hams fills – shall I say? – a fragrant place in my recollection ...'[117]

The End of the Affair

In the 1890s, Adderley's dispute with Birmingham was to settle for a final time, and in this, Chancery played no direct part. Some informal contact between Adderley and dignitaries from Birmingham led to meetings and an exchange of correspondence in 1891, in which a path for settling the dispute and dropping the suit was outlined. An arrangement in 1892 was reached between Adderley and Edward Lawley Parker, Birmingham's mayor, such that the suit was to be dismissed and all proceedings stayed on receipt by Adderley of a sum of £5,000 (plus costs) from the corporation, for 'cleaning the River Tame along its course through the Hams Estate' under the direction of Adderley with no admission of any liability on the part of the corporation.[118] Although the receipt of the monies was acknowledged in January 1893, the order dissolving the injunction had to await the authority of the Attorney-General, in whose name the suit had been pursued, and the suit came to a final conclusion in Chancery in February 1895. This action by Charles Adderley against the sewerage authorities of Birmingham, which had

---

[116] Vince, *History of the Corporation of Birmingham IV*, 166.

[117] Childe-Pemberton, *Life of Lord Norton*, 297.

[118] Letter from Norton, 28 February 1892, Norton Archive, 2640/2; 'Heads of Agreement for Dismissal of Suit', 1 June 1892, Norton Archive, 2393A/11; Vince, *History of the Corporation of Birmingham IV*, 81–2.

first found a formal hearing in the Court of Chancery in July 1858,[119] hence ended an astonishing *thirty-seven years* later, in 1895.[120]

One further legal episode, in 1908, must be recorded: it demonstrates that all Birmingham's efforts to abate its sewage pollution nuisance at Hams Hall were unable to raise the quality of the Tame enough to avoid legal liability for nuisance at Chancery. Hence, legally and according to Chancery, the sewage pollution nuisance along the Tame still existed, at an unlawful level, well into the twentieth century. In 1908, the Court of Chancery nuisance suit, Attorney-General v Birmingham Tame and Rea District Drainage Board was brought, as a relator action, by the town authorities of Tamworth, the town next along the Tame downstream of Adderley's Hams Hall. The problem was again effluent passing into the river which 'had not been freed from all excrementitious or other foul or noxious matter before being poured into the stream, and that it consequently seriously affected and deteriorated the purity and quality of the water.'[121]

Birmingham's sewage authorities were again found liable for the nuisance and the Court of Chancery awarded an injunction restraining them from allowing the deterioration of the quality of the water of the Tame as it flowed past their sewage outlets. But, again, although the legal liability of the defendants was established, the court remained unwilling to put the injunction into immediate force. Justice Kekewich's view, on what was almost the *fifty-year* anniversary of Adderley's first Chancery judgment, was to allow Birmingham 'reasonable time':

> I think the defendants deserve gentle treatment. [The plaintiff] must take into consideration all the difficulties which beset the defendants in dealing with the vast problem entrusted to them – a problem, be it observed, involving practical questions of the highest importance to the community at large. ... [T]he Court would be extremely reluctant to allow process to issue unless and until the defendants have had a reasonable time for remedying the present state of affairs and have neglected to use the opportunity thus afforded to the best advantage.[122]

The issuing of the injunction was subsequently discharged, but on technical grounds not relevant to the argument here.

---

[119]   Appearances in Chancery directly concerning the dispute occurred in July 1858, March 1871, February 1872, July 1872, November 1872, April 1873, June 1873, August 1873, January 1874, November 1874, April 1875, November 1881, February 1886, December 1887, April 1890 and January 1892.

[120]   After Charles Adderley (Lord Norton) died in 1905, his son sold off the extensive Hams Hall farm estates in 1911, and Hams Hall and park was sold in 1919, to Birmingham Corporation (of course).

[121]   *Times*, 14 October 1908; Attorney-General v Birmingham, Tame and Rea District Drainage Board (1908) 2 Ch. 551; (1910) 1 Ch. 48; (1912) AC 788 (HL).

[122]   Ibid.

By this stage, as the Edwardian period progressed, Birmingham's sewage authorities, always eager to be at the forefront of sanitary engineering advances, were already putting septic tanks and bacterial-based filter beds at the centre of their treatment processes. The introduction of new biological treatment methods would eventually provide a workable solution to the sewage problems along the Tame.

Lessons from Birmingham

The dispute between Charles Adderley and the Birmingham sewage authorities over sewage in the River Tame was a protracted affair and one that remains preeminent among the river sewage pollution dilemma cases. It was the first to come to Chancery and proved the most long-lasting and intractable and contains a number of elements of the dilemma that will be seen to reoccur in the other cases under study.

Vice-Chancellor Page Wood and Vice-Chancellor Bacon were both steadfast in rejecting the argument that the balance of convenience was relevant to the legal situation, and both supported the riparian stance on the responsibilities of water users to maintain water quality for others. Further, the liability of Birmingham as responsible for the sewage nuisance in the Tame was never in doubt at any stage. Yet at no time were the sewers of Birmingham or the outfalls into the Tame at Saltley ever stopped by the court. The historical context of the dispute shows that this was achieved by a number of means.

Chancery itself, in its attempts to settle the dispute, while clear on liability, proved very willing to allow delays and suspensions to the imposition of the injunction and sequestration remedies. At some points, paradoxically, Chancery is recorded as requiring the plaintiffs not to enforce the writs that Chancery has just awarded. The court also made orders contingent on Birmingham carrying out preferred actions, which amounted to Chancery making administrative requests and orders.

The disputants themselves can be seen to be acting at times (self-interestedly) to further mutual agreements that would end the dispute and attempted and failed negotiations are recorded between Adderley and Birmingham. But there were also successful agreements, involving pecuniary payments, which both suspended the dispute for a time and, finally, ended it.

And Birmingham, at least after 1870, made great efforts to abate the nuisance it was causing in the river by applying what treatment methods it had available and even contemplated diverting its sewer outfall beyond Adderley's property. But as demonstrated, the available treatment methods proved insufficient to abate the physical nuisance to the satisfaction of Chancery (or Mr Gladstone).

For the protracted action(s) concerning the pollution of the Tame, covering a full half-century, undoubtedly the most striking feature remains the clear unwillingness of the courts, at the crunch, to enforce the injunctions and writs of sequestration arising from the actions and non-actions of the Birmingham sewerage authorities. The dilemma posed by the mutual incompatibility of legal precedent and social benefit in the Tame pollution cases must have been most evident to the judicial authorities. The Court of Chancery *in action* was very aware of the practical consequences of their decisions as regards social efficiency. Little else can explain the Court of Chancery failing to enforce emphatically its decisions. In line with guidance from Posner's conjecture, we might have expected Chancery's judges to be reluctant decisively to enforce seemingly economically inefficient decisions, and this is what we see. What the historical context of the case most clearly shows is that the Court of Chancery was able *formally* to maintain individual landowner and riparian rights and the law of nuisance; while *effectively* allowing the town of Birmingham to continue, for four-plus decades, its polluting activity along the Tame, to the social advantage of its large population.

Chapter 6
Delays and Contingencies: Leeds and Barnsley

The history and context of Birmingham's protracted dispute at Chancery with Adderley, presented in the last chapter, introduce many features that will be seen again in the other case studies being examined. One feature that reoccurs concerns how Chancery allows delays and extensions to time limits to the legal remedies applied to enforce liability judgments. Indeed, Chancery was sometimes willing to allow oft-repeated delays and extensions before injunctions became operative, to an extent that the injunction would come into force only when the nuisance for which the injunction had been sought was known to be unlikely to be violated. The cases of Leeds and Barnsley, the subjects of this chapter, are clear examples of such. In these instances, Chancery is shown as willing to stand as a supervisor and guarantor that the concerned sanitary authorities were working towards, if not in fact achieving, full abatement of the nuisances arising from their actions.[1] In consequence, the cases show Chancery was more concerned to 'settle the dispute' than it was to uphold and enforce legal rights and standards as traditionally assumed.

Leeds: Attorney-General v Leeds (1870)

> ... if the Corporation were really busying itself to remove the nuisance complained of, ample time for the completion of the works would be allowed.[2]

By the mid-Victorian era, Leeds, as the centre of the Yorkshire woollen trade, had become an important and thriving English town, one of the largest of the day, with a population in 1871 of some 370,000, more than treble that of 1801. The River Aire is the major river of the area; it passes through a busy industrial landscape and collects the tributary waters of a number of valleys, many with their own industry, before flowing close to Bradford and then through Leeds, eventually to join the River Calder to meet the tidal Humber estuary at Goole.

---

[1] Merthyr Tydfil provides another instance, see Leslie Rosenthal, 'Sewage Pollution of the Taff and the Merthyr Tydfil Local Board (1868–1871)', *Merthyr Historian*, 23 (2012): 70–93.

[2] *Leeds Mercury*, 18 April 1870. The *Leeds Mercury* was the most significant local Leeds newspaper of the era, and sympathetic to the Liberal-run Leeds town council of the day.

Formally and administratively for the period that concerns us, the ancient Borough of Leeds was run by the Town Council of the Corporation of Leeds as established by the Municipal Corporations Act of 1835.[3] Pressure for better public health facilities and civic improvement for the town led to the passage of the Leeds Improvement Act of 1842, which aimed at enabling the provision of better streets, water and drainage for the area. Robert Baker, reporting on Leeds for Chadwick's *Sanitary Report* in 1842 paints a vividly grim picture of the town at that time:

> ... the lower parts [Leeds's poorer areas] which lie contiguous to the river and the Becks or rivulets are dirty, confined, ill-ventilated and in many instances self-sufficient to shorten life, and especially infant life ... furthermore disgusting particularly on account of a general want of paving and drainage, for the irregularity of their buildings, for the violation of the common decencies of life, in the abundance of refuse and excrementious matter lying around in various directions ... here and there stagnant water, and channels so offensive that they have been declared to be unbearable, lie under the doorways of the uncomplaining poor; and privies so laden with ashes and excrementious matter as to be unusable, prevail till the streets themselves become offensive ...[4]

New sewerage network plans were commissioned by Leeds Corporation and a scheme from John Wignall Leather in 1848–9 was eventually accepted that would install mains sewers and connections for the (first) drainage district formed by the townships of central Leeds, Hunslet and Holbeck.[5] The *Leeds Mercury* was supportive:

> The Leeds Town Council acting in some measure doubtless under the influence of the fact that Leeds has for some weeks been the worst place in England for the Cholera have at length resolved to enter upon a great and effectual plan for the drainage of the town.[6]

Wignall Leather's sewerage scheme, which commenced, effectively, in 1850, required driving two main sewers under the town, parallel to the Aire, intercepting and collecting the existing sewage flows and proposed a new network of drains and sewers for the district. The sewer contents would be discharged into the river

---

[3]   After the reorganisation of local government in 1888, Leeds became a County Borough and in 1893 the town received a Royal Charter to become the City of Leeds.

[4]   Robert Baker, 'Report on the Condition of the Residences of the Labouring Classes in the Town of Leeds in the West Riding of York', in Chadwick, *Sanitary Report*, 349–50.

[5]   John Wignall Leather, *Leeds Sewer Contracts*, (Leeds: H.W. Walker, 1850), Leeds City Library, Local History Collection, L352.63 L483; David Sellers, *Beneath our Feet: The Story of Sewerage in Leeds* (Leeds: Department of Highways and Transportation, Leeds City Council, 1997).

[6]   *Leeds Mercury*, 6 October 1849.

at Thwaites Mill, Knostrop (Knowesthorpe). This outfall lies just one-and-a-half miles downstream from Leeds town centre, on land then owned by the Meynell-Ingrams (Viscount Irwin) of Temple Newsam, and Leeds paid a rental of £300 per annum for this access. Over time Leeds obtained ownership of the land here and it became the core location of Leeds's main sewage processing works up to modern times. By 1855, the main sewers of the new network were in place in the town itself,[7] with a single outlet at Knostrop dumping the entirety of Leeds's sewage, very cheaply and totally untreated, into the river: and the river sewage pollution along the Aire began to mount.

Through the 1860s, the sewage pollution of the Aire became serious enough for the *Leeds Mercury* to begin a campaign:

> A town has not gained any large population before it finds the necessity of sewers to take away the offal and refuse which would otherwise breed pestilence in its midst. For a time the remedy answers ... It then begins to be found that the sewage of a large town poured into a comparatively small river is productive of the greatest evils ... The once pure water which might be drunk with pleasure becomes thick and slimy, full of decaying matter, and at length in hot seasons a black deposit is found on the banks, emitting a stench horrible to the nostrils and ruinous to the health of all who live on the river banks ... Thus it is with the Aire as it flows amidst banks of black mud, like a river of ink, beneath Swillington Bridge.[8]

And continued the campaign with:

> Our rivers [including] the Aire as it flows by Knostrop are converted into huge open sewers and ooze along through their banks of black slime, pouring forth pestilential vapours throughout every yard of their courses.[9]

In 1867, the Aire and Calder rivers were the subject of one of the investigations of the Royal Commission on Rivers Pollution Prevention where it was reported: 'With very few exemptions the streams of the West Riding of Yorkshire run with a liquid which has more the appearance of ink than of water'; and that not one of the sewage and industrial outflows from Leeds, or from the other major towns along the Aire and Calder, was even subjected to basic screening.[10] At Leeds, the commission recorded:

---

[7] *Leeds Mercury*, 15 August 1857, reported 'Sensation' at the Town Council meeting when the current cost of the new sewage system at £137,000 was revealed, compared to its initial estimate at £80,000 in 1850.

[8] *Leeds Mercury*, 21 November 1862.

[9] *Leeds Mercury*, 27 November 1862.

[10] Royal Commission on Rivers Pollution Prevention of 1865, *Third Report*, 1867, xxi.

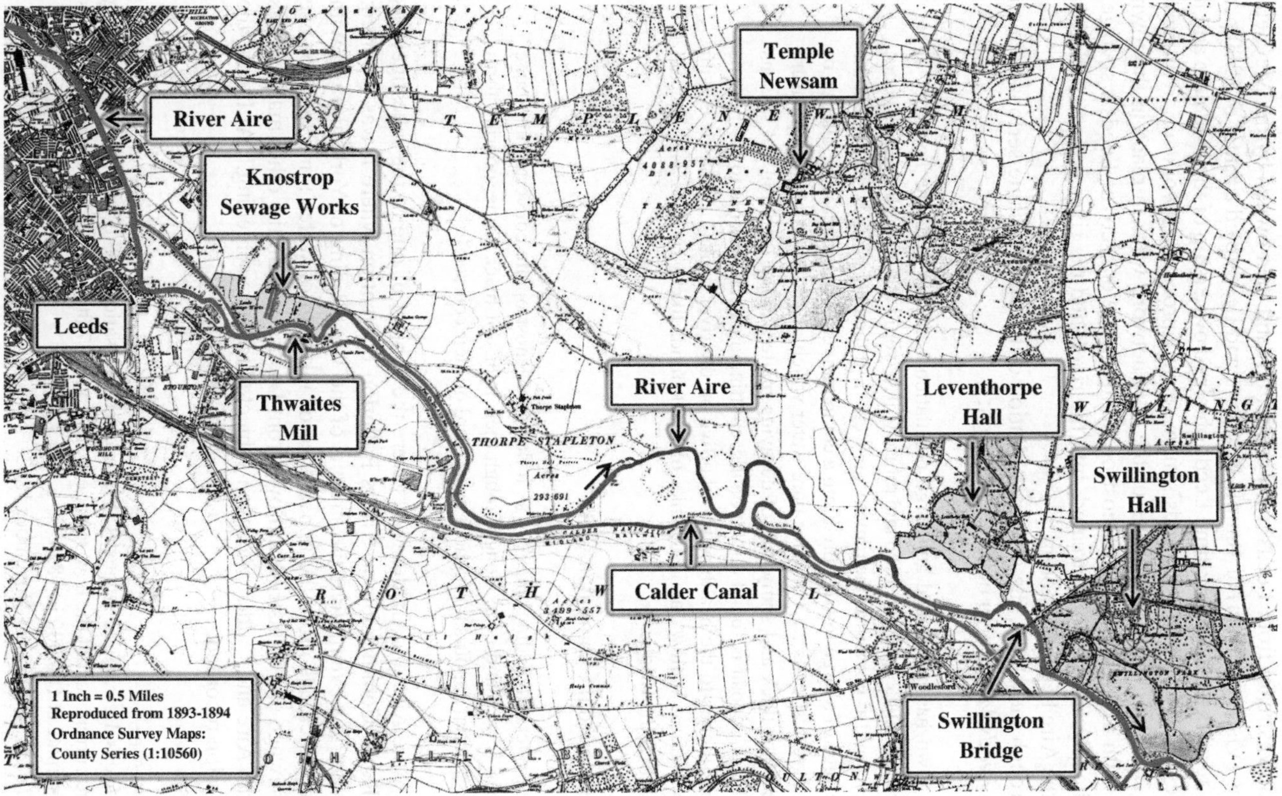

Map 6.1   Leeds and the River Aire

The whole of the becks flowing through the town are fouled with waste refuse from dyeworks, tanneries and the various other manufactures, from their source beyond the municipal boundaries to the Aire. Carcasses of dead animals float down until intercepted by shoals and banks, where they remain to become putrid and most offensive.[11]

The Mayor of Leeds himself joked to the commission that if a handkerchief were to be put into the Aire it would be dyed blue,[12] and another contributor reported the state of the Aire at Swillington as 'frightful and wretched' and reported having to 'put my hand over my mouth and run' when crossing Swillington bridge.[13] Despite this, throughout the 1860s, Leeds continued to expand its sewer network and, in 1866, a second main drainage district, St John's, was formed and added to the system. Complaints about the increasing pollution of the Aire were now being regularly received by the town authorities[14] and a councillor announced that: '... it was a scandal to the town that the river remained in the state it was ... one of the curses of Leeds.'[15] Notwithstanding the scandal, in 1869 the council moved to extend connections of the main sewer system to a third large drainage district made up of adjoining townships. It was only at this stage, towards the end of 1869, that Leeds town council began to consider putting any sort of treatment process in place at the sewage outfall; in preparation in January 1870, the council purchased a small five-acre site at Knostrop from the Meynell-Ingrams of Temple Newsam and negotiated to buy twenty acres more.[16]

For the troubled landholders downstream, these first steps towards treatment offered too little promise of relief and the proposed extension of the mains sewers of Leeds to a third drainage district was probably the final straw. Notice was received by the Leeds Town Clerk in September 1869 that a relator action over sewage nuisance in the Aire was to be heard before the Court of Chancery.[17] The instigators of the suit were two local landholders at Swillington, where the Aire was the colour of ink and Swillington Bridge had to be crossed with mouths covered.

The Swillington Relators

The two landholders acting as the relators standing behind the Attorney-General's name in the Attorney-General v Leeds suits of 1870 were Sir Charles Hugh

---

[11] Ibid., 39.

[12] Ibid., 164. The Mayor was Henry Oxley (1803–90).

[13] Ibid., 206.

[14] Leeds Corporation, Leeds Streets and Sewage Committee Minutes, 31 July, 28 August 1868; 22 January, 20 August 1869, West Yorkshire Archives Service, LLC9/1/9–11, Leeds.

[15] *Leeds Mercury*, 7 December 1869.

[16] Leeds Corporation, Leeds Streets and Sewage Committee Minutes, 19 January 1870.

[17] Leeds Corporation, Leeds Streets and Sewage Committee Minutes, 3 September 1869.

Lowther and John Towlerton Leather, neighbours in the village of Swillington, three or so miles downstream of the Knostrop sewage outfall.

Sir Charles Hugh Lowther (1803–94) had been blind since childhood scarlet fever and he had inherited a baronetcy and the estate of Swillington Hall from his brother in 1868. His extensive land holdings at Swillington comprised a large area of mixed industrial, domestic and agricultural property, including canal side developments and a colliery.[18] Lowther's home at Swillington Hall itself, which dated back to before 1655, actually overlooked the River Aire at Swillington Bridge. It was Lowther's land agent on the estate, William Pollard, who, in November 1866, had testified before the Rivers Pollution Royal Commission on the increasingly polluted, unpleasant and near intolerable state of the Aire at Swillington.[19]

Much more can be told of John Towlerton Leather (1804–85), the second relator, who was Lowther's neighbour, living at Leventhorpe Hall,[20] also close to the Aire. Towlerton Leather was an active and energetic Leeds-based civil engineer and contractor, prominent at a national level. Unfortunately, he is best remembered as having been responsible for designing the Dale Dyke Dam, constructed to help provide Sheffield's new water supply. On its completion in 1864, the dam collapsed, killing 270 in the Great Sheffield Flood.[21] Towlerton Leather's subsequent reputation as an engineer was dented by this disaster but his career nevertheless continued to thrive and he subsequently successfully designed and contracted for numerous civil engineering projects around Britain.[22] Closer to home, Towlerton Leather founded the Hunslet Engine Company in 1864, and was the owner of the Waterloo Colliery Company at Thorpe Stapleton, both enterprises situated at Leeds hard by the Knostrop sewage outlet on the Aire.

Towlerton Leather was first cousin to John Wignall Leather who, as noted above, designed and planned the Leeds sewerage network. The two engineers were members of an extensive Leather dynasty of Yorkshire-based engineers over the late eighteenth and nineteenth centuries, prominent enough that four chapters of Binnie's *Early Victorian Water Engineers* concern the members and adventures of the family. Towlerton Leather married Wignall Leather's sister, Maria Leather (1811–49), so Towlerton and Wignall Leather were both cousins and also

18   Lowther's younger son, James Lowther (1840–1904) served as a Conservative MP for over thirty years, becoming Secretary of State for Ireland. Lowther's grandson, Charles Bingham Lowther, sold off Swillington Hall in 1920 and the bulk of the rest of the estate of over 2,000 acres in 1935 (J.C. Bartle, *Sale of the Swillington Estate*, (1935), Leeds City Library, Local History Collection, Q Yorkshire SW1 333).

19   Royal Commission on Rivers Pollution Prevention of 1865, *Third Report*, 206–7.

20   Leventhorpe Hall was built in 1774, designed by John Carr, and remains an attractive property today.

21   Geoffrey Amey, *The Collapse of the Dale Dyke Dam, 1864* (London: Cassell, 1974).

22   Binnie, *Early Victorian Water Engineers*; David Leather, *Contractor Leather* (Ilkley: Leather Family History Society, 2002).

brothers-in-law. Father to Wignall and Maria Leather was George Leather (Jnr) (1786–1870). George (Jnr) and his engineering firm had been the consultants for Leeds for their new water supply network, which included Bilberry Dam, above Holmfirth in Yorkshire. This dam failed in 1852, causing the Holmfirth Flood, killing 81, which, remarkably, remained Britain's worst recorded flood disaster until the Towlerton Leather-designed Dale Dyke Dam failure in 1864. George (Jnr) was found culpable for the Holmfirth disaster and retired from active engineering to become land agent for the Meynell-Ingrams: he lived at Knostrop New Hall[23] and his post-engineering career would have included responsibility for managing relations with Leeds over their Knostrop sewage outlet site.

Attorney-General v Leeds (1870) and Appeal

On 2 March 1870, Attorney-General v Leeds was heard in the Court of Chancery before Vice-Chancellor James.[24] For the complainants, a number of affidavits, including one from Lowther's butler, were presented,[25] arguing that the sewage entering the river at the Knostrop outfall was a cause of the state of the Aire as it passed by the estates at Swillington being 'so foul that fish could no longer live in it … and unfit for cattle to drink', and that 'five miles below the town it can be smelt for as much as a mile from the banks and it is almost impossible for anyone to live near it.'[26] As defendants, Leeds made little attempt to dispute the foul state of the river, but argued that long before it reached Leeds the Aire was a foul and polluted stream, receiving the drainage of a populous manufacturing district including the towns of Skipton, Keighley, Bingley, Shipley and Bradford. Leeds also contended that the 'balance of convenience' was with Leeds and a greater nuisance would arise if the sewers were stopped, with George Jessel for the defence,[27] contending, rather uncharitably:

> Were they to imperil the health of a quarter of a million of people because some one's wife was sick, and some one's daughter for a reason which did not even transpire, had to go away? It was well known that all stinks were not injurious to health [but there was] evidence as to the injury the town of Leeds would receive if the injunction was granted.[28]

---

[23] Knostrop New Hall has disappeared from the Knostrop site, a victim of urban development, as has Knostrop Old Hall, home from 1870 of the splendid Yorkshire painter, Atkinson Grimshaw (1836–93).

[24] Sir William Milbourne James (1807–81).

[25] Court of Chancery Records: Pleadings, C16/545/A10; *Times*, 3 March 1870; *Leeds Mercury*, 5 March 1870.

[26] Court of Chancery Records, ibid.

[27] George Jessel (1824–83) was to serve as Master of the Rolls in Chancery from 1873.

[28] *Leeds Mercury*, 5 March 1870.

Large expenditures, it was contended, had been made when the sewers had been installed, and no complaints had come from the present relators. Further, Leeds was empowered, they argued, if not directly then by implication, to pour their sewage into the river by their 1848 Leeds Improvement Amendment Act, some clauses of which had been drawn from the Towns Improvement Clauses Act of 1847, a general act, and this had bestowed statutory powers to use the river. This final argument had previously been proposed by Birmingham in their dispute with Adderley in 1858 and had been comprehensively dismissed by Page Wood.[29]

Vice-Chancellor James lost little time in concluding that a most offensive nuisance had been produced by the actions of the defendants and that the case against Leeds was fully made out. James dismissed all Leeds's arguments, carefully explaining, again, that the 1847 Towns Improvement Clauses Act was explicit in requiring that nothing contained in that act could authorise a nuisance: thus whatever powers might be imported into the 1848 Leeds Improvement Act must necessarily be powers also not authorising the creation of a nuisance. He reserved his drollest sarcasm to allow that Leeds:

> ... seemed to have been under the same delusion which had affected the corporations of other large towns in England in supposing that the sewage of a large place could be turned into a river without causing a nuisance. The existence of this nuisance having been proved, the question then arose whether the corporation of Leeds, by their act of 1848 had obtained a privilege which, as far as he [James] was aware, had not been given to any other town in England in draining into their river without regard to any nuisance that might be created.[30]

Vice-Chancellor James ordered the defendants to restrain with immediate effect from 'making any new sewer, and from allowing any such sewer to communicate with their main sewers' and that with regard to the sewage outflow they refrain:

> ... from the second day after the close of the Parliamentary Session of 1871 [August 1871], from causing or permitting the sewage of Leeds, or any part of it, to pass through their main sewer into the river Aire, unless sufficiently purified and deodorized so as not to be a nuisance.[31]

James's order of March 1870 allows a delay of *eighteen* months until August 1871 before this injunction would come into force to put Leeds Corporation under threat of contempt and sequestration. James allowed this delay, he said, to give Leeds time to go to Parliament for a private bill to legitimise their situation by acquiring specific powers or authority: Leeds made no attempt to do this. In effect, the order

---

[29]   See Chapter 5 above.
[30]   *Times*, 3 March 1870.
[31]   Ibid.

gave Leeds eighteen months of contingent grace to purify and deodorise its sewage outflow before the injunction would come into force.

Back in Leeds, the Town Council was divided about the court's orders, with some members arguing that they were only being forced to do that which they were willing to do, and about to do, anyway, but they quickly resolved to reappear at Chancery to appeal the original decision.[32] Not everyone believed there was any point to an appeal and the *Leeds Mercury* was eminently sensible:

> [The Town Council] are in the trying position of being ordered to discontinue a nuisance without the slightest means of preventing it. Under these circumstances we can well understand the anxiety they feel ... Yet we think the resolution to which they have come was a mistake. ... it was intimated at the time, and is well understood by all parties that if the Corporation were really busying itself to remove the nuisance complained of, ample time for the completion of the works would be allowed. Under these circumstances the injunction amounts to nothing more than a decree that the Leeds Town Council shall not defile the river by pouring all the filth and abominations of the town into a stream but scantily filled with water. So reasonable, we might almost say, so righteous, an injunction ought not to be withstood.[33]

Clearly the nature of Chancery's supervisory stance with regard to its enforcement of river pollution disputes was understood, by the *Mercury* at least, even in 1870.

The appeal was quickly held, on 9 June 1870, at the Court of Appeal in Chancery, before Lord Hatherley (William Page Wood) and Sir George Markham Giffard (1813–70).[34] It lasted only a day and rehearsed no new arguments. Again, the court rejected the argument that the Aire was already decisively polluted by other users, pointing out that though the river was polluted before it received Leeds's outflow, the landowners on the banks were fully entitled to restrain the additional pollution. Similarly, it was held that, though the main sewer had been completed sixteen years before proceedings were taken, the court could interfere at the suit of the landowners as the pollution had vastly increased over the period. Finally, the court upheld the earlier decision rejecting the argument that Leeds had statutory authority to create a nuisance through powers enshrined in the Leeds Improvement Act of 1848 derived from the Towns Improvement Clauses Act of 1847. Hence the appeal failed and the earlier decision of Vice-Chancellor James in the original case was decisively and unanimously upheld. Lord Hatherley found that:

> ... the conclusion the Vice-Chancellor has come to is correct. The Defendants must either abate the evil – whatever difficulties may be imposed in their way –

32 *Leeds Mercury*, 16 April 1870.
33 *Leeds Mercury*, 18 April 1870.
34 Attorney-General v Leeds Corporation (1870) L.R. 5 Ch.App. 583.

or they must go to the Legislature; and, no doubt, the Legislature will be ready to afford a remedy if they find the evil is such as is deserving of it.[35]

The counsel to go to Parliament echoes that of James and that of Hatherley's own earlier advice in Attorney-General v Birmingham (1858), but Leeds made no attempt to obtain such statutory exemption, and no town was to pursue this course before Wolverhampton did so in 1891. Leeds in 1870 turned its attention to the installation of a sewage treatment plant along the Aire.

Leeds's Treatment Regime

Having comprehensively failed to divert the legal challenge in the courts, Leeds Town Council were now forced to confront their position that, after August 1871, the substantive part of the injunction would restrain them to purify and deodorise their outflows so as not to create a nuisance. Leeds then looked to what steps it could take, albeit, and explicitly, restricting themselves to methods which would not unduly strain the patience and pockets of their ratepayers.

In May 1870, Leeds Council received a report from a group of council members who had explored the available possibilities for sewage treatment at other English towns, and had outlined their opinions on the methods being applied elsewhere.[36] The report came to an unfortunate conclusion in being 'very favourably impressed' with the flawed ABC process as applied by the (sensitively named) Native Guano Company at Leamington Spa. The council resolved to approach the company with a proposal for them to deal with Leeds's sewage, initially as a test of the patented ABC system they used, which relied on tank-based chemical precipitation using a mixture based on alum, blood and clay.[37] Leeds Council believed there could be £2 profit per ton from the fertiliser derived from the sludge produced and planned a twenty-nine year concession to be granted to the Native Guano Company. Leeds would provide the required buildings, equipment and land and the company would fund and apply the ABC process, with fifteen percent of the profits being returned to the Corporation. The test would start with one-seventh of the sewage flow being treated, increasing to one hundred percent as the method became proven effective.

Unfortunately, as described above in Chapter 3, the ABC method, in practice, not at Leeds, Leamington or anywhere else, ever proved either effective or economically viable as a sewage treatment process in other than restricted experimental situations. Just weeks after Leeds's decision to endorse the process,

---

[35]   Ibid.

[36]   Leeds Corporation, Leeds Streets and Sewerage Committee Minutes, 6 May 1870. Visits went to Worksop, Croydon, London, Hertford, Rugby, Bradford, Harrogate, Leicester, Birmingham, Coventry and Leamington Spa: a number of these also had severe legal problems.

[37]   *Leeds Mercury*, 12 May 1870; Leeds Corporation, Leeds Streets and Sewerage Committee Minutes, ibid.

Frankland's damning Rivers Pollution Commission report on the ABC method was published in July 1870.[38] It concluded that the method was little better than basic settling and could not clean the sewage sufficiently to allow admission into rivers; any fertiliser derived, the report continued, would be of little commercial value; the very ABC works were likely themselves to be offensive enough to cause a nuisance; and reiterated that only land-irrigation-based methods, using sewage-farm-like approaches, were viable. However, Leeds thought themselves unable to apply sewage-farm irrigation treatments: there were no easily obtainable and suitable sites available close to the city; the local industrial waste and its special dye and wool-grease (lanoline) content made irrigation less effective; and, not least, it would be (too) expensive as a method.[39]

Scepticism over the Native Guano Company scheme at Leeds soon emerged. In late 1870, Leeds town council saw motions for Leeds to abandon the ABC experiment and heard comment that 'ABC was not worth a rap' and 'worthless'.[40] But Leeds persisted with the ABC method throughout the early 1870s, clearly on the basis that it was required that they be seen to be seriously engaged in sewage treatment in order to show the Court of Chancery they were doing something. The Town Clerk was remarkably open in laying out Leeds's strategy with regard to the court orders they faced:

> It would be useless to ask for a relaxation of the injunction if we were not prepared to show that after the two years' delay which had taken place that we had a scheme in hand and were carrying it out. If we asked for an extension of time on the grounds of something else turning up, we would be laughed out of court.[41]

Leeds's contract with the Native Guano Company finally foundered in March 1873 when financial and technical problems forced the company to ask to be released from their agreement. Leeds Corporation then took over responsibility for treating the town's sewage and, predictably, Leeds subsequently switched from the ABC method to the more widely used lime-precipitation process, which was cheaper and not patented. The town had by 1873 acquired from the Temple Newsam estate an area of land totalling around twenty-six acres on which to expand the works at Knostrop. By 1874, a purification method could at last be applied to the whole of Leeds' normal dry weather sewage flow.[42]

The twenty-six acres was to remain the entire area that Leeds had for sewage treatment over the next thirty-plus years, until the first decade of the twentieth century, and the lime-precipitation process introduced by Leeds was used

---

[38] Royal Commission on Rivers Pollution Prevention of 1868, *Second Report*, (The ABC process), 1870.

[39] *Leeds Mercury*, 12 May 1870.

[40] *Leeds Mercury*, 15 October 1870.

[41] *Leeds Mercury*, 27 February 1872.

[42] Heavy storm rainfall would require sewage flow to pass into the Aire untreated.

continuously by the works at Knostrop over the same period.[43] The treatment applied was basic chemical precipitation. Briefly, incoming sewage was mixed with the lime and led through two rows of six settling tanks, used alternatingly, to precipitate out the more solid sludge, the remaining wastewater being allowed to pass directly into the river. The settled sewage sludge in the tanks was removed and left to dry in huge open sludge lagoons at Knostrop, over periods lasting months until manageable. No profitable exploitation of the final product proved possible and Leeds eventually had to offer cartage for the canny Yorkshire farmers to take it away.[44] For the river, as we know, lime addition does provide deodorising and disinfectant effects which can temporarily retard putrefaction, and most of the liquid run-off should take only a day or two down the Aire to reach the wide tidal expanses of the Humber Estuary.

Back at Chancery

While developing and constructing the tanks and works at Knostrop progressed after 1870, Leeds soon found it required longer protection from the injunction which was still due to come into force in August 1871 when the initial eighteen-month period of grace ran out. In July 1871, Leeds returned to Chancery to apply formally for an extension of time to meet the requirement that their sewage be purified and deodorised, arguing that although they had already spent £10,000 they would need a further eighteen-month period of grace to meet the requirements of the court's orders. Lowther and Leather responded that they were content for an extension to be granted, but only for six months so as to see what improvements Leeds were able to make in that time. With the bench agreeing that this was a handsome offer, a six-month extension was agreed and a further extension, for the other twelve months followed in February 1872. Then, as this time began to run out in February 1873, a further extension of twelve-months was agreed between the parties,[45] with Leeds stressing how their new buildings and works were being constructed at Knostrop and how they were now treating one million gallons of their sewage per day.[46]

Up to 1874, Leeds encountered few problems in obtaining these further suspensions to the substantive order issued in 1870, but Leeds was well aware that the extensions, while protecting the town council, also extended the period when, given the Chancery orders, new sewerage facilities and drainage connections

---

    [43]   Far-sightedly, Leeds allowed various small-scale experimental sewage treatment processes to be tried out on site, but none proved effective (*Leeds Mercury*, 6 June 1877).

    [44]   *Leeds Mercury*, 9 January 1885.

    [45]   Court of Chancery Records: Cause Book, C32/10/A104; Court of Chancery Records: Orders, C33/1175/2627, C33/1183/541, and C33/1195/556.

    [46]   *Leeds Times*, 22 July 1871, 1 March 1873.

could not be provided for the people of their town.[47] In February 1874, with the sewage works at Knostrop expected to be completed imminently, the Town Clerk reported that he had been in communication with the solicitors for Lowther and Leather. Although the works would not actually be fully finished and in working order by the time specified, they were progressing so well that, the Clerk reported, he expected that there would be 'no difficulty' with the relators on the expiry of the final suspension of the injunction in March of 1874. The Town Clerk's report was that:

> The suspension of the injunction expires this week but it is not expected that any legal proceedings will be taken in the London courts on the subject ... it is unlikely that the Chancery Court will be moved on the matter, or that any proceedings will be pressed against the Town Council.[48]

The Town Clerk's correspondence with the relators' solicitors had included detail on the progress of the treatment works at Knostrop and had asked for reassurance that a further application to the court might be unnecessary. The response received back was formal and hardly definitive, saying it was up to the Corporation to decide if a new suspension application at Chancery was necessary and warned:

> ... if we may estimate future performance on the basis of the past we cannot feel much confidence in the purification being so fully effected, no promise is even ventured upon. We feel however certain that if the nuisance is not fully removed in terms of the injunction before the hot weather sets in the Corporation may expect some decided measures being taken to obtain such relief as the law will give.[49]

Still, confident that their works could now, in 1874, satisfy the requirements of the injunction, Leeds decided not to return to Chancery to seek a new extension to the period of suspension of the injunction, due by March 1874. So at this point, then, Leeds's final suspension was allowed to run out.[50] After February 1874, nearly five years after the complaint was first filed, back in October 1869, Leeds became subject to the full force of the injunction awarded on the motion of the Attorney-General on behalf of the relators, Lowther and Leather.

---

[47]   Leeds Corporation, Leeds Town Council Minutes, 13 February 1873, West Yorkshire Archive Service, Leeds, LL2/1/13–16.

[48]   Leeds Corporation, Leeds Town Council Minutes, 19 February 1874.

[49]   Leeds Corporation, Leeds Utilisation of Sewage Sub-Committee Minutes, 4 March 1874, West Yorkshire Archive Service, Leeds, LLC9/5/1–2.

[50]   '... said injunction was by order dated the 29th day of February 1872 suspended until the 1st day of March 1873 be further suspended until the 2nd day of March 1874 ...' Court of Chancery Records: Orders, C33/1195/556.

There exists no record of further actions in this Chancery dispute over the sewage pollution of the Aire. The legal context therefore ends with an intriguingly circular conclusion. The injunction is allowed (by the defendants) to come into force only when the situation is such that the defendants are convinced a nuisance that might violate the injunction no longer exists.

The example of the legal action over Leeds's sewage pollution of the River Aire over the period 1870–75 provides another instance of Chancery's use of delayed and contingent orders as a means of managing a sewage pollution dispute. Chancery, while periodically checking the abatement process, was able to stretch the period of grace allowed before Leeds had to face the injunction, extended from an initial eighteen months to four full years. Even then, the parties were aware that further extensions would be available from Chancery if requested. It was only when Leeds was convinced that the engineering it had under way would satisfy the injunction's requirement that its effluent be 'purified and deodorised', did Leeds decide to allow the Chancery injunction to come into force.

After 1874: Something in the Aire?

For Leeds Town Council, the lime precipitation process at Knostrop remained a success simply through enabling the council to avoid, after 1874, further Chancery proceedings and sequestration actions by the relators. In practical sewage engineering terms, the overall success or failure of the Knostrop works, once established, in dealing with Leeds's sewage problems in the Aire is more open to debate. On the positive side, by the end of 1874, Leeds claimed that their sewage-water effluent was able to pass into the Aire 'in a condition to pass into the river without polluting it' with the water 'remarkably clear and smelling only to a slight extent of lime'[51] and, in 1878, that the deodorising works was able to 'turn the water, perfectly clear and harmless, into the river again.'[52] In 1880 Leeds Town Council made a notable visit to the works, where they declared the effluent to be 'sufficiently clear to meet the requirements of the injunction'; the Mayor was able to describe the effluent flow as 'like a trout stream'; and, pricelessly, 'several members were persuaded to taste it and they declared it to be free from any nauseousness.'[53] In 1885, the council claimed that the works had secured 'clear effluent water at the lowest cost yet attained',[54] and in 1887 that 'the sewage works [was] going on satisfactorily without complaint from any quarter.'[55]

Others, however, disagreed: for example, 1875 proved a trying year. In April, a neighbouring sanitary authority complained that 'the whole of the [Leeds] sewage is being poured into the river without any attempt at purification ... poured into

---

51   *Leeds Mercury*, 23 December 1874.
52   *Leeds Mercury*, 15 October 1878.
53   *Leeds Mercury*, 16 September 1880.
54   *Leeds Mercury*, 9 January 1885.
55   *Leeds Mercury*, 10 August 1887.

the river almost as it comes from the sewers',[56] to which Leeds's Town Clerk replied unconvincingly that 'the whole of the sewage had been treated from time to time during the last six months.'[57] The works at Knostrop was not designed or conceived to be able to cope with treating all of Leeds's sewage flow all the time: in periods of storm water, sluices opened to allow the sewers direct entry into the Aire; and temporary problems led to interruptions in the treatment processes at irregular intervals. In August 1875, the Town Clerk admitted that 'amounts of unpurified sewage are still allowed into the Aire',[58] and, in November 1875, John Attfield's report on the effluent at Knostrop contained the judgment that '... by the standards of the River Pollution Commission this effluent must be deemed polluting and inadmissible into any stream in respect of organic matter and sewage matter.'[59] Leeds was perhaps fortunate not to have had to defend their situation at this point at the Court of Chancery, five years after the injunction had been obtained and just eighteen months after it came into full force.

With time, as Leeds grew and developed, the treatment works at Knostrop became increasingly outgrown and out-dated. In the 1890s the restricted twenty-six acre site had become decisively unsatisfactory, no longer able to cope with Leeds's existing demands and deliberately not clearing all the sewage flow: finding space for the sludge lagoons was especially problematic. By 1896, the council admitted the Knostrop works and processes were inadequate: 'it is now generally recognized that further purification is necessary and that precipitation must be followed by land filtration.'[60]

Meanwhile, whatever the success of the sewage works, the general state of the Aire remained appalling. In 1880, the Aire was depicted as 'a black, noisome stream ... bobbing up and down is the carcass of a dead dog.'[61] In 1887, the *Leeds Mercury* campaigned that it would be natural to urge Leeds Corporation to proceed (under the 1876 Rivers Pollution Prevention Act) against polluters of the Aire, 'if only the Corporation were not the worst offender' and described the river as black, stinking, offensive and poisonous, with 'bubbling signs of fermentation', and likely to be the cause of spread of epidemic disease.[62] The *Mercury* continued:

---

[56] Leeds Corporation, Leeds Sewage Utilisation Sub-Committee Minutes, 28 April 1875.

[57] Leeds Corporation, Leeds Sewage Utilisation Sub-Committee Minutes, 8 September 1875.

[58] Leeds Corporation, Leeds Streets and Sewage Committee Minutes, 18 August 1875.

[59] Leeds Corporation, Leeds Sewage Utilisation Sub-Committee Minutes, 19 November 1875. John Attfield (1835–1911), a former student of Frankland, was Professor of Practical Chemistry to the Pharmaceutical Society of Great Britain.

[60] Thomas Walter Harding and W.H. Harrison, *Report on experiments in sewage disposal*, (Leeds: Jowett and Sourry, 1905), Leeds City Library, Local History Collection, L352.63 L517, 6–5.

[61] *Leeds Mercury*, 14 May 1880.

[62] *Leeds Mercury*, 26 July 1887.

> Pollution has become so bad, so alarming, indeed, and so notorious that ratepayers must insist upon knowing the extent of the peril we are facing ... Thousands are already suffering: thousands more may any day have their very lives imperiled through the neglect that ought now come to an end. The ratepayers will look to the Council to do its duty in this serious matter ...[63]

The town council defended itself that there was little purpose in Leeds acting alone when much of the pollution of the Aire arose elsewhere, especially from Bradford's effluent carried in the notorious Bradford Beck. A wider river conservancy body covering the Aire and Calder basin was needed, to follow the pattern for Birmingham and in Lancashire for the Mersey and Ribble river basins. Such an institution appeared when the West Riding of Yorkshire Rivers Board was established in 1894, covering the west Yorkshire region and its abused watercourses.[64] The new Rivers Board was given enhanced powers to prosecute under the 1876 Rivers Pollution Prevention Act and employed its own inspectorate of ten inspectors to police the area. This was just the independent guardianship of the Aire and Calder river basin that had been recommended by the Rivers Pollution Prevention Royal Commission back in 1867. One of the new Board's first targets became the ineffectiveness of Leeds Corporation's Knostrop works. As early as December 1894 the Board pointedly declared: 'The Board thought the time had come when the Leeds people should do something beyond putting off the matter from year to year.'[65]

Eventually, having continuously badgered and bullied Leeds and having witnessed more than a decade of Leeds's multi-postponed and frustrated plans for improved treatment of its sewage, the Rivers Board, in February 1907, instituted legal proceedings against Leeds Corporation over their sewage pollution of the Aire.[66] Rather than a contingent injunction under nuisance law, in July 1907, to avoid a conviction under the powers of the Rivers Pollution Act, Leeds agreed a formal consent order before Justice Grantham at the Yorkshire Assizes.[67] The order suspended any prosecution by the Rivers Board for twelve months, but required that Leeds would seek Parliamentary approval to authorise a complete sewage disposal scheme and that they would ensure that any flow of sewage discharged into the Aire would not exceed a stated, measurable, standard of

---

[63]   *Leeds Mercury*, 11 August 1887.

[64]   Under the West Riding of Yorkshire Rivers Act (1894), see John Sheail, 'The institutional development of river management in Yorkshire', *The Science of the Total Environment*, 194/195 (1997): 225–34.

[65]   *Leeds Mercury*, 19 December 1896.

[66]   West Riding of Yorkshire Rivers Board, Domestic Sewage and Solid Refuse Committee Minutes, 7 February 1907, West Yorkshire Archive Service, Wakefield, C1001/2/4/3.

[67]   Justice William Grantham (1835–1911).

quality.[68] Thereafter, with the passing of the Leeds Corporation Act in 1908, a new expanded sewage works was authorised for the site at Knostrop, with more land purchased from the Temple Newsam estate now owned by Viscount Halifax.[69] In 1911 a new Leeds Corporation sewage works was inaugurated, though these works were not completed until 1925.[70]

The dispute over Leeds's sewage pollution of the River Aire provides the first of the two disputes described in this chapter displaying a series of delays allowed by Chancery in face of the river sewage pollution dilemma.

Barnsley: Attorney-General v Barnsley (1873, 1874)

The interests of the public and the landowners [are] paramount to any right or interest of the town of Barnsley.[71]

The river sewage pollution dispute at Chancery involving Barnsley provides a second example where the injunction awarded by Chancery was delayed and not allowed to come into force until physical abatement of the nuisance was such that the injunction would not be violated. Barnsley is another English town of the West Riding of Yorkshire. It lies between the large cities of Leeds and Sheffield with, in the 1870s, a population of about 25,000. Situated squarely on the rich South Yorkshire coalfield and surrounded by famous and immensely productive

---

[68] 'Rivers Board v Leeds Corporation: Terms of Order Settled by the Domestic Sewage and Refuse Committee at their meeting on the 24 July 1907. Order to be suspended for 12 months. During that time, Corporation to obtain Act of Parliament to enable them to carry out complete sewage disposal scheme. The Corporation to commence forthwith to deal and to continue to deal with the whole of the dry weather flow of sewage so that the suspended solids in the effluent discharged to the river shall not exceed 10 parts in every 100,000 parts. On default of compliance with either condition, penalties to accrue from date at £50 per day. If Act of Parliament obtained, liberty to apply for further suspension.' West Riding of Yorkshire Rivers Board Minutes, 19 July 1907, West Yorkshire Archive Service, Wakefield, C1001/2/1.

[69] Edward Frederick Lindley Wood (1881–1959), Third Viscount Halifax, later First Earl Halifax, had inherited Temple Newsam in 1904 and, in 1922 sold the entire estate to Leeds City Council (*Times*, 20 September 1922). Lord Halifax was a major political figure of the twentieth century serving as Foreign Secretary 1938–1940 and was a rival to Churchill as Prime Minister in 1940. His grandfather, the First Viscount Halifax (Charles Wood) had been one of the relators in the river pollution case against Barnsley. In 2010, Temple Newsam Hall remains a major local tourist attraction for Leeds: nearby, Knostrop is still the site of Leeds's main sewage works and the area retains a local reputation for its 'pong'.

[70] Sellers, *Beneath our Feet*, 16.

[71] Lord Justice James, *Barnsley Chronicle*, 14 February 1874.

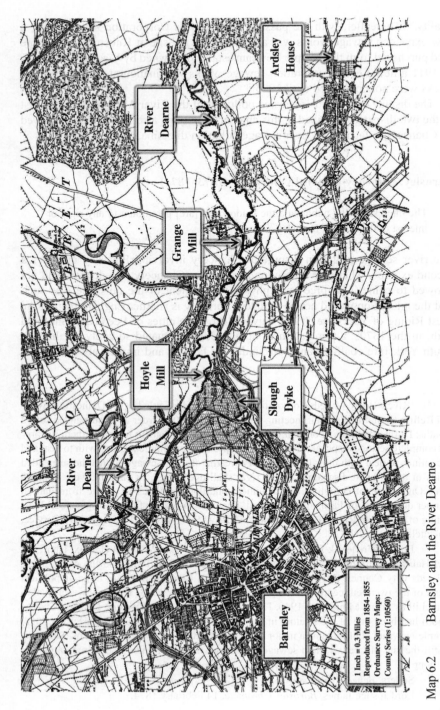

Map 6.2   Barnsley and the River Dearne

1 Inch = 0.3 Miles
Reproduced from 1854–1855
Ordnance Survey Maps:
County Series (1:10560)

collieries, Barnsley's highly industrial economy was at this time becoming increasingly dominated by the coal industry.

Administratively, from 1853, a Local Board of Health was responsible for the public health of the town but, in 1869, Barnsley became a corporate borough and the sanitary duties of the town were taken on by the new Barnsley Borough and its town council. The borough inherited from the Local Board the beginnings of a sewerage network utilising a main drain and sewer running into the Sough Dyke, a minor stream (more an open ditch) which ran through the town and acted as a conduit taking the town's effluent into the River Dearne a little way to the north-east. The Dearne, which joins the River Don about six miles east of Barnsley, flows close to the town but it is hardly a substantial waterway. At Hoyle Mill where the Slough Dyke sewage outfalls into the Dearne, the river is barely six paces wide and three feet deep.

By 1870, it was clear that new and comprehensive sanitary investment was required. A report of that year described Barnsley as 'filthy and disgusting'; found 'privies dilapidated ... some most wretched dwellings, scarcely inhabitable' with 'cesspools ... overflowing and running on the surface [and producing] noxious gases'; and warned of potential disease epidemics.[72] In October 1870, Barnsley's town council resolved to provide a full sewer system to Barnsley's Old Town area.[73] But the extended sewer network would add substantially to the raw, totally untreated sewage (370,000 gallons per day) already finding its way, via the Sough Dyke, into the River Dearne. The new proposals provoked legal action from a group of landowners below Barnsley who held property in the Dearne Valley downstream of the sewage outfall at Hoyle Mill. These complainants now began to take up with the town council the sewage pollution evident along the Dearne:[74] in September 1871 notice was served that an injunction was being sought from the Court of Chancery restraining the Corporation from continuing to pollute the river.[75] It took until December 1873 for the suit to come to the Court of Chancery.

The Four Relators

There were four relators in the action brought in the name of the Attorney-General against Barnsley: Francis Taylor, Richard Micklethwait, Earl Fitzwilliam and Viscount Halifax. Of the four, the latter two were well-known and nationally-celebrated individuals but it is the first two relators, much less well-known, who were the most active individuals and the prime movers of the action against Barnsley.

---

[72] Borough of Barnsley Town Council Minutes, 27 December 1870, Vol. 1, 1870–76, Barnsley Archive and Local Studies, Barnsley Library.

[73] Borough of Barnsley Town Council Minutes, 18 October 1870.

[74] Borough of Barnsley Town Council Minutes, 7 March 1871.

[75] Borough of Barnsley Town Council Minutes, 5 September 1871.

Francis Howard Taylor (1822–98) and his neighbour Richard Micklethwait (1831–88) were both holders of modest estates along the Dearne. Francis Howard Taylor was one of the Taylor entrepreneurial family at the centre of Barnsley's then-important linen manufacturing industry.[76] The firm of Thomas Taylor and Sons ran linen cloth weaving mills in Barnsley and in the 1880s Taylor's Mill in Peel Street, Barnsley, employed 800 people and housed 400 power looms. Francis Taylor had purchased, in 1845, the estate of Middlewood Hall, Darfield, and the hall still stands, about four miles down the Dearne from where the sewage entered the river at Hoyle Mill. Richard Micklethwait was a member of a prominent South Yorkshire family with agricultural and coal-mining interests in the area, and he had an estate at Ardsley House, now a hotel, at Ardsley just one mile or so from Hoyle Mill.

From the testimonies of the affidavits presented to Chancery, Taylor and Micklethwait could have picked from a number of landowners of the Dearne valley to join them as relators for the nuisance action,[77] but Earl Fitzwilliam and Viscount Halifax had the advantage of being especially prominent figures of the time. The Rt. Hon. William Thomas Spencer Wentworth Fitzwilliam (1815–1902), Sixth Earl Fitzwilliam, owned the vast Wentworth Woodhouse estate and was among the richest men in the country. Earl Fitzwilliam had been MP for various constituencies before inheriting the earldom and becoming head of a family that had exploited the coal and other minerals of wide land holdings for industrial ventures through which they had accrued huge wealth during this period.[78] The family seat, Wentworth House at Wentworth Woodhouse, is cited as the largest private house in Britain and the estate sits plumb on what was one of the richest coal seams in England, five or six miles from Barnsley. The Rt. Hon. Charles Wood (1800–85), First Viscount Halifax, who owned Hickleton Hall, was an influential politician of the period. Sir Charles Wood had been Liberal MP for several constituencies, including Halifax, between 1826 and 1866, serving in senior cabinet posts, including as Chancellor of the Exchequer under Lord John Russell, and he had become Viscount Halifax in 1866.[79] Hickleton Hall close to the river, four to five miles down the Dearne valley from Barnsley was his family seat.[80] Although Earl Fitzwilliam and Viscount Halifax were to remain silent

---

[76]   John Goodchild, *Golden Threads – Barnsley's Linen Industry in the 18th and 19th Century* (Wakefield: Wakefield Historical Publications, 1983).

[77]   Court of Chancery Records: Pleadings, C16/693/A93. C.E.B. Wright, Edward Parker and Mr Montegue are cited as willing to have become relators.

[78]   John T. Ward, 'The Earls Fitzwilliam and the Wentworth Woodhouse Estate in the Nineteenth Century', *Bulletin of Economic Research*, 12 (1960): 19–27. For speculation on the story of the fall of the house of Fitzwilliam see Catherine Bailey, *Black Diamonds*, (London: Penguin Books, 2008).

[79]   David Steele 'Wood, Charles, First Viscount Halifax (1800–1885)', *Oxford Dictionary of National Biography*, (Oxford University Press, 2004). His grandson, Edward Frederick Lindley Wood was to become an even more prominent politician, see above.

[80]   Hickleton Hall is now a *Sue Ryder* care home.

partners in the suit with Taylor and Micklethwait, these four individuals constitute a challenging set of relators for Barnsley to face in the dispute in 1873.

Attorney-General v Borough of Barnsley (1873)

Two years after the case was first filed, Attorney-General v Borough of Barnsley was held over three days, 8–11 December 1873, in the Court of Chancery before Vice-Chancellor Hall.[81] In the weary words of the *Times*:

> ... the case presented the usual features of these sewage pollution cases which have been so frequent of late in the Court of Chancery ... as usual in cases of this sort, the pleadings were very voluminous; and the evidence of witnesses, both scientific and others, lengthy and conflicting.[82]

The relators asked that the defendants in particular might be restrained:

> ... from causing or permitting any sewage or other noxious or offensive matter from the intended new sewer ... to pass into the main sewer or to be conveyed into the river by any other channel ... to prevent the discharge into the river of any sewage or other noxious matter ... under the control of the defendants.[83]

Twenty-nine affidavits testifying to the nuisance being caused along the river were presented. These told of the calamitous effects of the ever-deteriorating purity of the Dearne on the husbandry of the fish, cattle and sheep of the landowners and the working conditions of their tenants and workers, and described the effects of the sharp decline in water quality and increases in stench since the new sewage network at Barnsley had been begun. The most striking evidence came from Charles Popplewell (1837?–81?) long-term tenant and miller at the Burton Grange Mill on the Dearne just a half-mile down from the sewer outflow. Popplewell presented graphic testimony about both the deterioration of the river quality since Barnsley's sewers had opened and the consequent malevolent effects on his family and workers. The river had become filled with putrid mud, he said, with its surface covered with black slime and with the water made unfit for any agricultural purpose so even pigs could not drink it. Three of his workers had been forced to quit his employ on account of sickness. Two local doctors attributed local disease outbreaks, including typhoid in Popplewell's family, to the state of the river.[84]

For Barnsley, the defence put forward three grounds for rejecting the application: firstly, that there was no nuisance; secondly, that even if there were,

---

[81]   Sir Charles Hall (1814–83).

[82]   *Times*, 12 February 1874.

[83]   Court of Chancery Records: Pleadings, C16/693/A93; *Barnsley Chronicle*, 13 December 1873; *Sheffield Daily Telegraph*, 11 and 12 December 1873.

[84]   Court of Chancery Records, ibid., 8–10.

it was inappropriate for the Attorney-General to have participated, for it was not a *public* nuisance; and, thirdly, that Barnsley had a continuing and *bona fide* right to discharge sewage into the Dearne in the manner done. Vice-Chancellor Hall rejected all Barnsley's objections to find in favour of the complainants and issued an uncompromising decree restraining the defendants from:

> ... continuing to permit the discharge into the river Dearne of any sewage or other noxious or offensive matter from the Borough of Barnsley or any works within the same or the existing main sewer or by any other channels or means whatsoever under the control of the defendants.[85]

The injunction, requiring total cleansing of the sewage or the stopping of the sewer outfall into the Dearne, was delayed to begin on 22 May 1874, giving Barnsley Town Council under five months to find some way of meeting these requirements. As the local newspaper was to ponder:

> What course will be adopted we do not pretend to guess at, but the Corporation will have little more than four months in which to provide for the disposal of our sewage and, therefore, the action must be prompt and decided. The corporation, clearly, has its hands full ...[86]

The first action the corporation took was to waste some of this time by appealing the decision.

Attorney-General v Borough of Barnsley (1874)

The appeal was quickly heard, over a single day again in Chancery. It took place just over one month after the original hearing, on 12 February 1874, before Lord Justice James (who had presided over Leeds's Chancery suit in 1870), Lord Chancellor Palmer and Lord Justice Mellish.[87] Barnsley's arguments were, again, that any nuisance involved was private and minor, as very few persons were affected, and that the town had a prescriptive right to do what was complained of. The Court seemed to have had little trouble coming to a decision. Lord Justice James noted that as Barnsley's use of the river for sewage and the nuisance caused was only recent, Barnsley could have no prescriptive rights in the matter and that the evidence presented at the original hearing showed conclusively that the pollution, rather than minor, made the water 'unfit for almost any purpose'. As for the nuisance being private rather than public, James responded: 'If the

---

[85]   Court of Chancery Records: Orders, C33/1200/3230.

[86]   *Barnsley Chronicle*, 13 December 1873.

[87]   *Times*, 13 February 1874. Lord Chancellor Roundell Palmer (1812–95), First Earl of Selborne, Sir William Milbourne James (1807–81) and Lord Justice Sir George Mellish (1814–77).

poisoning of the river for miles, the impregnating of the air for a great distance on both sides was not a public nuisance it was very difficult to say what was a public nuisance.'[88] Lord Justice James's judgment also contains a further judicial rejection of any implied balance of convenience argument. James says that what Barnsley argued was:

"We [Barnsley] admit that there is a pollution, we admit that the pollution is produced by the sewers, and we are taking carefully into our consideration what we can best do to reconcile the interests of the complainants and the interests of the ratepayers" ... But [Barnsley] are not entitled to act as arbitrators. The interests of the public and the landowners were paramount to any right or interest of the town of Barnsley.[89]

James concluded that: 'the plaintiff's case was wholly made out, and that of the defendants wholly failed' so the appeal was comprehensively and unanimously dismissed by the three justices and the earlier order affirmed.[90]

Hence, after February 1874, Barnsley was faced with dealing with an injunction coming into force on 22 May, barring them from discharging sewage or other noxious material into the Dearne. But, around that time, Barnsley was able to obtain in chambers at Chancery, by consent, a first six-month extension to their period of grace. This was to be the first of a series of extensions, mostly for six-month periods, allowed to Barnsley with the agreement of the relators. The cause books record no less than twelve such extensions taking the dispute to January 1882, some ten years after the first applications of the relators to Chancery and eight years after the first formal hearing at Chancery.[91] Over this period, the sewage outfalls into the Dearne were never stopped while Barnsley concentrated on attempting to ensure that what was going to enter the Dearne was no longer 'sewage' nor 'noxious or offensive'. By the time the injunction was allowed by Barnsley to finally come into force, all sides must have known that the situation was such that Barnsley would no longer be in danger of failing to meet the conditions set by the terms of the injunction.

Barnsley's Response

Having comprehensively failed in February 1874 to divert the basic legal challenge in the courts, Barnsley Town Council began to consider what treatment to apply to their sewage to attempt to abate the nuisance. A delegation toured a number of towns (including Birmingham and Leeds) and reported back, in September 1874,

---

[88]   *Barnsley Chronicle*, 14 February 1874.

[89]   Ibid.

[90]   Court of Chancery Records: Orders, C33/1207/418.

[91]   Court of Chancery Records: Cause Books, C32/11/1871A94 and Depositions, J15/1516/1411.

with sensible and realistic recommendations for sewage treatment.[92] They concluded that purely chemical or mechanical precipitation treatments would be likely to be ineffective; that no available scheme would provide profit through producing agricultural fertiliser; and that land irrigation and filtration schemes in some combination was most likely to be effective 'for future immunity from complaint or litigation'. The report recognised that land irrigation would require large amounts of expensive, suitable, nearby land and was especially firm that it 'cannot recommend perseverance in any scheme of simple precipitation'.

John Bailey Denton, leading designer of land filtration and irrigation sewage farming systems at the time, was invited to meet with the Barnsley town council's Sewage Committee, and was asked to provide a detailed scheme for the treatment of Barnsley's sewage.[93] By December 1874, a report and plan from Bailey Denton was received, which would require Barnsley to acquire around one hundred acres of land for a site suitable for a mixed intermittent downward filtration and irrigation treatment scheme.[94] A prime possible location was an area of land at Burton Grange to include Burton Grange Mill itself; the site, it will be recalled, of miller Charles Popplewell's home and unhappy workplace. Popplewell's corn mill, and most of the adjacent land, was owned by another formidable character, the splendidly-named Lieutenant-Colonel Adolphus Ulick Wombwell.[95] Colonel Wombwell would be party to a long-running negotiation with Barnsley Town Council over his land and the siting of Barnsley's sewage farm.

Bailey Denton's plan was straightforward and parallels his earlier scheme that was widely considered (not least by Bailey Denton) as having provided a successful treatment works at Merthyr Tydfil.[96] Barnsley's sewage which currently passed down the Sough Dyke towards the Dearne outfall at Hoyle Mill would now be intercepted and diverted by pipe for about one half-mile to the Burton Grange Mill site. Here, on the new sewage farm, there would be settling tanks; thirty acres of land (three areas of ten acres each) prepared with under-draining pipes for intermittent filtration; and seventy acres for surface broad irrigation. This land treatment would provide the cleaning process required before the residual wastewater was allowed to enter the Dearne. The set-up cost, excluding acquiring

---

[92]   Borough of Barnsley, 'Report to Members of the Town Council', 28 September 1874, Barnsley Library, B628.3. It seems unlikely that Bailey Denton had nothing to do with the content of this report.

[93]   Borough of Barnsley Town Council Minutes, 27 October 1874.

[94]   Borough of Barnsley, 'Report of J Bailey Denton Esq., CE, upon the disposal of the sewage of Barnsley', 1874, Barnsley Library, B628.3.

[95]   Colonel Adolphus Wombwell (1834–86), late of the 12th Lancers, was the second son of Sir George Wombwell (1769–1846), the Third Baronet Wombwell of Wombwell. The village of Wombwell, birthplace of the First Baronet, lies a mile down the Dearne from Burton Grange.

[96]   John Bailey Denton, *Sewage Disposal: Ten Years' Experience*, (London: Spon, 1885), 51–7.

the land, was estimated at £17,770.[97] Outline approval for Denton's plan was quickly agreed by Barnsley Town Council in December 1874.[98]

The speedy pursuit of a workable plan for the solution to their sewage problem now slowed through 1875 as the town council contemplated the expense required and searched for methods of raising the finance. High priority became obtaining the Mill and land at Burton Grange Farm from Colonel Wombwell and he proved canny enough to exploit the situation by himself threatening another Chancery action. Wombwell's threat, in May 1875, in a letter to Barnsley Town Council accompanied an expanded and disturbing description of the plight of the Popplewell family at the Mill:

> The effects of the exhalations from the water ... in the mill are extraordinary. The painted woodwork has been changed in colour in a most remarkable manner and the corrosion of iron-work about the wheel is very rapid. The tenant himself is at the present time suffering from blood poisoning and two medical men have warned him against the consequences, not only to himself but to his wife and family, if he do [sic] not escape the place without delay. This is a state of things that demands the immediate attention of the Corporation both on moral and pecuniary grounds ... The tenant has a fair right to expect his landlord [Col Wombwell] to protect him, and if no arrangement be come to by which the nuisance will be abated without a day's unnecessary delay he [the tenant] would be fully justified in calling upon him to apply for an injunction ...[99]

Barnsley town council was eager not to add a Wombwell/Popplewell injunction to their problems[100] and resolved that negotiations start with owner and tenant at the mill over the purchase of Burton Grange Mill and eighty or so more acres of Colonel Wombwell's Burton Grange estate.[101] A deputation went to Wombwell to ask the price required for his properties at Burton Grange and he is reported to have initially asked an unacceptable sum of £30,000, including compensation for Popplewell.[102] Arbitration settled the central matters for a total of £19,585

[97]   'Report of J Bailey Denton Esq', 10–11.
[98]   Borough of Barnsley Town Council Minutes, 19 December 1874.
[99]   *Barnsley Chronicle*, 26 May 1875.
[100]   Barnsley Borough already faced a second legal action at the time over drainage and sewage. In August 1872 Guy Senior of the beer-brewing firm of Paul and Guy Senior (the Barnsley Brewing Company) began a suit against Barnsley Town Council over pollution of the Sough Dyke, next to their brewery site at Beevor Hall. The case, eventually settled by arbitration, continued until 1882. (Borough of Barnsley Town Council Minutes, 6 August 1872, 27 August 1878, 1 July 1879, 13 June 1882.)
[101]   Borough of Barnsley Town Council Minutes, 25 September 1875. Barnsley would need approval from the Local Government Board and eventual parliamentary approval for the scheme.
[102]   Borough of Barnsley Sewage Works Committee Minutes 1875–82, Barnsley Archive and Local Studies, Barnsley Library, 4 May 1876. Popplewell himself was to

in August 1876, but associated problems over more minor legal and other costs was to extend into another time-consuming and litigious process, even involving another trip to the courts in 1877.[103] Finally, in April 1878, the freehold of the land was conveyed to the corporation.[104]

While the arbitration over the purchase price proceeded, construction of the new sewage farm was allowed to begin at the Burton Grange site. In December 1875, Bailey Denton delivered detailed plans for the new conduits and settling tanks and for the preparation of the land drainage to take the intermittent downwards filtration scheme.[105] In May 1876, after contracts for the required work had been settled, the formal ceremony of turning the first sod for the new Barnsley Sewage Farm at the Mill was performed by Mayor Carter, before a rather limited crowd of eight interested gentlemen: 'The party, shortly afterwards, through the kindness of Mr Popplewell, partook of wine in that gentleman's residence.'[106] Physically, the works were substantially completed in 1877 but, as the town council was reminded in 1879, '... until the Court of Chancery is satisfied with the effluent the works cannot be considered as complete.'[107]

Barnsley proved reluctant to allow the relators' Chancery injunction to come into force so long as there remained any risk of the relators returning to court for a writ of sequestration. But in 1881, the town council was told by its surveyor that the report on the effluent from the works was 'very satisfactory'[108] and in February 1882 the surveyor's opinion was that the corporation sewage treatment works had now fully satisfied the requirements of the Court of Chancery in the matter.[109] No further motions by Barnsley to extend the period of grace before the injunction came into force are recorded after June 1882. And the relators did not move to act against Barnsley once the injunction was allowed to come into force.

No doubt, the Burton Grange sewage works relieved some of Barnsley's contribution to the pollution of the Dearne valley. There were no further complaints from adjoining landowners and no further threats of legal proceedings arose from

---

receive £750 of compensation for his loss of business.

[103]   Wombwell v Barnsley Corporation (1877) 41 JP 502. Wombwell was still receiving payments with respect to these costs well into 1879, (Borough of Barnsley Town Council Minutes, 29 July 1879).

[104]   The price paid was reported as £254–£296 per acre for an area of 78 acres. Barnsley does not seem to have got a bargain, as they were to pay only £175 per acre for the adjoining 11 acres of land in 1889. (Borough of Barnsley Town Council Minutes, 16 April 1878; J Henry Taylor, *New Sewage Purification Works*, (1909), Barnsley Archive and Local Studies, Barnsley Library, B628.3; Borough of Barnsley Town Council Sewage Committee Minutes 1882–94, Barnsley Archive and Local Studies, Barnsley Library, 31 December 1889.)

[105]   Borough of Barnsley Town Council Minutes, 7 December 1875.

[106]   *Barnsley Chronicle*, 6 May 1876.

[107]   Borough of Barnsley Town Council Minutes, 12 August 1879.

[108]   Borough of Barnsley Town Council Minutes, 22 February 1881.

[109]   Borough of Barnsley Town Council Minutes, 14 February 1882.

the relators. The *Leeds Mercury* was able to report (though perhaps pointedly) that Barnsley 'by means of the sewage farm, has removed all contamination from the Dearne, so far as Barnsley is concerned.'[110]

Barnsley's experience over the pollution of the Dearne shows many of the features common to the way the river sewage pollution disputes evolved in this Victorian era. Despite its vocal objections to the notion of balance of convenience arguments and maintaining the paramountcy of the interests of the public and landowners, Chancery in practice did not act to enforce restraints that might have put in jeopardy Barnsley's use of the Dearne or stop its sewerage network. In order to achieve this, extensive use was made of repeated delays to the imposition of the injunction Chancery had awarded against Barnsley which, albeit with the consent of the relators, acted as contingent threats encouraging the continued attempts to improve the quality of the wastewater outflows. So long as Barnsley was seen by the relators and Chancery to be applying itself to solving the problem at the root of the dispute, further extensions to the period of grace before the injunction came into force seemed available on demand. From 1874 to 1882 the series of twelve recorded motions by Barnsley for extensions to these delays were all successful.[111]

In the end, the legal dispute became a decade-long affair, but Barnsley seems to have been sympathetically treated by the relators and by Chancery as the treatment works slowly became installed. Finally, in 1882 when the injunction was allowed to come into force, on Barnsley's decision not to seek a further extension, all sides would have known the investments at the sewage farm over the previous decade meant Barnsley could fulfil the conditions of the injunction, as confirmed by the town's surveyor. The effect was to impose a barrier only when it was known the barrier would be ineffective.

The Pollution of the Dearne?

Barnsley's new sewage treatment works was, however, only able to treat Barnsley's effluent to the limited standards available to Victorian sanitary engineering technology. At Burton Grange, modifications to the sewage farm were adopted almost continuously over the following twenty years to attempt to improve its effectiveness, including the purchasing of additional land and the adoption of extra chemical precipitation processes not part of Bailey Denton's original plans. Bailey Denton, who had lauded the success of his scheme at Merthyr, was unable to claim the same success for his Barnsley scheme, describing it as merely 'satisfactory' and blaming its shortcomings on the clayey soil along the Dearne.[112]

---

[110]   *Leeds Mercury*, 20 June 1887.

[111]   5 June 1874, 19 November 1874, 10 March 1875, 29 July 1875, 11 November 1875, 1 June 1876, 9 November 1876, 2 August 1877, 4 December 1879, 3 June 1880, 13 January 1881, and 30 June 1881 (Court of Chancery Records: Cause Books, C32/11/1871A94).

[112]   Denton, *Sewage Disposal*, 14.

In 1889, the Barnsley Medical Officer of Health reported the River Dearne below Hoyle Mill as again 'unsatisfactory'[113] and by 1893 complaints to Barnsley town council were again mounting about sewage in the river.[114] A report for the West Riding of Yorkshire Rivers Board said of the Dearne, 'the stream is much polluted by domestic sewage and by treated and untreated trade refuse almost from its source to the junction with the Don' and reported that after treatment at the Barnsley sewage farm 'the effluents are nearly always unsatisfactory.'[115] The state of the Dearne was as pressing a concern for the Rivers Board as was the state of the Aire, and the recommendations it urged for changes to the treatment works at Burton Grange were only some among a large number of improvements being recommended for the river. In truth, to have shown any improvement at all, the River Dearne would have needed much more than even a perfect sewage treatment regime at Burton Grange could have provided. By 1900 the combination of domestic sewage from many sources, along with industrial pollution from innumerable plants along the valley was making even the identification of serious sources of nuisance in the Dearne next to impossible.

Lessons from Leeds and Barnsley

For both Leeds and Barnsley, Chancery was called upon to make judicial decisions about the rights and wrongs of the disputes and, thereby, fairly and justly apply the principles of equitable law in determining the liabilities of the suits: this was duly achieved. More illuminating is how Chancery managed to deal with the river pollution dilemma in these disputes in the way it applied the remedies and enforcement of the liability decisions it made. For Leeds and Barnsley, Chancery did this by allowing long series of delays to the actual application of the orders it issued. This, it is argued, amounted to Chancery supervising and overseeing the towns' progress towards abating their sewage nuisance to a level where the violation of the injunction became unlikely. In this way, the towns' vital means of disposing of their sewage was never interrupted.

In the next chapter, two further river sewage nuisance disputes are examined, and here we can examine what happened when towns found liable for sewage nuisance failed to meet, adequately, the contingencies of the orders Chancery had issued.

---

[113]   *Leeds Mercury*, 18 September 1889.

[114]   Borough of Barnsley Town Council Sewage Committee Minutes, 26 September 1893.

[115]   H. Maclean Wilson, Report to West Riding Rivers Board upon River Dearne (Confidential), Wakefield, 6 December 1902, Barnsley Library, B628.39, 1.

Chapter 7

The Threat of Sequestration: Leamington Spa and Tunbridge Wells

For Leeds and Barnsley, lengthy series of delays to the effective enforcement of the injunctions issued by Chancery enabled the towns to institute treatment regimes which abated the nuisances enough such that when the injunctions became operative, no violations were likely. For both Leeds and Barnsley the relators concerned consented, mostly sympathetically, to the extensions and delays to the enforcement of the Chancery injunctions. For Leamington Spa and Tunbridge Wells, both Chancery and the complainants concerned proved less accommodating.

For the complainant, the advantage of injunction over compensatory damages is that future acts of nuisance will be restrained. If an issued injunction is violated, with further offences proven, then the offender risks being found in contempt of court. In the river sewage pollution disputes where the offender is a local sanitary authority, the threat from the court is then that the assets of the authority, financial and physical, can be sequestered into the control of the court and the agents of the plaintiff.

Among the river sewage pollution cases of the Victorian period, there are a number of instances where claimed violation of injunctions led to requests for sequestrations. Typically, successful requests for sequestration orders were themselves delayed or suspended or made contingent on some condition set by the court, and the sequestration although 'granted' by Chancery is neither issued nor actually put into force. Birmingham, as we have seen, is one example, but other examples of delayed or contingent sequestration orders include, as we shall see in further chapters, Wolverhampton and Harrogate. The records have unearthed only three river sewage pollution cases where sequestration orders were unconditionally and actually awarded and put into force by the Court of Chancery: at Banbury, Leamington Spa and Tunbridge Wells. In no dispute were the sewer outflows to the rivers halted directly by the actions of the court.

At Banbury, John Spokes, a miller at Twyford Mill on the River Cherwell, downstream of Banbury, Oxfordshire, obtained a Court of Chancery injunction in February 1865 that would restrain, from July 1865, the Banbury Local Board from polluting the Cherwell with the town's sewage. In November 1865, Banbury having done nothing to restrain their sewage and, crucially, having failed to ask Chancery for a longer delay, Spokes applied for and was granted a sequestration order following Banbury's contempt in violating the February order. Banbury appealed against the award but this was rejected by Chancery in December 1865. Spokes could now have had writs of sequestration prepared and delivered to the

Banbury authorities by bailiffs to enforce these orders. But rather than enforcing the sequestration in this way, Spokes chose instead to await the results of Banbury's new promises and new-found zeal to put all its sewage through a new local sewage irrigation scheme. Although awarded by Chancery, no sequestration was actually enforced by the plaintiff, Spokes, and no actual writs of sequestration were delivered to the authorities at Banbury.[1]

Only at Leamington Spa and Tunbridge Wells, following suits for sewage pollution nuisance, were writs of sequestration authorising bailiffs to take control of the assets of the sanitary authority actually prepared and delivered to the officials concerned: here the town authorities' assets were *actually* sequestrated. Still, in neither case did the sequestration last much more than a matter of days before new court orders lifted the sequestration orders. And in neither case were any interruptions apparent to the provision of public amenities or to the sewerage systems of the towns.

Leamington Spa: Heath (and Field) v Wallington (1865)

'By their heedless acts they have murdered the innocent fish in the placid waters of the Leam …'[2]

Leamington (Royal Leamington Spa), like Tunbridge Wells, provides an example where the Court of Chancery's supervisory role, in actually spelling out what needed to be done to the sewage treatment regime to alleviate the legal problem, is clearly shown. It was the reluctance of Leamington to do that which the court required that precipitated the issuing of the sequestration orders.[3]

The town of Royal Leamington Spa is situated near Warwick and Coventry in the West Midlands of England, and lies on the River Leam, less than a mile from the Leam's convergence with the River Avon at Warwick. Based upon the health-inducing quality of its numerous saline water wells, the town prospered as

---

[1]   Court of Chancery Records: Pleadings, C16/232/S126; *Banbury Guardian*, 2 March 1865; *Times*, 2 March 1865; *Spokes v Banbury Board of Health* (1865) LR 1 Eq 42; *Times*, 27 November 1865; *Banbury Guardian*, 30 November 1865; *Times*, 16 December 1865; *Banbury Guardian*, 21 December 1865; Banbury Local Board Minutes, 1856–86, 18 December 1865, Oxfordshire Record Office, Oxford, BOR/2/X/i.

[2]   *Leamington Spa Courier* (hereafter, *Courier*), 8 July 1865. The *Courier* was the major local (weekly) newspaper for the town during the nineteenth century. Its editor from 1865–78 was Thomas Joseph Burgess (1828–86) and to him we owe thanks for the *Courier*'s entertaining and 'sometimes outspoken or even libellous' comment (Lyndon F. Cave, *Royal Leamington Spa: A History* (Chichester: Phillimore, 2009): 94).

[3]   Leamington Spa's sewage problems are discussed in Christopher Hamlin, 'Muddling in Bumbledom: On the Enormity of Large Sanitary Improvements in Four British Towns, 1855–1885', *Victorian Studies*, 32 (1988): 62–9.

a spa during the nineteenth century, and it was fashionable enough to be patronised by royalty: Princess Victoria had visited the town in 1830, and after becoming queen she authorised Leamington Spa to style itself grandly as Royal Leamington Spa in 1838.[4] Administratively, over the period considered here, a Local Board of Health held responsibility for the sanitary arrangements for the town and its small 20,000 population,[5] from 1852 until the incorporation of the town into a formal Borough in 1875.

The River Improvement Scheme and Sewage

In the 1850s, the Local Board took note that in order to compete with the other spa towns of the period in England, some productive investment in the town's infrastructure would be necessary. Especially pressing was the state of the River Leam, which had the potential for being a fine asset for a town eager to attract visitors, but which was as yet mostly unimproved and even responsible for periodically overflowing and flooding portions of the town. The river also served as the repository for the smelly and untreated contents of the town's sewers: at this time the dwellings of the town were almost completely equipped with WCs. John Hitchman (1806–67), local surgeon and deeply concerned member of the Local Board, wrote of the Leam that its pollution and odour was such that:

> The minds of strangers have been acted upon most prejudicially by this state of the river and they have questioned the salubrity of the town ... the effluvium thus occasioned has often driven strangers out of the town and rendered it highly objectionable to those obliged to remain.[6]

The Local Board commissioned ambitious improvement plans for the town in the early 1850s and settled in 1856 on a river improvement and sewerage plan from their town surveyor, Joseph Fox Sharp (1831–1908). Sharp's scheme involved widening, straightening and deepening the Leam, moving a weir and altering some islands to speed the flow of the river. One of Lord Warwick's mills would be purchased and removed. The river would be lined with embankments and promenades, parks, ornamentation and boating lakes would be established. For new sewerage, along the river banks would be laid intercepting sewers to collect existing drainage and deliver it to a new sewage works to be constructed on the south bank next to, and hidden by, the railway viaduct across the Leam. At the works, the sewage would be deodorised and treated by additions of milk of

---

[4] 'The Borough of Leamington Spa', in *Victoria History of the County of Warwick*, (ed.) L.F. Salzman, (Oxford: OUP, 1951): 155–61.

[5] The Leamington Spa Local Board had fifteen elected members with three-year terms. Their rather formal minutes are at Leamington Local Board Minutes, CR1563/176–9, Warwickshire Record Office, Warwick.

[6] *Courier*, 30 October 1858.

lime and led through four settlement tanks or canals (allowing about two hours of settlement): the liquid allowed to pass on into the river through new outfalls below the town; and with the settled sludge 'residium' drawn off every six weeks to be removed to a place of storage. The whole scheme was an extensive investment for the town and squarely aimed at enhancing its attractions for visitors as a health spa and resort. But it would require difficult, if not fraught, negotiations with Lord Warwick and other landholders and there would have to be a public enquiry and London's approval to sanction the £20,000 of loans needed for the work. It took until October 1859 for the first sod to be turned in the construction of the new improvements.

Within the larger project, the design of the lime-settlement sewage treatment to be applied at the new sewage works became increasingly subject to uneasy comment from a number of objectors.[7] Lord Warwick at Warwick Castle on the Avon just a mile or so downriver was an especially influential and wary local observer:[8] earlier, Lord Warwick had offered to provide land for sewage farm irrigation facilities for Leamington, which offer had been rejected. One of Lord Warwick's mills had been needed for the river improvement scheme and in 1858, as part of his contract to sell, Warwick had insisted the new sewage treatment process at Leamington must be certified as a success by an inspector from the General Board of Health in London: to provide 'ultimate approval of the deodorising works.' The Earl remained sceptical and was still warning in 1860: 'I have seen danger to the river Avon.'[9] On the Leamington Local Board, Hitchman, too, remained a consistent critic of the sewage plan, pressing for an irrigation-based scheme and for the separation of storm water. Following the public enquiry required to authorise the loans needed for the development plan, Henry Austin,[10] the Inspector from London, had reported:

---

[7]   *Courier*, 24 November 1860.

[8]   George Guy Greville (1818–93) 4th Earl of Warwick.

[9]   *Courier*, 24 April 1858. Certification of the cleanliness of the effluent entering the Leam was anyway required by the Public Health Supplemental Act of 1852 (section 2). Sewage discharged into the rivers Avon or Leam had to be 'certified to be free from such matters by the General Board of Health under their hands and seal, after examination and report thereon by one of their superintending inspectors' (William Cunningham Glen, *The Law Relating To The Public Health*, (London: Butterworths, 1858): 73). The General Board of Health ceased to exist in late 1858 which caused later complications.

[10]   Henry Austin (1812?–61) is better known to history as friend and brother-in-law to Charles Dickens, having married Dickens's sister, Letitia Mary, in 1837: the Austin and Dickens families are together registered as visitors at the surgery where Charles and Letitia's father, John Dickens, was to die on the night of the 1851 census. Austin was Secretary to the General Board of Health (1848–52) and later Chief Inspector under the Public Health Act and the Local Government Act from 1858 until his early death. See Christopher Hamlin, 'Austin, Henry (1811/12–1861)', *Oxford Dictionary of National Biography* (Oxford: Oxford University Press, 2004).

[Although] no doubt much of the solid and offensive matter will be separated by this process, I am by no means prepared to say that the operation will be attended with the desired success ... the sewage will, in the absence of other treatment, still flow off in a state somewhat offensive both to sight and smell.[11]

The Board's response to this criticism was to urge the critics to wait until the sewage works was complete when, they maintained, their fears would be assuaged. In June 1862, both the river improvement scheme and the new sewage works were opened with the usual Victorian show and love of ceremony. Over Leamington's successful river-side improvements, even the *Courier* could declare: '... we cheerfully admit that the town is indebted to [the Local Board] for the attainment',[12] but the sewage works proved a dismal and disappointing failure.

With the works in operation, evidence of its poor design quickly appeared with reports of the banks of the Leam being covered in thick layers of black fermenting mud and the Avon transformed into a common sewer. Lord Warwick demanded the certification of the sewage works, as required by his earlier contract for his land sale. With the General Board of Health and its inspectors no longer existing, it was agreed that Leamington's Local Board would hire Robert Rawlinson to inspect the works, and he visited in November 1862 and July 1863. When released in December 1863, Rawlinson's review concluded that the settling and liming regime was failing to deal with the fermentable content of the effluent, resulting in the black matter, bubbling gas and general offensiveness being produced in the river.[13] Rawlinson recommended that the settling tanks at the works be extended to filter the effluent wastewater further before discharge and concluded he would be unable to provide a certification that the works were 'satisfactory' until this work was done at least. The Board immediately had his recommendations carried out but, in July 1864, when Rawlinson again inspected the river and the works he was still unable to provide the certification of success required by Lord Warwick. When later confronted by the claim that 'Mr Rawlinson cannot certify that your works are successful ...' the Board could only weakly respond that they had not this time actually asked him for a certificate.[14]

Although Lord Warwick would have topped any list of likely candidates to have instituted legal action for nuisance at this time against Leamington's Local Board,[15] when actions were taken they were in the names of two less aristocratic and more middle-class residents, Thomas Heath and Alfred Field.

[11]   *Courier*, 24 November 1860.
[12]   *Courier*, 5 July 1860.
[13]   *Courier*, 5 December 1863.
[14]   *Courier*, 1 July 1865.
[15]   Indeed, Ben Pontin actually does incorrectly cite the Earl of Warwick as the plaintiff in the Leamington Spa sequestration dispute: similarly, Pontin also incorrectly cites Louisa Ann Ryland as the relator in John Spokes's 1865 dispute with Banbury described above.

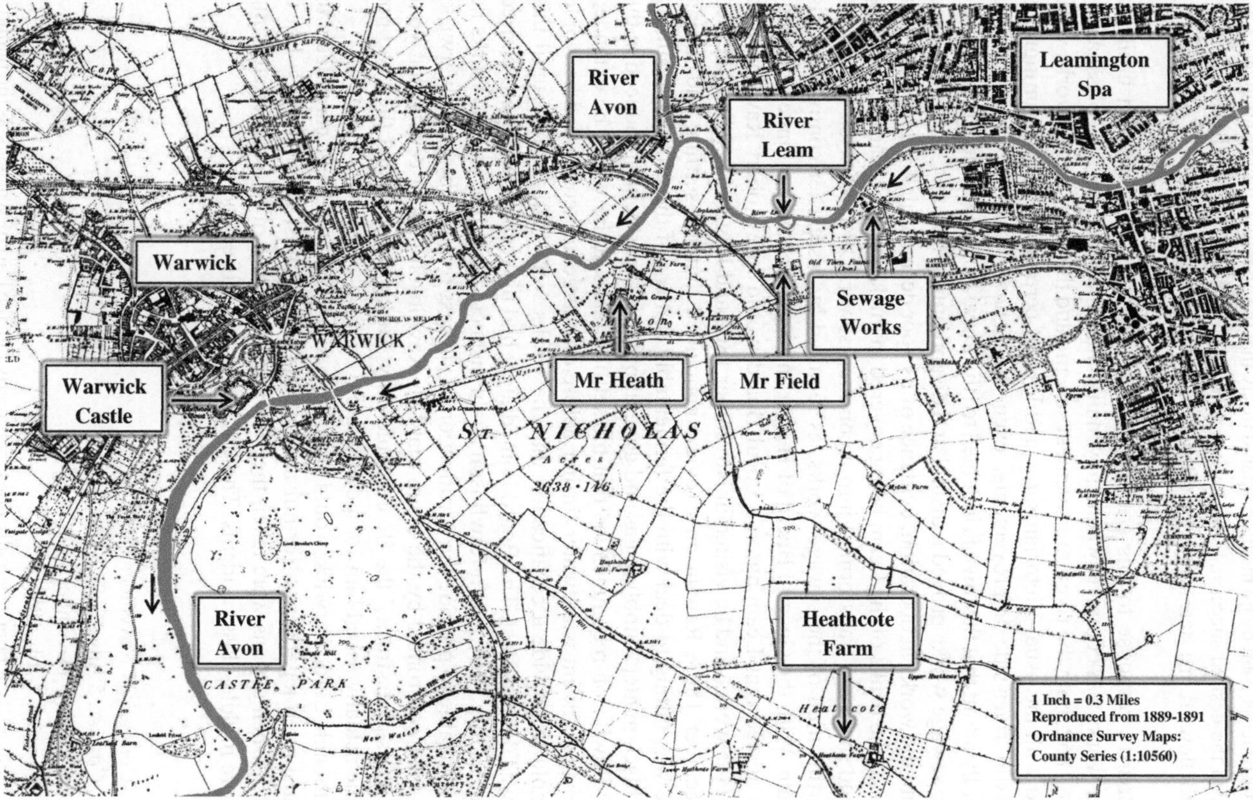

Map 7.1   Leamington Spa and the River Leam

Heath v Wallington (1865) and Field v Wallington (1865)

On 29 June 1865, the twin actions of Heath v Wallington and Field v Wallington began in the Court of Chancery before Vice-Chancellor Page Wood:[16] the two causes were coordinated to the extent that Field's action was always considered only a parallel adjunct to Heath's case and is often ignored in reports.[17] The defendant in both causes was Richard Archer Wallington (1821–74), solicitor and attorney, who, as Clerk to the Leamington Local Board of Health, was given the honour of standing in for Leamington's town authorities. The major plaintiff was Thomas Heath (1802–72), a long-term resident with his family, at Myton Grange, Myton, on the Avon, just below the convergence of that river with the Leam. Little more than a mile separated his property from the new sewage outfall. Both Thomas Heath and his son were solicitors and Thomas Heath had acted as officer for various public bodies in Warwickshire including being prominent in opposing Leamington's unsuccessful bid in 1856 to extend its town boundaries. The Local Board heard him described as someone able to get his law much cheaper than the Board could: a man 'who grew his own mutton'.[18] The complainant in the parallel suit, Alfred Field (1814?–84), was Heath's neighbour, resident at Leam House in Myton.[19] Field was an international trader and merchant in hardware products and his firm, Alfred Field & Co., founded in Birmingham in 1836 had, in the 1870s, branches in Sheffield, Birmingham and New York marketing a range of brands of tools, silver plate, cutlery and razors.

The two suits at Chancery opened with Heath's representatives presenting the (traditional) collection of local resident and expert evidence on the increasingly offensive state of the river since the sewage works opened, along with the usual tales of dead fish and cattle that refused to drink the water. Especially telling here were description of deposits of black mud 'two-to-five feet thick' on the banks of the Leam and Avon and the glaring absence of any Rawlinson certificate as to the success of the sewage treatment works.[20] The defence responded with evidence from their experts and other local witnesses that as it was impossible for any such

---

(Ben Pontin, 'Nuisance Law and the Industrial Revolution: A Reinterpretation of Doctrine and Institutional Competence', *The Modern Law Review*, 75 (2012): 1027.)

[16]   Now a veteran, Page Wood had heard the river sewage pollution actions against Birmingham and Banbury.

[17]   *Courier*, 1 July, 8 July 1865; Court of Chancery Records: Pleadings, C16/209/ H246 and C16/200/F112.

[18]   *Courier*, 8 July 1865.

[19]   The irony of having complainants named Heath and Field pursuing an environmental pollution cause seems to have inexplicably escaped general notice. A Mr Wood will additionally appear as a plaintiff in the next chapter.

[20]   Certification was required both in relation to Warwick's farsighted contingent land-sale contract and also because of the 1852 Supplementary Public Health Act, as explained above (*Courier*, 23 August 1862 and 8 July 1865).

problems to be due to their new plant, so other sources of the pollution must be to blame.

Vice-Chancellor Page Wood reviewed the admissions of the defendant's experts that there was foetid scum present and floating in the river and that the sewage works was not big enough to manage the task asked of it. He concluded that there was no doubt the Leamington Local Board was liable for causing a nuisance and that Thomas Heath was entitled to restrain Leamington's present discharge of sewage in 'its noxious and offensive state'. But Page Wood was insistent that rather than awarding an immediate binding injunction, there should be a further enquiry, not, he said, to consider again whether a nuisance existed but as to 'what should be done to remedy it' at the sewage works:

> Let an enquiry be made in Chambers, what steps ought to be taken, and what works executed by the Defendants, for the purpose of rendering the sewage, prior to its discharge into the said river Leam so free from noxious and offensive matter as that such discharge shall not occasion a nuisance to the Plaintiff ...[21]

Here is strong evidence of the supervisory role Chancery was willing to play in these disputes: if the General Board of Health no longer existed to provide certificates of good practice, then Chancery would.

The detail of the enquiry was to be handled by the Chief Clerk in Chancery who would produce a certificate detailing what steps were to be taken at the Leamington sewage works.[22] And once the certificate of the Chief Clerk was available, Heath would be able to apply for an 'injunction to restrain further discharge of sewage into the River Leam unless and until such steps shall have been taken, and such works executed as shall be specified in the certificate'. When the parties met in chambers with the Chief Clerk, on the 15 August 1865, it was decided that the proper course would be for the complainants, Heath and Field, to prepare the proposal that would form the basis of the certificate the Chief Clerk would present for the Leamington Board. Therefore, at this stage, no restraining injunction yet formally existed. The contents of the Chief Clerk's certificate, when issued, would provide the contingencies upon which any injunction would be based. The actions of the court might, perhaps, be interpreted as attempting to ensure that changes at the works or to Leamington's overall treatment regime would have rendered the necessity for an injunction to have been removed.

At this point in 1865, it could have happened that Leamington would move seamlessly towards a broad irrigation solution to its sewage treatment problems and the English legal system would be able to move on to other matters. Lord

---

[21]   *Courier*, 8 July 1865.

[22]   In Chancery, while the trials and injunction hearings were the domain of the judges, the majority of the rest of the work in Chancery Chambers was done by the Masters. The duties of the clerks at the Court of Chancery was to act as assistants to the judges and Masters and included case management, post-trial accounts and (as here) enquiries.

Warwick wrote to the Local Board pointing out that their experiment with lime deodorisation of the sewage at the sewage works had been a total failure, but also that he was (still) willing to offer again to accept (on reasonable terms) Leamington's sewage being pumped to his farms nearby at Heathcote: in the absence of acceptance he threatened (again) to no longer tolerate the present nuisance in the rivers.[23] At the same time, Robert Rawlinson wrote to the Board privately to give his opinion that such pumping and irrigation was the only solution he could see to Leamington's problem.[24]

In August 1865, the heavyweight pair John Frederic La Trobe Bateman and John Thomas Way[25] inspected the sewage works at Leamington for the Chief Clerk's certificate and damningly reported that 'the process has not succeeded in so clarifying or purifying the sewage as to prevent it becoming a nuisance' and that no recommended alterations to the works could be suggested that would be of any benefit.[26] Further, they argued, given suitable land existed nearby (the four hundred acres of Lord Warwick's land on offer) to which the sewage could be pumped and there made 'innoxious' by irrigation at a cost of less than £10,000, this would be their recommended policy. This Bateman-Way report and its recommendations provided the content of the Chief Clerk at Chancery's certificate handed on to a hearing before Vice-Chancellor Page Wood in November 1865.[27] At the hearing, however, Leamington objected that the Chief Clerk's instructions had been to enquire what steps were to be taken to improve the treatment *at the sewage works* before the sewage should be discharged into the river, and that the Chief Clerk had therefore gone beyond the powers conferred on him by the Vice-Chancellor's decree by recommending a scheme that would keep the sewage from the works and the sewage water from being discharged into the river at all. Page Wood responded that perhaps, then, Leamington themselves might now propose some course of action of their own for the works.[28]

So Leamington's Local Board set their surveyor, Thomas Barry,[29] to prepare an alternative scheme and in December 1865 he presented a report that became the basis for the town's response.[30] Barry argued that the proposals, survey and

23   *Courier*, 19 August 1865.

24   Leamington Local Board Minutes, 25 August 1865.

25   John Frederic La Trobe Bateman (1810–89) was an eminent water engineer and President of the Institute of Civil Engineers ('Bateman, John F La Trobe, 1810–89', *ICE Minutes of Proceeding*, 97 (1889), 392 –8). John Thomas Way had been a member of the Commission on Rivers Pollution Prevention of 1865, alongside Robert Rawlinson.

26   *Courier*, 9 December 1865.

27   Ibid.

28   *Courier*, 18 November 1865.

29   Thomas Denville Barry (1815?–1905) was an Irish-born architect and engineer. His turbulent time at Leamington ended in December 1869, when he was dismissed by the Board over matters of private practice.

30   *Courier*, 6 January 1866.

conclusions of the Bateman-Way report were faulty and their plans mistaken, badly-costed, over-expensive and could provide no guarantee of success. Instead, Barry lauded the existing set-up at the sewage works, implausibly describing the existing scheme of filtering and settlement in the tanks and canals as 'the most perfect method yet known.' His counter-proposals were simply to double the length of the settling tanks/canals at the works, add to the system additional ventilators and more filter screens, close off an inlet in the river where offensive floating matter gathered and clean, clear and scrape the bed and banks of the Leam to remove the black deposits. Once the river was cleaned, Barry contended, it would become obvious that no problems in the river were being caused by the Leamington works. The clinching argument for the Local Board was presumably that Barry estimated his scheme was likely to cost £500–£700, compared to his estimate of £15,000 for the Bateman-Way scheme: so, despite the misgivings of some critics, Leamington resolved to take this proposal back to Chancery.[31]

When Vice-Chancellor Page Wood was presented with this new plan in February 1866, he ordered that Leamington carry out the scheme Barry suggested, with reasonable time to be allowed.[32] Even so, Page Wood expressed some scepticism over the new proposals, saying 'I cannot but have grave doubts whether your works will succeed' and required the Chief Clerk to certify that the reformed works, when completed, were fulfilling the promises made.[33] The plaintiffs were anyway assured they were still free to pursue proceedings for an injunction for nuisance at any time under the terms of the original decree. Ominously, in a note to the Local Board, Heath and Field are reported as saying that they remained completely indifferent to whether the present sewage works were extended or not, their aim being for the river outfalls to be stopped.[34] Furthermore, they said, were the Bateman-Way land irrigation scheme to be adopted they would allow Leamington the most ample amount of time to carry it out, but, if the river outfalls remained, they were prepared to seek the heaviest legal sanctions they could obtain.

Injunction and Sequestration Order, April to November, 1866

Heath and Field followed up their threat by applying to Chancery just weeks later, on 21 April 1866, for the full injunction that they had been promised at the hearing in February in the event that the works required in the Chief Clerk's March certificate were not completed; these, of course, were Leamington's own suggestions as contained in Barry's plan. No affidavits were offered by either side, and Heath's argument was simply that as the works specified in the order had not been completed the issue of the injunction was unarguable (indeed so, given

---

[31]   Leamington Local Board Minutes, 5 December 1865.
[32]   *Courier*, 24 February 1866.
[33]   *Courier*, 3 March 1866.
[34]   *Courier*, 23 April 1866.

even tenders for the work would not be opened until mid-May). Leamington's response was to argue that they needed more time to carry out the work. But Vice-Chancellor Wood noted that the works required by the revised Barry scheme did not amount to very much engineering, and that Leamington, with goodwill, could have begun to improve the situation long before. He, therefore, gave Leamington until 1 June 1866 to comply, with liberty to extend this deadline.

Leamington at this point had worked themselves into a quite tight spot. Chancery had saved them from a nuisance injunction being served by requiring an enquiry into the changes necessary at the works and by allowing a period for the changes and the cleaning of the river to be completed. Now time was catching up. Not completing the changes would trigger the injunction and an immediate sequestration on the violation of the terms of the certificate; if the changes were made and (as likely) did not completely cure the problems it would lead to an injunction and immediate sequestration on the continuation of the nuisance. Leamington now faced a contingent injunction with well-specified conditions to be attained to avoid the issuance of the injunctive order.

For Leamington's Local Board, April and May 1866 offer much evidence of panic and refusal to confront the facts in face of their sewage problems.[35] On 15 May, a delegation from the Board went down to the sewage works to review the situation along the Leam at a time when the river was low and the banks more fully exposed. The editorial in the *Courier* painted a less than idyllic picture: '... we shall not soon forget the sight that met our eyes or the stench that found its unwelcome way to our nostrils' and continued by describing deposits of filthy black feculent sediment from six inches to eighteen inches deep, poisoned riverside flora and fauna and how an inky fluid arose from disturbing the river waters.[36] The editorial concluded with: 'the present system of deodorization is an utter failure and ought to be altered and abandoned ... a miserably inefficient system.'[37] The subsequent meetings of the Local Board in May 1866 were rowdy and abusive affairs, centred on a motion that 'the sewage be disposed of in some way otherwise than at present.'[38] The proposal, from Hitchman, was backed by a sensible plan and pathway out of the town's problem: if Leamington would abandon its sewage

---

[35]   Leamington Local Board Minutes, 16 April, 7 May, 15 May, 22 May 1866.

[36]   *Courier*, 19 May 1866.

[37]   This sparked a lengthy feud between the Leamington Local Board and the *Courier*, with the *Courier* advocating the replacement of the Local Board by an incorporated Borough and the Board withdrawing its advertising from the paper. The *Courier* responded: 'Smarting under our criticism ... the Clerk and Chairman ... show their miserable spite' (9 June 1866).

[38]   A letter in the *Courier* from 'Jacobus' (Editor Joseph Burgess?) observed sagely: 'If some genius yet unborn – some historian of a future generation – should endeavour to serve his country by collecting and publishing the selected debates of the local boards of this country we might expect to find the doings – or misdoings – of the Leamington Board enlivening many a dull page of the stupendous annals; but if the eyes of the recording genius

plans using the river outfalls, Lord Warwick (again) publicly offered a general promise of land for a land irrigation scheme and Thomas Heath (again) publicly offered a general promise of legal truce and as much time as required.[39] The Board proceedings included fierce outbursts, personal attacks and slanders, walkouts, legal challenges and the childish refusal of the chairman to allow motions to be tabled. On one side one member confessed to being 'astonished' by so great a nuisance as had been witnessed during the river visit with another declaring: '... the town was fast asleep and did not discern the danger ahead'; while on the other side, some still flatly denied the existence of any nuisance at all on the river.[40]

The confusions and panic of May for the Leamington Board, led, firstly, on 19 May 1866, to the Board voting to reject both Heath's and Lord Warwick's offers and gamble to continue with Barry's plan to make do with cleaning the river and making minor adjustments at the sewage works. Then, a week later on 26 May 1866, in an extraordinary new about-face, the motion to find an alternative means of dealing with the sewage was re-introduced, during a special meeting of the Board, and *passed*. Now, with the (1 June) date of the coming into force of Heath's injunction only days away, the Board finally formally endorsed the policy that 'as soon as practicable the sewage to be taken out of the river Leam and distributed upon the land' and arranged to apply to Lord Warwick for terms to follow the Bateman-Way scheme.[41]

Sensibly choosing to put his trust in the High Court rather than with the paper promises of the unreliable Leamington Local Board, Thomas Heath calmly went back to Chancery on 8 June 1866, for the injunction he had been promised earlier in April. As the Leamington Board had failed to prepare any motion to extend the period of suspension for this hearing, the injunction was now issued and restrained the Local Board, under penalty of £5,000, '... from discharging into the River Leam ... any sewage or water containing sewage unless and until such steps shall have been taken and works executed ...' as specified in the Chief Clerk's certificate of 22 March (Barry's scheme).[42] The order, signed by the Master of the Rolls, Lord Romilly, was issued on 11 June 1866, and, simply, disallowed any sewage

---

should happen to rest upon the debate of Tuesday last we can fancy that his countenance would be lighted up with the supremest satisfaction' (26 May 1866).

[39]   Lord Warwick offered '... [if] the Board formally resolve to abandon their present system of dealing with the sewage ... his Lordship will, so far as the circumstances of his property allow, be disposed to give his favourable consideration to any reasonable proposal the Board may make with a view to the application of the sewage to the land.' Thomas Heath offered '... if the Board are prepared ... to remove the outfall of the sewage works so that no sewage whether filtered or not shall hereafter pass into the Leam or Avon above my residence, I shall not object to such reasonable time being given for the execution of the necessary works ...' (*Courier*, 19 May 1866).

[40]   Ibid.

[41]   Leamington Local Board Minutes, 11 June 1866.

[42]   *Courier*, 16 June 1866.

being discharged into the Leam until Barry's scheme was completed. As the works specified in Barry's scheme had not yet even been awarded to contractors, let alone completed, any sewage allowed to run into the Leam would be a violation of this now active injunction and constitute a contempt of court, punishable not only by the fine of £5,000, but, traditionally, by a sequestration of the assets of the violator until the fine was paid and the contempt discharged.

The situation might have been saved if repetitious vacillations had not continued on all sides through 1866. Lord Warwick suddenly became reluctant to provide the promised land at Heathcote for the sewage irrigation farm, claiming obligations made in new contracts with tenants as the problem, and, so, the Board had to search for other suitable sites. The Board even temporarily switched back to supporting Barry's river-outfall policy when elections intervened to alter the balance of Board personalities; but then switched back again.[43] The *Courier* continued its bewilderment at the Board's decisions, citing their 'suicidal course' and 'petty cavilling', calling for incorporation of the town and accusing the Board of having 'ceased to be harmless incapables, but who now mean mischief.'[44]

So, with no reliable policies in place at Leamington, on 8 November 1866, Thomas Heath and Alfred Field returned to Chancery with affidavits showing that over the months of July, August, September and October nothing had been done of the required improvements at the sewage works and that, centrally, the sewage had continued to flow as before into the Leam.[45] In reply, the Local Board maintained that they were still diligently pursuing land for the planned irrigation farm and (dubiously) claimed that the work at the sewage plant would be completed by the middle of November 1866. But confusion then arose over whether, in fact, so much as a signed contract for the work at the treatment site yet existed.[46] The hearing was adjourned to determine the disputed existence of this contract and the hearing resumed in January.

When reconvened on 17 January 1867, the complainants in the suit reiterated that the Local Board had reneged on what they had promised to do and had breached the injunction. Further, they argued that 'unless the sequestration were issued the defendants would do nothing.'[47] Leamington's defence rested solely on their claim that they had done all they could and that a sequestration would not help the situation, only hindering their sincere efforts to comply with the court's order. Vice-Chancellor Wood's opinion was that he had no discretion in the matter, in that if Leamington could not purify the water they did not have the option of pouring it into the river: one 'could not put the sewage in his drawing-room because there is no other convenient place to put it on, and you could not therefore put it

---

[43] *Courier*, 9 June, 16 June, 23 June, 7 July 1866.

[44] *Courier*, 6 October 1866.

[45] *Courier*, 10 November 1866.

[46] The Board only agreed to clean the Leam as late as 23 November 1866 (Leamington Local Board Minutes).

[47] *Times*, 18 January 1867.

on this gentleman's ground no more than in his drawing-room or anywhere else.'[48]
There had been, Wood continued, ample time since March 1866 to construct the
necessary works, so he had no option but to order the sequestration.

The *Courier* responded in typically stylish form:

> Leamington is in Chancery. The town is sequestrated. The parish brooms and
> wheelbarrows are to be seized by the myrmidons of the law. The very ugly Town
> Hall will shortly be in possession of the messenger of the Court of Chancery and
> the very handcuffs of the Police force will be sold ...[49]

Sequestration Imposed, August 1867

Although the order authorising the sequestration was available from Chancery
from January, it was not until late August 1867 that Thomas Heath actually moved
to enforce sequestration on the town. Even by this time, Leamington had done
nothing to clean the river and little to advance the other works required by the
certificate. Writs of sequestration were signed at Chancery, dated 2 August 1867,
and were delivered on the 20 August, to various agents of the Local Board,
including to the bank, treasurer and sheriff's office. The sequestrators were thereby
empowered to take control of the property and finances of the Board until such
time as the Board had fully answered their contempt and, as enforced, this would
leave the Board with no funds to meet current expenses.[50]

The *Courier* summarised the history of the affair:

> ... at last the sword has fallen. Leamington is in Chancery! The whole property
> of the town is sequestered! Our rulers are bewildered; their advisors are at sea;
> and we have the supreme felicity of knowing that we have been living in a Fool's
> Paradise. The history of the sewage difficulty is the history of a blunder, carried
> on by blunderers ... When complaints were first made by the plaintiffs in the
> Chancery suit, those complaints were treated with scant courtesy, which is now
> being returned in kind. They denied the nuisance, they refused concessions, they
> drifted into the Chancery suit with its enormous expense, and when the nuisance
> was proved, they proposed to do foolish things. They proposed to lengthen
> their depository canals and cleanse out the river ... We were asked to carry out

---

48   Ibid.
49   *Courier*, 19 January 1867.
50   The Local Board's finances were (also) managed somewhat ill-advisedly. The
Board had no bank accounts of its own so financial matters were conducted personally by
the Board's Treasurer, through whom the Board's revenues were paid and received. The
Treasurer at the time was the manager of the local Lloyds Bank; and when Lloyds proved
tardier than a rival local bank in offering temporary loan facilities designed to circumvent
Chancery's sequestration orders, the Board's financial affairs were churlishly transferred to
a new Treasurer at the rival bank.

our own proposal – it was met by a quibble. No attempt was made to carry it out ... the board should at once proceed rigorously to work to acquire the land necessary for irrigation ...[51]

The Board responded to Thomas Heath by issuing, in August, a notably unconvincing and unapologetic apology and the woolliest of pledges:

... regretting the circumstances over which it had no control have delayed the cleaning of the river from the Sewage Works to the Avon but as soon as the obstacles ... are removed the Board pledges itself to proceed with the same so it may be completed if possible within the next two months.[52]

They asked on this basis that Heath withdraw the sequestration notices. Heath replied that any such withdrawal of a court order was out of his hands and would require a Chancery ruling.[53]

Little wonder Thomas Heath and the *Courier* were frustrated with Leamington's leisurely lack of action: eighteen months since Leamington had promised what they had *themselves* proposed as required of them by the (revised) Chief Clerk's certificate and none of it yet achieved. Contracts for the improvements at the sewage works itself had been issued, but no work had begun, despite the Board's claims. Further, the promised cleaning of the river Leam down to the junction with the Avon was proving a much tougher and more expensive proposition than had been anticipated by Barry. The engineering required the building of a half-mile long temporary canal beside the Leam through which some of the water could be diverted while the cleaning of the river banks proceeded, but gaining the permission of the landholders involved and authorisation from the Board of the detail of the contracts took until September 1867.[54]

After the sequestration writs were delivered in August 1867, Leamington certainly proved rather quicker in responding to the legal challenges arising from the dispute than it had been in responding to the sewage engineering ones. Within days of the sequestration writs being served, the Board managed to organise a hearing for a postponement of the action before Chancery's vacation judge, Vice-Chancellor Malins, at the judge's local Angel Hotel in Godalming, Surrey,

51   *Courier*, 24 August 1867.
52   Leamington Local Board Minutes, 26 August 1867.
53   Leamington Local Board Minutes, 28 August 1867.
54   Leamington Local Board Minutes, 3 September 1867. More rowdy scenes occurred at this Board meeting, gleefully reported by the *Courier* (7 September 1867) as: '... another of those amusing contretemps which owing to the irascibility or excitability of certain members so frequently crop up as a relief to the monotony of the irrepressible sewage question ... [members] appeared to be competing for the prize for the production of the greatest amount of noise with the least modicum of sense.'

on 5 September 1867.[55] Heath's case was simply that the Board, no matter how much time and leeway was given them, continued to do nothing and since the sequestration writs were remedies already awarded after full consideration of the circumstances, further review was irrelevant.[56] Leamington argued they had begun the work at the sewage plant required by the court's orders and that the sequestration would now halt their attempts to carry out these improvements just when 'the works are being pushed on with the utmost vigour.'[57] Indeed, they submitted '... so completely are our operations paralysed that if the Clerk to the Local Board had not put his hand in his own pocket we should not have been able to pay the labourers who attend to these deodorizing tanks, the police of the town or the lighting and so on'. They also asked why the complainants, who, since January, had refrained from enforcing the sequestration for over seven months, just now decided to serve papers at a point when Vice-Chancellor Page Wood was unavailable to hear any pleadings. Leamington, therefore, asked for a suspension of the sequestration to complete the work that was now in hand. Vice-Chancellor Malins while recalling that his colleague Page Wood had said 'it was the worst contempt of court that ever came under his notice', proved sympathetic to the argument that Page Wood would be better informed to pass judgment when normal Chancery sittings resumed. So Malins allowed a suspension of the sequestration writs until 7 November 1867, ordering that until that time the financial affairs of the Local Board be again freed from restraint.[58]

In the event, the short period of fifteen days or so from the serving of the sequestration writs on 20 August 1867 until the orders were relieved by Malins on 5 September 1867 covers the entire period of sequestration suffered by the Leamington Board. To have had any very noticeable effect on the ordinary affairs of the town the sequestration would have had to have persisted for much longer than it did and even the barest of effects on the work of the Board are difficult to discern.[59] For example, while the writs froze the contents of the Board's financial accounts, both of Leamington's banks stated openly that they were willing to set up temporary loan facilities to allow the Board to circumvent the effects of the sequestration writs that had been served.

---

[55]   Vice-Chancellor Sir Richard Malins (1805–82). The building housing the Angel Hotel remains but not as a hotel: it was, reputedly, later a venue where an early Fleetwood Mac appeared.

[56]   *Courier*, 7 September 1867.

[57]   Ibid.

[58]   'Notwithstanding the order of 17 January 1867, the Court order payment by the sequestrators of all monies, if any received by them, to the Treasurer of the Local Board and order the sequestrators to permit the Board to receive all monies as if no sequestration had issued until after 7th November ... on an undertaking in the meantime to proceed with all due diligence in executing the works of the certificate of 22 March 1866 ...' (ibid).

[59]   It was reported that Lloyd's Bank did refuse, only temporarily, to cash a cheque for £53 for police and other wages.

The major effect seems to have been to motivate the Local Board into realising that they must have something substantial in the way of riverside workings to show when appearing again before Vice-Chancellor Page Wood in November. So they pushed ahead with the engineering works along the Leam required by the Chancery certificate. At a later public enquiry, the Clerk to the Local Board admitted that they had had to hasten to ensure that they could show the work to be in progress for fear the sequestration would be reinstated at Chancery: 'I deny', he said, 'we treated the sequestration as a matter of no importance. It frightened us out of our wits.'[60] It was also revealed that the costs of the river cleaning alone had amounted to £1,800, an amount many times larger than surveyor Barry's estimates, and that the contractor had at times employed a huge workforce of 100–140 men on the job.

Nevertheless, enough was achieved to satisfy Chancery. The final legal episodes of the affair of Leamington's sequestration took place when Vice-Chancellor Page Wood heard the suit again on 25 November 1867. Both sides were able to agree that the works required by the Chief Clerk's certificate had now been completed and that the writs of sequestration in this branch of the dispute could be discharged,[61] albeit with Heath's counsel obtaining reassurance that there was no bar to possible future actions concerning the pollution nuisance in the river.

After the Lifting of the Sequestration

Leamington's sequestration had arisen from their failure to fulfil the requirements of Chancery's supervisory certificate, but the pollution nuisance problem with Heath still remained. The Board recorded in 1868, with faint self-praise, that there was now 'scarcely any black scum' on the river, and admitted guiltily that 'the sewage works had never been properly worked since they were first established and had never proved themselves sufficient for the work given them to do.'[62] Thomas Heath again threatened to return to Chancery over his nuisance dispute as early as June 1868, and the Local Board debated whether to revise and expand the existing sewage works beyond the requirements of the Chancery certificate.[63] Heath and Field, they rightly suspected, would never be satisfied until any river discharge was stopped and they were anyway still bound by their earlier proposals and promises that they would move, in the longer-run, to an irrigation system, a strategy that was very slowly evolving.

At this point, the Board was tempted by an offer from the Native Guano Company with their ABC sewage treatment system, to conduct some experiments,

---

[60]   Some townsfolk had claimed the circumstances of the awarding of the contract for the river cleaning had been over-hasty to the extent of illegality but the subsequent Home Office public enquiry dismissed the charge (*Courier*, 1 February 1868).

[61]   *Courier*, 30 November 1867.

[62]   *Courier*, 27 June 1868.

[63]   Leamington Local Board Minutes, 16 June and 22 June 1868.

from autumn 1868, to demonstrate the efficacy of their chemical precipitation method at the Leamington sewage works. The events that followed provided much evidence for the Rivers Pollution Prevention Commission's pointed report on the ineffectiveness of the ABC treatment method.[64] The Commission's description of its visits to Leamington's sewage works in 1869 and 1870 show the works as a ramshackle affair and picture the river below the works being heavily polluted with sewage fungus, putrescent, thick, black mud and much suspended organic debris in the water.[65] There was, anyway, a storm of local complaints to the Board about the Native Guano Company's time at the sewage treatment works and, in March 1871, the company was given notice to quit.[66]

Meanwhile, alongside the stop-gap methods continuing at the sewage works, more long-term solutions emerged. In 1868, the Leamington Local Board agreed with its smaller neighbouring villages to form a joint sewer authority and to apply land irrigation treatment.[67] Crucially, the plan with Lord Warwick for a broad irrigation treatment scheme was resurrected. In April 1869, the Board announced that Lord Warwick would take the whole of the area's sewage to be pumped in its raw, untreated and unfiltered state, to be used in the broad irrigation of his farms at Heathcote.[68] For this privilege, Lord Warwick would pay Leamington an annual fee of £450 and take responsibility for any legal challenges that might arise from any pollution of the local rivers. Leamington would provide the initial pipelines and pumping facilities, deliver the effluent and maintain the network. The project would remove Leamington's sewage entirely from the Leam, but would not come cheap. A two-and-a-half-mile-long pipeline to the Heathcote site was required; and the town would build, on the existing sewage treatment site, a pumping station and engine house and install steam engines to move 800,000 gallons per day of the town's sewage over a small valley and up again to the small plateau at Heathcote.[69]

The thirty-year contract and agreement with Lord Warwick was finally settled and signed in May 1870;[70] and in May 1871 the cornerstone was laid of the 'handsome' new red-brick Leamington Pumping Station with its 90ft chimney shaft. By October 1871, the building was complete and the twin rotary beam steam-powered pumping engines began operations.[71] At Lord Warwick's Heathcote farms

---

[64]   Royal Commission on Rivers Pollution Prevention of 1868, *Second Report*, (The ABC process), 1870.

[65]   Ibid., 14.

[66]   Leamington Local Board Minutes, 6 September 1869, 7 June, 7 March, 21 March 1871.

[67]   Leamington Local Board Minutes, 27 July, 1 September, 8 September 1868.

[68]   *Courier*, 3 April, 10 July 1869; 'Plan for Heathcote Farm', Warwick Record Office, CR1886/M607 and CR1886/M35.

[69]   Leamington's capital costs for the scheme came to over £16,200 and the annual pumping costs were over £1,000 (*London Standard*, 17 October 1874).

[70]   Leamington Local Board Minutes, 3 May 1870.

[71]   *Courier*, 28 October 1871.

a total of 331 acres had been prepared to receive the sewage effluent which, now raised 130 feet above the pumping station, would be distributed by gravitation and sluices around the site. Up to 1,000 acres were available at the site. Even the *Courier* was enthusiastic:

> Ratepayers of Leamington may congratulate themselves on being freed from the entanglements of the vexed sewage question and a consequent immunity from sequestrations or injunctions on account of the pollution of the river.[72]

And so it proved. With the sewage outfalls to the river closed, no further legal suits or serious complaints with respect to Leamington's sewage pollution of the Leam are recorded and the Heathcote broad irrigation farm provided a genuine solution to Leamington's sewage pollution problem along the Leam and Avon. The farm was to become cited favourably: 'The effluent water ... was sufficiently purified to be admitted into the river, as not a trace of sewage could be detected in the clear and inodorous stream which flowed from the meadows into the watercourses'.[73] Crucially, the town was small enough and had ample suitable land available for basic irrigation techniques to be effective and Heathcote provided a broad irrigation solution for sewage treatment of the area until well into the twentieth century.[74] The report for the Royal Agricultural Society in 1876 provides a fine bucolic ending to this narrative:

> No complaint has ever been made of any annoyance occasioned by irrigation ... [outflow] at Heathcote is clear, bright and sparkling, like water from a spring, all organic impurities having been left behind to fertilise the soil. ... The brook is fragrant with meadowsweet and willow-herb, while haws and blackberries are ripening on its banks.[75]

Finally

It is clear that the responsibilities taken on by Chancery at Leamington Spa in the 1860s and 1870s included many more supervisory and managerial roles than traditional views might have expected. Vice-Chancellor Page Wood at Chancery was immediately concerned not simply to enforce the duties of Leamington's Local Board towards Heath and Field by issuing injunctive remedies, but to spell out what was expected of Leamington to alleviate the problems: to discover 'what

---

[72]   *Courier*, 21 October 1871.

[73]   Local Government Board, *Sewage Disposal Report*, 19–23.

[74]   Leamington's contract with Lord Warwick was renegotiated over time, reflecting perhaps a falling value for native guano. In 1886, Lord Warwick's payment to Leamington was reduced to £225 per annum and in 1899 the agreement reversed, with Leamington contracting to pay Lord Warwick for the sewage treatment services he was providing, of £500–£600 per annum.

[75]   *Courier*, 19 August 1876.

should be done to remedy it.' So Leamington was presented with certificates specifying the engineering to be conducted to avoid the issuance of an injunction and with checks specified to ensure the requirements were fulfilled. It was only when pressing evidence was presented showing the extent to which Leamington had failed to attain these conditions that sequestration orders were issued. When the sequestration writs were finally served, they remained in force only for around two weeks, and no damage was done to Leamington's usual public service activity. Sequestration's bark proved rather worse than its bite.

Ultimately, Leamington was shown to be one of those fortunate towns where a combination of small population, favourable local soil conditions and land availability could allow irrigation adequately to treat the sewage produced. The Local Board made poor, even incompetent, decisions with regard to its sewage treatment and it took serious action and contingent threats from the legal system for them to finally gird their loins for the financial outlays that would free them from their problems.

The other river sewage pollution dispute which saw the actual issuance, delivery and enforcement of sequestration writs during the period, was at Tunbridge Wells.

Tunbridge Wells: Goldsmid v Tunbridge Wells Improvement Commissioners (1865)

In the case of Goldsmid v the Tunbridge Wells Improvement Commissioners, the town of Tunbridge Wells polluted with its sewage effluent the property of the Goldsmid family at Somerhill and were forced through Chancery actions to abate the nuisance. In common with Leamington, sequestration orders were not only awarded and issued, but writs of sequestration were served and delivered in the town and the sequestration was actually *enforced.* As with Leamington, also, the enforcement was quickly lifted and suspended by Chancery so that no major observable ill-effects resulted for the town's performance of its civic duties. Notwithstanding the truth of the affairs, the tales told of these cases and their outcomes remained rather like moral fables to warn councillors in other jurisdictions of the threats of such suits.

The Civic Background

The town of Tunbridge Wells sits firmly in the deep south of England in Kent close to the border with Sussex.[76] Its permanent population was small in the Victorian era, only about 8,300 in 1841, but trebled to around 24,300 by 1881. Like Harrogate

---

[76]   The 'Royal' in the present-day name Royal Tunbridge Wells was added in 1909. The town should not be confused with the very close neighbouring town of Tonbridge (from whence its name is derived), which lies just five miles to the north, close to Somerhill, the Goldsmid residence.

and Leamington, it was, and remains, a celebrated spa town, becoming, during the Georgian period, a very fashionable resort, attracting the most prominent national celebrities of the day. The Tunbridge Wells Improvement Act in 1835 set up a supervisory body of Improvement Commissioners for the local governance of the town and in 1860, the commissioners took on the powers of a Local Board.[77] It is with the Tunbridge Wells Improvement Commissioners constituted as a Local Board that the river sewage dispute with the Goldsmids arose.

Tunbridge Wells is situated on the top and two sides of an elevated ridge on the edge of the Weald and the topography of the area also plays a part in the unfolding of this story. The geology of this ridge produces the springs and wells for the spa town and although the original chalybeate spring lies on the southern side of the ridge (within the famous Pantiles area), the expansion of the town in the mid-1800s developed new residential and commercial sites on the higher parts of the ridge and over the top, on the northern watershed. The plan of entrepreneur John Ward in the 1830s was to develop the Calverley estate on Mount Pleasant and his Calverley Park project aimed to produce a large new community of fashionable villas, terraces, parks and shops aimed forthrightly at the highest and most exclusive end of the market.[78] This development opened up the northern side of the Tunbridge Wells ridge. To provide a new water supply for his developments Ward also exploited the existing Calverley springs, which provided one source for the Calverley Brook watercourse flowing northwards, which eventually fell into the Goldsmid's lake at Somerhill. Another source feeding this watercourse was a drainage culvert across the previously open fields of the area, which was by 1860 serving as a main sewer for the new housing on the northern side of the ridge. The increased flow of domestic sewage from this sewer, combined with an ever-reducing flow from the Calverley spring to dilute it, formed, after the sources merged, an ever-more-toxic mixture feeding the Calverley Brook (or Bourne Stream), the watercourse flowing northwards and bound for Goldsmid's lake.

Although there was sewerage effluent running into the streams flowing both northwards and southwards from the Tunbridge Wells ridge, no systematic treatment was provided. But some opportunistic, informal cleansing of the Calverley Brook did exist. At the Colebrook estate owned by William Arthur Smith, just north of Tunbridge Wells, the land was managed to include an irrigation scheme which channelled off some of the water through carrier ditches parallel to the brook. This acted as a broad irrigation manuring scheme that extracted nutrition from the sewage in the water. Its aim was the enhancement of the agricultural productivity of the farmland, not the purification of the brook, so the scheme was, for example,

---

[77] There were now twenty-four commissioners serving three-year terms with one-third standing annually for election by higher-rated property holders. It took until 1889 for a Borough Charter to establish a town council with mayor, six aldermen, and twenty-four elected councillors.

[78] John Ward (1779–1855) was a successful property developer who had been MP for the rotten borough of Leominster in 1830. His Calverley estate extended to 874 acres.

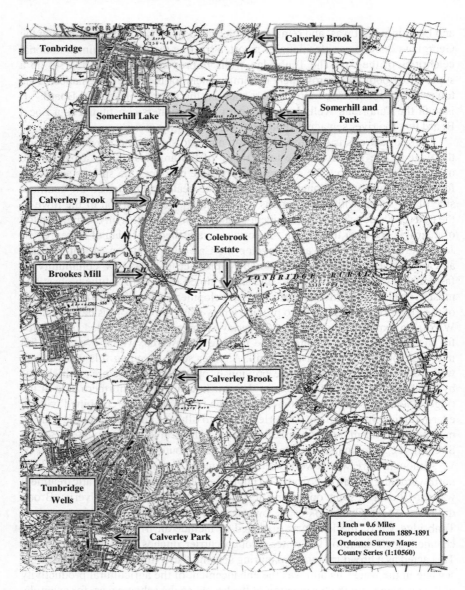

Map 7.2   Tunbridge Wells and the Calverley Brook

switched off during the summer months when any defaecation of the stream surely would have been most welcome. Other natural features along the route of the stream, like marshy areas, mill-ponds, bays and pools, would also have promoted cleansing of the effluent, but these were not adequate to still the growing unease at Somerhill over the volumes of sewage matter being brought down.

Frederick David Goldsmid's Complaint

The Somerhill estate, of above 4,000 acres, begins about four miles north of the edge of Tunbridge Wells, with, at its focus, Somerhill House and Somerhill Lake.[79] By the 1850s, the estate was in the possession of the Goldsmid family, having been purchased in 1849 by Sir Isaac Lyon Goldsmid (1778–1859) and then, on Sir Isaac's death, passed to his (second) son, Frederick David Goldsmid (1812–66), who was briefly MP for Honiton.[80] Later, the Somerhill estate, in 1866, and the baronetcy, in 1878, were inherited by Frederick David's son, Sir Julian Goldsmid (1836–96), who himself served as MP for various constituencies, including St Pancras.

The formal aspects of the disputes between the Goldsmid family and Tunbridge Wells began during the summer of 1864. In June of that year, the increasingly unpleasant state of Somerhill Lake and at the Priory Mill, enhanced by the warmth of the season, was brought to the attention of Frederick David Goldsmid, by his land agent, who blamed the pollution on sewage run-off in the Calverley Brook flowing down from Tunbridge Wells. Goldsmid quickly had these suspicions confirmed by consultation with the ever-active water engineer John Bailey Denton, and in August 1864 complained to the Tunbridge Wells commissioners. The letter included:

Gentlemen, It has lately come to my knowledge that in the prosecution of your drainage works for the town of Tunbridge Wells the sewage of the said town or of a considerable portion thereof is discharged into an ancient brook or stream which has heretofore flowed from or near to the said town to the River Medway and … through the Somerhill estate (of which I am tenant for life in possession)[81] for a length or space of nearly two miles and supplies the lake in Somerhill Park … You have in fact converted the entire bed of the stream into a common sewer… [and] the lake has become very foul and impure; unwholesome to cattle and dangerous to health. Now I give you notice … to take all requisite measures to abate this nuisance … and in default of your doing so I shall be obliged to take such measures as I may be advised to compel you to.[82]

---

[79]   The estate was scenic enough, in 1811, for William Turner of Oxford (not to be confused with J.M.W. Turner) to paint a fine landscape, 'Somer Hill', there.

[80]   The Goldsmid family has a more distinguished history than can be adequately reviewed here. Sir Isaac Goldsmid renewed the family's banking-based fortune in the early nineteenth century and became influential enough to be awarded the first Jewish hereditary baronetcy in 1841. Sir Isaac's eldest son (and Frederick's older brother) Sir Francis Henry Goldsmid (1808–78), became MP for Reading in 1860 only two years behind the first Jewish MP to sit in the Commons (Lionel de Rothschild in 1858).

[81]   The use of 'tenant for life in possession' was a traditional way of preserving a landed estate intact through succeeding generations.

[82]   Court of Chancery Records: Pleadings, C16/204/G114, Letter, 16 August 1864.

The Tunbridge Wells commissioners failed to realise how serious was the situation they would face with Goldsmid and made no response before October 1864 when they replied rather weakly that to act they would have to await some unspecified future national-level legislation and that, anyway: '... no complaints of this nature have ever before reached [us].'[83] Goldsmid quickly responded, sarcastically:

> I expected that the commissioners of Tunbridge Wells while they have been actuated by a desire to preserve and promote the health of their town and the vicinity would have felt it incumbent upon them, as soon at least as their attention had been called to a state of affairs so prejudicial in every way to the health and well-being of a more distant locality produced by their operations, to take steps to mitigate the evil and which I am advised it would be quite competent for them to do under their existing powers instead of referring me to the uncertainty of future legislation ...[84]

In November 1864, Goldsmid asked Chancery for an order to restrain the authorities of Tunbridge Wells from 'causing or permitting the sewage and other offensive matters draining from the town to be discharged or flow into the Calverley brook or pollute the lake or mill-stream or stream' on Goldsmid's estate.[85]

The suit of Goldsmid v Tunbridge Wells Improvement Commissioners opened a year later, on 16 November 1865,[86] before the Master of the Rolls, Sir John Romilly, in the Rolls Court.[87] Goldsmid's case was supported by numerous affidavits and evidence from residents and experts arguing the nuisance to be substantial, increasing and attributable to the untreated sewage coming from the town. The defendants responded with arguments that their sewage was fully cleansed by the private irrigation scheme and ponds along the stream and that any contaminating organic matter in Goldsmid's lake must come from other farms and sources along the valley.[88] The defence maintained that any nuisance was trivial; that an injunction could not be issued on the basis of future *potential* injury, as this assumes that the defendants will so neglect their duty as not to take proper precautions; and that the court must respect the public interest so some sacrifice should be expected of private individuals with regard to sewage and towns (the balance of convenience argument).

---

[83]   Ibid., Letter, 1 October 1864.

[84]   Ibid., Letter, 7 October 1864.

[85]   Ibid., Bill.

[86]   Goldsmid v Tunbridge Wells Improvement Commissioners (1865) LR 1 Eq 161.

[87]   Sir John Romilly (1802–74) became Baron and Lord Romilly from the beginning of 1866.

[88]   Including an eccentric argument blaming rotting leaves and leaf mould from the trees along the banks, from a competent scientist, Charles Heisch (1820–92), Professor of Chemistry at Middlesex Hospital.

Romilly concluded that the existence of a substantial nuisance to Goldsmid's lake and property was fully proven and he was satisfied the potential for the sewage pollution to increase would indeed be manifested. He dismissed the argument that an injunction could not be issued on the basis of future potential pollution, on the basis that waiting for the actuality to occur might itself provide a presumptive right for the polluters to continue to do so.[89] As for the balance of convenience proposition put by the defence, Romilly firmly rejected the argument, maintaining that: '... private rights are not to be interfered with'. An order was issued on 24 November 1865:

> ... to restrain the Defendants from causing or permitting the sewage and other offensive matters draining from the town of Tunbridge Wells to be discharged into the Calverley Brook or stream in such manner as injuriously to affect the water of the brook as it flows through the Plaintiff's land.

But the situation is rather more complex than any reading of the order might imply. Romilly was, in fact, not willing simply to restrain Tunbridge's pollution of the stream. The application of the injunction was both delayed and made *contingent* on Tunbridge's actions in attempting to abate the problem, as the surviving shorthand transcript of the proceedings reveals. The following is the exchange recorded between the Master of the Rolls (Romilly) and John Rolt[90] (counsel for Goldsmid) when the order was made:

> Master of the Rolls: I will make the Order then that you may let the matter stand if you please until the last day of Hilary Term [Easter 1866] in order that you may see what steps they have been taking in the meantime.

> Rolt: Your Honour will stay any action on the Order till then?

> Master of the Rolls: ... I do not stay the execution of the Order. I pronounce the Order to restrain them. The Order for the injunction goes at once; but if you were to come for any compulsory forces because they had not obeyed the Order I should not enforce it until at least the last day of Hilary Term *and not even then if I found they were taking steps to prevent it.* [My italics]

> Rolt: They will have further time if they show cause for that purpose?

> Master of the Rolls: Yes...[91]

---

[89] And the case set a precedent on this point.

[90] Sir John Rolt, QC MP (1804–71).

[91] Court transcript 'Goldsmid versus The Tunbridge Wells Commissioners', 24 November 1865, Tunbridge Wells Archives, Tunbridge Wells Art Gallery and Museum.

So the injunction order was formally pronounced and issued but could not be effective in any way for four-plus months and not even then if Tunbridge Wells could show they were taking steps to abate the causes of the nuisance: a contingent injunction. Even an unpractised eye would recognise the problem Romilly was having in forcefully 'executing' the order while simultaneously and demonstrably not 'enforcing' it. Posner's contention, that common law judges had a preference for rules enforcing efficient outcomes, might have guided us to expect to see judges struggling in this way.

Surprisingly, given the leniency with which they were being treated, Tunbridge Wells decided, at the next meeting of the Local Board in December 1865, to appeal this decision. The appeal against the Master of the Roll's decision followed at the Court of Appeal in Chancery beginning on the 24 February 1866, before Lord Justice Turner and Lord Justice Knight Bruce.[92] Tunbridge Wells argued, again, that the present injury felt by Goldsmid was trivial and that there could be no grounds for the intervention of an injunction on the presumption of possible future injury. Lord Justice Turner for the bench responded that they were satisfied that a nuisance existed that was sufficiently serious to affect the value of Goldsmid's estate and that the Tunbridge Wells commissioners had no prescriptive or other right to continue it. Further, he continued, the evidence was that the nuisance had been and was still increasing and that it would continue to grow, with increasingly serious and substantial consequences to the value of the estate. The appeal court thereby ordered that the appeal should be dismissed, on 24 March 1866.

A week earlier, on 18 March, Frederick David Goldsmid had died in London, aged 53, and his son Julian became the tenant for life in possession of Sommerhill.[93]

Tunbridge Wells's Sewage Scheme

It was only with the failures at Chancery that the Tunbridge Wells Improvement Commissioners seemed to realise that their sewage problems were not going to go away quickly: they had been convinced that there could be no case against them.[94] At the end of 1865 the commissioners started looking seriously for a solution and hired John Lawson as their consulting water and sanitary engineer.[95] Lawson's first report was delivered in February 1866 and proposed a typically bold and

---

[92]   Goldsmid v Tunbridge Wells Improvement Commissioners (1866) LR 1 Ch App 349; *Times*, 26 March 1866. Lord Justice Sir George James Turner (1798–1867) and Lord Justice Sir James Knight Bruce (1791–1866).

[93]   On 28 March 1866, Julian Goldsmid also became Liberal MP for Honiton in an uncontested by-election for his father's vacant parliamentary seat (*Times*, 29 March 1866).

[94]   Tunbridge Wells *Gazette*, 4 August 1865.

[95]   Minutes of the Tunbridge Wells Improvement Commissioners Sewage Outfall Committee, 30 December 1865 Tunbridge Wells Archives. John Lawson (1824–73) was recommended by his friend Robert Rawlinson, whose engineering firm Lawson had taken over ('Lawson, John, 1824–73', *ICE Minutes of Proceedings*, 38 (1874): 315–7).

ambitious Victorian engineering solution. Noting the siting of Tunbridge on its ridge and having inspected the areas to the north and to the south of Tunbridge Wells, Lawson concluded that while there were eminently usable sites to the south, no suitable sites for an irrigation farm existed to the north, in the valley of the Calverley Brook, that could treat the sewage from the northern two-fifths of the town. He proposed, in what we might call Plan 1, that a new tunnel should be cut under the town. The sewage from the northern portion of the town would be led southwards through this tunnel to join with the south-flowing sewage from the remainder of the town, to be treated together and utilised at a single sewage irrigation works below the town to the south-west, at Groombridge.

To divert this portion of the town's sewage away from the natural northward watershed direction would need a tunnel nearly 4,000 feet long, and up to 80 feet deep. The sewage tunnel would stretch from near the goods station to near the passenger station, parallel to the railway tunnels which had earlier been cut through the ridge to bring rail lines to the town. With the north-bound sewage carried away southwards, Goldsmid's problem would be solved and only one rather than two sewage treatment sites would be required.[96] By early May 1866, initially with surprisingly little vocal opposition, Lawson's Plan 1 was accepted by the commissioners. In June 1866, after being consulted, Julian Goldsmid at Somerhill demanded the town set up temporary works to treat the sewage in the northern valley until the tunnel solution could come on line. But nowhere to place a temporary treatment plant could be found in the northern valley as no owner would volunteer their land. Up to December 1866, now twelve months after the original injunction hearing, the Tunbridge Wells commissioners had, in fact, neither turned a single sod nor cleared an inch of land in pursuit of purifying their sewage. They did not, it transpired, even have in Plan 1 an acceptable scheme: Plan 2, closely pursued by Plan 3, would soon appear.

Julian Goldsmid's Complaint

From late 1866 through 1867, while confidence in the commission's sewage treatment Plan 1 declined, the legal dispute with the Goldsmid estate continued to escalate. Julian Goldsmid proved as impatient as his late father had been in defending his rights at Somerhill. In June 1866, Goldsmid's representative wrote to the commissioners, complaining that '... so far from being abated, the nuisance has been increased since the injunction'[97] and in July 1866 Goldsmid's agents began the process for enforcing the court order and eventual sequestration. Even the Tunbridge Wells *Gazette* begrudgingly acknowledged Goldsmid's position:

---

[96] John Lawson, 'Report to the Chairman and Members of the Sewage Outfalls Committee', 1866, Tunbridge Wells Archives.

[97] Tunbridge Wells *Gazette*, June 8 1866.

... a man was not obliged to wait until the water and air about him were poisoned before seeking to avert the evil. So far, no fault attaches to either side – Mr Goldsmid having a grievance had every right to seek redress; the commissioners [can] do no more than defend their position ...[98]

The motion for a writ of sequestration for violating the injunction of 24 November 1865 was heard by Lord Romilly in the Rolls Court on 26 July 1866 but, with Goldsmid's agreement, this was allowed to stand, to give time for the commissioners to carry out an informal agreement that had been reached between the two parties' engineers, Lawson and Bailey Denton. But the agreement, which involved a promise of temporary treatment works along the Calverley valley, was never made binding, and collapsed with the town's continuing inability to acquire land for the site. Renewal of legal action became inevitable.

On 20 November 1866, a new hearing of the motion for sequestration began at Romilly's Rolls Court. Goldsmid asked for the sequestration of the '... personal estate and the rates, issues and profits of the real estates of the defendants, the Tunbridge Wells Improvement Commissioners, until the further order of this court ...', with the argument that: 'During the spring and summer months, April, May and June we have waited and nothing was done ... the sewage still runs into our stream ... They have done nothing and have avoided doing what was possible.'[99] For Tunbridge Wells, the argument was that they were still attempting to fulfil their promises of the earlier putative agreement. 'We have done all we could', they said, 'as quickly as we could' but required more time. The sequestration motion was again postponed by Romilly, now until February 1867, 'to see what they have done.'[100]

In December 1866, engineer Lawson presented a new report to the commissioners defending his Plan 1 against growing local criticism that it was over-expensive and overambitious and to allay fears that the proposed sewage tunnels might divert the springs and poison the water of the spa town.[101] For a second opinion, the commissioners had already hired Joseph Bazalgette, from whom a report was received in February 1867.[102] Bazalgette's new plan, Plan 2, proposed dropping Lawson's sewage tunnel idea and using instead pipes lain within the railway tunnels and cuttings that already existed in the town. This

---

[98]   Tunbridge Wells *Gazette*, June 22 1866. A staunch supporter of the Commissioners, this was just about the last time the *Gazette* showed any sympathy for Goldsmid's position.

[99]   Court transcript, 'Goldsmid versus The Tunbridge Wells Commissioners', 20 November 1866, Tunbridge Wells Archives.

[100]   Ibid.

[101]   Memorandum from John Lawson, 'To the chairman and members of the Tunbridge Wells Local Board', 17 December 1866, Tunbridge Wells Archives.

[102]   Joseph William Bazalgette, (1819–91), Engineer to the Metropolitan Board of Works, and soon to be knighted in 1875 for his extraordinary work on London's sewers and the Thames embankments.

would have been a far less expensive venture, which alone would have given it weight with the commissioners.

In February 1867, the commissioners successfully asked Chancery for a further postponement for time to further consider Bazalgette's Plan 2: so that the next hearing in Lord Romilly's court would not take place until August 1867. Well before then, however, in March 1867, Plan 2 was fatally scuppered by the flat refusal of South-Eastern Railway to allow its tunnels to carry the town's sewage pipes and over the summer of 1867, the town moved on to a new, simpler, but still-to-be-announced Plan 3, which dispensed with tunnels entirely.

When the time came for the postponed Rolls Court hearing on 1 August 1867, Lord Romilly first query to Goldsmid's team was: 'They have done nothing, I suppose?' Goldsmid's counsel responded they had done 'worse than nothing', and proceeded to describe how nearly two years had now been wasted by the commissioners to no effect.[103] Tunbridge Wells, it was contended, had broken their promises of quick action in diverting the sewage from the Calverley Brook; Lawson's Plan 1 had been rejected and Bazalgette's Plan 2 had failed and no third new plan (Plan 3) had appeared. If, Goldsmid's counsel continued, their Plan 3, as suspected, involved Tunbridge Wells reconsidering and re-surveying the northern valley for a permanent site for a sewage farm, even more time would be required for enquiries and Parliamentary approval: 'One year and three quarters is already utterly lost'. Lord Romilly contributed that 'It will be the same story this time next year.'[104]

Counsel for Tunbridge Wells admitted their (still quite vague) new Plan 3 would indeed be re-examining the case for a sewage farm in the north, but the bulk of the defence case remained that sequestration was unhelpful and inappropriate:

> ... when the members of the Local Board meet they will not have a table nor chairs on which they can sit, nor papers nor pens with which they can write and take the minutes of their proceedings. They will have a sort of perambulatory meeting, walking about in the room, because they have no chairs to sit on. That is the sort of order your Lordship is asked to make.[105]

Tunbridge had nothing to show in response to the contingencies holding back the original injunction; there was sewage pollution continuing in the Calverley Brook; and there was not even a viable plan for remedial engineering. Romilly reluctantly concluded:

> [Tunbridge] must take the order for sequestration. I have no option. The nuisance is not prevented and has not been for a year and a half. It is not for me to say how

---

[103] Court transcript 'Goldsmid versus The Tunbridge Wells Commissioners', 1 August 1867, Tunbridge Wells Archives, 11.

[104] Ibid., 17.

[105] Ibid., 31.

it is to be done ... I have no option in these matters. I can do nothing more than enforce the order of the court.[106]

And with this, in August 1867, Goldsmid was placed in possession of an active order awarding sequestration, unsuspended and without even the admonition of the court that it should not be served on the officers of Tunbridge Wells: a straight, non-delayed and non-contingent order. But Goldsmid did not move immediately to deliver his writs.

During the summer of 1867, while the courts had been moving towards sequestration, the Tunbridge commissioners had formally rejected all their earlier plans for tunnels and sent their engineer, Lawson, to resurvey the northern Calverley valley in search of a suitable sewage farm site.[107] Plan 3 emerged as the commissioners realised there was, after all, suitable land to support an adequate irrigation scheme in the northern valley: so the option re-emerged for a two-sewage-farm solution (one for the northbound and one for the southbound sewage). William Arthur Smiths's land at Colebrook Park had always been a possible site in the north but Smith, earlier in December 1866, had wanted £25,000 for the 100 acres required and £100,000 for the whole estate including Smith's house, the Great Lodge. This had been, at the time, too excessive a demand for the commissioners.[108] Now Lawson found another suitable area, to the west of the railway line, comprising Brookes Mill and Farm and Moat Farm.[109] Moat Farm was part of Goldsmid's estate.

Plan 3, now proposed by Lawson, would involve 10,000 feet of pipeline to take the sewage from the northern sewage outlet, through two large preliminary straining tanks, to these farms, and then through open carriers across this area applying broad irrigation treatment before the effluent waters re-entered the Calverley Brook. Statutory instruments at this time had recently eased the acquisition of the legal powers that Tunbridge would require for this plan but they would still need authorisation from a public Inquiry under a Home Office Inspector.[110] Not needing traditional formal parliamentary approval would reduce the opportunity for Goldsmid to organise parliamentary blocks and obstacles but before Tunbridge was able to organise the authorisation process needed for Plan 3, Goldsmid served his sequestration letters on the town.

---

[106]   Ibid., 34–5.

[107]   Tunbridge Wells Improvement Commissioners, Sewage Outfalls Committee Minutes, 6 July 1867.

[108]   'Report of the Proceedings of the Sewage Outfalls' Committee', 20 August 1867, Tunbridge Wells Archives.

[109]   The absent owner of the 46-acre Brookes (or Brokes) Farm was the Rev. William Wilkin Stephens (1792?–1868) an Anglican clergyman 'without cure of souls'.

[110]   William H. Michael, *The Sanitary Acts*, (London: H. Sweet, 1867); Tunbridge Wells *Gazette*, 25 October 1867.

'The Town of Tunbridge Wells under Sequestration'

It was not until 11 December 1867 that, on Goldsmid's request, the Master of the Rolls issued writs enabling bailiffs (Commissioners of Sequestration) to take full power and authority over:

> ... the lands tenements and real estate of the defendants, the Tunbridge Wells Improvement Commissioners, and to collect take and get into our hands not only the rents and profit of their real estate but also all their goods chattels and personal estate and detain and keep the same under sequestration in our hands ... and require you to pay and deliver over to us all moneys property and securities for money [of the Improvement Commissioners] ... and we require you not to part with or dispose of any of such monies property or securities for moneys other than to us.[111]

Similar orders went to the commissioners, their bankers, collectors and solicitors, and further letters ordered all books of account and rate and assessment books held by agents of the commissioners to be handed over to the court's agents: these letters were dated the 17 December 1867.

It is unclear why Goldsmid waited for so many weeks between the award of the sequestration order by Lord Romilly in August 1867, and his obtaining and serving the writs on the commissioners in mid-December of that year, but the writ-serving did follow swiftly the issuing by Tunbridge Wells on 15 November of the notices required for the public Inquiry on Plan 3. That plan, it will be recalled, required buying Goldsmid's Moat Farm. The Tunbridge Wells *Gazette* believed that Goldsmid's action in December was in retaliation for the final dropping of the tunnel plans that would have taken the northern sewage to the south, far from Goldsmid's property: the *Gazette* went on to predict gloomily: 'the salaries of the police force and all the other officers of the town will have to go unpaid ... The paving, drainage, lighting and cleaning of the streets may also have to be suspended.'[112]

Tunbridge immediately looked to Chancery to obtain a suspension of the sequestration writs and Tunbridge's case was now much stronger as its Plan 3 was actually advancing. So on 1 January 1868, Tunbridge Wells was back before Lord

---

[111] Notice, 'Copy: Notices served under Sequestration', 17 December 1867, Tunbridge Wells Archives.

[112] Tunbridge Wells *Gazette*, 20 December 1867. The tone of the *Gazette* leader might be viewed by some as unduly provocative, including as it did, the addresses of Goldsmid's Tonbridge and London homes alongside reference to the taking of a 'pound of flesh'. Especially as, only recently (and uncharacteristically, perhaps, for Tunbridge Wells) the town had been provoked into violent street demonstrations in the notorious 'Webber riots' of 1864 (see C.W. Chalkin, *Royal Tunbridge Wells – A History*, (Chichester: Phillimore, 2008): 83).

Romilly at the Rolls Court asking for an order suspending the writ of sequestration.[113] Their argument was that effective steps were being taken with their Plan 3 to stop the nuisance at the core of the dispute but that the sequestration was in fact hindering them in carrying out the work required to comply with the wishes of the court. Counsel for Goldsmid innocently contended that they had neither received, nor even did they want to receive a penny of the funds that had been sequestrated from the town's bankers, which now rested in a separate account: 'we do not want to handle the money …', they said.[114] Tunbridge, however, protested that they would not be able to pay their police and they would be left, eventually, 'totally unprotected from violence and robbery.'[115] In the end, with Goldsmid willing to allow the commissioners' funds to be accessed and agreeing not to interfere further with the commissioners' duties until the Plan 3 Inquiry had reported, Romilly was willing to suspend the sequestration until the Inspector reported. But Tunbridge preferred that their motion (for suspension of the sequestration order) be refused so they could quickly go to appeal.

The appeal was held two weeks later,[116] before the Lord Chancellor,[117] sitting alone, on 16 January 1868 in the Lord Chancellor's Court. Counsel for Tunbridge Wells described their situation in awaiting approval for their plans (Plan 3): the Home Office Inquiry was now due to take place only a week ahead on the 23 January. The Lord Chancellor reasonably asked why, then, with Tunbridge Wells doing all this, was Goldsmid pressing his suit?[118] Goldsmid's counsel responded that there was no guarantee the Home Office Inquiry would approve Plan 3, and, anyway, they had already offered not to press the sequestrations until the Inquiry reported, an offer which the commissioners had rejected. The Lord Chancellor concluded that postponing any actions on a suspension of the sequestration until the decision of the Home Office Inquiry would be the best course and decided the motion of Tunbridge Wells was to stand over until 8 February: 'It may be

---

113   Court transcript, 'Goldsmid versus The Tunbridge Wells Commissioners', 1 January 1868, Tunbridge Wells Archives.

114   Ibid., 7.

115   Ibid., 10.

116   Tunbridge Wells *Gazette*, 17 January 1868.

117   The appeal was heard by the Lord Chancellor alone by special leave, as both the Lord Justices of Appeal had previously been employed as counsel in the dispute. The Lord Chancellor was Frederic Thesiger (1794 –1878), First Baron Chelmsford. Thesiger had been vocal in the 1850s in opposing Jews sitting in parliament: 'by giving a seat to the Jew in the Legislature of this country they would give a fatal blow to Christianity, which was intimately interwoven with every department of the State'. Nothing of such attitudes is discernible in his dealings with Jewish MP Julian Goldsmid's suit. (148 Parl. Deb. (3d ser.) *10 December 1857*, 479; *Times*, 7 October 1878).

118   Court transcript 'Goldsmid versus The Tunbridge Wells Commissioners', 16 January 1868, Tunbridge Wells Archives.

absolutely necessary to enforce [the sequestration] but I hope not', conceded the Lord Chancellor.[119]

The Home Office Inquiry on Tunbridge's Plan 3 took place in Tunbridge Wells under Inspector Arnold Taylor beginning on 23 January 1868 and continued for three days. Evidence was taken from a number of witnesses including the engineers Lawson and Bailey Denton and representatives of the principal parties involved. Although vociferous objections to Plan 3 were raised on Goldsmid's behalf, Tunbridge's scheme was ultimately approved by Inspector Taylor.[120]

The Dispute Settled but on to Plan 4

With their Plan 3 approved, the commissioners, on the 7 February 1868, went back to Chancery to petition for the suspension of the writ of sequestration. One week later, with both parties agreeing, the Master of the Rolls ordered a suspension of the sequestration orders until 22 May 1868 and it was not further re-imposed: so the Tunbridge commissioners were formally free once again to collect their rates and draw their cheques on their bankers.[121] The period of sequestration had lasted from 17 December 1867 until 14 February 1868. The only recorded effect was that the town's finances remained in disarray for a while,[122] with the commissioners reporting that their accounts were in a poor state and they were uncertain 'positively what was the real amount they had in hand.'[123]

Then, following the favourable public Inquiry authorising Plan 3 and having successfully stumbled over the major preliminary hurdles, as if the sleepwalker had awoken, the Tunbridge Wells commissioners summarily *dropped* their Plan 3 together, with all its remaining anticipated complications. The only landowner in the northern valley who had been voluntarily willing to deal with the commissioners over a suitable sewage treatment site had been William Arthur Smith who had, at Colebrook Park, the existing small land irrigation scheme using the Calverley stream, but the commissioners had earlier baulked at the price asked. Now a new plan, Plan 4, was constructed, which was based on an agreement for Smith to sell 110 acres for £20,000 and for Goldsmid to voluntarily sell a small neighbouring parcel of thirteen acres for £1,000.[124] On 6 April 1868, a special

---

[119]   Ibid., 19.

[120]   Tunbridge Wells *Gazette*, 24 January, 31 January 1868.

[121]   Tunbridge Wells *Gazette*, 7 February, 21 February 1868.

[122]   Tunbridge Wells *Gazette*, 28 February 1868 carried the request: 'Town Rates: seeing that the finance of the town has been greatly disarranged by the effects of the sequestration ... we hope all ratepayers in arrears will so far assist the Board of Commissioners by paying the same ...': some reluctant ratepayers had no doubt considered the sequestration a blessing.

[123]   Tunbridge Wells *Gazette*, 6 March 1868.

[124]   Little trace remains of what must have been interesting prior behind-the-scenes negotiations, but the initiative for the deal seems to have come from Smith.

meeting of the Tunbridge Wells Improvement Commissioners accepted the new Plan 4.[125] The Smith land at Colebrook Park had always been the most acceptable site for any northern treatment farm but a major factor in the decision to take up this new scheme must have been that it also came with Goldsmid's blessing and an end to the dispute.

In a formal document, Goldsmid and Tunbridge agreed: that Goldsmid would not oppose the new scheme at Colebrook; that the sequestration would be further suspended for, at least, twelve months after 22 May 1868; and that Goldsmid would sell his thirteen acres at the agreed price.[126] It took until August for the parliamentary authorisations for the new scheme and its financing to be obtained: and in September 1868 the first tenders for the sewage farm were sought. The formal legal conveyancing of both the Goldsmid and Smith land was completed in May 1869.[127] Following this, what became known as the Northern Sewage Farm quite quickly took form. Before long, sewage was being applied to the new sewage irrigation lands at Colebrook and, in 1869, it was reported, 'brocoli' (sic) was being planted.[128]

Although the substantive issues were settled at this point, other aspects of the dispute lingered much longer, indeed for another five years. Until the associated matters of damages, lake- and stream-cleaning costs and legal costs were settled, Goldsmid wished to retain some means of exerting pressure on Tunbridge and so the sequestration orders continued to be suspended rather than discharged.[129] Even though the new sewage works were claimed to be complete in 1872, it took until July 1874 for the dispute to be ended at which time the Master of the Rolls (now Sir George Jessel) determined the outstanding claims for costs and, finally, ordered the absolute discharge of the order of sequestration.[130] The injunction, of course, remained, but was now no longer deemed to be being violated. With this, the dispute between Tunbridge Wells and the Goldsmid estate finally ended.[131]

---

[125]   Tunbridge Wells *Gazette*, 10 April 1868.

[126]   Memorandum 'Provisional Agreement between Julian Goldsmid and the Tunbridge Wells Improvement Commissioners', 1 June 1868, Tunbridge Wells Archives.

[127]   'Conveyance and Grant' 31 May 1869, Tunbridge Wells Archives.

[128]   The Northern Sewage Farm at Colebrook was successful enough for, in 1874, the Royal Commission on Rivers Pollution Prevention of 1868 (*Fifth Report*, 217) to note: 'No complaint has been made of the state of the stream into which the effluent water flows nor is there any cause for complaint even in hot weather, or of the remedial process itself'. In 1876, the Local Government Board (Sewage Disposal Report, 27) reported that no complaints had been made since the lifting of the sequestration. Colebrook remains the site of the local sewage works to this day.

[129]   Six-month suspensions of the sequestration order were allowed in May 1869, November 1869, and in May 1870; and twelve-month suspensions began in December 1870.

[130]   Tunbridge Wells *Journal*, 4 July 1874.

[131]   The River Pollution Prevention Commission of 1868 (*Fifth Report*, 217) reported the costs to Tunbridge Wells of Goldsmid's suit, including enquiry and law costs,

Lessons from Leamington and Tunbridge

Goldsmid v Tunbridge Wells again shows Chancery using contingencies in the issuing of orders with regard to river sewage pollution suits. Romilly explicitly here states that he will not enforce his orders if the authorities of Tunbridge Wells are taking steps to deal with the problems in the stream. The sequestration eventually issued followed only when Tunbridge Wells could clearly be seen to be taking no steps at all to satisfy Chancery's requests that something be seen to be being done.

Leamington Spa (in August 1867) along with Tunbridge Wells (in December 1867) constitute the only river sewage pollution disputes of the era where sequestration writs were issued, enforced *and delivered*. But once delivered, for both Tunbridge Wells and Leamington Spa, the consequences of the enforced sequestration, in the event, involved minimal discomfort and disorder for the towns. In Leamington Spa the sequestration lasted only for a matter of days before the courts suspended the writs, and in Tunbridge Wells although the sequestration period formally lasted a little longer, no serious effects may be discerned. Neither town suffered the horrors of stopped sewers nor did violence and disorder arise from the threatened absence of police and policing. No officials on the responsible boards and authorities had their personal property attached. Indeed, sequestration seems, in both of these cases, as with Banbury, to have acted as just another goad or inducement for local authorities to put in place abatement processes adequate for Chancery to avoid having to decide that an injunction had been violated. For both Leamington Spa and Tunbridge Wells, the crisis with Chancery arose from failure to respond to Chancery's attempts to settle their disputes by requiring specific tasks of them. Leamington failed to respond dutifully to conform to Chancery's requirements contained in the Chief Clerk's certificates, and Tunbridge Wells dithered over and failed to provide Chancery with definite and agreed plans for the implementation of their sewage treatment.

For Tunbridge Wells, an urban fable spread, echoing the fancies of the defence's oratory at the 1 August 1867 hearing that imaginatively anticipated perambulatory meetings of the commissioners after their conference table and chairs had been taken by the sequestrators. This was exemplified by the identical accounts in any number of local newspapers reporting for Tunbridge that: 'sequestrators ... have seized the chairs, tables, rate books and the other property of the Commissioners, who have no alternative but to discharge their servants'.[132] This was not true. Perhaps the most important consequence of the cases of these 'sequestered towns'

---

compensation, and land preparation, had amounted to £87,243.

[132] The identical common wording occurs in accounts in: *Birmingham Daily Post* and *Manchester Courier* (23 December 1867); *Manchester Weekly News, Burnley Gazette, Leeds Times, Hereford Times, Leicester Chronicle, Yorkshire Gazette, Louth & North Lincolnshire Advertiser*, and *Hertfordshire Guardian* (28 December 1867); *Whitstable Times* (4 January 1868); and *Buckingham Herald* and *Chester Chronicle* (11 January 1868).

was to provide a myth for other threatened town councils to frighten themselves with, so to push them into the expenditure and effort required to get their sewage treatment regimes to the state-of-the-art level of the time.

Chapter 8

Negotiation and Settlement: Harrogate and the St Helens Canal

No practitioner of the law, observing the processes of the civil courts as they operate day-to-day, could deny the existence and importance of mutual agreements for the settlement of disputes. These may arise as a consequence of the courts encouraging parties to come to a settlement or may occur entirely away from the formal setting of the law courts. It is certain that private negotiation of terms of settlement, rather than the formal process of judicial weighing of law and facts and legal judgment, provides the more common means by which civil disputes come to a conclusion. In this chapter, two water pollution disputes are examined that were ended by negotiation and openly acknowledged monetary settlements between the parties, with little intervention by the courts.

The first of the two case studies concerns Harrogate's sewage pollution of the Oak Beck to the nuisance of William Wood and his bleachworks. The dispute, which covered a period from 1870 until 1876, illustrates, straightforwardly, a protracted Chancery action settled by monetary negotiation: some might say the town bought off the disputant. The second of the case studies is earlier than this, and describes a 'ghost' suit brought by William John Legh in 1859 against the St Helens Canal and Railway Company over the pollution of the Sankey Brook. Here the settlement occurred before even the first hearing at law, and as such would normally leave little or no trace. However, for this dispute enough evidence remains of what transpired to outline the course of most of the negotiation: it serves as an instance of what would usually be lost and thereby illustrates part of the source of the selectivity bias which makes empirical testing of aspects of the Coase theorem so problematic. Mutual negotiation and the Coase theorem will often inform the economist's first thoughts in disputes over nuisance and pollution, but care must be exercised if examples are found to be sparse: the very sparseness may be due to mutual private settlement taking disputes out of the records. In such circumstances, as in others, 'absence of evidence is not evidence of absence.' Court records may not be a source of evidence from which an unbiased sample may be selected about how, in practice, disputes such as those concerning river sewage pollution are terminated.

Harrogate: Wood v High and Low Harrogate

Harrogate in Yorkshire, the setting for Wood v the Improvement Commissioners of High and Low Harrogate was, in the eighteenth and nineteenth centuries, as today, a tourist centre famed as a spa based upon its exceptional mineral waters. The spa water has an astonishingly sulphurous taste which makes it virtually undrinkable and, therefore, for some at least, incalculably health-inducing. As the 1840s opened, the two neighbouring and then separate village communities of High Harrogate and Low Harrogate found themselves under pressure to update their local government regimes to provide the civic and urban improvements needed to cope with the rising number of visitors to the area. To remain attractive as a resort, specific public and communal amenities in the town needed careful handling. In particular, there was a need to protect and control access to the wells and springs of medicinal water, the very source of Harrogate's attraction, and to regularise control over the Stray, the 200-acre area of parkland and common grassland shared between High and Low Harrogate. As many of the public wells central to the local cure lay within the Stray, unrestricted visitor access to this area was essential; but while this access was not threatened, formal ownership of the Stray lay (until 1893) within the hands of 'gatekeepers' who retained ancient medieval usage rights alongside rather carelessly exercised responsibilities for general maintenance. The Harrogate Improvement Act of 1841 was mainly concerned to normalise the rules, responsibilities and uses with regard to the Stray.

As part of its reforms, the 1841 act joined together the communities of High and Low Harrogate under the governance of a Harrogate Board of Improvement Commissioners. The Board of Improvement Commissioners remained in existence for another forty-three years, until 1884, and was the responsible local governing body at the time of the nuisance action described here.[1] The commissioners had a limited power to raise loans and levy local rates alongside limited executive power over a tight selection of public amenities in the town which included optional, but not obligatory, license to construct common sewers, culverts, drains and watercourses. Not much was expected of local governance in Harrogate at mid-century; and, to be blunt about it, not much was delivered. Alongside a lack of finance there was also a paucity of enterprise, vision and competence among the commissioners. In 1855, the Improvement Commission took on the parallel guise of constituting themselves as a Local Board of Health, and, eventually, in 1884, the Board of Improvement Commissioners ended its existence when Harrogate

---

[1]   Harold Hyde Walker, *History of Harrogate under the Improvement Commissioners 1841–1884* (Harrogate: Manor Place Press 1986), 30–43. The Board had twenty-one commissioners, elected for three-year terms by higher rate-paying local landholders: seven of the commissioners being elected in rotation each year. Voter eligibility rules were remarkably flexible: no gender, age or citizenship restrictions were specified and multiple votes (up to twelve) were available for those with increasingly higher rate-paying responsibilities.

acquired the apparatus of mayors and town council under incorporation under the Municipal Corporations Act of 1882.

In the 1850s, except for the hotels, sanitary hygiene in Harrogate was still basic: WCs and sewers were not commonplace for the 4,500 or so permanent residents. In 1855, there existed no general network of underground sewers in the town. A single main sewer directed most of the flowing drainage and effluent of the town through the area of the Cheltenham Grounds, in Low Harrogate, along a part-open culvert to fall into the Coppice Beck and away northwards to the Oak Beck and to the River Nidd.

In 1856, the commissioners moved to fully cover this culvert down to the junction with the Coppice Beck after visitors to Low Harrogate were said to be cutting short their stays because of the 'unpleasantness' of the area.[2] This moment marks the beginning of the town's efforts properly to drain the town and lay a network of sewers. Over the following few years, drainage plans and proposals emerged for various parts of the town, and new sewers were laid both by the commissioners and by private developers, in a rather piecemeal manner, to service portions of the town.[3] However, a poor record of success for general improvement projects from the commissioners over the 1850s indicated a lack of professional polish at this time and led to the blunt and worrying characterisation that 'the commissioners of the 1860s had inherited a reputation for incompetence.'[4]

Harrogate's population was still small, at around 6,500 in the 1860s, but the town was growing and developing quickly and it needed sewerage suitable for respectable Victorian visitors. In 1864 and 1865, the town surveyor, John Ellis, presented a full, but complicated, plan for a network of sewers for the town.[5] There would be intercepting sewers to catch the new and existing drainage and three outlets into the streams and becks flowing northwards and southwards out of the town to carry away the unpleasantness from under the visitors' noses. No treatment of the effluent was proposed before discharge into the streams and because of this, and other criticisms raised, revisions of the scheme were made to include having basic settling tanks at each sewer-river outfall, which now numbered five. The extra settling tanks and outlets raised the overall cost to an estimated £4,300, and the project was authorised in late 1866 and construction began in 1867. Half-way through the year, the project then collapsed while only half-completed, as the relationship between the surveyor Ellis and the town soured over (unsubstantiated) accusations of either corrupt or inefficient practices by the surveyor and disagreements over salaries and private practice. So Ellis resigned in April 1867. In addition, the landowners at the proposed sewer outlets organised objections to the plan and flatly refused to allow the proposed settling tanks on

---

[2]   To indicate the restricted finance available to the commissioners, the cost of this culvert cover-up, at £490, amounted to one-half of their annual revenues.

[3]   Walker, *History of Harrogate*, 201–7.

[4]   Walker, *History of Harrogate*, 254.

[5]   Walker, *History of Harrogate*, 259–75.

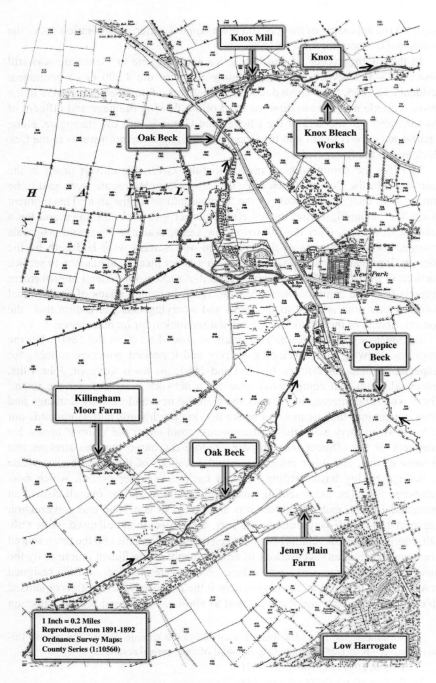

Map 8.1   Harrogate and the Oak Beck

their land.[6] Even as the new sewer network for the town was being installed a new scheme was going to be needed for dealing with the effluent.

When the new surveyor, James Richardson, was appointed in October 1867, he advocated a sewage farm using broad irrigation for treating Harrogate's sewage as replacement for Ellis's proposed scheme of five scattered settling tanks.[7] Richardson argued that a single sewage farm north of Harrogate would be able to treat successfully all the town's effluent when piped there. The problem with such a proposal had always been that the heavy soil of the area might be unsuitable for broad sewage farm irrigation, but Richardson maintained that so long as enough land was employed, and usage and rotation managed efficiently, such a farm would be a viable option. There were advantages to be had from such a change. Only a single outlet for the cleansed wastewater outflow, from the sewage farm into the Oak Beck, would be required; multiple current disputes over the setting tanks would be ended; and it would deal with complaints about potential pollution of the River Nidd now coming from neighbouring Knaresborough.[8] The commissioners jumped at the new proposal, even given the new scheme's higher price tag of £7,000, and a delegation moved to obtain the land required, which took about eighteen months to organise.

The sewage farm and works proposed was to use contiguous land, near the gasworks, made up from two existing farms. One was the Jenny Plain Farm, owned by the Duchy of Lancaster. Terms to take a twenty-year lease on the thirty-two acres of this land were quickly settled in 1867 and work began in October 1868 on preparing this part of the sewage farm. But negotiating for the neighbouring parcel of sixteen acres of church land, controlled by the Rector of Ripon, proved more troublesome: Harrogate decided to proceed with just the larger Jenny Plain Farm portion while negotiating for the rest, which was not finally obtained until May 1870.

The gap in time that appeared, between the cancelled but part-completed Ellis scheme of 1867 and the establishment of the new Richardson scheme and sewage farm after 1870, is important for the events that follow. The expanded Harrogate sewer network sent an increased flow of untreated sewage into the Coppice Beck. The hiatus between the two schemes left a nuisance in the small brooks to the north of Harrogate of serious consequence to William Wood at Knox.

---

[6] *Harrogate Advertiser*, 5 October 1867.

[7] James Richardson's appointment at Harrogate lasted until 1875 when he, too, fell out with the commissioners about private practice. James was the brother of John Richardson, Borough Surveyor of Halifax, who had been temporarily appointed in 1867 as a consulting engineer for Harrogate to help assess their sewage plans.

[8] *Harrogate Advertiser*, 2 November 1867; Royal Sanitary Commission, *Second Report*, 1871, C.281, 94.

William Wood and the Knox Bleachworks Settlement, 1868

The plaintiff and complainant in this dispute, William Wood (1821–77), was, in the mid-1860s, the tenant of thirteen acres of land, and proprietor of the Knox Bleachworks, on Knox Lane (Old Trough Lane), on the south side of the Oak Beck near Knox, which lies about two miles, as the water runs, from the edge of Harrogate. The Oak Beck is fed by the Coppice Beck after the latter flows through Harrogate, the two streams joining about one mile from the bleachworks. The textile bleaching process then in use required large quantities of water, which Wood took from the Oak Beck, the major reason for the bleachwork's situation on its banks. The presence of a linen textile bleachworks at the centre of this pollution story is not without some irony. The chloride of lime bleaching powder that Wood was using contains calcium chloride and calcium hypochlorite, both of which have disinfecting and sterilising properties, and so their presence in sewage-polluted water should tend to improve water quality. But the decomposition of bleaching powder releases toxic chlorine gas, with weed-killing properties, and can be a serious environmental nuisance.[9]

William Wood, born in Spofforth near Harrogate, had plied his trade as a bleacher of linen and other textiles around Yorkshire, and the censuses trace his progress to Beverley in 1851, Guisely, near Leeds, in 1861 and thereafter at Knox. Intriguingly, William's wife was Phillis Exelby whose brother, George Exelby, was prominent in local affairs in Harrogate: he was a Harrogate Improvement Commissioner from 1875 until 1884 and chairman of the Board in 1881. The Victorian bourgeoisie of Harrogate must have formed quite a small world.

In 1866, William Wood discovered that the quality of his bleached linen output at his Knox Bleachworks was being damaged by impurities in the water and, in 1867, an investigation determined that the cause was pollution from sewage in the Oak Beck.[10] Wood first complained to the Improvement Commissioners in August 1867 and more formally, through his lawyers, in November 1867 asked for compensation for the damage to his product. Receiving no response, in May 1868 Wood filed a bill in Chancery seeking an injunction to restrain the commissioners from continuing to convey their sewage into the Oak Beck and sought damages for previous injury and loss of trade.[11]

The Harrogate commissioners, in June 1868, obtained legal opinion and were told that Wood would probably win an injunction hearing and that a settlement should be sought. Negotiations between the parties then followed and proceeded until November. As reported to the board, an offer of £500 for costs was first accepted and then declined by Wood amid confusion over what was and what was not included in the deal, and then Wood countered that for a £1,000 settlement,

---

[9]   The site of Wood's bleachworks at Knox even today displays abnormally poor vegetation.

[10]   Letter from William Wood, *Harrogate Advertiser*, 16 May 1868.

[11]   Court of Chancery Records: Pleadings, C16/539/W114.

specified to include all legal costs, damages and loss of trade, alongside 'a satisfactory arrangement as to the time when the nuisance will be discontinued', he would withdraw the Chancery suit.[12] On inspecting Wood's books, the commissioners declined this offer, and Wood made a new offer to accept £500 plus £5 per week for future damages up to May 1869 for a total of £725. Wood's lease would expire at that date and, by that time, the sewage farm was expected to be in operation, so ending any pollution. This offer was again turned down by Harrogate and Wood reduced his asking price still further to £680. After these hair-raising exchanges, Harrogate offered £580 to cover past and future damages (up to May 1869) plus covering Wood's legal costs. This was accepted and confirmed all round during December 1868, and the commissioners congratulated themselves that they had avoided the considerable expense of a Court of Chancery action.[13] If only.

Wood had required that the deal should include a 'satisfactory arrangement' about when the nuisance would end. Here Harrogate promised, specifically:

> That the defendants [Harrogate] shall not after the 31st of May 1869, cause or permit the drains of the district under their control, or any of them, to discharge into the stream or watercourse flowing into the Oak Beck, any sewage matter or foul water whatsoever, or otherwise pollute the water of the Oak Beck.[14]

It was this part of the contractual agreement that was to cost Harrogate dear in the next part of the dispute. The commissioners had been badly advised. Even if no damage or demonstrable nuisance were being caused, it would be difficult to evade a charge of allowing 'any sewage matter or foul water whatsoever' to enter the Oak Beck.

As early as May 1869, Wood was back pointing out to the commissioners the continuing fouling of the Oak Beck and he complained again in August 1869.[15] It transpired that Wood's tenancy was not to end in 1869, as Harrogate believed. Wood had renewed and extended his lease on the bleachworks for a further five-year period, and had even taken a short tenancy at the nearby, corn-grinding, Knox Mill. Wood maintained that this was because he had believed Harrogate's promise of clean water would be delivered, but Harrogate believed that it was a ploy to extort yet more damages from them. Indeed, early in 1870, Wood did ask for a meeting to discuss an extension of their settlement saying '… we think terms could be arranged', but Harrogate brushed off the approach, specifically declaring Wood had '… no ground of complaint left to him.'[16] In November 1870, Wood served notice that he had filed a new bill asking for an injunction at the Court of Chancery.

[12]   *Harrogate Advertiser*, 5 December 1868.
[13]   Ibid.
[14]   Court of Chancery Records: Pleadings, C16/689/W228; *Harrogate Advertiser*, 6 June 1874.
[15]   *Harrogate Advertiser*, 15 May 1869.
[16]   *Harrogate Advertiser*, 12 November 1870.

This time, showing faith in the efficiency and effectiveness of Richardson's new expensive (but too small) sewage works and with backing from technical analyses of the water by consulting chemists, Harrogate allowed the case to proceed slowly to a full hearing at Chancery: this was eventually heard in 1874.

Meanwhile, Wood ceased to operate his bleachworks at Knox in 1871 because, he said, it had become valueless to him owing to the pollution, but in 1873, anticipating the end in 1874 of his new lease, he took out another new five-year tenancy extension. The situation for the town was now becoming serious. If Harrogate had congratulated themselves because they thought they had had the best of the first round of their dispute with Wood in 1868, they now faced a sound thrashing in the following rounds.

The 'Battle of the Bleachworks',[17] 1874–5

The four-day formal proceedings in Wood v Harrogate Improvement Commissioners (1874) began before Vice-Chancellor Bacon at the Court of Chancery on Thursday 28 May 1874.[18] William Wood, through his counsel, asked for an injunction, not, primarily, to restrain Harrogate from committing a nuisance, but to stop them from continuing to breach the contract they had entered into when the first settlement with Wood had been finalised. The effect was identical. At the centre of Wood's current case was that plenty of evidence existed that at least some Harrogate sewage was failing to be directed to the new irrigation works and this was basically all that Wood required for his case that Harrogate's commitment had been broken. Nevertheless, Wood's case further contended that, with all the sewage of Harrogate now directed northward via the Coppice Beck and given the growth of the town, the state of the stream was anyway worse than it had been in 1869 when the agreement was to come into force. The state of the Oak Beck around Knox and at Knox Mill was described as filthy, offensive and stinking and the fecund contents of the mill dam, removed after cleaning, was able, it was said, to be sold for agricultural manure. At the bleachworks, witnesses said, the water continued to be unusable for bleaching purposes. Affidavits, witnesses and expert opinion attested to the continued presence of sewage pollution in the beck and the unfitness of the water for use at Wood's bleachworks. John Bailey Denton was used as an expert witness and he maintained that Harrogate's sewage could not be adequately purified by the broad irrigation methods now being used at the sewage farm.

Harrogate denied that they had breached their commitment, which was, the Board contended, only intended to last until April 1869, so that Wood had 'come to' any nuisance or broken contract past that date. They further held that any sewage nuisance from their sewers and works had anyway been trivial and no

---

[17]   The designation 'Battle of the Bleachworks' is from Walker, *History of Harrogate*, 259.

[18]   Wood v High and Low Harrogate Improvement Commissioners, (1874) 22 WR 763; *Harrogate Advertiser*, 30 May, 6 June 1874.

substantial injury could be resultant: testimony was presented from experts and other bleachers of the district who maintained that the waters were clear and clean and suitable for bleaching and flatly contradicted the evidence from Wood's side. The defence even contended that the problems with the quality of output at Wood's bleachworks were more to do with Wood's professional competence than with the water quality. Harrogate also charged that the earlier agreement with Wood had only whetted Wood's greedy appetite for further payments, to which Vice-Chancellor Bacon astutely responded: 'Your objection is like Sheridan's, who objected to paying creditors because it only encouraged them.'[19]

Vice-Chancellor Bacon was intrigued that: 'Among the many nuisance cases that have come before this court this is the only one that I recollect which has been founded upon a positive plain contract' and noted that the 'mere infraction of the agreement entitled the plaintiff to relief.'[20] In coming to a judgment, he pointed out that that there was ample evidence that the Coppice Brook was, and remained, a common sewer under Harrogate's control with quantities of feculent matter passing directly into the Oak Brook, and that this had caused sufficient damage to Wood's business that he had had to suspend his operations at the Knox Bleachworks. Crucially, Harrogate had not found it possible to refute the contention that *some* sewage under the authority of the commissioners had been allowed to enter the local streams at points below the irrigation works and this straightforwardly violated the 1869 agreement. Given the breach of the agreement, Wood was, Bacon concluded, entitled to compensation and to an injunction which he ordered, dated 4 June 1874: 'prohibiting Harrogate from discharging into the stream flowing into the Oak Beck any sewage matter or foul water whatsoever, or otherwise fouling or polluting the waters of the Oak Beck.'[21] What had been an agreement now became a formal legal obligation in the form of the injunction. Time was allowed for Harrogate, so that the injunction was to come into effect during January 1875, around six months hence.

Harrogate now determined to appeal the decision and the appeal was held before the Lord Chancellor (Lord Cairns) and Lord Justice James in a two-day hearing during the second week of December 1874.[22] There seems to have been very little point to the appeal. It did not give Harrogate more time as it was held and settled before the injunction was to come into effect and Harrogate seems to have done nothing in the meantime to change its sewage treatment regime or to renegotiate terms with Wood. The same arguments from Harrogate that had failed to move the court in the original hearing were rehearsed again and similarly failed again. The case turned on the agreements and settlement that had been made in 1868 and 1869. The Lord Chancellor's opinion was that the agreement of May 1869: 'to all intents and purposes gave the plaintiff the same rights against

---

[19] *Harrogate Advertiser*, 6 June 1874.
[20] Ibid.
[21] Ibid.
[22] *Harrogate Advertiser*, 19 December 1874.

the defendants as he would have if an injunction had been issued against them, except that he could not enforce his rights in the same way that he could if an injunction had been granted [by threat of sequestration through contempt]' and that Harrogate had fallen entirely short of what they had committed themselves to do.[23] The court dismissed the appeal and upheld the original decision to award an injunction without bothering to hear Wood's side at all, but gave Harrogate some more time, until April 1875, to comply fully.

Short further extensions of time (until November 1875) were then allowed by consent following the court's supervisory suggestion that Harrogate employ Bailey Denton to provide advice and suggestions for improvements to their sewage disposal methods. Bailey Denton's response was to favour, of course, intensive intermittent irrigation through deep under-draining at the Jenny Plain sewage farm, which was too small and unsuited, he maintained, for broad irrigation. But the commissioners rejected these suggested improvements. Following this, when a new application was made by Harrogate for a further extension beyond November 1875, Wood's team objected, pointing out that Harrogate had done nothing to improve the situation since the injunction had been ordered. Vice-Chancellor Bacon decided he was unable to extend the suspension: Chancery never reacted well to having its suggestions underappreciated and its supervisory role spurned.

Harrogate would therefore face the full force of the injunction from November 1875, and a sequestration order would be likely to follow. Richard Ellis, the chairman of the Improvement Commissioners, publicly criticised the Chancery decision, maintaining that the water of the Coppice Beck below the sewage works was 'perfectly innocuous, clear as crystal and fit to drink ... as clear as spring water'. Rather undiplomatically, given the situation, Ellis also turned on Wood and declared that 'it was a disgrace that a town like Harrogate should be so harassed and hampered by a person who had been carrying on a little small business in a shanty', adding that he 'supposed £200 would purchase [Wood] up and yet, forsooth, they had to go to all this large expense to satisfy a little interest of this sort.'[24]

Richard Ellis may have been particularly exercised because he had been part of an earlier and near farcical attempt, in April 1875, to negotiate an end to the dispute.[25] He had heard informally that the freehold of the Knox Bleachworks and the adjoining land was being offered for sale. Along with another commissioner, James Lomas, he rushed off to meet the owner, the Ripon-born Dowager Baroness

23   Ibid.

24   *Harrogate Advertiser*, 7 August 1875. Richard Ellis (1821–95) was a major figure in the history of the town, sometimes called the father of Victorian Harrogate: he was later Mayor from 1884–7.

25   *Leeds Mercury*, 21 April 1875.

Grace du Bois de Ferrieres, then living in Tenbury.[26] A private deal for the freehold was successfully closed for £2,000, and Ellis and Lomas triumphantly reported back to the Harrogate board who immediately agreed to take the property from them at the same price. However, this coup was of little immediate or significant consequence and might even be considered comic. William Wood was in firm possession of a five-year lease signed with the owner in 1874: the commissioners of Harrogate were now in deep dispute with one of their own tenants.

'Obknoxious' Sequestration Order and Settlement,[27] 1875–6

The injunction had only been fully in force for weeks from November 1875 before Wood returned to Chancery to move for an order of sequestration before Vice-Chancellor Bacon, on 9 December 1875. Wood's counsel presented evidence on the present and continued pollution of the Oak Beck, attested by affidavits from expert chemists and engineers and argued that any changes instituted by Harrogate had been insufficient to match the commitments required by the original agreement and the Chancery injunction of June 1874.[28] In short, Harrogate had 'openly acted in defiance of the order of the court'. Harrogate, in their defence, argued the case that they now had in hand plans for an extensive and well-planned expansion and extension of their sewerage system and again presented unconvincing affidavits affirming the cleanliness and purity of the water courses at Knox: 'the water is as pure as some of the water supplied by water companies to the populace to drink'.[29]

Vice-Chancellor Bacon could do little but grant the sequestration request, reported as believing that:

> There was no evidence on which he could rely that the nuisance did not exist. … [And] the disobedience had been wilful. In this case the defendants had the advice of Mr Bailey Denton but not adopting his suggestions and acting on their own opinion, sending more sewage matter than they had previously done on the irrigation farm which was inadequate to deal with the sewage previously sent there, they had practically disobeyed the order and injunction of the court.[30]

Note how Bacon draws attention to Harrogate's rejection of Bailey Denton's court-approved supervisory suggestions. Bacon therefore issued the sequestration order sought, but, in line with the pattern set, allowed a suspension of two months before the order was to be enforced: the critical date to be 9 February 1876. Both sides would now expect yet another hearing at that time.

---

26   The Dowager Lady Grace (1807–97) was the widow of the Second Baron, Augustus du Bois de Ferrieres (d. 1867).

27   The pun is from the *Harrogate Advertiser*, 11 December 1875.

28   Ibid.

29   Ibid.

30   Ibid.

The suspicions of Harrogate's earlier surveyor had been correct in believing that the local heavy soils would cause problems for the application of broad irrigation processes to the treatment of Harrogate's sewage. The limited forty-eight acres of the Jenny Plain Sewage Farm was unable to provide adequate purification and deodorisation using simple surface irrigation alone, because the clay soil became over-saturated and the liquid sewage flowed too quickly and ineffectively over the surface.[31] Although Harrogate had rejected Bailey Denton's plan for under-drained intermittent irrigation (on the basis of cost) they had replaced this plan, earlier in 1875, with an alternative scheme from their new surveyor, E. Wareham Harry. This new scheme would require the acquisition of a much larger irrigation area at the 247-acre Killingham Moor Farm (sometimes Howard's Farm), which lay to the west of the Jenny Plain Farm site. There would also be new intercepting and main sewage pipes to make sure no untreated Harrogate sewage entered the Coppice Beck. And the outflow from the treatment farm would be carried through even more pipework installed alongside the Oak Beck so the wastewater would enter the stream only at a point further along and *below* the Wood bleachworks at Knox. Desperate and ultimately successful negotiations continued with the owners and the tenants at Killingham Moor Farm until October 1875 and until December 1875 with the Local Government Board in London for a £8,000 loan. The irrigation design to be installed at Killingham Moor was even rejigged to include some deep under-draining.[32] But none of this had been enough to influence Vice-Chancellor Bacon's opinion at the end of 1875.

At the turn of the year, as the 9 February 1876 deadline approached, both sides must have been eager for a settlement. Harrogate could not risk failing again at Chancery and becoming a humiliated victim of an actual sequestration of their rates and assets and, in consequence, have an even more costly treatment scheme enforced on them. And Wood would lose his power to extract a settlement if Harrogate's new scheme was effective with the sewage outflow diverted downstream or if sequestration led to the enforced imposition of, say, a court-approved version of Bailey Denton's treatment plans.

William Wood approached the Harrogate board on 29 December 1875 saying that he was willing to discuss terms and a meeting was then arranged. Wood's terms were reported as being that he would accept £1,000 plus damages as determined by the court, or £7,000 for his lease and to clear everything else except legal fees alone.[33] The commissioners were able to bargain this down to £5,000 plus legal fees, and this arrangement was nearly finalised on 3 January when confusion arose over the certification of the legal accounts. A certain amount of strategic bluff must have been invoked at this point, as the stand-off, ostensibly over legal fees alone, persisted until 15 February when a final meeting determined the legal fees payable

---

[31]   'The Harrogate Sewage Farms', *The British Architect*, 18 May 1877, 305.

[32]   *Harrogate Advertiser*, 22 January 1876.

[33]   Walker, *History of Harrogate*, 274.

at a fixed £1,650 to go with the £5,000.[34] These amounts might be compared to the £4,000 paid in 1878 by Harrogate for the freehold of the whole of Oak Beck Farm.[35] In exchange for these payments, Wood undertook comprehensively:

> ... to cancel and abandon his agreement with the Commissioners, to relinquish the Chancery suit, remove and dissolve the sequestration, to give up his lease of the Knox Bleach Works, and allow the free use of Oak Beck for all time for the outflow of the sewage works of the Commissioners without any interference by himself or any of his agents or tenants at any time hereafter.[36]

Wood relinquished the bleachworks on 6 April 1876 and received the final instalment of his settlement on 3 May 1876.

The Harrogate commissioners were overjoyed to see the end of the affair, which, bluntly, had not done much overall to alleviate their reputation for incompetence. The commissioners' own post-mortem discussion on the agreement, on 21 February, actually considered (but rejected) outright stupidity on their part; although the discussion did point out instances of poor strategy and lack of complete truthfulness in their dealings both with Chancery and Wood.[37] There was also deep unease about the size of Wood's pay-off, with some commissioners considering the settlement to have been more akin to extortion than negotiation. Still, there was relief that the affair was over, and with it was an end to the threat posed to the tourist trade arising from the damage to the reputation of its waters from any continuing controversy over sewage. One commissioner even argued the Wood suit had done the town incalculable good giving it 'sanitary arrangements second to no town in the kingdom'. After the board endorsed the final arrangement and settlement (by ten votes to three), Chairman Richard Ellis concluded the debate with a sentiment with which a number of other town authorities would have agreed: 'A Chancery suit was a game at which local boards were ill-equipped to play – the proceedings were so intricate and delicate. He hoped he would not live to see the town engaged in another. (Hear, hear).'[38]

Concluding Remarks

The suit of Wood v Improvement Commissioners of High and Low Harrogate began in 1868, but with the first Chancery bill being withdrawn and the renewal

---

[34] The *Harrogate Advertiser* (8 January 1876) reported that Wood had initially demanded a £22,000 settlement based on claims of foregone profits of £1,700 per annum at the Knox bleachworks.

[35] And with the impolitic £200 that Richard Ellis had thought Wood's enterprise was worth.

[36] *Harrogate Advertiser*, 26 February 1876.

[37] Ibid.

[38] Ibid.

of the suit in 1870, took until 1876 to be resolved. Alongside the series of negotiations over settlement, the history includes suspensions of injunctions and impositions of supervisory orders and also an example of the suspension and delay of a sequestration order by Chancery. In addition, the dispute shows how the Court of Chancery could react harshly when its judges felt the defendants were wilful in disobeying orders and insufficiently respectful of their (supervisory) suggestions regarding abatement. Overwhelmingly, however, the context of the dispute provides a fine case study of the river pollution dilemma being resolved through bargaining and negotiation between the parties. In this case, the defendants had to settle twice, first in 1868 and then again in 1875/6, when to end the dispute they finally bought both the freehold and the lease of the property concerned. As such, this case study fits the guiding arguments of the Coase theorem.

The competing offers involved in Harrogate's negotiations with Wood as they groped towards a settlement of the dispute are reasonably well-documented. A large part, at least, of the evidence remains and many details of the negotiation process are retained and may be followed even after a century or more. It is clear, however, that the extent and practical relevance of bargaining and negotiation between parties in nuisance disputes is obscured by the methodological problem of the absence of evidence when such disputes and their settlement by negotiation can occur far beyond the recording of the formal legal process and the notice of publicly-available media. This point is illustrated by the case study that follows which concerns a water pollution dispute of the period where negotiation was used to settle the case in circumstances where no court had yet played a role, nor was ever going to.

St Helens Canal: Legh v St Helens Canal and Railway Company (1859)

The suit, Legh v the St Helens Canal and Railway Company, concerns an obscure private nuisance dispute that was scheduled to be heard in August 1859. The defendant was a private commercial company and the complaint was filed to be held under the Queen's Bench Division at the Liverpool Assizes and primarily involved industrial pollution of water rather than sewage pollution.[39] Paradoxically, the case is revealing and of interest because of its very obscurity.

The dispute's lack of celebrity is not surprising, given its failing to be referenced in any of the usual legal sources and with no great question of law at issue. The importance of the case for our purposes is that it is exactly an example of a nuisance case that, following negotiation between the parties, was withdrawn from the legal process and the case never went before the court for a formal hearing. There are no public legal orders or bills or petitions to be discovered regarding the case. A monetary settlement was reached privately. Indeed, it is surprising that Legh v the

---

[39]   Although sewage effluent from the town of St Helens was also a contributing contaminant.

St Helens Canal and Railway Company (1859) has any public record at all. The case highlights that it is simply not possible to determine just how many Victorian legal disputes over river pollution were being similarly settled before the formal judgment of the court was even sought, let alone delivered. The same argument applies, of course, through to today. But this is one such 'ghostly' dispute where most of the course of events can be reconstructed, because of the existence of private letters and papers retained in the archives of a distinguished landed family.

During the 1850s and 1860s, the economy of the St Helens area of south Lancashire included important industrial concentrations of glass-making and other manufacturing, collieries and metal smelting and foundries. Crucially, given the local availability of coal and salt, chemicals and alkali (soda) production had become the dominant speciality of the area and its villages had grown rapidly into populous, important and smelly towns.[40] Chemicals and alkali production were activities widely and correctly renowned for their ill effects on the environment and the local area had become covered with vast tips of sulphurous and other noxious waste.[41] One lament for the area's environmental quality, in 1854, will suffice to set the scene:

> Look at the once crystal brooks, formerly swarming with fish, now one stream of poison, the fogs and vapours rising from which are indeed shameful. Surely, when it has, and continues to turn copper, silver and gold in people's pockets as they walk the streets, is it not sure to hurt both vegetable and animal life, when we know that it is impregnated with arsenic, muriatic [hydrochloric] and other strong acids? Some days the appearance of the brooks are orange, others blue, next green, perhaps the following, a foamy milk colour. Fertile fields are forever ruined, once grand and majestic trees are now leafless and branchless stumps. Our once good hedges are also laid low, and if these smokes and vapours do these things, can it be wondered that ... these pages might be filled with horrifying accounts of the dangerous state of the town.[42]

---

[40]   Theo Cardwell Barker and John Raymond Harris, *A Merseyside Town in the Industrial Revolution: St. Helens, 1750–1900* (London: Frank Cass, 1993).

[41]   Richard Hawes, 'The Control of Alkali Pollution in St Helens 1862–1890', *Environment and History*, 1 (1995): 159–71. Legislation specifically aimed in particular at regulating the noxious outpourings from the Leblanc alkali production process was passed as the Alkali Act, 1863, to become a landmark in environmental law. St Helens was also the site for an important air pollution nuisance case: Tipping v St Helens Smelting Company (1861–73) All ER Rep Ext 1389; see Simpson, *Leading Cases*, Chapter 7.

[42]   Letter, *Northern Daily Times*, 3 November 1854.

The Dispute

The defendant in the prospective case was the St Helens Canal and Railway Company. The company owned, in the area of Merseyside to the east of Liverpool, a canal and a railway, both of which, individually, have illustrious claims within the economic history of the industrial revolution. The canal part of the company dates back to 1755 when the Sankey Navigation was authorised. With its 1755 date, the Sankey Navigation predates the Bridgewater Canal of 1761, which is usually cited as the first English canal of the industrial revolution, but the Sankey Navigation was originally constructed, in places, as its name implies, by embanking and deepening the Sankey Brook, allowing the Bridgewater Canal, built to stand entirely separate from any existing watercourse, to gain its historic citation.

The purpose of the Sankey Navigation was to move the coal of the St Helens area collieries over about ten miles through Newton-le-Willows and Winwick, on past Warrington, to Fiddler's Ferry on the Mersey riverside, and from there to be moved on to the docks and industry of Liverpool. Soon the navigation was improved and developed by the Sankey Brook Navigation Company and, as competition with the railways emerged in the 1830s, the Merseyside canal link was extended to Widnes. Even the canal's name developed, from the Sankey Navigation to the Sankey Canal to the altogether more respectable-sounding St Helens Canal. The competition had come from an early railway company, the St Helens and Runcorn Gap Railway, which in 1833 opened a route from St Helens to Widnes. This railway, too, has historical importance as it was among the very earliest purpose-built railways in Britain, opening just three years behind the celebrated Liverpool and Manchester Railway. Competition between the St Helens canal and the newly-built St Helens railway led to the rival companies bringing each other close to failure and so, as competing companies often do in such circumstances, they merged, in 1845, to form the St Helens Canal and Railway Company: the party to the dispute of 1859.[43]

By its nature, where the parties to a dispute have no public responsibilities and come to some mutually agreed solution to settle and withdraw a suit before any hearing, little if any record of the progress of the dispute is normally available. That fortuitously, for this dispute, records for one party are available, is due to the plaintiff being a man of substance and a political grandee, so that an archive of

---

[43]   The merged company did not itself long survive as an independent body. In 1864, the London and North Western Railway formally took over the company as a whole; and in its turn, became part of the giant London Midland and Scottish Railway. Both railway and canal traffic along the original St Helens to Widnes routes gradually declined: the canal was progressively abandoned up to the 1950s until closure in 1963 and the railway route finally closed in the 1980s.

his papers and affairs has been preserved, including documents, letters and notes relating to the case.[44]

The plaintiff was William John Legh (1828–98) of Lyme Park in Cheshire, heir to a family with a notable history traceable back to before the fourteenth century.[45] The Leghs were enormously wealthy and not frightened of litigation over nuisance from industry. In 1851, William Legh's father, Thomas Legh, had sued James Muspratt of St Helens, a dominant figure in the British alkali industry, and successfully forced Muspratt to move his soda works.[46] William John Legh, himself, was to become MP for Lancashire South from 1859 to 1868 and for Cheshire East from 1868 to1885. Though never a political force and never attaining high political office, he was raised to the peerage as the first Baron Newton of Newton-in-Makefield in 1892.[47] The Leghs were substantial landowners in north Cheshire and south Lancashire, recorded in the early 1880s as owning 13,800 acres of land in the area.[48]

In 1858, Legh's land agents became aware of problems mounting for some agricultural land close to the Sankey Brook near St Helens. Tenants for the land were becoming more difficult to find and the rentals available had fallen steeply, due, it was thought, to the agricultural land becoming increasingly damaged over the previous ten years. A flood from the nearby canal had earlier, in July 1853, led to the St Helens Canal and Railway Company paying compensation to local farmers, and this must have influenced the course of events later in 1859. Legh's locally-based agents quickly confirmed that the current difficulties with the land were due to water pollution, and set about obtaining more formal confirmation and evidence. It could not have been a difficult task to surmise that the water of the Sankey Brook might be the source of the problem. The Rivers Pollution Prevention Commission later noted the 'exceedingly offensive smell' of the Sankey Brook and reported:

> ... it is no exaggeration to say that this brook renders the country within two miles of its banks uninhabitable, except under a penalty of so much discomfort as few would be prevailed upon to endure.[49]

---

[44]   Legh Family of Lyme Park Archive, Greater Manchester Record Office, E17/123/1 (hereafter Legh Family Archive).

[45]   The house at Lyme Park remains a national treasure, owned by the National Trust.

[46]   Simpson, *Leading Cases*, 178. Thomas Legh (1793–1857) had been MP for the rotten borough of Newton, historically in the 'pocket' of the Leghs.

[47]   *Hansard* has him as making zero contributions to their records in the Commons over these spells.

[48]   John Bateman, *The Great Landowners of Great Britain and Ireland*, (London: Harrison, 1883).

[49]   Royal Commission on Rivers Pollution Prevention of 1868, *First Report* (Rivers Mersey and Ribble), 34.

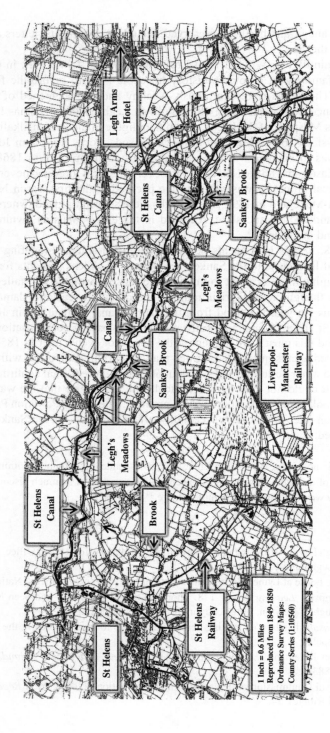

Map 8.2   St Helens and the Sankey Brook

In July 1858, Legh's lawyers instructed William Rothwell and Son, a firm of local land surveyors, to assess the water meadows along the Sankey Brook as it flowed eastwards from St Helens. Water meadows are grassland fields subject to periodic flooding from neighbouring watercourses and are farmed accordingly, usually for pastoral. Legh's meadows lie in a locality where the Sankey Brook and the Sankey Canal interact and feed each other at many points, sometimes they are only a few yards apart. For their survey, Legh's surveyors were asked to consider damage to all the fields in the locality, not just those owned by Legh, and to look for possible causes for any damage. Rothwell's report was duly submitted, dated 17 July 1858.[50] It concluded that there was, indeed, substantial damage evident in these grassland meadows, with some meadows described as 'completely destroyed' and the cause of the damage was attributed as being 'solely from being covered at floods with water containing poisonous matter ... and also by a constant soakage from the canal of the same poisonous water.' The report found that in places the 'water is now very strongly impregnated with deleterious matter ... so as to completely destroy vegetation', and it would take, the report continued, many years to restore the meadows so affected.

As to the sources of the damaging pollution, Rothwell was able to point to the runoff from 'great accumulations of waste from various chemical works' making up embankments to the canal and railway, and also to discharges of deleterious matter from glassworks and chemical and smelting works.[51] Untreated effluent from the St Helens town sewer also contributed but was not considered serious. The Sankey Brook could receive these poisonous discharges directly both from the industrial premises themselves and also via soakage and seepage and wet weather overflows from the canal. The report contained opinion on the extent of damage done to each meadow and the names of both the owners and the tenants of the lands. A list of the major polluting sources was also included in Rothwell's report and nine locations were detailed where, it was held, seriously polluting matter was being discharged into the watercourses. The St Helens Canal and Railway Company appears as one of these major polluting sources, with reference to the damaging seepages from the canal and the company's use of chemical waste as canal embankment material. Legh's legal advisors now looked to the legal process for redress.

Counsel's advice was sought from barrister John Horatio Lloyd.[52] His opinion pointed out a number of potential problems any suit seeking redress from the nuisance along the Sankey would face.[53] Lloyd was adamant that the case should not be taken through Chancery as the nuisance had by then been continuing for too extended a period: an injunction would not be imposed, so, he argued, damages

[50] William Rothwell, 'A Report on the State of the Water Meadows', 1858, Legh Family Archive.
[51] Ibid.
[52] John Horatio Lloyd (1798–1884) had been Liberal MP for Stockport, 1832–4.
[53] 'Case: For the opinion of Mr John H. Lloyd', 20 November 1858, Legh Family Archive.

should be sought through the common law courts. Lloyd also believed it inadvisable to attempt to sue any of the collection of individual industrial enterprises named among the polluters, as each would claim their own contribution to the poisoning of the water to be negligible as compared to the rest. However, Lloyd did believe that an evident nuisance existed and recommended a strategy of indictment of the canal company alone as a viable course. This was, he continued, because the canal company carried statutory obligations with regard to the maintenance of water quality; they had used chemically noxious waste to construct embankments for their railway; and they had been 'supine' in failing to curb the use of their canal and adjacent areas as a waste tip for the local chemical and alkali plants.

So communications with the St Helens Canal and Railway Company commenced in February 1859, demanding compensatory damages and that the company undertake to cease polluting the Sankey Brook.[54] The company replied that they must 'disclaim any responsibility' for polluting the Sankey Brook,[55] and the legal process was initiated.

Legh's lawyers had already begun to accumulate evidence to support the case for nuisance, contending that 'the trees and bushes on the banks of the brook are killed' and 'the cattle of [Legh's] tenants cannot drink the water and all the fish (if this is worthy of mention) are destroyed'.[56] Testament collected included that: 'The smell from the Sankey Brook is at times almost intolerable as every person must know who may have the misfortune to live near its banks ...'[57] Experts were gathered, and Legh was willing to aim very high for consultants on the chemistry of the pollution, including an attempt to engage science superstar Michael Faraday, who politely declined.[58] Legh eventually settled for engaging lesser heavyweights, Angus Smith and Frederick Crace-Calvert,[59] who, in August 1859, reported on

---

[54]   Letter, Beaumont, Urmson and Davies to Sinclair, 28 February 1859, Legh Family Archive.

[55]   Letter, Sinclair to Beaumont, 15 April 1859, Legh Family Archive.

[56]   'Legh v St Helens Canal & Railway Co – Request to draw up the Declaration', undated, Legh Family Archive.

[57]   Letter, John Thomson of Sankey Sugar Works to Beaumont, 15 November 1858, Legh Family Archive.

[58]   Letter, Michael Faraday to Beaumont, 19 May 1859, Legh Family Archive. Michael Faraday (1791–1867) had interests in sewage pollution, having testified before the Select Committee on Metropolis Sewers in 1834, and he later warned of the olfactory and other implications of the sewage pollution of the Thames after a river trip in 1855 (*Times*, 9 July 1855). Lyon Playfair (1818–98), later First Baron Playfair, politician and MP, President of the Chemical Society and part of Faraday's group at the Royal Institution, also declined an invitation to consult.

[59]   Angus Smith (1817–84) was a pioneer in environmental science and head of the inspectorate established under the Alkali Acts, see Hawes, 'The Control of Alkali Pollution in St Helens'; Christopher Hamlin, 'Smith, (Robert) Angus (1817–84)', *Oxford Dictionary of National Biography* (Oxford: Oxford University Press, 2004). Frederick Crace-Calvert (1819–73) was Professor of Chemistry at the Manchester Royal Institution, see J.K. Crellin

the chemical pollutants in the waters of the canal and brook.[60] Reports on the monetary value of the damage inflicted upon the Sankey Brook water meadows of the area were obtained from Rothwell and from Thomas Dobbs in July 1859, and estimated at £2,000.[61]

Settling the Dispute

Legh's legal team also approached the other owners of the neighbouring damaged meadows to ask for authorisation to negotiate on their behalf with the canal company,[62] and a series of meetings with the more cooperative of the other landowners involved were held through 1859 at the Legh Arms Hotel in Newton-le-Willows.[63] The first meeting, in March 1859, unanimously and formally agreed that the canal company be indicted for nuisance, and the second meeting, in June, similarly resolved to support the preparations being made by Legh to further the legal process.[64]

The timetable for the Liverpool Assizes assigned the case to be held in late August 1859, but from the beginning of that month events began to move quickly to a sudden conclusion. It seems that the St Helens Canal Company began to think it a good idea to avoid the full hearing. On 6 August 1859, William Mercer (Legh's land agent) reported to R. Davies (one of Legh's legal representatives) on a meeting held with the St Helens Canal Company's representative, Arthur Sinclair, which included the beginnings of an offer of settlement:

> This afternoon I saw Mr Sinclair who seems much put out of the way at our proceedings against his company. He says they are willing to take the whole of Mr Legh's land at the former rental so as to put him in as good a position as he

---

'Calvert, Frederick Crace- (1819–73)', *Oxford Dictionary of National Biography* (Oxford: Oxford University Press, 2004).

[60] 'Chemical Analysis', 10 August 1859, Legh Family Archive.

[61] 'Report: Legh and the St Helens Canal Company', July 1859, Legh Family Archive.

[62] Rothwell had provided a list of the owners of lands adjoining the Sankey Brook who might have interests in Legh's action. With their relevant acreage they were: William J. Legh, himself (87 acres); Lord Lilford (81 acres); Reverend F.G. Hopwood (56 acres); Executors of Estate of John Bridge (14 acres); Henry Hatton (28 acres); Samuel Brooks (24 acres); J&J Johnson (2 acres); Dr Thomas Gaskell (24 acres); John Shaw Legh (3 acres); John Hanniwell (5 acres); and Joseph Greenough (17 acres). (Untitled note from Rothwell, 18 July 1859, Legh Family Archive.) The Legh Arms still exists at the site in Mill Lane, Newton-le-Willows, but the original Legh Arms Hotel suffered a devastating fire in 1865.

[63] At the 10 March meeting were Hopwood, Gaskell, Greenough, Brooks, Hatton and Mercer (for Legh) ('Minutes', 10 March 1859, Legh Family Archive).

[64] At the 24 June meeting were Mercer, Brooks, Selby, Greenough and William Legh ('Minutes', 24 June 1859, Legh Family Archive).

was in before the dumpings took place by the brook. We must talk this over on Monday next.[65]

When further talks took place between Davies and Mercer and Sinclair on 11 August, the written note of the meeting indicates the canal company began its campaign by taking a tough stance. The company was recorded to have been willing to take, at its former, undamaged, rent, a 50-year or 100-year lease on Legh's damaged meadows but required permission to dump chemical waste on them, though not to increase the nuisance. Finally, the company 'refused to pay a penny in damages' and was not willing to agree to offer a similar deal to the other landowners apart from Legh.[66] Legh's representatives seem to have had little trouble in turning down this first offer.

The Legh Arms Hotel group of landowners met for a third time on the 12 August in the absence of Sinclair from the St Helens Canal Company (who had promised to attend). The minutes lay out the terms the company would have to accept for Legh's advisor, Mercer, to recommend to Legh that the action be withdrawn.[67] The substantive content of these terms included: that Legh's lands be taken on for a lease of twenty-one years, with rent set by Legh's side; the land to be left in a fit state at the end of the term; and £100 to be paid for past damages and £200 for legal costs. The meeting enthusiastically approved these terms as a 'fair' basis for a withdrawal of the suit.

The terms outlined at this meeting proved to be very close to those by which the dispute was finally ended. Although the case was due to begin at Liverpool on the 25 August, a contract over a half-crown stamp was signed on the 24 August 1859 to withdraw the action. It read as follows:

> *Legh v St Helens Canal and Railway Co.* We agree that the record in this action shall be withdrawn on the following terms. That the defendants shall take a lease of the plaintiff's land … damaged by the Sankey Brook and Canal at the best agricultural rental at which it has been let during the last ten years for a term of twenty-one years from the second day of February last. The defendants to covenant to leave the land in good order for agricultural purposes at the end of the lease and to lay no chemical waste upon the land without the plaintiff's consent being first obtained and to do no act thereon which can be considered a public nuisance. The defendants to pay the Plaintiff £100 in satisfaction of all injury sustained by him and to pay £300 for costs. … [Any] matters of difference arising out of this agreement to be settled by a Barrister to be mutually agreed upon.[68]

---

[65]   Letter, William Mercer to R. Davies, 6 August 1859, Legh Family Archive.

[66]   'Notes', 12 August 1859, Legh Family Archive.

[67]   At the 12 August meeting were Hopwood, Gaskell, Mercer, Selby, Hatton and Greenough ('Minutes', 12 August 1859, Legh Family Archive).

[68]   'Legh v St Helens Canal and Railway Co', 24 August 1859, Legh Family Archive.

The settlement is signed by Arthur Sinclair for the St Helens Canal and Railway Company, approved by William Legh, and formally dated and witnessed. The reader will recognise how close these terms are to those outlined by Mercer, except that the final terms include £300 for legal costs rather than the £200 cited earlier.

A final meeting of the Legh Arms Hotel landowners was held on the 29 August 1859.[69] The group unanimously approved the terms by which Legh's action had been ended and considered the arrangement made a fair basis for settling their own individual but still outstanding claims against the company. The meeting agreed that no further legal action would be taken by the group so long as satisfactory settlements were made between individual members and the company and that they would contribute *pro rata* (in proportion to the extent of land ownership) to Legh's legal costs as incurred already. In a letter of the 29 August, Lord Lilford, owner of the second largest spread of meadowland involved, but who had kept aloof from the Legh Arms group, indicated his reluctant acceptance of the existing terms agreed.[70] Despite one or two moans about the agreed settlement from other owners, there exist no records of more court actions for nuisance taken against the St Helens Canal and Railway Company for polluting the Sankey Brook following this date. Therefore, it is probable, though not certain, that individual landowners within and without the Legh Arms Hotel group were able to make satisfactory arrangements with the company to settle their own individual cases.

Concluding Remarks

Despite it being a dispute where it is less clear where the socially efficient outcome lies, the process and context of the dispute between Legh and the St Helens Canal and Railway Company in 1859, in its quite straightforward and somewhat unexceptional way, nevertheless shows some useful features and provides some valuable lessons. Above all, it is an example where a negotiated settlement did result and the settlement emerged at a point prior to any formal hearing at the Liverpool Assizes, which in consequence did not take place. This case study, therefore, is a rare example illustrating the possible selectivity bias that affects arguments about evidence relating to the relevance of negotiated settlements and the Coase theorem. In this instance, it is only thanks to a fortuitous survival after a century and a half of quite full records from one side of the dispute, that enables any examination at all of the subject, content and outcome of the dispute.

It should also be noted that Legh was not the only disputant in this action, though he was demonstrably the most active. It is often argued that the existence of numerous parties to a nuisance, through opening the process to free-riding and holding-out among the group, makes negotiation and settlement more costly and difficult, and, therefore, less likely. Problems along such lines seem to have been

---

[69] 'Minutes', 29 August 1859, Legh Family Archive. At the meeting were Hopwood, Gaskell, Mercer, Suttle (for Brooks), Hatton and Greenough.

[70] 'Letter', 31 August 1859, Legh Family Archive.

of little relevance here and it may, to the contrary, have been that the threat of a series of further individual actions in fact spurred the canal company to an early out-of-court settlement. Importantly, the context of the dispute illustrates that even where there exists a number of victims, it is still possible for a negotiated settlement to occur: Legh's individual negotiations became the norm for the rest of the group, with Legh asking merely for a contribution to his costs, making him, perhaps, classifiable as a charitable political entrepreneur.

Those concerned with the debate over the effectiveness of the civil law of nuisance in the protection of the environment might also note that the final agreement signed by Legh contains no clause requiring any abatement or reduction in the defendant's actions that might in the future reduce their pollution-producing activities along the Sankey valley. When the disputants agreed to a mutual settlement, the legal nuisance ended: the physical nuisance did not.

Lessons from Harrogate and the St Helens Canal

The two disputes, at Harrogate and with the St Helens Canal and Railway Company, settled by negotiation and monetary side-payments, serve, therefore, as illustrative examples of a further means by which nuisance disputes like those of the river sewage dilemma can end.

It may be that disputes that result in formal courtroom hearings have earlier passed through episodes where offers of negotiated solutions have arisen, but for any of a number of possible reasons, failed: Birmingham's dispute with Adderley, it will be recalled from Chapter 5 above, contains such an instance. One of the case studies of the chapter to follow similarly concerns a situation which, while seemingly ripe for a simple negotiated settlement to enable the ending of the dispute, was, rather, ended by a further possible means by which nuisance disputes may be terminated: diverting the polluting effluents away from the complainant is the subject of the following chapter.

Chapter 9

The Tactic of Diversion: Northampton and the Brinsop Hall Coal Company

Because of the special nature of water pollution in rivers, one possible strategy that may be followed by polluters to offset or abate any legal nuisance is simply to divert polluting materials through other channels so the complainants are no longer affected. This provided a tempting solution for a number of the defendants among the towns involved in sewage pollution cases, though in no case is there evidence that Chancery explicitly encouraged such solutions. But Chancery will only notice complaints and petitions brought to its attention by plaintiffs, so a diversion of polluting materials away from the complainant can satisfy legal demands and orders but yet do nothing for the general environment. We can, then, see *legal* abatement of the nuisance while the *physical* pollution continues unaffected, elsewhere.

To illustrate the tactic of diversion as a response to river pollution suits, the two case studies covered in detail here include, as defendants, both a town sanitary authority and a private enterprise. The town authority is that of Northampton, which was sued for nuisance and found liable for the sewage pollution of the River Nene. Under the threat from Chancery, instigated by complaints from millers along the river, Northampton *three times* diverted its polluting material to satisfy and placate these complainants. The problem with diversion as a tactic is that each time it is exercised, the effluent is brought closer to new potential complainants at points further downstream and this consequence is evident for the events along the Nene. The second case concerns a private nuisance river pollution case involving two commercial enterprises at Hindley, near Wigan, Lancashire, where a textile mill entrepreneur sued a colliery company over the colliery's pollution of the mill's water supply. Here the polluting material from the pit was also diverted to satisfy the complainant, but not to re-enter the same stream further downstream, but into an entirely separate watercourse.

The temptation to use the tactic of diverting polluting effluents past or away from complaining parties was by no means confined to the two examples examined in this chapter. In cases already examined, for Birmingham and Harrogate, the sanitary authorities prepared plans that would have carried their (treated) sewage outflows by pipeline to empty into the streams further downstream of the complainant's property. Similarly, a further example concerns the situation at Halifax, Yorkshire, at the end of the 1860s. Following the partial development of Halifax's sewer network, and in the absence of any treatment of the existing effluent, the town's Hebble Brook became increasingly disgusting.

The Holdsworth brothers, as relators behind the name of the Attorney-General, sought an action at Chancery, in July 1869, for public nuisance against Halifax Corporation.[1] The Holdsworths (one of whom had twice been Halifax's mayor) were owners of Shaw Lodge Mills, a substantial textile mill on the brook, close to the existing sewage outlet. The Corporation was found liable for the nuisance and then faced an injunction, from 1 June 1870, restraining their sewage outfall into the brook.[2] The town reacted with a two-step abatement scheme. Firstly, the Goux privy-pan system was introduced to serve the as-yet unsewered parts of the town. Secondly, for the existing effluent using the sewers, the town laid an iron pipeline along the bed of the Hebble to carry the sewage flows from its existing outfall two miles further down the Hebble before discharging into the stream, still untreated, at Salterhebble.[3] This diverted the offending sewage away from both the Holdsworths and other potential complainants in Halifax town to abate the legal nuisance involved. But the Hebble is a tributary of the River Aire, whose physical pollution problems, as seen, for example, at Leeds, would have been little abated by the diversion strategy followed by the Halifax authorities.

The pollution of the River Nene below Northampton, and the Borsdane Brook as it flowed into Hindley, provide illuminating examples of the use of the tactic of diversion in face of liability for nuisance caused in rivers.

Northampton: Harrold v Markham (1869) and Monk v Northampton (1872)

The sewage pollution of the River Nene by the sanitary authorities of the historic town of Northampton had led to a barrage of complaints over decades before the case of Harrold v Markham (1869), and the formal legal history of the dispute continued for a lengthy period after 1869. The episode includes a further example of Chancery issuing a sequestration order on the town authorities with no sequestration in fact ever occurring, and there was a second, subsequent, separate and successful injunction application to Chancery by another complainant over the same nuisance, in Monk v Northampton Improvement Commissioners (1872). However, in its historical context, the dispute over the pollution of the Nene is most distinguished in being a prime example of the multiple use of sewage *diversion* as a tactic for tackling the river sewage dilemma. Northampton managed, on three separate occasions, to divert its sewage outfall beyond the proximity (and noses) of a sequence of complainants.

---

1   Court of Chancery Records: Pleadings, C16/543/A48.

2   *Halifax Courier*, 10 July 1869.

3   Local Government Board, *Sewage Disposal Report*, 53–6.

Background to the Dispute

Northampton is the county town of Northamptonshire, and has been for centuries the preeminent centre for the trade and manufacture of boots and shoes in Britain.[4] The town lies on a bend just to the north and east of the River Nene, which itself flows east, eventually to empty into The Wash and the North Sea.[5] The oldest part of the town was built on a hill, which rises about one hundred feet above the valley floor. The small but sharp rise allows the town to avoid flooding from the river, which can spill onto the water meadows of the Cow Meadow, Midsummer Meadow and Calvesholme that lie to the south, along the river's otherwise flat flood plain. This topography played some part in the sanitary development of the town. For the governance of the town,[6] for the period of concern here, local authority was split between the Northampton Board of Improvement Commissioners, responsible for the important infrastructure, including roads, drains and sewers, and the Northampton Town Council, responsible for law and order and for collecting the local rates, including the levy that funded the Improvement Commissioners' activities.[7] The town council gradually accumulated additional powers and finally took over the duties of the Improvement Commissioners when the latter disbanded itself in 1875. But when the pollution disputes occurred in Northampton, around 1870, there existed both a town council and a Board of Improvement Commissioners and it was the Board that was the defendant at Chancery.[8]

At Northampton, as elsewhere, the ditches and gutters provided to drain the public highways of the town gradually attracted household and industrial effluvia as well as run-off from the streets, so the Improvement Commissioners found themselves having to provide and develop a more formal system of covered drains and sewers. Given the geography of the location, the content of the merged systems flowed into the brooks and ditches that drained the water meadows of Cow Meadow and Midsummer Meadow and emptied into the River Nene

---

[4]   The old but weak joke had it that: 'This town stands on other men's legs' ('The Borough of Northampton' in *Victoria History of the County of Northampton*, (ed.) William Page, (Northampton: Northampton Borough Reprint, 1998): 29).

[5]   The river's name varies between Nene, Nen and Nenn; and is variously pronounced locally, 'nen' and 'neen'.

[6]   Cynthia Brown, *Northampton, 1835–1985: Shoe Town, New Town* (Chichester: Phillimore & Co, 1990), 42–3.

[7]   The powers of the Improvement Commission derived from the Northampton Improvement Act of 1843. There were forty-eight commissioners, with a quarter of the board turning over annually, chosen by an electorate restricted to the higher-rated of the local resident ratepayers. Northampton Town Council with mayor, six aldermen and eighteen elected councillors, dates from 1835.

[8]   Northampton became a county borough with the features expected of English local government in 1888.

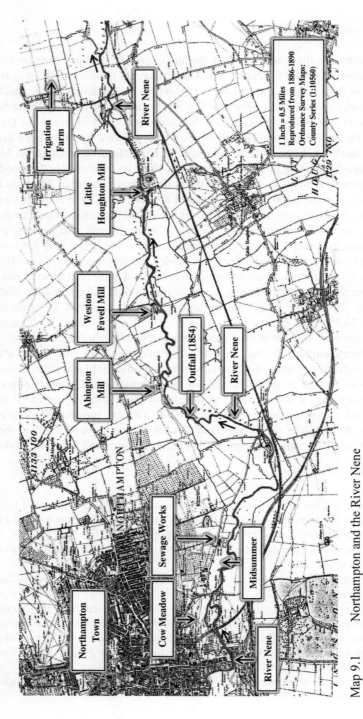

Map 9.1   Northampton and the River Nene

Irrigation Farm

River Nene

Little Houghton Mill

1 Inch = 0.5 Miles
Reproduced from 1886-1890
Ordnance Survey Maps:
County Series (1:10560)

Weston Favell Mill

Abington Mill

Outfall (1854)

River Nene

NORTHAMPTON

Sewage Works

Cow Meadow

Northampton Town

Midsummer

River Nene

along the low-lying flood plain to the south of the town.[9] By 1850, the growth of the town and the innovations of domestic WCs were developing serious sewage nuisances along the flood plain and in the river, and complaints to the Improvement Commissioners reporting the rising levels of unpleasantness were accumulating.[10] But improvements to the drainage over the southern meadows proceeded only slowly and consisted mostly of taking this sewage outfall further away from the town. In 1854, much of the sewage of the town was being directed, untreated in any way, via both culverts and open ditches, through the Cow and Midsummer Meadows and the Abington Brook, and into the Nene just ahead of the Abington Mill.

Northampton Sewage and Sewage Works, 1854–68

Abington Mill on the Nene was owned by Lord Overstone.[11] Overstone, a banker, was one of the wealthiest men in Britain, holding extensive landed estates to the east of Northampton and with a reputation as a leading economist of his day.[12] But the tenant and miller at Abington Mill was Thomas Merry who, together with his family, are recorded in both the 1861 and 1871 censuses. Merry, the miller, along with Overstone's land agents, had been active at this time in directing complaints

---

[9]   Northampton's Cow Meadow is cited as far back as the twelfth century, in connection with a meeting between Henry II and Thomas a Becket. It has provided open common and parkland for the town since the early 1600s: the earliest recorded cricket match in Northamptonshire was played there in 1741 and in the mid-nineteenth century the area became a municipal park. Sadly, in 1935 Cow Meadow lost its historic name and was prosaically renamed Becket's Park.

[10]   *Northampton Mercury* reported: 'noisome malaria' and 'pestilential vapours' of the water meadows (19 February 1848); the 'filthy ditches' of Cow Meadow (12 November 1850); the 'foul' state of the Nene (22 November 1851); the Cow Meadow area 'disgusting' and 'extremely prejudicial to the health of the town' (23 February 1850); 'if the nuisance were not immediately remedied, pestilence and death would ensue' (31 July 1852); 'nuisance at the outlet of the sewer ... was assuming a very formidable shape' (8 April 1854); and for the Nene 'the stench from dead cats and dogs festering in the sun, decomposing vegetables and sewage matter was such as to be dangerous to all inhabitants' (10 June 1854).

[11]   Samuel Jones Loyd (1796–1883) became Lord Overstone in 1850 after serving as MP for Hythe. He had inherited from his father a large fortune and Overstone Park, near Northampton, as well as the running of the family bank, which eventually comprised the core of the current Royal Bank of Scotland. In 1876, Overstone's estate was of over 30,000 acres (Bateman, *The Great Landowners of Great Britain and Ireland*; Michael Reed, 'Loyd, Samuel Jones, Baron Overstone (1796–1883)', *Oxford Dictionary of National Biography*, (Oxford University Press, 2004).

[12]   Walter Eltis, *Lord Overstone and the Establishment of British Nineteenth-Century Monetary Orthodoxy* (Oxford: University of Oxford Discussion Papers in Economic and Social History, No. 42, 2001).

to the Improvement Commissioners about the state of the Nene, and had threatened legal action for nuisance.

The Improvement Commissioners had reacted to the many complaints about the state of the Nene by developing a sanitary plan for the town in 1854 which included intercepting sewers running south of the town to collect the sewage and carry it across the water meadows to a small sewage works to be constructed to the east of Midsummer.[13] This first sewage works would be minimal, with just two filtering tanks, operating alternately, and using charcoal to filter out the solid matter to be sold for manure, with the remaining wastewater flowing on into the Nene. The running of the sewage works was entrusted to a leaseholder but after operations began, serious problems emerged: commercial profit proved elusive and the simple filtering treatment system installed was never able to cope with the ever-increasing volume of sewage. Complaints continued.[14] In July 1858, John Hyde Pidcock,[15] newly appointed as the town surveyor, presented a damning report on the sanitation of the town which warned: 'the prospect, then, at present before you is that of an inadequate supply of water, wells contaminated, sewers choked up and noxious effluvia your habitual atmosphere' and, reviewing Northampton's 'frightful' death rate concluded with: 'it is the water ... which is killing you'.[16] Pidcock's advice was to take on the public ownership of the local water company to assure water supply quality, phase out the wells, middens and cesspits and institute full sewer coverage and a water carriage and WC system for the town.

Complaints about inadequate sewage treatment continued.[17] In December 1859, Pidcock recommended a new sewage works setup, based on four (later six) tanks arranged in parallel, with lime and chlorate of iron to be added to aid settling and deodorising and this restructuring was finally in place and operating at the end of 1861. Every two-to-three weeks, as the depositing tanks became filled, the solid matter was dug out, run into pits at the site, mixed with the scavenged ashes of the town, dried and, when manageable, sold on to farmers. For its time, and subject to the usual penny-pinching by the Board, this £6,000-worth of improvements was just about state-of-the-art, though, as we know, likely to provide an ineffective treatment. All the while, and despite Surveyor Pidcock's rash promise that the

---

[13]   *Northampton Mercury*, 10 June 1854. The sewage works later became known as the Houghton Road Sewage Works: somewhat less lyrical than had 'East of Midsummer Works' become its name.

[14]   *Northampton Mercury*, 6 September 1856, 8 May 1858.

[15]   Pidcock (1819–85) remained an energetic town surveyor to successive Northampton civic authorities for thirty-five years. When he finally retired, aged sixty-six, in 1884, the town neglected to pay him the pension that had been promised: he died the following year.

[16]   *Northampton Mercury*, 24 July 1856.

[17]   The *Northampton Mercury* recorded the works described as an 'intolerable nuisance' (4 September 1858); 'dilapidated; in fact they were not working at all' (4 June 1859); 'perfectly useless' (9 July 1859); and reported Overstone threatening that 'unless the sewage nuisance was abated legal proceedings would be instituted' (8 October 1859).

outflow from the renovated works would be clean enough to drink, the complaints failed to cease.[18] Especially influential was a new legal threat in July 1862, from Lord Overstone's solicitor, who was instructed:

> ... to take immediate proceedings against the Commissioners ... to recover damages for an injury done to his lordship's land by reason of their having constructed their sewer so that the sewage and filth flowing from the town of Northampton, or some portion thereof, passes through a stream or watercourse which runs through lands of his lordship near the town and thereby poisons the water so as to render it wholly unfit for the cattle ...[19]

In response, the Board sought expert opinion and outside consultants were called in to appraise the situation, but they found little wrong with the setup.[20] Through the middle years of the 1860s, the ditches through the water meadows were cleaned and covered and new machinery and more tanks were installed at the sewage works.[21] These moves may have placated Lord Overstone's legal threat but were not enough to still other complaints.[22]

Northampton's first overt use of the tactic of diversion of its sewage outflow beyond a complainant occurs at this time. It had been on the Board's agenda for a while to end the problems with Overstone's miller, Thomas Merry, by taking the sewage outfall by pipe beyond Merry's Abington Mill to empty the sewage wastewater into the Nene further downstream.[23] If the sewer outfall emptied into the outlet of the Abington Mill, where the river speeded up beyond the mill's weir and mill race, there would be a bigger drop for the drains carrying off the flow from the sewage works, and this would keep the culverts clearer and move the effluent more quickly into the river. This would be combined with more improvements, scheduled for 1866, both at the sewage works and with the ditches and culverts running through the water meadows. And, of course, diverting the sewage would remove the source of the complaints and legal threats coming from Merry and his landlord, Overstone. The major problem with the plan was that moving the sewage outflow point further downstream beyond Abington Mill moved it that much closer to the next mill on the river, Weston Favell Mill.

Only expensive new investment in a sewage farm irrigation scheme could have helped Northampton along the Nene at this time. Frankland and the Rivers

---

18 *Northampton Mercury*, 4 May, 10 August, 9 November 1861.
19 *Northampton Mercury*, 9 August 1862.
20 *Northampton Mercury*, 8 November, 22 November 1862.
21 *Northampton Mercury*, 8 April, 22 April 1865.
22 *Northampton Mercury*, 4 April, 5 December 1863. The residents of Billings Road protested about 'vast accumulations of filth' at the works (*Northampton Mercury*, 5 March 1864) and Dr Hunter of the Privy Council reported 'nuisances dangerous to health' (Medical Officer of the Privy Council, *Seventh Report*, No. 3484, 1865, 526–8).
23 *Northampton Mercury*, 8 October, 5 November 1864.

Pollution Prevention Commission of 1868 visited in May 1868 and looked askance at Northampton's setup. They found the outflow liquid apparently clear and innocuous but, after analysis, discovered the presence of 'large amounts of putrescible organic material', with putrefaction only being delayed by the chemicals. Their opinion on the chemical and filtration treatment being applied at Northampton was blunt: 'we consider this as nearly useless.'[24]

Harrold v Markham (1869)

The first complaints to the Improvement Board from Weston Favell Mill came in July 1865, when the mill's then owner and miller, George Spokes,[25] complained of 'pestilential vapours': the board replied that the situation would be transformed with the new improvements to the sewage works, which were, as described above, scheduled for 1866.[26] But, in June 1867, George Spokes died and the mill was sold. The new owner was Richard Harrold, who paid £2,350 for the property. Harrold was an experienced and capable miller in the trade and he proved to be much less tolerant of the nuisances and rather more impatient with the Improvement Commissioners than Overstone's estate had been.[27]

After 1867, with the new sewage outfall pipe into the Nene now placed behind Merry's Abington Mill, the outflow point was now within about 800 yards of Harrold's recently purchased Weston Favell Mill. Harrold began to apply, repeatedly, to the Northampton Commissioners for relief from the effects of the sewage being issued into the Nene, sending letters to Pidcock, the surveyor, in August 1867 and to the Board directly in September 1867 and July 1868 to which he received no reply.[28] In August 1868, after Harrold complained again to the commissioners and threatened to file for an injunction, a delegation from the board visited his mill but reported back that the river was not too bad, this in spite of observing there were

---

[24]   Royal Commission on Rivers Pollution Prevention of 1868, *First Report*, 1870, C 37, 58.

[25]   George Spokes (1829–67) was born in Weston Favell and is recorded as miller and farmer at Weston Favell Mill in the 1851 and 1861 censuses. It has not been possible to establish any connection to the Spokes family of Twyford Mill on the Cherwell, the complainants in Banbury's sewage pollution dispute.

[26]   *Northampton Mercury*, 8 July 1865, 9 September 1865.

[27]   In the 1851 census, Richard Harrold (1825–1906) is a miller at Oxford. By 1861 Harrold had become the manager of the New Union Mill Company in Birmingham, at a time when 10,000 loaves per week were being distributed by the Board of Guardians to the poor of the town and the Union Mill was a major supplier. During this time the *Birmingham Daily Post* (6 March 1862) carried a vehement denial from Harrold over a rumour that 'inferior' flour was being supplied to the local workhouses.

[28]   Northampton Improvement Commissioners Minutes, Book II (1865–71) 14/9, 2 September 1867, Northampton Improvement Board Archive, Northampton Record Office; *Northampton Mercury*, 29 July 1868.

numbers of dead fish to be seen there.[29] Another commissioner, refusing, as he said, to tell untruths about the nuisance, admitted there was 'no question that the sewage did affect Harrold's mill and the Commissioners would have a bill filed against them and would not have a leg to stand on.'[30]

Harrold's response was an ultimatum from his solicitor, W.S. Adams, dated 11 August 1868:

> Gentlemen, Mr Harrold of Weston Favell Mill, Northampton, has consulted with me on the subject of the sewage of your town being discharged into the river close to the above mill which causes a nuisance to him and his family and an injury to his property. He states that he addressed complaints to you ... to which complaints no reply or attempts to remedy the evil has been adopted by the proper authorities... Unless before the 20th August [they] undertake to remove the nuisance, in writing, my client will file a bill in Chancery and seek relief to have the nuisance removed...[31]

Markham, the clerk to the Northampton Improvement Board, replied, denying the existence of any nuisance caused by their actions and, indeed, asserted the Board had adopted every means to prevent such nuisances. Adams responded that this reply was:

> ... by no means satisfactory to my client ... The fish, as you must be aware, have been destroyed, as reported in your local papers, and my client and his family and workmen have suffered from this nuisance in health and are likely to do so again. [Without reassurances] my client will seek without further delay relief in Chancery.[32]

A bill of complaint was duly filed by Harrold in Chancery against the Board on 30 September 1868 with the defendant formally named as Arthur Bayley Markham, clerk and solicitor of the Board. The Board responded with questionable declarations that the water at the outfall was nonetheless 'fit to drink.'[33]

The suit of Harrold v Markham opened before Vice-Chancellor Sir William Milbourne James at Chancery on 16 July 1869.[34] Harrold asked for restraint on Northampton's sewage outfall causing pollution to the river and injury to his

---

29   *Northampton Mercury*, 8 August 1868.
30   Ibid.
31   *Northampton Mercury*, 5 September 1868.
32   Ibid.
33   Northampton Improvement Commissioners Minutes, 4 November 1868.
34   Sir William Milbourne James (1807–81) had only been appointed to the Court of Chancery in January 1869 and he became Lord Justice of Appeal in Chancery on 2 July 1870.

property, and for damages for past injury.[35] Harrold's case contended that at his Weston Favell Mill, the River Nene was:

> ... foul and contaminated and the filthy, unwholesome and offensive state of the river was constantly increased by reason of the acts of the commissioners [and Harrold was] injured and damnified in his business as a miller and he and his family and workmen ... suffered great and incessant discomfort therefrom.[36]

Twenty-three affidavits were presented to back up these claims, testifying to offensive and unendurable stench, filthy and feculent scum on the river, hundreds of dying fish, and sickness caused to Harrold's customers and workers. Thomas Merry contributed the story of his mill's part in the history and his view that one George Moss had actually died from the effects of the sewage nuisance. Expert witness William Odling reported he had examined the Nene in September 1868 and found a disturbing stench, black bubbling decomposing mud, dead fish, black weeds and the smell of stale sewage.[37] If not yet putrid, he submitted, the outfall water was putrescible and certainly capable of causing nuisance and ill-health to the Harrolds. His chemical analysis of the Nene, he said, showed good clear water upstream of the sewage outfall at Abington Mill, but downstream of there, and at Weston Favell Mill, there was a large increase in organic matter and the river was 'merely diluted sewage.'[38]

Northampton's defence was that the waters of the Nene had not been pure and wholesome for twenty years and that, despite the increasing population of the town, they had improved the sewage situation by installing, they claimed, 'the best and most sensibly conducted works in the country.' Anyway, they argued, their prescriptive and statutory rights allowed them to drain sewage into the river: 'but not to create a nuisance', interjected Vice-Chancellor James.[39] The admittedly 'offensive, foul and foetid' smell and condition of the river in 1867 was primarily due, continued the defence case, not to domestic sewage but to the tanning and dyeing industry in the town and the low rainfall and dry summer just experienced. It was purely temporary. Evidence also came from Pidcock and Northampton's eminent consulting engineers, Thomas Hawksley and Sir Charles Fox,[40] who

---

[35]   Court of Chancery Records: Pleadings, C16/501/H208.

[36]   *Northampton Mercury*, 24 July 1869.

[37]   William Odling (1829–1921) had both medical and chemistry qualifications and succeeded Michael Faraday as Fullerian Professor of Chemistry at the Royal Institution in 1868.

[38]   *Northampton Mercury*, 24 July 1869.

[39]   Ibid.

[40]   Sir Charles Fox (1810–74) was among the first rank of British civil engineers of the Victorian era (the 'cast-iron man'). Fox had earlier helped construct and drive one of the Rainhill Trial railway engines and collaborated with Joseph Paxton in designing the Crystal Palace for the 1851 Great Exhibition, for which he was knighted. Fox was a friend

maintained that on the occasions of their separate, but recent, visits to the scene, there had been no evidence of gross sewage pollution. Hawksley said that he had not perceived any sewage matter nor discoloration nor any consequence of sewage contamination at the mill, and that he knew of 'only one other sewage works as perfect as these works in the town of Northampton … I may describe the works and the operation carried on therein as excellent'. Fox, too, was sure that the water delivered out of the works could not be the cause of any complaint by Harrold, with no offensive smell found in river, works or culvert and with the works excellent, well-established and appropriate.[41]

The deeply conflicting testimony presented by the two sides proved puzzling to the court, and Vice-Chancellor James dutifully ascribed this to the different times and dates to which the evidence was obtained and to the coming on-line of improvements at the works. His view was that there was no reason to disbelieve the affidavits of Hawksley and Fox for the defence, so it must be that no practical nuisance could have been existing currently at the sewage outfall. Nevertheless James was satisfied that the plaintiff had suffered a very substantial nuisance from the foul sewage pollution in the past:

> No doubt that was occasioned by the peculiar state of the summer – very hot and dry – when the Nene, like most of the streams of the country, had shrunk to very small dimensions. But that did not justify the defendants in committing a nuisance … [42]

Hence, despite his sympathy for Northampton's case, in order to protect Harrold and his property from similar problems in the future, Vice-Chancellor James decided that Harrold was entitled to have a decree to restrain Northampton from 'turning water into the river in such a manner as to cause a nuisance or an injury to the plaintiff'. One aspect of Vice-Chancellor James's decree caused, it is clear, some confusion. The wording of the order that James suggested allowed that any temporary or accidental discharges from the sewage works, resulting perhaps from the continuing alterations at the sewage works, to be construed as a violation, opening the way for Harrold to immediately return to Chancery for a sequestration order. So Northampton's counsel asked James for protection from this possibility, and James responded that he would not grant a sequestration under those circumstances and, further, that he would not consider the absence of any alterations of the sewage works as a breach of his injunction which he added into his order: 'so as not to compel them [Northampton] to make any alteration to the existing works until the 1st of June next'.

---

of John Pidcock, whose career had begun within Fox's company. (Robert Thorne, 'Fox, Sir Charles (1810–1874)', *Oxford Dictionary of National Biography* (Oxford: Oxford University Press, 2004).)

[41]   *Northampton Mercury*, 24 July 1869.

[42]   Ibid.

Although James sympathised with Northampton's situation and complimented them on conscientious efforts at the sewage works, even the most favourable reading of the formal order, as it was issued, cannot be interpreted as much of a victory for the Improvement Commissioners.[43] Chancery's order did not stop Northampton from continuing to outfall its sewage effluent into the Nene (which Harrold had not, in fact, asked for), but it did require an end to the nuisance being caused. Indeed, the order reads like a straightforward nuisance injunction allowing twelve months leave for the necessary alterations to be made: in effect, a contingent injunction. This, it transpired, is exactly the way that the Court of Chancery did indeed later interpret the order. But, back in Northampton, the outcome of the 1869 hearing was widely interpreted as a triumph for the town. The leader in the *Northampton Mercury* mistakenly gloated that Harrold had neither successfully won his case, nor had been awarded an injunction[44] and the next meeting of the Improvement Commissioners crowed that no damages had been awarded Harrold and that they had gained a 'favourable position': 'Mr Harrold's case had failed ... now he could not move for a twelve-month ...'[45] Fatally, the Board complacently decided that 'They might safely leave themselves in the hands of Vice Chancellor James.'

Harrold v Markham (1870)

It did not take long for the warming weather of the summer of 1869 to heighten the effects of the outfall effluent from the Northampton sewage works enough to renew the complaints about the state of the river. Harrold's solicitors maintained that the nuisance was becoming worse than ever and, for the very day of the earlier hearing at Chancery, Joseph Campion, a local farmer, while carrying hay near Harrold's mill, reported that 'the nuisance was then abominable.'[46] The commissioners again visited the mills of both Harrold and Merry, but again found not a sign of any problem to engage them: and one commissioner rather uncharitably contributed to the 'balance of convenience' debate with: 'is it not better that one family should suffer a nuisance if it could not be avoided than that half Northampton should be poisoned.'[47]

---

43   The critical part of the order reads: 'That an injunction be awarded perpetually to restrain the Northampton Improvement Commissioners, their servants, agents and workmen, from causing or permitting the drain and sewers situate within their limits to discharge into the River Nene any sewage or sewage matter or foul water so as to cause a nuisance or injury to the plaintiff. But the injunction is not to operate so as to compel the said Commissioners to make any alteration or addition to their Sewage Works before the 1st June 1870.' Northampton Improvement Commissioners Minutes, 24 July 1869.

44   *Northampton Mercury*, 24 July 1869.

45   *Northampton Mercury*, 7 August 1869.

46   *Northampton Mercury*, 4 September 1869.

47   Ibid.

Later, at the end of 1869, realising practical strategies had to be considered, the Improvement Commissioners prepared a list of the possible alternative courses they might take, including simply bowing to any new complaint from Harrold at Chancery and relying on subsequent advice from Chancery-appointed experts to determine an appropriate engineering process.[48] At the least, this shows that Chancery was being viewed not only as a source of judicial decisions, but also as a source of guidance for on-going technical matters: in short, as providing an overseeing role. In the event, more by default than decision and hampered by the absence of funds and legal authority to do much other than let events take their course, the twelve-month period of grace passed with little-to-nothing achieved. Northampton did engage consultants Hawksley and Letheby to advise on improvements to the existing sewage works, but the pair failed to even appear at Northampton before April 1870.[49] Their report was only received in May 1870, much too late for anything to be achieved before the expiration of the twelve-month period of grace.[50] In June 1870, the Board learned that Richard Harrold was going back to Chancery.

On 14 July and 21 July 1870, Harrold's nuisance case against the Northampton Improvement Commissioners was renewed at the Court of Chancery. Harrold now asked for a sequestration of Northampton's Improvement rates and a forfeit of £5,000 for disobeying the injunction of July 1869. The judge this time was Vice-Chancellor Bacon, who had succeeded Vice-Chancellor James after James's appointment as Lord Justice of Appeal just a week earlier.

The hearing on 14 July turned out to be a quick and quite straightforward affair as regards the substantive issues.[51] The case for the plaintiff was simply that Northampton had had little short of a year to put their works in order: as testified by affidavits from a number of sources, and admitted even by the Board and their agents, the nuisance at Weston Favell Mill had, if anything, increased. At the sewage works, the Board had failed to do a thing: their consultants, Hawksley and Letheby, could only now, belatedly, suggest a regime of more chemicals to enhance the failed system of chemical deodorisation (which would itself need another six months grace). Harrold's counsel pleaded that his client needed protection: 'we want a sequestration because the injunction has proved absolutely inoperative … [the defendants] had no intention of doing anything to comply with the order.'[52] Vice-Chancellor Bacon agreed that the 'evidence is uncontradicted'.

---

[48]   Northampton Improvement Commissioners Minutes, 25 October 1869.

[49]   Henry Letheby (1816–76) was an analytical chemist. He and Hawksley collaborated in consultation for other sewage disputes, for example at Banbury: their usual recommendation was ever-heavier chemical applications. (Christopher Hamlin, 'Letheby, Henry (1816–1876)', *Oxford Dictionary of National Biography* (Oxford: Oxford University Press, 2004).)

[50]   Northampton Improvement Commissioners Minutes, 2 May 1870.

[51]   *Northampton Mercury*, 16 July 1870.

[52]   Ibid.

Given Harrold had, according to Vice-Chancellor Bacon, proved his case fully and that wilful violation had ensued, Harrold's application for sequestration orders and forfeitures might be expected, perhaps, simply to proceed. But this did not happen. Bacon said he thought:

> ... sequestration is a very rude and clumsy kind of machinery ... very unsatisfactory ... we want to see the Commissioners acting as upright, honest and earnest men, desirous of doing what they can to remedy a great injury they have done another. [53]

The Vice-Chancellor then adjourned the hearing for a week. If Bacon was hoping that some privately negotiated settlement or contractual agreement on an engineering solution might emerge between the two parties, he was to be disappointed. The hearing resumed as arranged on 21 July 1870 and mostly heard the arguments of the earlier session again. Vice-Chancellor Bacon again condemned Northampton, citing:

> ... clear and uncontradicted evidence that the injunction had been broken ... they seemed to have thought they were masters of the situation and that the injunction was a dead letter to them till it was convenient to them to comply with it.[54]

One new contribution offered by Northampton, and in the nick of time, was the tentative possibility of a sewage farm to be established on some specific land down the Nene: but this plan had not yet even gone before the Board of Improvement Commissioners and would require a substantial extension of time. Vice-Chancellor Bacon responded by saying that he could do no other than formally grant an order of sequestration, but, giving the defendants credit for sincerity and noting the plaintiff was willing to grant more time, an extension of time could be found and delivered.[55] Hence, Bacon asked the plaintiff to delay any enforcement of the sequestration order and the £5,000 forfeiture until after 1 November 1870.[56] This gave Northampton another four months to produce a viable scheme. Chancery's role as facilitator and manager, steering and cajoling Northampton into enhancing and improving its treatment regime seems clear.

---

[53]   Ibid.

[54]   *Northampton Mercury*, 23 July 1870.

[55]   Harrold's attitude was accommodating: 'If the Commissioners did right and showed an earnest desire to remedy the evil complained of, reasonable time would be given' (ibid).

[56]   Other local authorities again heard confused and over-exaggerated tales of the events. Birmingham was later told that, for Northampton, sequestration was made of the 'income of the Corporation and it was only by a representation that the peace of the town was endangered that a sufficient sum of money was allowed to pay the police' (*Birmingham Daily Post*, 2 August 1871).

This time, at last, Northampton moved quickly. The next meeting of the commissioners, in August 1870, made several decisions for both the short-run and long-run, recognising that serious plans for the Nene, acceptable to Chancery, were required of them.[57] For the long-run, it was decided the only viable possibility was a sewage farm along the Nene valley to provide comprehensive irrigation treatment. For this, a parliamentary act would be needed to authorise the acquisition of the funds and compulsory purchase powers. An area just surveyed, in Ecton and Great Billing, mostly land from Ambrose Isted's estate, they determined, would provide a suitable site.[58] Surveyor Pidcock quickly produced plans for the sewage farm.[59]

More immediately, for the short-run, a meeting with Harrold gave reassurance to the commissioners that he was a 'man of sense' who would not enforce the sequestration were he sure the commissioners were in earnest. But to put a permanent end to the source of his complaint, a new diversion of the sewage effluent was put into effect. This would be done by extending the existing main sewer to outfall into the Nene further downstream, beyond Harrold's Weston Favell Mill. As soon as October 1870, three landowners along the route of the extended main had given consent for the conveyance through their land of the sewage in underground pipes, reasonable compensation had been agreed and the surveyor had begun the sewer extension work. Richard Harrold was informed the Commissioners hoped his trouble with sewage water was now terminated.[60] This constitutes the second use by Northampton of deliberate and considered *diversion* of the sewage effluent beyond the complainant.

The effluent outflow, however, now entered the Nene just ahead of Little Houghton Mill. Northampton's dispute with Harrold was firmly resolved by the diversion of the sewage outfall beyond his mill, but this brought the outfall that much closer to the next mill on the River Nene at Little Houghton, where resided Samuel Monk, another owner-miller.[61]

---

[57]   Northampton Improvement Commissioners Minutes, 3 August 1870; *Northampton Mercury*, 6 August 1870.

[58]   *Northampton Mercury*, 10 September 1870. Ambrose Isted (1797–1881) of Ecton Hall, Ecton, is described in the census rather bluntly as 'deaf and dumb from birth', but the Isted family was long-established there. Some church-owned property was also to be purchased.

[59]   'Plans and Sections of proposed outfall and irrigation works', 1871, Northampton Improvement Board Archive, Northampton Record Office, QS 122.

[60]   Northampton Improvement Commissioners Minutes, 12 September 1870; *Northampton Mercury*, 8 October 1870.

[61]   Samuel Monk (1833–89) was miller at Little Billing in the censuses for 1851, 1861 and 1871. His mill, which he gave up in October 1875, is variously called Houghton Mill, Little Houghton Mill and Little Billing Mill. Monk, aged eight, appears in the 1841 census at school in Northampton on the same page as George Spokes, owner and miller at Weston Favell Mill before Harrold: the social milieu of Northampton's millers may have been restricted.

Monk v Northampton Improvement Commissioners (1871)

The pollution of the river must have been very bad in the summer of 1870 and the disruptions caused by new sewer construction could not have helped. Letters to the *Northampton Mercury* describe the Nene near the outflow pipe as running with 'black filthy scum and the stench was unbearable', 'fish dead by thousands', with 'patches of scum and sewage', 'smell of sewage very bad' and, again, 'thousands of dead fish'.[62] The Improvement Commissioners even stopped denying the existence of sewage pollution nuisance in the river.

Samuel Monk had earlier made his unhappiness with the state of the river known to the Improvement Commissioners, and, in October 1870, they received formal notice that he had lodged a bill for a new nuisance writ at Chancery.[63] The commissioners would have no defence to the charge of causing a nuisance to Monk but they did now have a long-term plan for a new sewage farm, so Northampton would rely, as they stated publicly, on an injunction to Monk being awarded but then suspended until they could divert the sewage water again, this time towards permanent irrigation-based treatment at the new sewage farm.[64]

The new ambitious plans for the farm would need the passage through Parliament of a new Northampton Improvement Act in 1871. This would give authority to the Improvement Commissioners for purchasing up to 900 acres at Ecton (Great Billing) and for raising up to £180,000 in loans.[65] With the passage of the measure through Parliament, evidence to the committee stage of the process, in May 1871, revealed much about the poor sanitary conditions at Northampton at this time, as attested by Dr George Buchanan:

> ... pumps and wells were within four or five yards of cesspools. There were open privies, in numerous instances overflowing into the road; pigstyes and ash-pits stood close to back doors; open ditches of stagnant water; the ground in many places was sodden with privy oozings; houses were built back to back; and throughout, the sanitary arrangements were extremely defective ...[66]

The Northampton Improvement Act, which also sought authority to purchase the local water and gas suppliers, successfully passed through Parliament and received its Royal Assent early in July 1871.

---

[62]   *Northampton Mercury*, 30 July, 6 August 1870.

[63]   Northampton Improvement Commissioners Minutes, October 24 1870; *Northampton Mercury*, November 5 1870.

[64]   *Northampton Mercury*, 7 January 1871.

[65]   *Northampton Mercury*, 13 May, 20 May, 8 June 1871.

[66]   *Northampton Mercury*, 20 May 1871. George Buchanan (1831–95) was inspector and medical officer at the Privy Council Medical Department.

The hearing of Monk v Northampton Improvement Commissioners (1871) took place in the Rolls' Court at Chancery on 17 July 1871,[67] only days after the Northampton Improvement Act was finally passed, before long-serving Master of the Rolls, Lord Romilly. The court heard the history of Northampton's efforts to drain the town and the progressive construction of sewage works and multiply-extended sewers outflowing into the Nene.[68] Romilly was told how the complaints of Lord Overstone and Thomas Merry and the outcome of Richard Harrold's suit had resulted in the sewage outflow being moved on so it was now sited only 1,000 yards or so upstream from Monk's mill. From 1868, the court heard, the river had become so contaminated by sewage that the fish at the mill had been destroyed and the water:

> ... had become of a dark and filthy colour, gave forth a foul and fetid smell, and deposited at the plaintiff's mill and in many parts of the river, a black and stinking deposit, composed exclusively of solid sewage and feculent and stircoraceous [sic] matters.[69]

Monk, his family and his workforce, the submission continued, had suffered greatly and Monk now sought restraint of the pollution by injunction and asked for damages for the injuries already suffered. Northampton, in response, admitted the nuisance but argued that they were now in possession of statutory powers, in the form of their Northampton Improvement Act, to establish the sewage farm required to tackle the pollution, and asked the court for time to carry out the works. An injunction was duly granted; and duly suspended until January 1872.[70]

The Improvement Commissioners began its new sewage farm investment in August 1871. The farm would, initially, require the construction of two-to-three miles of new covered culverts and piping and the purchase of 335 acres of the land at Great Billing. The old sewage works beside Midsummer Meadow would be improved and retained for the preliminary extraction of solid sewage matter; the residual liquid effluent would be moved by pipe and gravity to the new irrigation farm where ditches and sluices would direct the effluent through broad irrigation at Great Billing before river discharge.[71] Work on extending the main culvert to the sewage farm would begin immediately and preparing the sewage irrigation land would start as soon as prices for the land had been settled, loans obtained and the harvest safely gathered in.[72] The plan was that, starting relatively small, the farm would be gradually expanded as experience was acquired and needs grew. Work

---

67 Court of Chancery Records: Pleadings, C16/662/M201.

68 *Northampton Mercury*, 22 July 1871.

69 Ibid.

70 The Northampton Improvement Commissioners Minutes, 1 January 1872, record a payment of £100 to Monk at this time, but no further details.

71 John Hyde Pidcock, 'Northampton and its sewage', *The British Architect*, 69 1875: 230–1.

72 *Northampton Mercury*, 26 August 1871.

progressed quickly enough such that in July 1872, the commissioners were informed 'the sewage water is now turned ... upon the farm so that the Commissioners will be relieved from the application from the millers and other persons who have hitherto suffered annoyance from the sewage water.'[73] By February 1874, the main drainage was complete, the other workings required at the farm site were close to completion, and 'a fine crop of mangolds' was being contemplated.[74]

With the establishment of the irrigation farm in 1872–4, no more is heard of the injunctions and sequestration orders obtained at Chancery by Harrold and Monk. Here, then, ends the part played by nuisance law and the civil courts in the history of sewage disposal at Northampton.[75]

In April 1875, the parallel local government administrations of Northampton ended when the Board of Northampton Improvement Commissioners resolved to dissolve itself and pass on to the Northampton Town Council all its duties and powers. It is, perhaps, a measure of the centrality and importance of the sewage pollution story at Northampton that the formal handing-over ceremony, the Northampton Improvement Commissioners decided, would take place at the Great Billing Sewage Farm.

Concluding Comments

The history of Northampton's legal disputes over the sewage pollution of the Nene shows a number of features shared by the context of other cases. Northampton was naïve at points in its actions over its sewage disposal and Chancery may again be seen as acting in a supervisory way by allowing and including contingencies and delays in its orders. But the most distinctive feature here is the way Northampton enthusiastically took up the strategy of diverting its troublesome sewage wastewater away from the complainant by shifting the sewage water outfalls ever further down the river Nene, and each time provoking a new complainant to come forward. Northampton managed three separate diversions: first in response to the complaints of Overstone and Merry; then in response to Harrold's court orders; and then following Monk's injunction.

As it stands, Northampton's use of diversion of its polluting effluent must be viewed as successful in the short-run, but unsuccessful in the long-run as a solution

---

[73]   Northampton Improvement Commissioners Minutes, Book III, (1871–75), 14/10, 1 July 1872.

[74]   *Northampton Mercury*, 7 February 1874.

[75]   However, general complaints about Northampton's sewage disposal methods did continue, (*Northampton Mercury*, 5 September 1874, 7 August 1875). In 1875 the Northampton Lunatic Asylum claimed it had caused inmate deaths there (Northampton Improvement Commissioners Minutes, January 6 1875). By 1890 the Great Billing sewage farm had expanded to seven hundred acres and, in 1892, new expansion and improvements were being adopted at the site (*Northampton Mercury*, 15 August 1890, 7 October 1892). The Great Billing site remains the location of the major local wastewater treatment works to the present day.

to its pollution problem: Northampton's commissioners were anyway eventually induced (perhaps forced) by Chancery to establish a conventional irrigation treatment works. The next case, however, shows a second example of the use of the physical diversion of polluting effluent in response to a nuisance dispute, and this was one where the defendants were ultimately completely successful in achieving their aims.

Brinsop Hall: Pennington v Brinsop Hall Coal Company (1877, 1882)

The dispute between Richard Pennington (Jnr) and the Brinsop Hall Coal Company concerns the pollution of a small Lancashire stream by a private colliery company to the nuisance of Pennington's cotton mill enterprise, another private company, sited in Hindley, near Wigan in Lancashire. So this was a private nuisance case brought between two single commercial operations. The historical context shows that the settlement of the dispute was a further example of the polluting party abating its legal nuisance by means of *diversion* of the offending material. But this river pollution case also underlines other points and arguments presented elsewhere in this book. The colliery company brought an explicit economic-efficiency (balance of convenience) argument to court which was thoroughly dismissed by Chancery but which, taken at face value, would have indicated the court's finding against the colliery to have been socially inefficient. As such, had the conditions of the Coase theorem been applicable, the historical context and subsequent course of the dispute should have shown a subsequent agreement emerging between the parties and, perhaps, some pecuniary settlement of the property rights involved. However, despite this dispute appearing to be almost a classic situation where a Coase-like negotiated settlement might emerge, there exists no evidence whatsoever of any such solution.

    This case, filed in 1875, was first heard in the Court of Chancery in May and June 1877, under Justice Fry, when the Brinsop Hall company was restrained by injunction from further polluting the Borsdane Brook; and a second hearing occurred in 1882 at Chancery before Vice-Chancellor Hall, when the coal company was accused of violating the terms of the injunction issued.

Richard Pennington (Jnr)

The plaintiff in the case was Richard Pennington (Jnr), a third-generation representative of the important Pennington cotton-spinning and weaving family, who took over the family-owned Worthington and Lowe cotton mills in Hindley when his father retired in 1863.[76] These mills were substantial cotton industry enterprises: in 1891, Worthington Mill boasted 43,000 spindles and 645 looms

---

[76]   Richard Pennington (Jnr) (1830–87) was the grandson of the company's founder, John Pennington (1770–1850), and son of Richard Pennington (Snr) (1799–1883). Another

and Lowe Mill 90,000 spindles. Lowe Mill was housed in what had earlier been a water-powered corn mill in Hindley and was situated next to the Borsdane Brook, from whence Pennington's factory had habitually drawn the water to supply the boilers of the steam-engines now powering the enterprise. It was the quality of the water drawn from the Borsdane that was the source of the dispute.

Richard Pennington (Jnr) was a prominent local figure. He was a JP and county squire who served as chairman of the Local Boards of Health both at Rainford, where he lived, and at Hindley, becoming a staunch supporter of local charities, the church and the local Conservative Party. Aping the Pennington baronets of Muncaster Castle, to whom his family was unrelated, he gave the name Muncaster Hall to his home in Rainford. Remarkably, one of Pennington's closest friends was the wealthy and eccentric fellow cotton spinning industrialist, William Whitacre Tipping of New Bold Hall, Wigan, who had learned his craft as apprentice to Richard Pennington (Snr). Tipping had been the plaintiff in the slightly earlier but widely celebrated industrial nuisance case of Tipping v St Helens Smelting Company.[77] Tipping had successfully fought this air pollution case through common law and equity courts and up to the House of Lords and the case clarified and firmly re-established strict liability rules under nuisance law. In the end the injunction awarded to Tipping forced the St Helens Smelting Company to move its offending plant elsewhere, to avoid further damaging Tipping's estate.[78] No doubt Tipping and Pennington had compared notes and shared experiences on their cases.

The family life of Richard Pennington and his wife Elizabeth presents an intriguing story and indicates a middle-class Victorian family at odds, perhaps, with general perceptions.[79] Elizabeth Cash was originally an independently-spirited operative among Pennington's mill workforce in Hindley. When Richard was unable to get parental approval for his lively relationship with her, in 1855 he moved in to live with her, and they had three children without (as they say) the benefit of a traditional blessing from the clergy. Eventually they married in 1861, but the union can hardly, thereafter, be called uneventful, even given their *sixteen* children. Marital problems arose, not least, but clearly not only, because of Elizabeth's passion for alcohol, and the couple separated in 1874, with Richard agreeing an annual stipend of £300 for his wife, conditional on her staying well away from the family in Rainford, and leading 'a chaste life'. In 1877, having

---

of the sons of John Pennington was Frederick Pennington (1819–1914) who was twice elected Liberal MP for Stockport.

[77]   Tipping v St Helens Smelting Company (1861–73) All ER Rep Ext 1389. Tipping (1820–89) was one of the two executors of Pennington's will and two of Pennington's many children carried 'Tipping' as their middle name.

[78]   Simpson, *Leading Cases*, Chapter 7.

[79]   There are parallels enough between the Penningtons' private story and the stances and characters of Manchester playwright Stanley Houghton's *Hindle Wakes* of 1910 to intrigue any admirer of that play as to Houghton's sources, but no firm connections are apparent.

learned of her liaisons and 'misconduct' with both a Mr Whitehead and a Mr Cranshaw (once a gamekeeper at Muncaster Hall) Pennington sued for divorce and was granted a *decree nisi* in 1878, at which point the £300 stipend ended. But in 1879, when Pennington petitioned to have his divorce made absolute, the Divorce and Probate Court learned of Pennington's own earlier adultery with a servant, and dismissed his petition and revoked the *decree nisi*. In 1880, Elizabeth, though now living with an Alf Clayton, described as a comic music hall singer, became a charge on the relief authorities in Manchester who unsuccessfully sued Richard for her maintenance. Elizabeth was characterised at this point as being 'of intemperate habits' and 'living in a state of riot and debauchery.'[80] Back in Rainford, aged 93 in 1929, she died, forty years after her husband. Shamelessly, she was able to comment, possibly from experience, on the mores of the 1920s: 'If the young ladies of my time had carried on like they do today they would have been locked up.'[81] After Richard died in 1887, his will required equal shares of his estate be divided among his many children, so his businesses and properties were sold, and the cotton industry connections of the Pennington family gradually ended.[82]

Pennington v Brinsop Hall Coal Company (1877)

The defendant in the dispute was the Brinsop Hall Coal Company, a colliery company with a single mining site at Westhoughton and one of many such enterprises exploiting the rich coal seams near Wigan. There had been an earlier pit at Brinsop Hall operated in a small way by brothers William and John Nathaniel Longworth up to the early 1870s, but they had sold out to an investment group which included Horace Mayhew. Mayhew's group, in January 1874, formed themselves into the Brinsop Hall Coal Company Ltd, capitalised at £130,000 and, once in possession, the company greatly expanded the colliery's activities and increased its output of steam and household coal with new investment in new pits sunk and colliery light railways installed. At its peak, around five hundred workers were employed at the site. The local area was a major producer of coal and the company's mine was one of a huge number on the South Lancashire coalfield: a thousand pits are popularly believed to have existed within five miles around Wigan. The Brinsop Hall site lies about two miles north of Hindley, alongside the Boundary Ditch, which feeds the Borsdane Brook that flows on southwards to pass the site of Pennington's Lowe Mill.

In many ways, Pennington v Brinsop Hall Coal Company (1877) is an unexceptional, even run-of-the-mill, private nuisance dispute heard in Chancery

[80] *Sunderland Echo*, 8 November 1879; *Manchester Times*, 24 January 1880.

[81] Ron Dagnall, *The History of Muncaster Hall* (Rainford: Rainford Civic Society, 1988).

[82] A fourth-generation connection is indicated by the establishment in 1896 of the Hindley Twist Company Ltd, which had five Pennington sibling shareholders (*Manchester Courier*, 7 September 1896). The company was liquidated in 1920.

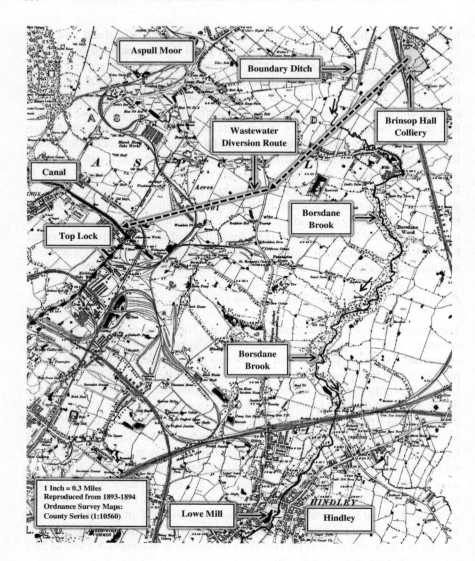

Map 9.2   Hindley and the Borsdane Brook

in May and June 1877, before Justice Fry.[83] The argument of the complainant, Pennington, was that the colliery used the Boundary Ditch and the Borsdane

---

[83]   Pennington v Brinsop Hall Coal Company (1877) 5 Ch. D. 769. Sir Edward Fry (1827–1918) was both a noted judge and a zoologist (J.E.G. de Montmorency, 'Fry, Sir Edward (1827–1918)', *Oxford Dictionary of National Biography*. (Oxford: Oxford University Press, 2004)).

Brook to dump its liquid mine run-off and waste, which included sulphuric acid, iron sulphides and other pollutants.[84] As mixed with the water drawn off from the Borsdane at the Lowe Mill in Hindley, this polluting material had then attacked and corroded the steam engine boilers and other equipment at the cotton mill, causing material damage and cost to the mill operation. Lowe Mill, it was claimed, had been able, over the previous forty years, to use the waters from the Borsdane for their processes without problems.

The defendants, the colliery company, responded that while they admitted pumping wastewater containing acids and pollutants into the Borsdane Brook, they denied any legal liability or responsibility for the damage described. Their argument was that the colliery had a right to continue pumping wastewater into the stream, and, anyway, they claimed any substances in the water from their premises would have been fully dispersed and diluted by the point the water reached Hindley and would have 'had entirely lost their deleterious character and become innocuous before they reached the Plaintiff's mill.'[85] And the water was already polluted from many other sources, the colliery added, so that any additional waste from their sources could not be established as the sole cause of any injury to the mill equipment.

Of particular note, the company presented in explicit form a 'balance of convenience' defence. The company claimed that the colliery was worth £190,000, and had a 500-strong work-force and would have to close as a consequence of being found liable for the nuisance were an injunction to be awarded, as there existed no possible alternative means of disposal of the wastewater from their mine. On the other hand, they claimed, the costs to the plaintiff of any harmful effects derived from the pollution in the water taken from the brook was trivial, merely some corrosive damage to the boilers of the mill, worth at most £100 per year. Hence on a social scale, the net effects of the imposition of an injunction would be highly negative, and, in economic welfare terms, economically inefficient. One of the reasons for the case being well-referenced is due to the explicitness of this economic inefficiency argument advanced by the defence.[86]

The case had an unexceptional and predictable outcome. In line with the established principles of English law concerning nuisance and balance of convenience arguments, both then and now, and in line with a riparian view of water rights, the arguments presented by the defence were all rejected at Chancery by Justice Fry who found the colliery liable for the nuisance cited. Fry decided that a permanent injunction would be the proper remedy and the Brinsop Hall Coal Company was restrained by order from:

> ... discharging water from their mines and colliery into the stream so as to
> cause an injury to the Plaintiffs' mill, engine, boilers and works, or other of

---

[84]   Court of Chancery Records: Pleadings, C16/1030/P120.

[85]   Ibid.

[86]   Stephen, *The Economics of the Law*, 81; Tromans, 'Nuisance', 91.

their premises ... or so as to cause the stream to flow to the Plaintiffs' mill and premises in a state less pure than that in which it flowed thither previously to the commencement of the Defendants' pumping.[87]

Compensatory damages for injury previously sustained and legal costs were awarded to Pennington, and a three-month delay in the imposition of the injunction was allowed for the coal company to find some means of conforming to the strictures of the order issued.

In the event, despite the claim that the colliery would have to close were Chancery to award the injunction sought, the colliery and the Brinsop Hall Coal Company duly managed to survive the imposition of the injunction. As Justice Fry clearly surmised, the colliery was able successfully to find a means of dealing with the injunction. Simpson succinctly warns us that: 'litigants normally tell lies'[88] and, indeed, as Mark Twain's Huck Finn has it, 'I never seen anybody but lied, one time or another.' It was not for another fifteen years, in 1892, that the Brinsop Hall Coal Company, then still employing 400 operatives at the mine, gave notice that they proposed to liquidate the company and close the colliery. No blame was attributed to the injunction: the sole reason given was that 'all the workable coal of the colliery has been secured.'[89]

It is also notable that there exists no hint of a Coase-theorem-type negotiation or agreement between Pennington and the Brinsop Hall Coal Company to settle the dispute, despite the situation seeming ripe for such a solution. After all, had Pennington's costs from the effects of the pollution amounted only to the £100 per annum as claimed by the colliery, direct compensatory payments would surely have provided a viable solution. The absence of a negotiated settlement may be surmised because, in 1882, Pennington again sued the Brinsop Hall colliery, this time asking Chancery to issue a sequestration order against the coal company alleging that they had breached the 1877 injunction. The material supplied for this second hearing in 1882 reveals how the dispute evolved in the wake of the original injunction.

Pennington v Brinsop Hall Coal Company (1882)

The second Chancery hearing between Pennington and the Brinsop Hall Coal Company began in Chancery nearly five years later, on Saturday 11 February 1882, this time before Vice-Chancellor Charles Hall.[90] Pennington now alleged a breach

---

[87]   Pennington v Brinsop Hall Coal Company, 774.

[88]   Simpson, *Leading Cases*, 11, though he later amends this to 'Litigants always lie', 184.

[89]   *London Gazette*, April 13 1892; *Liverpool Mercury*, August 1 1892.

[90]   Vice-Chancellor Charles Hall had previously overseen the Barnsley suit in 1874, see chapter 6 above.

of the earlier injunction,[91] and asked for an order for the sequestration of the assets of the Brinsop Hall Coal Company along with the committal to prison for contempt of the company's managing director, Horace Mayhew.[92]

Horace Mayhew had been brought up in Wigan, becoming a member of the Institute of Mechanical Engineers in 1867 and is recorded by the censuses in Wigan in 1871 and 1881 as a mining engineer. Following his association with the group who set up the Brinsop Hall Coal Company in 1874, Mayhew's fortunes leapt, and by 1881 he had become a county magistrate for Lancashire (alongside Richard Pennington) and managing director of the company.[93]

Pennington's argument in court in 1882 was that the Brinsop Hall Coal Company, under Mayhew's direction, had wantonly and persistently violated the 1877 injunction. The violation, it was argued, was proven by the continuing presence in the Borsdane Brook of mineral deposits and 'ochry water', a phenomenon often associated with, and an indicator of, water pollution from mining. When acid mine washings mix water, oxygen and iron pyrites, chemical reactions precipitate out iron hydroxides and rust, leaving distinctive ochre-coloured sediments and discolouration in and along watercourses. A number of affidavits were submitted by Pennington presenting evidence supporting the contention that not only did such pollution exist in the Borsdane, but that it originated from the Brinsop Hall King (No. 4) Pit and could have come from no other industrial site. Evidence was also presented that the measures put in place at the pit after the earlier 1877 injunction, to pump the troublesome wastewater away from the Borsdane Brook, had proven faulty and had not, anyway, been in operation for some time, so resulting in the re-commencement of the nuisance. The colliery maintained that its new pumping network, pipe system and drains, installed since the first hearing, made it impossible that they were to blame. The specifics of the case came to rest on three occasions when the colliery reluctantly admitted that through December 1881 and January 1882 the colliery may have, albeit accidentally and inadvertently, allowed some wastewater to escape into the Borsdane watercourses, leading again to the temporary and, they maintained, innocuous discharges into the brook.

After three days of hearing the evidence in the case, which he complained of as being 'overlaid with evidence', Vice-Chancellor Hall concluded that there was ample proof that substantial breaches of the injunction had occurred, certainly

---

[91] *The Wigan Observer*, 15 February 1882.

[92] Pennington also wanted the engine man at the colliery committed for contempt.

[93] In 1891 and 1901, Horace Mayhew (1845–1926) is a 'colliery owner' and Deputy Lieutenant in Flintshire, living in Broughton Hall, near Chester. He then became involved in a disastrous Canadian coal mining speculation in 1905. Millions of dollars were raised to exploit coal deposits in Nova Scotia and to develop a whole new city called Broughton, dependent on the new collieries. Over-ambitious from the start, in 1907 the scheme and the new company collapsed without having sold a lump of coal. Mayhew died back in Chester and the town of Broughton, Nova Scotia, is currently recorded with a population of twenty-four.

on more than merely the three instances documented, and agreed that there was serious cause for complaint by Pennington, even though the violations had now ceased.[94] But Hall noted that the colliery defendants had done much to alleviate the situation since the original injunction had been awarded, though not without 'imperfections they must deal with as best they can to set right, as I have no doubt they will'. He concluded:

> I do not think it is incumbent on me to do otherwise than order the defendants
> to pay the [legal] costs; and I think that if I do that ... I shall effectuate what is
> meant to be effectuated, that is to say, that such defects as there are in the pipes
> will be put right. I shall therefore order the defendants to pay the costs of the
> application and make no other order.[95]

So, despite the finding of real and serious breaches of the earlier injunction, no sequestration order was issued against the colliery and no compensatory damages were awarded to Pennington.[96] As is clear, the Vice-Chancellor appears much more concerned to ensure the engineering defects of the colliery's wastepipes had been adequately repaired and re-secured than to compensate the victim for the proven nuisance or judiciously right any wrongs inflicted and assure future compliance. He is content to note the source of the dispute had now been removed. And Horace Mayhew was not committed to prison for contempt.[97] No further action is recorded in connection with the dispute between Richard Pennington and the Brinsop Hall Colliery Company.

The Abatement of the 1877 Nuisance

For our purposes, the specific outcome of the second phase of the dispute, regarding the sequestration hearing in 1882, is not of primary interest. What the 1882 hearing on the petition for sequestration provides is a rare opportunity to see how the two private organisations dealt with the court's 'socially inefficient' decision in the first, 1877, case. The second hearing in 1882 details and preserves the historical information which will normally, especially after such a passage of time, otherwise remain absent and, likely, undiscoverable.

From the evidence presented, rather than any solution arising from negotiation, it is clear that the colliery company attempted to abate the legal nuisance in 1877

---

[94]   *The Wigan Observer*, 15 February 1882.

[95]   Ibid.

[96]   There are hints in the report of the hearing that Vice-Chancellor Hall suspected that the pursuit of damages was Pennington's overriding motive for bringing the sequestration case. Another intriguing, if rather mad, possibility raised by one of the plaintiff's witnesses was that the colliery had made a 'secret drain' through which the polluted ochry waste was discharged into the Borsdane Brook.

[97]   Nor was the engine man (William Sharrock).

by *diverting* its mine wastewater to an alternative source. The 1882 hearing details the means and general path by which the elaborate diversion of the wastewater run-off from the mine away from the Borsdane Brook was originally effected. The colliery first collected its wastewater in a settling pond next to the pit and then drained this by pumping the water away through a four-inch pipe network. Although the exact route of the pipeline is now lost, testimony from a number of witnesses gives the rough course as follows and as indicated on Map 9.2. From the settling pool at the King (No. 4) Pit at Brinsop Hall, the wastewater was piped under the Liverpool and Yorkshire Railway embankment, and pumped due west to cross the Boundary Ditch stream marking the Union and LBD (local board district) boundary. It was around this point that the new pipe and network system had failed, spilling the ochry wastewater and re-polluting the watercourses of the Borsdane Brook down to Pennington's mill in Hindley. From the Boundary Ditch the pipeline led west and crossed William Coates's farm (Ainscough Farm) and Bradshaw Lane in Aspull, finally reaching its new destination to empty into the canal system at Top Lock, where the Leeds and Liverpool Canal and the Lancaster Canal merge. The total length of the new pipeline was about one-and-a-half miles and involved skirting the higher area of Aspull Moor. In short, the abatement of the original pollution of the Borsdane Brook after the award of the 1877 injunction was achieved by diverting the polluting material of the colliery away from the Borsdane Brook and into an alternative watercourse, namely the Leeds and Liverpool Canal.

To present-day eyes, this solution may look rather extravagant and expensive, but it would have been more workaday for the skills of Victorian mining engineers. Still, on the face of it, the opportunity for the colliery company to buy off Pennington at the time of the original 1877 injunction and come to some negotiated compromise agreement seems irresistible. This dispute was between private organisations. It was not made more complex by the involvement of public bodies like Local Boards and town corporations, who faced restrictions in raising funds and loans and would always have had to withstand public scrutiny of expenditures and outlays where the issue of side-payments might be viewed as unethical or possibly corrupt. Here was a private nuisance dispute between two disputants with no other interested parties involved. The damages being inflicted on Pennington's boilers could be easily and cheaply compensated: if the figures are correct, by only £100 per annum. The major parties involved can even be shown to be connected socially, as Mayhew and Pennington were fellow Justices of the Peace. Nevertheless, Brinsop Hall chose to invest in building a mile-and-a-half pipeline snaking around a hillside and requiring appropriate pumping engines and long-term running expenses, to dispose of its wastewater in the local canal. The supporter of Coase theorem approaches to such arguments would have to contend that, for the colliery company, the diversion of the colliery wastewater outfall to the canal must have been the cheaper alternative.[98] In the end, readers will have to come to their own conclusion.

The case of Pennington v Brinsop Hall Coal Company provides a further example of the abatement of a water pollution nuisance by means of a diversion of the offending wastewater. On this occasion the diversion was not into the same watercourse downstream of the complainant, but into an entirely different watercourse.

Lessons from Northampton and Brinsop Hall

A policy of diverting the polluting materials away from any complainants must have been a tempting solution for polluting offenders and Northampton along the River Nene and the Brinsop Hall Coal Company along the Borsdane Brook were by no means the only instances that can be found of the use of this strategy, as we have seen. However, whatever the temptation of such a strategy for defendants, the diversion of pollutants like sewage away from complainants to satisfy the requirements of the law appears generally cynical and it provides little reward for the natural environment. Although the *legal* abatement of water pollution nuisance can be successfully achieved by such a diversion, evidence of advantages for the general environment from what is merely a displacement of the material with no *physical* abatement of the offending pollutants remains elusive.

---

[98]   In fact, at least one other alternative means of disposal of the colliery's wastewater existed via the awe-inspiring Aspull Pumping Station system, which was running commercially from 1872. This system was centred on the Aspull Pumping Pit, which was situated a bare few hundred yards from Brinsop Hall itself. The Wigan Coal and Iron Company had set up this system to consolidate the draining of wastewater from its numerous local pits. From the Aspull Pumping Pit, huge steam engines pumped hundreds of millions of gallons of water per year through pipes and brick-lined tunnels under the Aspull Moor, including through the Great Haigh Sough, to discharge into the (well-named and no doubt ochry) Yellow Brook and then into the Douglas River, a mile-and-a-half to the west, beyond the canal. William Woods and Sons, a substantial local mining company that owned pits nearby, paid £500 per annum to share this system. By running its own piped wastewater disposal system, this alternative solution, too, was rejected by the Brinsop Hall Coal Company.

Chapter 10
Protection by Statutory Legislation: Wolverhampton

A further distinct means by which towns could gain relief from civil nuisance suits over any sewage pollution would be to go to parliament to gain statutory relief from prosecution. In practice, this possibility provided an uncommon solution for civic authorities and only the single example, at Wolverhampton, can be found for the Victorian period. Why more towns did not pursue this complete and comfortable option remains a puzzle. Perhaps most local authorities believed parliament would be unwilling to allow individual towns special privileges under the law not bestowed on all. But as we shall see, in the case of Wolverhampton, the obtaining of statutory relief from prosecution for nuisance proved time-consuming, but relatively straightforward.

For the period leading up to Wolverhampton's obtaining this relief, the town had been involved in a long-running river sewage pollution nuisance dispute with the Giffard family over the pollution of the Pendeford Brook and the River Penk, centred on the hearings of Giffard v Wolverhampton Corporation (1874) and Giffard v Wolverhampton Corporation (1886–91). The legal dispute with the Giffard family finally ended at a date almost simultaneous with Wolverhampton successfully obtaining their statutory protection – the Wolverhampton Corporation Act in 1891. As passed by parliament, this act exempted Wolverhampton from prosecution for nuisance over any *future* sewage pollution of the watercourses in question. But as originally drafted, one clause included in the bill specifically aimed to override the *existing* decisions of the High Court in requiring the suspension of both the existing injunction and the then-threatened sequestration in the on-going Giffard dispute.

Wolverhampton: Giffard v Wolverhampton (1874, 1886)

Wolverhampton is a large inland town (city since 2000) close by and just to the north-west of Birmingham, within the modern Metropolitan County of the West Midlands. It lies on the edge of the highly industrialised region known as the Black Country. Wolverhampton's population in 1880 was around 75,000 and growing quickly, but the geography of the area is such that there exists no sizeable watercourse in the vicinity that would not be quickly overwhelmed if utilised as a wastewater outfall for such numbers. In the nineteenth century this region was host to a bustling heavy-industrial economy utilising local coal mining and iron and steel production, with noted specialisms in tin-plating, galvanising and metal-based manufacturing. Wolverhampton grew strongly and even thrived as a Victorian industrial town, but the implications for its urban and social environment in the middle-to-late 1800s can only be uncomfortably imagined.

In 1848, Wolverhampton became a Municipal Borough and Corporation, governed by a town council of mayor, councillors and aldermen, and this authority remained responsible for the general sanitary condition of the town, including its drainage and sewerage, for the Victorian period.[1] These responsibilities were not always executed successfully. In an instructive episode beginning in 1854, the new town council failed heavily in an early and unsuccessful attempt to municipalise the local waterworks company by means of a parliamentary act. Part of the failure was due to the council finding it had had no legal powers to attempt the takeover in the first place. Similarly, it had, also, no legal access to funds to settle the outstanding fees it had incurred and was helpless as legal claims for these debts were served. One frustrated consultant engineer, Mr S. Hughes, assiduously pursued his claim for £1,224 and eventually issued a summons and then obtained a writ of sequestration in 1856 against the council's property. Bailiffs seized the historic mayoral robes, oak chair and mace and other council property, including police clothing and bedding, water-carts and even the town's fire engines: the cash from market tolls at the fat stock market was also seized. Eventually voluntary donations from councilmen and extra rates enabled the debts to be paid.[2] This event provided more serious consequences for a town from a sequestration order than any that can be discovered amid the numerous sequestrations granted by Chancery in any of the sewage pollution cases covered in the course of this book.

The council proved generally slow to provide the sanitary infrastructure the town required and Wolverhampton provided a poor health and mortality record over the 1850s. The town was picked out specially in the Registrar-General's 1862 review of the health of the nation, which noted the critical mortality rates for Wolverhampton being significantly above that expected and that '... the health of Wolverhampton is every year getting worse':[3] the *Times* urged Wolverhampton to emulate the Biblical leper Naaman to 'wash and be clean.'[4] Even in 1872, Wolverhampton's medical officer of health presented an account of the improved

---

[1]   There were twelve aldermen and thirty-six councillors with a third of the seats up for re-election by eligible ratepayers annually. See Frank Mason, *Wolverhampton: the Town Commissioners, 1777–1848* (Wolverhampton: Wolverhampton Public Libraries, 1976); and Frank Mason, *The Book of Wolverhampton* (Bucks: Barracuda, 1979).

[2]   *Worcestershire Chronicle*, 17 January, 24 January 1857; George Barnsby, *A History of Housing in Wolverhampton 1750 to 1975* (Wolverhampton: Integrated Publishing Services, 1976), 16.

[3]   Registrar-General of Births, Deaths, and Marriages in England, Twenty-Third Annual Report, No. 2977, 1862, xviii and xxv.

[4]   *Times*, 16 May 1862.

state of the town that would have seriously undermined any budding tourist industry. It first noted the persistence of the town's many open privies and continued:

> ... the exhalations from the vast open ashpits, containing as they do so much stagnant water and soapsuds, combined with want of cleanliness on the part of the poor, give rise to that amount of fever which is continually to be found in their dwellings. Another great cause of impurity in the atmosphere is due in a great measure to the keeping of pigs and the length of time the contents of the cesspools have been allowed to accumulate.[5]

As regards sewerage, from 1855 and for the following decade, a series of schemes were prepared and considered by the Corporation, but none went on to be implemented, either because of critical review or because of financial or legal obstacles. Finally, with most of the finance already in place, new plans from Anthony Morgan, lately Surveyor at Leamington, but now the new Wolverhampton Borough Engineer, were submitted and approved, in 1866. His plan envisaged two intercepting sewers circling the town connecting with a number of branch and subsidiary sewers across the town totalling thirty-seven miles, with the cost estimated at £40,000. The plan also included a sewage treatment facility. Originally the sewage was to be directed northwards to a sewage farm and works on the 270 acres of Alexander Hordern's Oxley Manor House estate just east of the Staffordshire and Worcestershire Canal.[6] Hordern objected to the scheme but agreed to allow passage over his land for the sewage pipes if Wolverhampton were to place its farm further to the west, on the other side of the canal, at Barnhurst Farm.

Barnhurst Farm was owned by Thomas Shaw Hellier of Rodbaston Hall, who proved willing to sell, voluntarily, and a price of £27,915 was negotiated for its 283 acres in 1870.[7] The site at Barnhurst Farm was, however, far from ideal. Wolverhampton's piped sewage was to be led here using only gravity. As a result, only the 130 acres of the lower-lying half of the farm (called the Low Level area) could be used to serve the bulk of the town's sewage, from districts containing over 60,000 of the town's populace. The higher-lying half of the farm (the High Level area), also of about 130 acres, could serve only to treat the sewage from the less-populace but higher-lying part of the town (with just 6–7,000 townsfolk). This reduced the useful area of the farm to below that needed for effective broad irrigation on the Low Level. Until the sewage works at the farm were substantially

---

[5]   *Birmingham Daily Post,* 7 September 1872.

[6]   Oxley Manor House had previously been owned by William Huskisson MP, famous as the first recorded human casualty of the railway age. On Hordern's death in 1870, the estate passed to his nephew, Alexander Staveley-Hill (1825–1905) who became the local MP, a leading critic of the Barnhurst Sewage Farm and an opponent of the Wolverhampton Corporation Bill of 1891.

[7]   Small areas also came from adjoining properties.

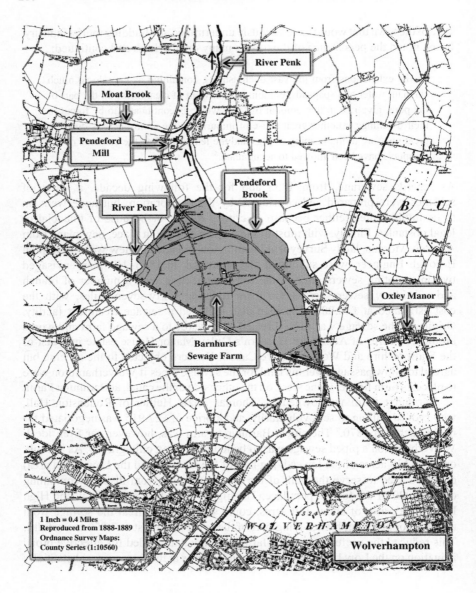

Map 10.1   Wolverhampton and the Pendeford Brook

improved, after 1890, the treated wastewater passing into the streams from the farm remained, bluntly, unacceptable.

This was unfortunate because, for all the procrastination, penny-pinching and, indeed, poor decision-making evident, Wolverhampton's ambitions for its new sewage treatment farm can still be seen as progressive and as intended to use the most up-to-date methods recommended by the Royal Commissions. The system would eschew chemical approaches and rely on the use of approved land-filtration methods with broad irrigation applied on a substantial sewage farm investment. The sewage would, thereby, be utilised to the benefit of the land, which would be cropped and grazed, with any financial surplus recycled to profit the town and its finances.

The design of the treatment process, though continuously reviewed, changed only minimally over the period of the disputes.[8] For the Low Level half of the farm, the sewage from the larger nine-tenths portion of the town would come into the farm over the canal aqueduct,[9] to be directed first into settling tanks. Here the more solid sludge was extracted to be mixed with ashes, pressed and transformed into manure cakes and the like and distributed to the farming community or transported away by boat down the canal. The remaining liquid was then allowed to flow out to surface irrigate the farm via the furrows, ditches, carriers, and sluices directing the effluent water around the property. Then, as hoped, cleansed and filtered by natural processes, it seeped and flowed off the farm into either the canal or the Pendeford Brook. For the Higher Level half of the farm, a second inflow pipe led the sewage onto the site to be used, via the carriers, for broad surface irrigation before similarly flowing off into the Wergs and Pendeford Brooks. The farm also contained two (then three) storm reservoirs which were intended to deal with excess flows to protect the farm being flooded after rain, but, in practice, these served as what amounted to permanent sewage-fed cesspools.

Throughout the period, the defects at the Barnhurst site undermined any efforts to treat the sewage effectively: the site was not big enough and the Pendeford Brook too small and slow-moving to cope with the outflow. Furthermore, after storm water flows, sewage-laden effluent could overflow the storm reservoirs and run through the farm straight into the brook untreated. And the nature of Wolverhampton's waste added special problems. The metal-based and galvanising sectors of Wolverhampton's industry produced industrial effluent containing large quantities of waste acid known as 'galvaniser's pickle' that proved poisonous not only to the fish and potability of the streams but also to the crops of the sewage farm: all adding further to the farm's poor performance. Galvaniser's pickle, containing acid and metal waste, is a by-product of hot dip zinc galvanising, a ferocious process that gives metal sheets a rust-proof zinc coating and was a method that Wolverhampton's manufactories pioneered from the 1830s.[10] The

---

[8]   'Plan of Barnhurst Sewage Farm', Giffard Family Archive, Staffordshire Record Office, D590/347/1.

[9]   A tiny pipe aqueduct carried the sewage over the Staffordshire and Worcestershire Canal onto the farm and a (newer) Sewerage Works Pipe Bridge remains, to this day, a minor feature of the canal.

[10]   Iron or steel metal sheets are first degreased with alkali caustic soda and then pickled in acid baths to remove any existing corrosion to strip the sheet back to base metal. The bare metal sheets are then dipped in molten zinc which reacts with the surface iron and

town faced a stiff task trying to get its manufacturing firms to keep such deeply noxious waste out of the sewers and, indeed, the general impact of the galvanising industry on Wolverhampton's Victorian environment can well be imagined.[11]

Giffard v Wolverhampton (1874)

The inadequately-cleansed wastewater outflow of the Barnhurst farm inevitably made its presence unwelcome in the Pendeford Brook, which formed part of the eastern boundary of the farm. The Pendeford Brook is tiny, and minor enough even to remain unnamed on the OS maps of the day.[12] As it flows north, the brook joins the marginally less tiny River Penk at Pendeford Mill, owned by the Giffards and neighbouring the Barnhurst Farm. By 1873 much of the area of Wolverhampton had had sewers laid and was being drained through the newly-developed network onto the sewage farm.[13] From this time, over the 1870s, complaints begin to emerge from a mix of landowners and their tenant farmers along the local rivers.[14] These complaints mark the first steps in the long-running sewage pollution dispute between Wolverhampton Corporation and the Giffard family: first father, Walter Peter Giffard; then son, Walter Thomas Courtnay Giffard. The dispute would continue until the 1890s.

Walter Peter Giffard (1797–1877) first complained to Wolverhampton about the pollution of the Penk and Pendeford Brook, on behalf of himself and his tenants, as early as 1871, just as soon as the Barnhurst site received its first sewage. Giffard was a major landowner along the Penk valley, and among his farms and properties was Pendeford Mill,[15] which immediately neighbours Barnhurst Farm and uses the water from the Pendeford Brook to fill its mill pond.[16] Giffard's representative met with the Town Clerk of Wolverhampton in 1872, but informal proceedings between the interested parties soon foundered and Giffard, with some of his tenants, sought formal writs for nuisance against Wolverhampton for causing pollution damage to their properties along the streams. This encouraged other

---

steel to bond in a series of zinc/iron alloys to provide the coating required. The spent acid, saturated with iron oxides, becomes the troublesome galvaniser's pickle waste.

[11]   *Birmingham Daily Post*, 6 February 1892.

[12]   Today, Pendeford Brook is even more elusive, having been straightened, rerouted, culverted and overtaken by the urban expansion of Wolverhampton. It now flows mostly underground, but a short section exists between Marholm Close and Blaydon Road, Pendeford. Wergs Brook has totally disappeared.

[13]   Wolverhampton was far from becoming a full water closet town. In 1895, Wolverhampton still had 13,500 privies served by a pan-closet collection system, costing the council £5,000 per year to service (*Birmingham Daily Post*, 24 October 1895).

[14]   *Birmingham Daily Post*, 9 November 1872.

[15]   'Map related to TS Hellier purchase', Wolverhampton City Archives, Map/80.

[16]   The Giffards' residence is the impressive Chillington Hall, in the midst of an estate of 4,000 acres at Brewood, about four miles to the north of Barnhurst.

landholders downstream of Barnhurst to seek writs as well and by 1874 there were ten complainants alleging damage against Wolverhampton when the first hearing for the dispute occurred at the Court of Exchequer and Pleas.[17]

At the hearing in November 1874, by agreement, it was ordered by Baron Gillery Pigott that the case of Giffard and others v Mayor Aldermen and Burgesses of the Borough of Wolverhampton would be settled as a Special Case under a court-appointed arbitrator. The arbitrator chosen was local land surveyor William Fowler, who was one of the Gravelly Hill relators in the Attorney-General v Birmingham (Davenport) dispute of 1870–6, which was described in Chapter 5. With his court-appointment credentials, Fowler as arbitrator was imbued with and carried all the powers of the original court, including the ability to call witnesses to testify on oath, award costs, make decisions as to liability and award damages. He would also be able to order, if required, improvements to be made at the sewage works and for cleaning and clearing the streams.

Fowler's arbitration began in May 1875 but the report and award was not published until November 1876.[18] His decisions went firmly against Wolverhampton. Along with Giffard, there were two other large landowners among the ten complainants, Robert Henry Fowler-Butler and Francis Monckton, and these three received a total of damages of £1,280. The seven other farmers shared another £600 of damages, which brought the damages faced by Wolverhampton up to £1,880.[19] However, as well as the compensation awarded for the pollution, Fowler ordered Wolverhampton to undertake extensive remedial work to improve the treatment process and reduce the potential for harm at Barnhurst. These required works are specified and detailed in the arbitration report, clearly demonstrating the role of the court (in the guise of the arbitrator) as a supervisory and managerial agent. The Corporation was required: to build a two-foot high waterproof bank along the eastern side of the farm to prevent any sewage water escaping or outflowing into the brooks except through two designated outflow points; to clean and deepen four miles of downstream brooks; and to build a third storm overflow reservoir and new settling tanks at the farm. The cost ran to nearly £10,000. Finally, Fowler issued what would have been, had it come directly from the court, a permanent injunction concerning the future disposal of Wolverhampton's sewage effluent, requiring that

---

[17]   In addition, in 1874 the Staffordshire and Worcester Canal required that Wolverhampton close the storm overflow outlet from Barnhurst into their canal.

[18]   'Award of Mr William Fowler', Wolverhampton City Archives, C-WCA/1891/5.

[19]   Ibid. Robert Henry Fowler-Butler (1838–1919) who owned Pendeford Hall, had been a career soldier, rising to Colonel and then Major-General. Francis Monckton (1844–1926) was resident at Stretton Hall, Penkridge and was Conservative MP for Staffordshire West between 1871 and 1885. Individually, Giffard was awarded £800, Fowler-Butler £300, and Monckton £180. For the seven others: Thomas Atkins, William Atkins, Sarah Beach, James Bennett, Brooke Chambley, Frederick Joseph Keeling, and James Lee, sums awarded ranged from £30 to £150.

no sewage or sewage water be allowed to pass into the Pendeford Brook without having first passed through the Barnhurst Farm treatment installation.[20]

Walter Peter Giffard died just three months after the arbitration was published, in March 1877 and before any of the works specified were begun. His son, Walter Thomas Courtnay Giffard (1839–1926), inherited both his father's property and his father's truculent attitude towards Wolverhampton's treatment of the Pendeford and Penk valleys. The dispute continued without a break.

Giffard v Wolverhampton (1886)

Fowler's arbitration and Giffard Senior's death did not even calm the dispute for long. As Wolverhampton, after 1877, began the work required by the Fowler arbitration, the Borough Engineer called a meeting of all interested parties in 1878, and this authorised some minor widening of the watercourses to facilitate the flow of the streams away from Barnhurst. Once the work was done, however, it became evident that it had gone well beyond that authorised; Walter Thomas Giffard considered substantial compensation from the Corporation was required.[21] It emerged that the brooks had been widened from the original ten feet or so, not by the one-to-two feet authorised, but had in fact been doubled in width over long stretches of the Pendeford and Penk and, indeed, by 'up to thirty feet' in others. Furthermore, it became clear that Giffard was not sympathetic towards the informal understandings that Wolverhampton claimed had already been agreed between the Town Clerk and his late father; and it became inevitable that a further round of litigation would ensue. The Town Clerk's view was 'a more ungracious and disgraceful attempt on the part of a landed proprietor to get money out of a Corporation never did exist than this one'.[22] A new arbitrator, Edward Ryde, had to be appointed in place of the exhausted William Fowler to determine the damages to be awarded to Giffard and his tenants over the over-widening issues and in June 1886, after a hearing lasting fifteen days, arbitration awarded the complainants a total of £1,050 (plus costs).

---

[20]   Wolverhampton were enjoined '… not to permit any water or sewage to pass from their lands at Barnhurst into the Pendeford Brook save through certain outlets or to permit any sewage or water whether storm water or otherwise to pass from the Borough of Wolverhampton through any sewers or drains belonging to the defendants or under their control into the Pendeford Brook or any of its tributaries without the same shall have been first passed through or over the lands of the Defendants at Barnhurst by way of purification by irrigation or percolation or through some or one of the storm reservoirs of the defendants at Barnhurst' (ibid).

[21]   'Heads of Agreement between W.T.C. Giffard and Wolverhampton Corporation', Giffard Family Archive, D590/818.

[22]   'Brief for Promoters of the Wolverhampton Corporation Bill', Wolverhampton Archives, C-WCA/1891/19, 15.

While the problems arising out of Fowler's arbitration of 1876 slowly unwound, the sewage pollution problems associated with Barnhurst continued. A private and confidential 1883 report on the sewage farm, commissioned from consultant engineer Edward Pritchard by the Corporation included: '[it] would be impossible to effectively purify the sewage of Wolverhampton by broad irrigation upon the small area of land available' and acknowledged 'the present failure of the sewage farm as a sewage purifier.'[23] Pritchard's drastic recommendations were to remodel the farm using intermittent (deep under-drained) filtration and more settling tanks; to drastically curtail the galvaniser's pickle in the sewage by some means; and to rebase the town drainage with separate outflow routes for rainwater and sewage for the town.

Through the early 1880s, a steady flow of complaints continued to be delivered to the town council about the pollution, including not only from the three big landowners, Giffard, Fowler-Butler and Monckton, but also from new sources,[24] including Alexander Staveley-Hill MP, now resident at Oxley Manor. In December 1884, invitations were distributed for a meeting of interested parties with a view to instigating new legal proceedings against Wolverhampton Corporation, and in March 1885 the Corporation received notice of a new action for an injunction about the sewage pollution of the Pendeford valley was to be brought by Giffard and a number of his tenants.[25]

The plaintiffs, in March 1885, had originally applied to the Court of Chancery asking for damages and an injunction to restrain the fouling of the Pendeford Brook, but the suit was transferred to the Queen's Bench Division at the insistence of Wolverhampton. Giffard and others v Corporation of Wolverhampton was begun at the High Court in London on 2 August 1886, with no defence offered by Wolverhampton. Justice Day held that: a) an injunction would be issued restraining Wolverhampton from discharging into the Pendeford Brook any further noxious matter; and b) that Justice Wills at the Birmingham Assizes, later that month, be empowered to ascertain the damages payable for the nuisance and to suspend the injunction, if appropriate, 'for the purposes of enabling the defendants either to

---

[23]   Edward Pritchard, 'Report No. 1 (1883)' in *Papers and Reports on Wolverhampton Sewerage 1878–1884* (Wolverhampton: Wolverhampton Corporation, 1884): 56–72, Wolverhampton City Archives, C-WCA/1891/7. Edward Pritchard had wide engineering experience and had been Surveyor at Warwick ('Pritchard, Edward 1838–1900', *ICE Minutes of Proceedings*, 141, 1900, 348–9).

[24]   Including the Seisden Rural Sanitary Authority and the Staffordshire and Worcester Canal company. (Wolverhampton Corporation Sewage Committee Minutes, 1859–1891, Wolverhampton City Archives, C-WCA/1891/2.)

[25]   Giffard's co-plaintiffs were William Atkins, Joseph Beach, Frederick Keeling, James Lee and Matthew Woodward. Atkins, Keeling and Lee had been part of the earlier group of complaints. Matthew Woodward was 'Miller, Maltster and Farmer' at Pendeford Mill.

adopt some new system, or, if possible, to apply the present system so that it might cease to be a nuisance.'[26]

The hearing at the Birmingham Assizes under Justice Wills, on 12 August 1886, was told how the opening of the Barnhurst sewage farm had transformed the Pendeford Brook from a trout stream, clear and lipid and a joy for sheep to drink, into a foul, yellow stream smelling dreadfully and flowing with acid and rust deposits, poisoning the neighbouring meadows, destroying their drainage, and killing the livestock.[27] After hearing the evidence, Justice Wills noted:

> There was a great difficulty in exercising a sound discretion in these matters, having regard to the impossibility of putting a sudden stop to the drainage of a large town; and on the other hand a desire ... to assert the sacredness of individual rights as against the operations of a very powerful Corporation.[28]

This, of course, is simply our familiar river sewage pollution nuisance dilemma, and Posner would have expected Wills to have had problems with enforcing the inefficient option. Wills suggested that an agreement between the parties might be the best solution with regard to both the damages payable and the length of suspension for the injunction, and, over-optimistically, sent the two sides away to meet. After two-and-a-half hours, the parties returned to announce little progress, which left Justice Wills to fill in the remaining gaps and hope that any future disagreement would be honourably settled. As regards damages, Wolverhampton was held liable for another £400 compensation payout, specific to the current suit. For the future, Justice Wills ordered that Constantine Moorsom,[29] an experienced land agent, would mandate new works at the farm, oversee the cleansing of the brook and determine damages payable, if any, until the injunction was to become operable. For the injunction, Justice Wills included a toughly-worded section restraining Wolverhampton from discharging into the Pendeford Brook: '... any excrementatious, filthy or noxious matter or sewage water contaminated or mixed therewith'. In order to give time for remedial work, the injunction was 'suspended for one year, with liberty to apply... for a (sic) further suspension.'[30]

Further Suspensions and Appeals (1887–9)

Wolverhampton's town council reacted to the 1886 hearing by Justice Wills with something between relief and triumph. The Town Clerk declared, to applause, that the town had come very well out of the proceedings, especially with regard to

---

26   *Birmingham Daily Post*, 13 August 1886.
27   Ibid. Sir Alfred Wills (1828–1912) was a native of nearby Birmingham. He is more widely celebrated as a pioneer of alpine mountaineering than as a High Court judge.
28   Ibid.
29   Constantine Richard Moorsom (1828–1919) was land agent to Earl Harewood.
30   *Birmingham Daily Post*, 13 August 1886.

the simple process put in place for new claims for damages to be simply referred to Moorsom's arbitration, which would save, he thought, much future legal and other expense.[31] A delegation of members of the council was sent away to visit sewage treatment plants in similarly placed towns and a number of engineers were then, in a leisurely manner, consulted over the problems at Barnhurst. It took until October 1887 for a scheme based on Pritchard's recommendations to be approved.[32] Under this plan, a new chemically-aided precipitation process would be introduced at the sewage farm alongside a new deep-drained irrigation set-up, while new drainage would be installed throughout Wolverhampton town to try to separate out the rainwater flow and direct this to other watersheds.

In July 1887, the first report from Moorsom, the court-appointed independent surveyor, recommended not undertaking any cleansing of the brook or making any new assessments for damages until the proposed improvements at Barnhurst were made. He nevertheless still reported 'intolerable nuisance' along the streams.[33] A new six-month extension to the suspension of the injunction was agreed by consent between Giffard and the Corporation. Moorsom's second report, in January 1888, noted that continuing work and the partial separation scheme had managed to reduce the flooding along the Pendeford, but still maintained the nuisance there had 'in nowise lessened.'[34] The parties reassembled before Justice Wills in March 1888 in chambers and a further twelve-month suspension was agreed with the wording of the suspended injunction allowed to be softened, now to restrain the Corporation from deteriorating '... the purity or quality of the water as it enters the plaintiff's lands.'[35]

At the end of January 1889, as this further suspension period began to be exhausted, Wolverhampton again applied for an extension, this time for twenty-four months, which would allow, they said, the final installation of the new improvements at Barnhurst and the completion of the new rainwater separation system in the town. This time, Moorsom's third and final report, in January 1889, was able to provide faint praise that, along the Pendeford Brook, the water was less foul and the smell less offensive than earlier.[36] But at the 11 February 1889 hearing, Justice Wills decided he was not empowered to grant a further suspension.

When Wolverhampton took the matter to the higher Divisional Court they agreed, on 30 April 1889, that Justice Wills indeed had no power to grant further extensions to the injunction. Formally, the problem here hinged on the original

---

[31]   *Birmingham Daily Post*, 12 October 1886.

[32]   *Birmingham Daily Post*, 9 August 1887.

[33]   'Mr Moorsom's Report (1887)', 8 July 1887, Wolverhampton Archives, C-WCA/1891/17. All Moorsom's reports are surprisingly skimpy.

[34]   'Mr Moorsom's Report (1888)', 31 January 1888, Wolverhampton Archives, C-WCA/1891/9.

[35]   'Brief for Promoters', 23.

[36]   'Mr Moorsom's Report (1889)', 18 January 1889, Wolverhampton Archives, C-WCA/1891/18.

order from Wills, which, by agreement: '... only provided that the Judge might order "a" suspension – that is, one suspension. The order did not provide for renewed suspensions from time to time.'[37] Wolverhampton received no sympathy from this court. The Divisional Court judges expressed general scepticism about Wolverhampton's case for a further extension and asked '... the suspension of the injunction has already lasted for two years. How long are these attempts to last?' And when the possibly dire consequences likely in Wolverhampton were the sewers to be stopped were raised, there was a dry response:

> If we restrain the sending of sewage into the brook, we are told we shall cause an epidemic in the town; if we allow it we are told we shall cause an epidemic in the country ... We are not to be frightened by such a threat as that, to poison a whole town with their sewage! ... It is, no doubt, a question of money.[38]

Having failed at the Divisional Court, Wolverhampton then applied to the Appeal Court. Here it was unanimously held, on 17 May 1889, that the Appeal Court had no jurisdiction in the matter and could not intervene. Nevertheless, the court requested of Giffard that a further six-month suspension be allowed and with an understanding that no more extensions or further suspensions would under any circumstances be available to Wolverhampton, this was agreed.[39]

Wolverhampton's general procrastination and reliance on judicial extensions of time was about to catch up with them. The very last and final six-month period of suspension would run out and the terms of the injunction would come into force towards the end of 1889. Inevitably, an application from Giffard alleging that Wolverhampton had breached the terms specified would then be served in the form of a sequestration motion.

The Writ of Sequestration (1890)

On 3 March 1890, the motion for a writ of sequestration in Giffard and others v Mayor and Corporation of Wolverhampton came before the Lord Chief Justice (Baron Coleridge) and Lord Justice Fry, in the Queen's Bench Division.[40] The hearing began with a recitation of the history of the legal dispute since March 1885, covering the injunction of 1886 and the suspensions of 1886, 1887, 1888 and 1889.[41] Counsel for the plaintiffs claimed that, over the period, nothing effective to remedy the nuisance had been done: 'the Corporation laughing in the face of

---

[37]   Giffard v Mayor and Corporation of Wolverhampton (1889) 5 TLR 434.

[38]   Ibid.

[39]   *Birmingham Daily Post*, May 18 1889.

[40]   Sir Edward Fry (1827–1918) had also heard part of the Pennington v Brinsop Hall Coal Company dispute.

[41]   *Birmingham Daily Post*, 4 March, 5 March, 1 May, 2 May 1890.

the Court.'[42] The plaintiffs' side painted the current condition of the water in the streams being beastly, foul-smelling and the colour of ink, with the Corporation applying a crude and ineffective treatment which they had done nothing effective to improve. In contrast, the Corporation responded by presenting a picture of their conscientious, arduous and successful attempts to tackle the expensive problems of sewage treatment in Wolverhampton. Following these presentations from the two sides, the court noted the very different opinions and conflicting evidence presented over current water quality in the streams and requested more detail and expert evidence: the case was adjourned for new affidavits to be prepared. When the hearing resumed, on 30 April 1890, there were still 'remarkable' contradictions in the opinions of the experts from the two sides and marked differences between the water samples presented by the two sides:

> ... one of the [defence] witnesses going so far as to say that the water of the Oxley Brook and the Pendeford Brook is pure water, quite free from sewage and fit for domestic purposes ...; whereas the [plaintiff] witnesses said the water was stinking, black and noxious.[43]

The bench was clearly unhappy with Wolverhampton's lack of energy and diligence in responding to the earlier injunction, confiding that 'we are unfavourable to the corporation' and thought that there was little doubt as to the defendants having disobeyed the injunction. Still, the court was concerned enough about the issuing of a sequestration that Justice Fry asked Giffard's counsel: 'What good can you get by a sequestration? ... it is a very serious matter to sequestrate a corporation.'[44]

On 5 May 1890, Justice Fry presented judgment. He called the Barnhurst farm a 'sewage swamp' and said that Wolverhampton's own evidence allowed that they had continued to pollute the streams contrary to the injunction. Fry further accused the Corporation of showing want of energy, dilatoriness and lack of due diligence in the period between 1885 and 1890, suspecting severe unwillingness to incur necessary expenditure; and contended serious neglect of duty in that no effort at all had been made to address the removal of the poisonous ferrous oxide and galvaniser's pickle acid from its effluent. Justice Fry even accused Wolverhampton of having manipulated the water samples they had presented at the hearing which 'showed that they wished to avoid enquiry upon the very point considered by the Court to be of special importance.'[45] There was enough evidence, he continued, to believe that disobedience had been wilful and that therefore a sequestration was appropriate and should be ordered to issue. However, despite all this, Fry concluded, he would order a further suspension of six months before enforcement

---

[42] *Birmingham Daily Post*, 4 March 1890.

[43] *Birmingham Daily Post*, 1 May 1890.

[44] *Birmingham Daily Post*, 2 May 1890.

[45] *Birmingham Daily Post*, 6 May 1890. Fry was alone: the Lord Chief Justice was indisposed.

of the sequestration. This was to finally allow a complete resolution of the confusion over the expert opinion on the current quality of the water.

In order to settle the matter, Justice Fry ordered that a skilled person appointed by the court (at Wolverhampton's expense) would report on the situation at Barnhurst to examine the court's views that the injunction continued to be breached in *both* wordings used in the two forms that the wording of the injunction had taken over the period of putative disobedience. The questions set to be reported upon by the expert were therefore whether: a) any 'excrementitious or filthy or noxious matter or sewage, or any water contaminated or mixed therewith' was sent into the brook from the sewage farm or works; and whether b) the 'purity or quality of the water of the brook … deteriorated thereby' as it entered the plaintiff's land.[46] In the event of another damning outcome confirming Wolverhampton's nuisance along the Pendeford Brook, the sequestration order would be put into effect. The skilled person appointed to carry out the report was the admirable Edward Frankland, Professor of Chemistry at the Royal Institution and ex-Chair of the Royal Commission on Rivers Pollution Prevention: a more suitably competent and eminent expert would have been impossible to find. Frankland's definitive report was completed in November and considered by the Queen's Bench in December, 1890.

As we shall see, in the event, Frankland's report worked out well for Wolverhampton, but while they waited for the results, as 1890 progressed, other events were also piling up to make Wolverhampton take the actions that made this dispute unique among Victorian town-sewage pollution cases. They went to Parliament for the Wolverhampton Corporation Act.

Wolverhampton: The Wolverhampton Corporation Act (1891)

One can, perhaps, understand the apprehension felt by the members of Wolverhampton's town council during 1890. They faced serious trouble with an active sequestration if the Frankland report were to reinforce the court's view of their culpability and poor management along the Penk and Pendeford valleys. But the council, furthermore, was also beset by other quarrelsome and litigious parties. Giffard, as we have seen, was only one of a number of complainants against Wolverhampton demanding that some improvements be made and/or that compensation and damages be paid for the effects of the Barnhurst works. Even landholders as far away as along the Trent and Severn rivers were now delivering complaints to Wolverhampton.

Giffard's old accomplices, Colonel Fowler-Butler and Francis Monckton, remained active complainants. In 1887, Fowler-Butler was claiming damage to his property of over £400 per year from sewage pollution, for which arbitration awarded him a total of £1,026 damages, and he continued, along with his tenants,

---

[46]   Ibid.

to make further annual claims.[47] Francis Monckton claimed damages totalling £5,000 in 1887, and Wolverhampton agreed a sum of £1,500 (plus brook-cleaning valued at £500) to settle his claim in 1888: to which Monckton responded by submitting new claims in August 1889 and February 1890. But these were by no means the only complainants. In 1888 there had been a joint meeting of landholders in the valley to express their discontent and there had been separate claims and complaints from Brooke Chambley at Coven Lawn Farm and from the neighbouring Seisdon Poor Law Union. In 1889 there were complaints from the millers at Stretton Mill and Engleton Mill, and from the Trent Fishery Board, the Cannock Poor Law Union and from Lord Hatherton, who reported the river in 'as filthy a state as ever.'[48] In 1890, Brooke Chambley sent the town council some poisoned dead fish from his part of the stream.[49] Indeed the complaints were such that representatives for the corporation spoke of a ring or conspiracy being laid against them to drive them entirely from the Penk valley and claimed that nowhere else had a corporation faced such 'persecution of litigation.'[50] Wolverhampton claimed that by 1890, and excluding Giffard's actions, they had faced demands totalling £8,484 and had already paid out £2,759 and expected more.[51]

So in 1890, Wolverhampton resolved to set in motion an ambitious attempt to extricate itself from litigation over its river pollution problems: Wolverhampton's mayor declared that 'no other way remained open than to settle the matter by Act of Parliament.'[52] They would protect themselves by the straightforward expedient of obtaining a Parliamentary Act exempting them from the common law of nuisance with respect to any pollution of the Pendeford Brook, and this would deal with Giffard at the same time. Other towns may have contemplated such a scheme, and Justice Page Wood had back in 1858 tantalised Birmingham with such a prospect, but no town had actually set out and done it.[53]

The Wolverhampton Corporation Bill, introduced in Parliament in February 1891, was entirely devoted to matters of Wolverhampton's sewers,

---

[47]   *Birmingham Daily Post*, 12 October 1887.

[48]   Wolverhampton Town Council Sewage Committee Minutes, Excerpts, 1859–1891, Wolverhampton City Archives, C-WCA/1891/2.

[49]   Ibid.

[50]   Wolverhampton got quite paranoid over these attacks, accusing its opponents of 'vindictiveness' and claimed to have become the victim of 'wicked treachery' (*Birmingham Daily Post*, 8 April 1892).

[51]   'Brief for Promoters', 26.

[52]   *Birmingham Daily Post*, 11 Nov 1890.

[53]   Wolverhampton's 'Brief for Promoters' claimed a (single) precedent existed in the River Lea Conservancy Act (1868) which included a clause reading: 'Nothing in this Act shall prevent ... Luton Local Board of Health discharging into the River Lea the sewage water or matter ... after such sewage matter has been subject to the process of purification known as Higgs' process', but this rather emphasises, perhaps, the novelty of the exemptions asked for by Wolverhampton.

sewage treatment, and sewage effluent, and included giving power to the town to obtain more land and to raise finance in pursuit of such purposes. Our particular interest[54] lies more with the content of the original Clause 5 and Clause 6 of the bill, both of which directly protected Wolverhampton Corporation, in perpetuity, from litigation on their sewage pollution. Clause 5 provided for the exemption of the Corporation from new actions in the courts concerning the effluent discharging into the Pendeford Brook: a complete defence to any new nuisance suit would be the possession by the Corporation of a certificate from the Local Government Board in London confirming the application to Wolverhampton's sewage of the 'best practicable and available means for deodorising and clarifying such effluent and rendering it harmless.'[55] The wording is in line with that used by the Rivers Pollution Prevention Act of 1876. The next clause, Clause 6, applied the same idea *explicitly* to Giffard's *current* Wolverhampton law-suits, requiring both the current injunction and sequestration to be suspended for as long as any certificate awarded from the Local Government Board remained in force.[56] Thus, the orders

---

[54]   By contrast, the *Leeds Mercury* was not interested at all: 'At the opening of the [Parliamentary] sitting some time was spent upon the Wolverhampton Corporation Bill ... and nothing of much importance happened' (18 February, 1891).

[55]   The relevant parts of Clause 5 read: 'The Corporation may subject to the conditions hereinafter in this section mentioned discharge or permit to flow into the Pendeford Brook and the tributaries thereof the effluent from their sewerage works and sewage lands; (1) The Corporation shall not discharge or permit to flow any effluent unless and so long only as they shall be using the best practicable and available means for deodorising and clarifying such effluent and rendering it harmless; (2) A certificate by an inspector appointed by the Local Government Board to the effect that the means used by the Corporation for deodorising clarifying and rendering harmless any such effluent are the best practical and available means shall in all courts and in all proceedings be conclusive evidence of the fact ...; (3) Any person aggrieved by the granting or the withholding of a certificate under this section may appeal to the Local Government Board against the decision of the inspector ...; (4) The Corporation shall pay compensation to any riparian owner or other person injuriously affected by the exercise of the powers of this section ...' ('Wolverhampton Corporation Bill', Wolverhampton City Archives, C-WCA/1891/21).

[56]   The original Clause 6 reads 'The injunction granted by the High Court of Justice (Queen's Bench Division) against the Corporation at the suit of Walter Thomas Courtnay Giffard and others and the said writ of sequestration and any proceedings that may be pending at the time of the passing of this Act for or in relation to the enforcement of such injunction shall be and the same are hereby suspended for a period of one year from the passing of this Act and for such further period or periods as the Local Government Board may after enquiry think fit to grant. Provided that if and when and wherever and so long as any such certificate as is referred to in the fifth section of this Act shall be in force the said injunction and all proceedings (if any) for or in relation to the enforcement thereof shall be ipso facto suspended from time to time and the production of such certificate shall be a conclusive answer to any application which may be made or which may be now or at any time hereafter pending before the Court to enforce the said injunction by any mode of execution whatsoever: Provided also that the granting of such certificate shall ipso facto

already awarded by the Queen's Bench would be absolutely overridden so long as the certification was in force. And that certification would be anyway based on less stringent criteria of cleanliness than the existing orders required and, indeed, less stringent than any injunction wording which was likely to emerge under common law.

In the event, these two clauses of the Wolverhampton Corporation Bill, with their notable exempting consequences, attracted unusual attention on the floor of the Commons to the bill's Second Reading (prior to its Select Committee hearings).[57] Alexander Staveley-Hill, MP for Kingswinford, and a neighbour at Barnhurst, organised the opposition and described the provisions sought as, simply, 'monstrous'.[58] Hill went on to argue:

> It simply amounts to an assertion that what is good against the rest of the world is not good against those who are bent upon breaking the law. ... And the Town Clerk [said] that what the borough wanted was relief against all persons who were likely to be litigants – that is to say, all persons who are likely to be injured, and he added that the object of the Bill was to give them "a right to do that which was at present wrong". I sincerely trust that the House of Commons will refuse to enable the Corporation of Wolverhampton or anybody else to do that which is at present wrong, and which will inflict a serious injury on their neighbours.[59]

Colonel Kenyon-Slaney, MP for Newport, maintained that setting aside specific and on-going decisions of the courts of law was indefensible and believed that the bill requested 'unusual and unreasonable powers that may be dangerous to the principles of justice and equity.'[60] Even Charles Ritchie MP, the current President of the Local Government Board, whose inspectors would have to provide the certification, thought the exempting clauses objectionable. In face of this, Clause 6 of the bill, seeking exemption from Giffard's existing Queen's Bench orders, was ordered to be dropped, without, it must be said, too much objection from Wolverhampton's MPs. It is likely its retention would have threatened the passage of the bill as a whole. Clause 5, on the other hand, although also thought novel, was retained and remained intact (with minor amendments) as the bill proceeded through the rest of its passage around Parliament. The Wolverhampton Corporation Bill received the Royal Assent in August 1891.

After this point, so long as Wolverhampton's sewage treatment processes were able to satisfy the Local Government Board's inspector and gain certification that its treatment plant was using the best practical and available means of treating its

---

operate as a discharge of the said writ of sequestration upon the Corporation paying all taxed costs incidental to such sequestration' (ibid).

[57]   350 Parl. Deb. (3d ser.) 17 February 1891, 830–32.

[58]   Ibid.

[59]   Ibid.

[60]   Ibid.

effluent, Wolverhampton would thereafter be protected from *any* new common law legal threats of nuisance arising from its actions along the Pendeford and Penk. Indeed, the Wolverhampton Corporation Act offered not only a complete defence for Wolverhampton against suits under civil law, it also afforded absolute protection against proceedings under the Rivers Pollution Prevention Act and any other existing or potential statute. As regards the certification from the Local Government Board required by the new act, the first certificate, covering twelve months from May 1892, was granted after an enquiry held in Wolverhampton in April 1892 by Colonel Walter Mardon Ducat,[61] and another certificate was issued in May 1893, covering the next two years. Wolverhampton was still obtaining certificates of exemption under the 1891 Wolverhampton Corporation Act well into the twentieth century,[62] and the town authorities invoked the act's power to evade a summons for polluting the Penk with sewage as late as May 1928.[63]

The Dispute Ends

The passage of the 1891 Wolverhampton Corporation Act may have freed Wolverhampton from *future* civil litigation over its sewage effluent, from Giffard and anyone else, but, with the dropping of the original Clause 6, the existing, *current*, legal problem with Giffard remained. While the Wolverhampton Corporation Bill was being prepared and steered through Parliament, the events concerning Giffard's motion for a sequestration before the Queen's Bench were also progressing towards a climax. In the event, this also ended satisfactorily for Wolverhampton. Edward Frankland's report on the two questions set by Justice Fry about the extent of the nuisance in the Pendeford Brook had been presented in December 1890.[64] While any independent observer could hardly view Frankland's responses to the questions as a ringing endorsement of Wolverhampton's situation, the town council unsurprisingly viewed the report as a triumphant vindication.

On the first question set, as to whether any excrementitious sewage water or noxious matter was sent into the Pendeford Brook, Frankland concluded that, as *presently* run (with its new improvements) no excrementitious matter or technically noxious matter could exit the sewage farm untreated and that, therefore, untreated sewage water was *not* currently being released into the stream. This was qualified by Frankland's view that the treated wastewater emerging was by no means fit for human consumption and that a large, close to unacceptable, amount of organic product from sewage was measurably present in the water. For the second question,

---

[61]   Colonel Walter Mardon Ducat (1837–1902) was Inspector at the Local Government Board, 1888–97.

[62]   An exemption certificate under the act was issued by the Ministry of Health in April 1928 (218 Parl. Deb. (5th ser.) 7 June 1928, 356–7).

[63]   *Nottingham Evening Post*, 20 March 1929.

[64]   'Report of Dr E Frankland', November 1890, Wolverhampton City Archives, C-WCA/1891/22.

of whether the purity or quality of the water of the brook was deteriorated as it entered the plaintiff's land, Frankland declared he could not find samples of water to enable a complete answer, as all sources for water samples were themselves contaminated by further sources and inflows. It was even possible, he said, that the water quality in the brook was *improved* after passing Barnhurst, given the addition to the flow coming from the uncontaminated Oxley Brook. However, more generally, Frankland found the purification level achieved at Barnhurst much too close for comfort to the limits prescribed by his Royal Commission and he recommended that a higher level of purification be achieved there. Nevertheless, he concluded, the works were well laid out, of an approved design and generally satisfactory and efficient. There was certainly no justification in Frankland's report for an immediate enforcement by the Queen's Bench of the sequestration order held by Giffard, and, so, the likelihood of any future execution became remote.

After the two parties were provided copies of Frankland's report, in December 1890,[65] Giffard's lawyer, R.N. Hearne, and Wolverhampton's Town Clerk, Horatio Brevitt, settled down to a long-drawn-out correspondence to come to an agreement to settle the dispute.[66] Pendeford Mill and Malthouse with its 81 acres, owned by Giffard and situated right next to the Barnhurst works, had been one of the properties that Wolverhampton had been eager to acquire to expand the works. Talks about its purchase began in January 1891 and, in 1892, a deal was agreed for £7,500.[67] At the same time, the two parties took up negotiations about settling the outstanding injunction and sequestration. On 21 January 1892, Wolverhampton offered to settle these actions and 'satisfy landlord and tenant' claims for £500 plus an agreement to clean the brooks to the satisfaction of Moorsom.[68] Giffard counter-offered in July 1893 with Hearne reporting that his client:

> ... will accept £2000 for the sequestration and injunction and in satisfaction of damages and costs to the present time ... Mr Giffard to apply to have the Injunction and Sequestration removed and their costs to be paid by the Corporation ...[69]

It took until November 1893 for Wolverhampton to sanction the £2,000 payment,[70] and then confusion arose over whether this amount included damages for Giffard's tenants and the extent to which Giffard could speak for his co-plaintiffs. Finally, in mid-January 1894, these details were settled and the dispute came to an end. The

---

65   *Birmingham Daily Post*, 2 December 1890.

66   See *Giffard Family Archive*, Staffordshire Record Office, D5827/2/6/24–40.

67   Letter from Brevitt to Hearne, 25 July 1892, *Giffard Family Archive*, D5827/2/6/28.

68   Letter from Brevitt to Hearne, 21 January 1892, *Giffard Family Archives*, D5827/2/6/32.

69   Letter from Hearne to Brevitt, 15 July 1893, *Giffard Family Archives*, D5827/2/6/35.

70   Letter from Brevitt to Hearne, 2 November 1893, *Giffard Family Archives*, D5827/2/6/36.

appropriate final word may be allowed to R.N. Hearne, in a note to Giffard: '... I can only say that I am even more anxious than yourself to get a settlement of this complicated and very disagreeable business.'[71]

Lessons from Wolverhampton

The history of Wolverhampton's sewage pollution disputes along the Pendeford and Penk waterways contains the unique occurrence of an English town successfully seeking protection from its legal challenges over sewage pollution nuisance by obtaining statutory exemption. This is another method which successfully deals with the legal aspects of the nuisance while doing little to tackle the physical nuisance that caused the problem.

Had other towns followed this course, and, perhaps, had Parliament been less unwilling than it proved to override common law on nuisance and landowner rights, this would have provided a complete strategy for Victorian society in seeking a solution to the town-sewage river pollution dilemma. It is tempting to think that had the funds and assets of large numbers of towns actually been sequestrated for extended periods and their activities seriously compromised, there would have been many more such approaches to statutory processes for relief. Or if civil courts had been less flexible in allowing towns time and leeway in approaching their sewage pollution suits and problems, might more general legislation have been introduced to protect them by overriding or replacing common law precepts? Had the pressure from towns to change statutory law in general to protect them from nuisance injunctions become irresistible, this might have provided an example of Demsetz's thesis in action.

But Wolverhampton's history also contains examples of other strategies seen in others of the case histories that have been considered. Whether the sale of land, farms and mills by the plaintiffs (for example by Giffard in 1893–4) might constitute evidence of the presence of negotiated, Coasian-type strategies is arguable, but must remain moot. Certainly there is much evidence of the unwillingness of the courts to apply strict remedies to enforce decisions that might be seen as economically inefficient, as Posner hypothesised. Further, for Wolverhampton, there were numerous instances of benefit-of-the-doubt being allowed to the town and numerous suspensions granted by the court so as to allow the dispute to persist over a surprisingly long period, here approaching twenty-five years. Again, as is common to many of the disputes instanced, the court acted as a go-between at points to encourage mutual negotiation for a settlement between the parties. And the Wolverhampton history contains clear evidence of the court acting in a supervisory capacity, specifying improving engineering works, requiring outside engineers to be consulted and ensuring experts provided continuing guidance to the town and reports back to the court.

---

[71]   Letter from Hearne to Giffard, 17 January 1894, *Giffard Family Archives*, D5827/2/6/38.

Chapter 11

Conclusions

'How odd it is that anyone should not see that all observations must be for or against some view if it is to be of any service' (Charles Darwin, 1861).[1]

At the centre of this study has been a series of reports on the historical context and outcomes of civil court actions for a set of Victorian towns in each one of which an example of the river pollution dilemma and its consequences has been shown. The cases have illustrated the process of increasing urbanisation and requirements for better sanitation for town-dwellers, including for the many ill-housed urban poor, that had produced new and expanded sewer networks, but had also resulted in the offensive defilement of local rivers from the resultant outflows of sewage effluent. Numbers of complaints from affected parties downriver produced a sizeable volume of actions at civil law for nuisance brought against the responsible sewage and sanitary authorities – and the complainants ranged from millers, through comfortable middle-class professionals, to small and large farmers and aristocratic landowners. Typically, we have seen the civil courts finding the towns liable under nuisance and issuing injunctive orders requiring abatement of the nuisance.

The state of sewage engineering at the time, and well into the twentieth century, however, was such that, at best, and for most situations, only partial physical abatement of the nuisance was possible by using the best (sewage farm irrigation) methods available to sewage authorities. Peremptory closure of sewage networks or sewage outlets into rivers would have had serious social consequences in the affected towns. The question was, therefore: how were the requirements of the civil law on nuisance, to the benefit of small numbers of rural landholders, to be reconciled with the provision and maintenance of healthy sanitary conditions for the vastly more numerous populations of towns, often demonstrably poor and disadvantaged? This was the river pollution dilemma.

As has been seen, most of the chapters have examined, case by case, the context and histories of river sewage and related river pollution disputes where nuisance liability led to the issue of injunctive orders. Special attention has been paid to the post-litigation history of events. These case studies have shown a number of means and strategies by which the disputes behind the river pollution dilemma were, in practice, tackled or settled. These means can be briefly summarised as: court

---

[1] Letter to Henry Fawcett, 18 September 1861, Darwin Correspondence Project, Cambridge University.

management and supervision of partial abatement; mutual private negotiation and settlement; diversion of the nuisance; and obtaining statutory exemption.

Court management and supervision of partial abatement

The cases of Leeds and Barnsley are examples where, following the initial liability finding, the issuing of a series of repeated delayed injunctions and contingent orders shows Chancery acting as a managerial or supervisory authority, ensuring that the town worked towards setting up abatement processes. At Leeds, extensions to the time limit on delayed injunctions stretched the process over five years, with periodic reporting of progress to Chancery and the relators, and only when Leeds was convinced that no further legal proceedings would ensue did the town, on its own decision not to pursue more extensions, allow the court injunction to come into force. At Barnsley a similar process is evident: here there were twelve returns to court and twelve extensions allowed by Chancery over a ten-year-long period before the injunction actually came into force, again when Barnsley was confident its actions would not violate the terms of the order. For neither Leeds nor Barnsley can strong cases be made that fully effective abatement did take place.

Further examples have been presented of case histories where there exists even more explicit evidence of a managerial/supervisory role taken by the court, with the court underwriting and even invoking what amounted to contingent injunctions or consent orders , specifying the future actions the local authority was required to take. One such example occurred at Leamington Spa where the court produced a Chief Clerk at Chancery's certificate containing instructions about how Leamington's treatment works had to be altered; and which if fulfilled would have headed off the complainant's injunction request. Another example appeared during Wolverhampton's arbitration hearing where detailed improvements required at the sewage works were specified. The court's employment of delayed injunctions and contingent orders and injunctions often afforded considerable leeway to offending towns, by upholding the formal liability-determining side of the judicial process while softening the effective remedial-corrective aspects.

Mutual private negotiation and settlement

It was also possible for disputant parties to come to private agreements leading to the withdrawal of the suit from the legal process. This will end the dispute and requires no action at all by the court itself. The agreement may or may not involve a monetary payment from one party to the other, and may or may not include a requirement relating to the physical abatement of the nuisance that led to the dispute. Such a solution is often associated with the economic arguments allied with the Coase theorem. Birmingham's seemingly interminable dispute with Adderley contains repeated evidence of private bargaining (both completed and not) at a number of points and was finally ended by a private arrangement, apparently completely independent of court process. The dispute over Wood's bleachworks near Harrogate was ended by Harrogate's purchase of both the freehold and lease of the bleachworks itself to forestall further legal involvement in a dispute that had stretched over more than six years. And the early water pollution dispute between Legh and the St Helens Canal and Railway Company presents a straightforward example of a negotiated solution to a dispute where private agreements involving monetary settlements were settled and signed even before any court hearing took place. No promise of any wastewater treatment or physical pollution abatement was part of either the Harrogate or the St Helens Canal settlement agreement. Abatement of the legal nuisance does not imply abatement of the physical nuisance.

Diversion of the Nuisance

Faced by a complaint from a riverside resident that their wastewater is causing a nuisance, it is tempting for defendants to react by trying to rearrange their waste disposal processes to avoid or bypass the complainant's property. Sewage authorities have, surprisingly often, seriously considered simply lengthening their sewage disposal pipelines to send sewage effluent to enter the river at a point away from the offended complainant. Birmingham's doomed choice of Dunton for a putative sewage farm must have been influenced by its being downstream of Adderley's Hams Hall. At Northampton, the sewage authorities diverted their culverts and pipes on three separate occasions to move the sewerage outflow away from a succession of complaining millers, further and further along the River Nene. In the water pollution dispute between Pennington and the Brinsop Hall Coal Company, the colliery company abated their nuisance by establishing a new mile-and-a-half-long wastepipe system that diverted its wastewater material away from the Borsdane Brook, to fall into an entirely different watercourse. Again, by diverting offending material in this way, the defending party is able to abate and relieve the legal nuisance and solve the legal side of the river pollution dilemma. But the physical pollution and polluting materials remain, albeit removed to another geographical place.

Obtaining Statutory Exemption

The threat of civil action over sewage nuisance, or any other tort, can be offset by obtaining Parliamentary grant of a statutory exemption to override existing common law rules. This was, uniquely, the strategy employed at Wolverhampton. When the number of civil claims over sewage nuisance became, the town believed, unbearable, the town successfully obtained a Parliamentary Act that gave the authorities protection from future civil court actions for sewage pollution nuisance. The obtaining of statutory powers to provide such exemption from the common law rules on nuisance would also exempt a town from the necessity of actually abating its pollution nuisance.

All of the case studies and disputes discussed in previous chapters, as well as other sewage nuisance disputes not extensively described here, fit into one at least of these categories. The categories are not mutually exclusive, and, as has become clear, some of the case studies, like Birmingham and Wolverhampton, over the course of their histories, can be seen to illustrate more than one of the generalisations.

It is also important to recognise that, over all the investigations where the pursuit of the context and subsequent history of sewage pollution nuisance disputes cases has been possible, some possibilities have failed to appear. These absences are also illuminating. Of especial note is that, in no case was a sanitary authority actually sequestered to an extent and for a long enough period of time for its sewerage activities to be seriously compromised. For Banbury a sequestration order was authorised but no writs were served or delivered. At Tunbridge Wells and Leamington Spa, where sequestration writs were served on town officers, the actual periods of effective sequestration lasted little more than days, and there was no discernible effect on their sanitation activities and processes. Further, in no case was a sanitary authority ordered peremptorily or required by the courts immediately to close down its sewage discharges into the rivers.

One conclusion that may be drawn from the series of case studies is that nuisance law in the civil courts is, by its very nature, fundamentally and functionally ill-equipped to play the role of society's protector of the environment: even were this to be desired. This is no consequence of bias or ideological bent on the part of the courts of law; nor, on the evidence, can it be attributed to such as the protection of one interest or class in society at the expense of another. The civil court's practical and day-to-day duty is to act as a conduit through which disputes are settled. At base, the process of the civil law of nuisance requires an aggrieved party to attend and present a complaint and the continuance of the case requires the continued presence of an aggrieved complainant. Satisfying the complainant to the extent that the complainant withdraws the suit will end the participation of the civil court, even when no abatement of the physical cause of the legal complaint is evident. And this is what we have seen to occur, periodically, among the river pollution disputes. Negotiation between the parties with one party buying off the complaint of the other ('purchasing property rights') fully settles the legal nuisance while having no necessary effect on the level of the polluting activity. Diverting sewage or waste effluent away from a complainant to some other place will presumably fully satisfy the complainant but again without necessarily having any effect on the amount of pollutant entering the environment. Parliament can bestow special privileges exempting polluting parties from violations under civil law. Legal disputes can end while the physical source of the dispute is still extant.

That the civil law system has such an inherent flaw in pursuit of, for example, river environment protection, might lead one to conclude that any success that may be perceived as derived from nuisance law in reducing excessive amounts of pollution should be viewed as a bonus worthy of celebration. With due regard to the warning of Ogus and Richardson that 'an analysis of the efficiency of the nuisance action as an instrument of pollution control presupposes an agreed definition of "pollution"', [2] it would be difficult to conclude, from the above case studies, other than the intervention of the courts was sometimes able to harry and cajole and threaten Victorian local authorities into setting up and improving sanitary arrangements and sewage treatment works. But even where the courts 'managed' abatement, improvements were only possible to the limits of the available technology. The overall effect by no means eliminated, but did, to an extent, reduce the general unpleasantness in the rivers concerned. For the time period considered, Victorian sewage treatment engineering never proved very effective and the state of the rivers remained (on absolute if not relative measure) wholly disgusting. Nevertheless it would be unfair to deny to civil law any effect in reducing whatever level of *excessive* pollution would have existed in the absence of river pollution nuisance suits. And the counter-factual standard is important. Evidence of even partial successes attributable to the application of nuisance law should not be ignored.

That excessive levels of pollution of the environment can persist even in the presence of a civil law of nuisance has not escaped comment and has long been a source of criticism. From the legal side:

> Nuisance law has never really reflected a concern for environmental protection as such. The primary focus of nuisance has been to define the rights and limitations attaching to the enjoyment of private property. Environmental damage is only relevant in so far as it poses a threat of harm to someone's proprietary interests. The wrong lies in the violation of property rights not in the destruction of the environment.[3]

For the economist, the argument would contend that the presence of transactions costs, free riding and system inflexibilities would result in too few public nuisance actions being pursued, with resultant unresolved external effects and an outcome for the environment displaying undesirably excessive levels of pollution.

There has also been a revived debate over Victorian nuisance law which originally arose from the proposition that special and extra reasons are required to explain why the *liability* decisions of civil nuisance law did not fully protect the environment and more fully hamper Victorian industrialisation.[4] In view of the evidence from the case studies above, it is clear that the influence of the application

---

[2]   Ogus and Richardson, 'Economics and the Environment', 288.

[3]   Joanne Conaghan and Wade Mansell, *The Wrongs of Tort*, 2nd edn (London: Pluto, 1999), 150.

[4]   Brenner, 'Nuisance Law and the Industrial Revolution', 403–33; McLaren, 'Nuisance Law', 155–221; Pontin, 'Nuisance Law and the Industrial Revolution', 1010–36.

of the common law of nuisance on the social condition and economic history of Victorian England cannot be determined by examining only court decisions on where liability lies, while ignoring basic questions of how legal remedies were being enforced and how, in practice, disputes came to an end.

To protect Britain's rivers more effectively from the ravages of industry and sewage the Victorians well knew the limitations of the civil law on nuisance. For the rivers, rather than civil law, statutory law was needed. And the Victorians were, moreover, perfectly capable of discerning the new regulatory framework that would be required to properly supply this protection. All this was outlined in the work, report and recommendations of the excellent Royal Commission on Rivers Pollution Prevention between 1866 and 1874. Enforcing the Royal Commission's recommendations would have seen statutory backing for the setting up of river-basin-wide authorities with independent inspectorates able to enforce, with penalties, violations of specified purity standards for materials being deposited in local rivers.

In the event however, the reforms urged by the Royal Commission failed to be implemented in the river protection statute that followed it, the disappointing 1876 Rivers Pollution Prevention Act. But the ideas of the commission can nevertheless be seen in the history of new institutions and pollution controls that were brought in for the UK over the course of the century that followed.[5] The major intellectual power of the Royal Commission, Edward Frankland, even knew that the essential key to the sewage problem was better technology. And it was, in the end, the new, better technology of biologically-based treatment regimes, rather than any legal changes, that has played much the greatest part in any success achieved since in defusing, dehorning and even solving the river pollution dilemma.

In considering a particular policy, even when the overall outcome on society is undeniably positive, some sectors of society may, nevertheless, be disadvantaged, absolutely, by the introduction of the policy. Considerations concerning the balance of effects between different parts of society are fraught with difficulty. It is often argued that in evaluating the impact of some new project that has effects on the environment, the welfare of future generations is typically undervalued, and the welfare of the present generation overweighed. The result is that a greater number of more environmentally-harmful projects are undertaken, to the benefit of contemporary society, with the environment becoming more damaged than would occur if the opinions of future generations about the environment they would inherit were to be available for inclusion. Along such lines, an unconventional, even contrary, opinion can arise in considering the sanitary conditions of life in the Victorian cities, especially for the urban disadvantaged. If the author might speak for himself: rather than claiming his welfare has been overly and unfairly harmed by the effects on his environment of the Victorian industrialisation project, he would say (along with, no doubt, many of his fellow 'future generation') that

---

    5   Samuel H. Jenkins, 'British water pollution control', *Environmental Science and Technology*, 4 (1970): 204–9.

he would willingly have allowed his level of welfare to have been reduced if by so doing the fearful conditions of the urban poor of Victorian Britain could have been relieved. But history cannot be rerun, only researched.

Bibliography

Manuscript Sources

Banbury Borough Archive, Oxfordshire Record Office, Oxford, BOR2/X.

Barnsley Corporation, Barnsley Archive and Local Studies, Barnsley Library, B628.

Birmingham Corporation Archive, Birmingham Central Library, Birmingham, BCC.

Court of Chancery Records, UK National Archives, Kew, C15, C16, C32, C33, J15.

Giffard Family Archive, Staffordshire Record Office, Stafford, D590, D5827.

Leamington Spa Local Board Archive, Warwickshire Record Office, Warwick, CR1563, C1886.

Leeds City Library, Local History Collection, Leeds, L352.63.

Leeds Corporation and County Borough Council, West Yorkshire Archive Service, Leeds, LL2, LLC9.

Legh Family of Lyme Park Archive, Greater Manchester Record Office, Manchester, E17/123/1–2.

Northampton Improvement Board Archive, Northampton Record Office, Northampton, 14/9–10.

Norton Archive, Birmingham Central Library, Birmingham, MS 917.

Royal Tunbridge Wells Archives, Museum and Art Gallery, Royal Tunbridge Wells, (uncatalogued).

West Riding of Yorkshire Rivers Board Archive, West Yorkshire Archive Service, Wakefield, C1001.

Wolverhampton City Archives, Wolverhampton, C-WCA/1891/5.

Printed Secondary Sources

Alchian, Armen A. 'Some Economics of Property Rights'. *Il Politico*, 30 (1965): 816–29.

Amey, Geoffrey. *The Collapse of the Dale Dyke Dam, 1864*. London: Cassell, 1974.

Anderson, Terry L. and Peter J. Hill. 'Cowboys and Contracts'. *Journal of Legal Studies*, 31 (2002): 489–514.

Ardern, Edward and William T. Lockett. 'Experiments on the oxidation of sewage without the aid of filters'. *Journal of the Society of Chemical Industry*, 33 (1914): 523–39.

Atiyah, Patrick S. 'Liability for Railway Nuisance in the English Common Law: A Historical Footnote'. *Journal of Law and Economics*, 23 (1980): 191–6.

Bailey, Catherine. *Black Diamonds*. London: Penguin Books, 2008.

Baker, John Hamilton. *An Introduction to English Legal History*. London: Butterworths, 1990.

Baker, Robert. 'Report on the Condition of the Residences of the Labouring Classes in the Town of Leeds in the West Riding of York'. In *Sanitary Report*, edited by Edwin Chadwick, 348–409. Report of Poor Law Commissioners, No. 007, 1842.

Barker, Theo Cardwell and John Raymond Harris. *A Merseyside Town in the Industrial Revolution: St. Helens, 1750–1900*. London: Frank Cass, 1993.

Barnsby, George. *A History of Housing in Wolverhampton 1750 to 1975*. Wolverhampton: Integrated Publishing Services, 1976.

Bartle, J.C. *Sale of the Swillington Estate*. Leeds, 1935. Leeds City Library, Local History Collection, Q Yorkshire SW1 333.

Bateman, John. *The Great Landowners of Great Britain and Ireland*. London: Harrison, 1883.

'Bateman, John F La Trobe, 1810–89'. *Institute of Chartered Engineers Minutes of Proceedings*, 97 (1889): 392–8.

Bator, Francis M. 'The Anatomy of Market Failure'. *Quarterly Journal of Economics*, 72 (1958): 351–79.

Bator, Francis M. 'The Simple Analytics of Welfare Maximization'. *American Economic Review*, 47 (1957): 22–59.

Binnie, Geoffrey Morse. *Early Victorian Water Engineers*. London: Thomas Telford Ltd, 1981.

'Birmingham New Sewage Works'. *The British Architect*, 6 October (1899): 248–9.

Breeze, Lawrence E. *The British Experience with River Pollution, 1865–1876*. New York: Peter Lang, 1993.

Brenner, Joel F. 'Nuisance Law and the Industrial Revolution'. *Journal of Legal Studies*, 3 (1974): 403–33.

Briggs, Asa. *Victorian Cities*. Harmondsworth: Penguin Books, 1975.

Brown, Cynthia. *Northampton, 1835–1985: Shoe Town, New Town*. Chichester: Phillimore & Co, 1990.

Brundage, Anthony. *England's Prussian Minister: Edwin Chadwick and the Politics of Government Growth, 1832–1854*. Pennsylvania: Pennsylvania State University Press, 1988.

Bunce, John Thackray. *History of the Corporation of Birmingham II*. Birmingham: Birmingham Corporation, 1885.

Butler, Michael R. and Robert F. Garnett. 'Teaching the Coase Theorem: Are We Getting it Right?' *Atlantic Economic Journal*, 31 (2003): 133–45.

Calabresi, Guido and A. Douglas Melamed. 'Property Rules, Liability Rules and Inalienability: One View of the Cathedral'. *Harvard Law Review*, 85 (1972): 1089–128.

Cave, Lyndon F. *Royal Leamington Spa: A History*. Chichester: Phillimore, 2009.

Chadwick, Edwin. *Sanitary Report: Report on an Inquiry into the Sanitary Condition of the Labouring Population of Great Britain*. Report of Poor Law Commissioners, Nos 006, 007, 008, 1842.

Chalkin, C.W. *Royal Tunbridge Wells – A History*. Chichester: Phillimore, 2008.

Chayes, Abram. 'The Role of the Judge in Public Law Litigation'. *Harvard Law Review*, 89 (1976): 1281–316.

Childe-Pemberton, William S. *The Life of Lord Norton*. London: John Murray, 1909.

Coase, Ronald H. 'Law and Economics and AW Brian Simpson'. *Journal of Legal Studies*, 25 (1996): 103–19.

Coase, Ronald H. 'The Problem of Social Cost'. *Journal of Law and Economics*, 3 (1960): 1–44.

Cocks, Raymond. 'Victorian Foundations?' In *Environmental Protection and the Common Law*, edited by John Lowry and Rod Edmunds. Oxford: Hart Publishing, 2000.

Conaghan, Joanne and Wade Mansell. *The Wrongs of Tort*. London: Pluto, 1999.

Cooter, Robert, and Thomas Ulen. *Law and Economics*. Addison-Wesley, 2000.

Corrigan, W.J. 'Sanitation under the Ancient Minoan Civilisation'. *Canadian Medical Association Journal*, 27 (1932): 77–8.

Crellin, J.K. 'Calvert, Frederick Crace- (1819–1873)'. *Oxford Dictionary of National Biography*, Oxford University Press, 2004: doi:10.1093/ref:odnb/4419.

Dagnall, Ron. *The History of Muncaster Hall*. Rainford: Rainford Civic Society, 1988.

Demsetz, Harold. 'Toward a Theory of Property Rights'. *American Economic Review*, 57 (1967): 347–59.

Denton, John Bailey. *Sewage Disposal: Ten Years' Experience*. London: Spon, 1885.

Dilks, David. *Neville Chamberlain*. Cambridge: Cambridge University Press, 1984.

Eltis, Walter. *Lord Overstone and the Establishment of British Nineteenth-Century Monetary Orthodoxy*. Oxford: University of Oxford Discussion Papers in Economic and Social History 42, 2001.

Escritt, Leonard Bushby, and Sidney Frank Rich. *The Work of the Sanitary Engineer*. London: Macdonald and Evans, 1949.

Farnsworth, Ward. 'Do Parties to Nuisance Cases Bargain after Judgment? A Glimpse Inside the Cathedral'. *University of Chicago Law Review*, 66 (1999): 373–436.

Finer, Samuel Edward. *The Life and Times of Sir Edwin Chadwick*. London: Methuen, 1952.

Flinn, M.W. 'Introduction'. In *Report on the Sanitary Conditions of the Labouring Population of Great Britain by Edwin Chadwick, 1842*, edited by M.W. Flinn Edinburgh: Edinburgh University Press, 1965.

'Frankland, Sir Edward, 1825–99'. *Institute of Chartered Engineers Minutes of Proceedings*, 139 (1900): 343–9.

Fraser, Derek. *Power and Authority in the Victorian City*. Oxford: Blackwell, 1979.

Friedman, David D. *Law's Order: What Economics Has to Do with Law and Why It Matters*. Princeton: Princeton University Press, 2001.

General Board of Health, (Henry Austin). *Report on the Means of Deodorizing and Utilizing the Sewage of Towns.* No. 2262, 1857.

Getches, David H. *Water Law in a Nutshell*. St. Paul, Minnesota: West Publishing Co, 1997.

Getzler, Joshua. *A History of Water Rights at Common Law*. Oxford: Oxford University Press, 2004.

Gill, Conrad. 'Birmingham under the Street Commissioners, 1769–1851'. *University of Birmingham Historical Journal*, 1 (1948): 255–87.

Gill, Conrad. *History of Birmingham, Manor and Borough to 1865*. London: Oxford University Press, 1952.

Glen, William Cunningham. *The Law Relating To The Public Health*. London: Butterworths, 1858.

Gooday, Graeme J.N. 'Playfair, Lyon, First Baron Playfair (1818–1898)'. *Oxford Dictionary of National Biography*, Oxford University Press, 2004: doi:10.1093/ref:odnb/22368.

Goodchild, John. *Golden Threads – Barnsley's Linen Industry in the 18th and 19th Century*. Wakefield: Wakefield Historical Publications, 1983.

Haddock, David D. and Lynne Kiesling. 'The Black Death and Property Rights'. *Journal of Legal Studies*, 31 (2002): 545–87.

Halliday, Stephen. *Making the Metropolis*. Derby: Breedon Books, 2003.

Halliday, Stephen. *The Great Stink of London*. Stroud: Sutton Publishing, 1999.

Hamlin, Christopher. *A Science of Impurity: Water Analysis in Nineteenth Century Britain*. Berkeley: University of California Press, 1990.

Hamlin, Christopher. 'Austin, Henry (1811/12–1861)'. *Oxford Dictionary of National Biography*, Oxford University Press, 2004: doi:10.1093/ref:odnb/40990.

Hamlin, Christopher. 'Edwin Chadwick and the Engineers, 1842–1854: Systems and Antisystems in the Pipe-and-Brick Sewers War'. *Technology and Culture*, 33 (1992): 680–709.

Hamlin, Christopher. 'Letheby, Henry (1816–1876)'. *Oxford Dictionary of National Biography*, Oxford University Press, 2004: doi:10.1093/ref:odnb/16520.

Hamlin, Christopher. 'Muddling in Bumbledom: On the Enormity of Large Sanitary Improvements in Four British Towns, 1855–1885'. *Victorian Studies*, 32 (1988): 55–83.

Hamlin, Christopher. *Public Health and Social Justice in the Age of Chadwick: Britain 1800–1854*. Cambridge: Cambridge University Press, 1998.

Hamlin, Christopher. 'Smith, (Robert) Angus (1817–1884)'. *Oxford Dictionary of National Biography*, Oxford University Press, 2004: doi:10.1093/ref:odnb/25893.

Hamlin, Christopher and Sally Sheard. 'Revolutions in Public Health: 1848, and 1998?' *British Medical Journal*, 317 (1998): 587–91.

Hardin, Garrett. 'The Tragedy of the Commons'. *Science*, 162 (1998): 1243–8.

Harding, Thomas Walter and Harrison W.H. *Report on Experiments in Sewage Disposal*. Leeds: Jowett and Sourry, 1905. Leeds City Library, Local History Collection, L352.63 L517.

'Harrison, John Thornhill, 1815–1891'. *Institute of Chartered Engineers Minutes of Proceedings*, 109 (1892): 405–7.

'Harrogate Sewage Farms, The'. *The British Architect*, 18 May (1877): 305.

Hassan, John. *A History of Water in Modern England and Wales*. Manchester: Manchester University Press, 1998.

Hawes, Richard. 'The Control of Alkali Pollution in St Helens 1862–1890'. *Environment and History*, 1 (1995): 159–71.

'Hawksley, Thomas, 1807–93'. *Institute of Chartered Engineers Minutes of Proceedings*, 117 (1894): 364–76.

Hennock, Ernest Peter. *Fit and Proper Persons*. London: Edward Arnold, 1973.

Hiley, Ernest Varvill. 'Birmingham City Government'. In *Birmingham Institutions*, edited by John Henry Muirhead, 87–139. Birmingham: Cornish, 1911.

Hodgson et al. 'Report on the State of the Public Health in the Borough of Birmingham'. In *Sanitary Report*, edited by Edwin Chadwick, 192–217, Report of Poor Law Commissioners, No. 007, 1842.

Howarth, William. *Wisdom's Law of Watercourses*. Crayford: Shaw & Sons, 1992.

Hunt, Tristram. *Building Jerusalem: The Rise and Fall of the Victorian City*. London: Phoenix, 2005.

Husband, Henry Aubrey. *Sanitary Law: A Digest of the Sanitary Acts of England and Wales*. Edinburgh: Livingstone, 1883.

Jenkins, Samuel H. 'British Water Pollution Control'. *Environmental Science and Technology*, 4 (1970): 204–9.

Jones, John Morris. *The Waters of Birmingham*. Birmingham: Birmingham Public Libraries, 1979.

Jones, Nicolette. *The Plimsoll Sensation*. London: Abacus, 2006.

Judd, Denis. *Radical Joe: A Life of Joseph Chamberlain*. London: Faber and Faber Ltd., 2010.

Kerly, Duncan M. *An Historical Sketch of the Equitable Jurisdiction of the Court of Chancery*. Cambridge: Cambridge University Press, 1890.

Kiralfy, Albert Kenneth Roland. *Potter's Historical Introduction to English Law*. London: Sweet & Maxwell, 1958.

'Lawson, John, 1824–73'. *Institute of Chartered Engineers Minutes of Proceedings*, 38 (1874): 315–7.

Leather, David. *Contractor Leather*. Ilkley: Leather Family History Society, 2002.

Leather, John Wignall. *Leeds Sewer Contracts*. Leeds: H.W. Walker, 1850. Leeds City Library, Local History Collection, L352.63 L483.

Lewis, Richard Albert. *Edwin Chadwick and the Public Health Movement*. London: Longmans, 1952.

Lijphart, Arend. 'Comparative Politics and the Comparative Method', *The American Political Science Review*, 65 (1971): 682–93.

Lobban, Michael. *The Common Law and English Jurisprudence 1760–1850*. London: Clarendon Press, 1991.

Local Government Board. *Fifteenth Report*. C.4844, 1886.

Local Government Board. *Sewage Disposal Report*. C.1410, 1876.

Lueck, Dean. 'The Extermination and Conservation of the American Bison'. *Journal of Legal Studies*, 31 (2002): 609–52.

Macmorran, James L. *Municipal Public Works and Planning in Birmingham 1852–1972*. Birmingham: City of Birmingham Public Works Committee, 1973.

Mason, Frank. *The Book of Wolverhampton*. Buckinghamshire: Barracuda, 1979.

Mason, Frank. *Wolverhampton: the Town Commissioners, 1777–1848*. Wolverhampton: Wolverhampton Public Libraries, 1976.

McCloskey, Dee N. 'The So-called Coase Theorem'. *Eastern Economic Journal*, 24 (1998): 367–71.

McLaren, John P. 'Nuisance Law and the Industrial Revolution – Some Lessons from Social History'. *Oxford Journal of Legal Studies*, 3(2) (1983): 155–221.

Medical Officer of the Privy Council. *Seventh Report*. No. 3484, 1865.

Mercuro, Nicholas and Steven G. Medema. *Economics and the Law*. Princeton: Princeton University Press, 1997.

Merrill, Thomas W. 'Introduction: the Demsetz Thesis and the Evolution of Property Rights'. *Journal of Legal Studies*, 31 (2002): 331–38.

Michael, William H. 'The Public Health Act, 1872: Its Defects and Suggested Amendments'. *The British Medical Journal*, 1(692) (1874): 443–6.

Michael, William H. *The Sanitary Acts*. London: H. Sweet, 1867.

Milson, Stroud F.C. *Historical Foundations of the Common Law*. London; Butterworths, 1981.

Montmorency, J.E.G. de. 'Adderley, Charles Bowyer, First Baron Norton (1814–1905)'. *Oxford Dictionary of National Biography*, Oxford University Press, 2004: doi:10.1093/ref:odnb/3034.

Montmorency, J.E.G. de. 'Fry, Sir Edward (1827–1918)'. *Oxford Dictionary of National Biography*, Oxford University Press, 2004: doi:10.1093/ref:odnb/33283.

O'Kane, Rosemary H.T. *Paths to Democracy: Revolution and Totalitarianism*. London: Routledge, 2004.

Ogus, Anthony I. and Genevra M. Richardson. 'Economics and the Environment: A Study of Private Nuisance'. *Cambridge Law Journal*, 26 (1977): 295–301.

Page, William (editor). 'The Borough of Northampton'. In *Victoria History of the County of Northampton*, 3, 1–67. Northampton: Northampton Borough Reprint, 1998.

Perin, Roberto Cavallo and Dario Casalini. 'Water Property Models as Sovereignty Prerogatives: European Legal Perspectives in Comparison'. *Water*, 2 (2010): 429–38.

Pettit, Phillip H. *Equity & the Law of Trusts*. Oxford: Oxford University Press, 2009.

Phillips, Anthony D.M. 'Denton, John Bailey (1814–1893)'. *Oxford Dictionary of National Biography*, Oxford University Press, 2004: doi:10.1093/ref:odnb/50168.

Pidcock, John Hyde. 'Northampton and its Sewage'. *The British Architect*, 69 (1875): 230–1.

Pontin, Ben. 'Nuisance Law and the Industrial Revolution: A Reinterpretation of Doctrine and Institutional Competence'. *The Modern Law Review*, 75 (2012): 1010–36.

Poor Law Commissioners. *Fifth Annual Report*. No. 239, 1839.

Poor Law Commissioners. *Fourth Annual Report*. No. 147, 1837–38.

Posner, Richard A. *Economic Analysis of Law*. Boston: Little Brown, 1972.

Posner, Richard A. 'The Law and Economics Movement'. *American Economic Review*, 77 (1987): 1–13.

Powell, J. Enoch. *Joseph Chamberlain*. London: Thames and Hudson Ltd., 1977.

'Pritchard, Edward 1838–1900'. *Institute of Chartered Engineers Minutes of Proceedings*, 141 (1900): 348–9.

'Rawlinson, Sir Robert, 1810–98'. *Institute of Chartered Engineers Minutes of Proceedings*, 134 (1898): 386–91.

Reed, Michael. 'Loyd, Samuel Jones, Baron Overstone (1796–1883)'. *Oxford Dictionary of National Biography*, Oxford University Press, 2004: doi:10.1093/ref:odnb/17115.

Registrar-General of Births, Deaths, and Marriages in England. *Twenty-Third Annual Report*. No. 2977, 1862.

Resnick, Judith. 'Managerial Judges'. *Harvard Law Review*, 96 (1982): 374–448.

Rosenthal, Leslie. 'Economic Efficiency, Nuisance, and Sewage: New Lessons from Attorney-General v. Council of the Borough of Birmingham, 1858–95'. *Journal of Legal Studies*, 36 (2007): 27–62.

Rosenthal, Leslie. 'Sewage Pollution of the Taff and the Merthyr Tydfil Local Board (1868–1871)'. *Merthyr Historian*, 23 (2012): 70–93.

Royal Commission on Health of Towns. *First Report*. No. 572, 1844.

Royal Commission on Health of Towns. *Second Report*. Nos 602, 610, 1845.

Royal Commission on Metropolitan Sewage Discharge. *Second Report*. C.4253, 1884–85.

Royal Commission on Rivers Pollution Prevention of 1865. *First Report* (River Thames). No. 3634, 1866.

Royal Commission on Rivers Pollution Prevention of 1865. *Second Report* (River Lee). No. 3835, 1867.

Royal Commission on Rivers Pollution Prevention of 1865. *Third Report* (Rivers Aire and Calder). No. 3850, 1867.

Royal Commission on Rivers Pollution Prevention of 1868, *First Report* (Rivers Mersey and Ribble). C.37, 1870.

Royal Commission on Rivers Pollution Prevention of 1868. *Second Report* (The ABC process). C.181, 1870.

Royal Commission on Rivers Pollution Prevention of 1868. *Third Report* (Woollen Manufactures Rivers). C.347, 1871.

Royal Commission on Rivers Pollution Prevention of 1868. *Fourth Report* (Scottish Rivers). C.603, 1872.

Royal Commission on Rivers Pollution Prevention of 1868. *Fifth Report* (Mining and Metal Manufactures Rivers). C.951, 1874.

Royal Commission on Rivers Pollution Prevention of 1868. *Sixth Report* (Water Supply). C.1112, 1874.

Royal Commission on Sewage Disposal. *Interim Report*. Cd. 685, 1901.

Royal Commission on Sewage Disposal. *Fifth Report*. Cd. 4279, 1908.

Royal Commission on Sewage Disposal, *Final Report*. Cd. 7821, 1914–16.

Royal Commission on Sewage of Towns. *First Report*. No. 2262, 1857.

Royal Commission on Sewage of Towns. *Second Report*. No. 2882, 1861.

Royal Commission on Sewage of Towns. *Third Report*. No. 3472, 1865.

Royal Sanitary Commission. *First Report*. No. 4218, 1868–69

Royal Sanitary Commission. *Second Report*. C.281, 1871.

Salzman, L.F. (editor). 'The Borough of Leamington Spa'. In *Victoria History of the County of Warwick*, 6, 155–61. Oxford: Oxford University Press, 1951.

Sandler, Ross and David Schoenbrod. 'The Supreme Court, Democracy and Institutional Reform Litigation'. *New York Law School Law Review*, 49 (2004–5): 915–42.

Sandler, Ross and David Schoenbrod. *Democracy by Decree: What Happens When Courts Run Government*. New Haven and London: Yale University Press; 2003.

Schultz, Stanley K. and Clay McShane. 'To Engineer the Metropolis: Sewers, Sanitation, and City Planning in Late-Nineteenth-Century America'. *The Journal of American History*, 65 (1978): 389–411.

Select Committee on Metropolitan Sewage Manure. *Report*. No. 474, 1846.

Select Committee on Sewage (Metropolis). *Report*. No. 487, 1864.

Sellers, David. *Beneath our Feet: The Story of Sewerage in Leeds*. Leeds: Department of Highways and Transportation, Leeds City Council, 1997.

Shavell, Steven. *Foundations of Economic Analysis of the Law*. Cambridge: Harvard University Press, 2004.

Sheail, John. 'The Institutional Development of River Management in Yorkshire'. *The Science of the Total Environment*, 194/5 (1997): 225–34.

Simpson, A.W. Brian. 'An Addendum'. *Journal of Legal Studies*, 25 (1996): 99–101.

Simpson, A.W. Brian. 'Coase v Pigou Re-examined'. *Journal of Legal Studies*, 25 (1996): 53–97.

Simpson, A.W. Brian. *Leading Cases in the Common Law*. Oxford: Oxford University Press, 1995.

Simpson, A.W. Brian. 'The Story of *Sturges v Bridgman*: the Resolution of Land Use Disputes Between Neighbors'. In *Property Stories*, edited by Gerald Korngold and Andrew P. Morriss, 9–40. New York: Foundation Press, 2004.

Skocpol, Theda. 'Emerging Agendas and Recurrent Strategies in Historical Sociology'. In *Visions and Method in Historical Sociology*, edited by Theda Skocpol, 356–91. Cambridge: Cambridge University Press, 1984.

Slaney, Robert A. 'Report on Birmingham'. In *Second Report*, Royal Commission on Health of Towns, 1–120, No. 602, 1845.

Smith, Henry E. 'Exclusion Versus Governance: Two Strategies For Delineating Property Rights'. *Journal of Legal Studies*, 31 (2002): 453–87.

'Smith, John Pigott, 1798–1861'. *Institute of Chartered Engineers Minutes of Proceedings*, 21 (1862): 594–5.

Spencer, John R. 'Public Nuisance – a Critical Examination.' *Cambridge Law Journal*, 48 (1989): 55–84.

Stanbridge, Henry Herbert. *History of Sewage Treatment in Britain*, 12 vols. Maidstone: Institute of Water Pollution Control, 1976–7.

Steele, David. 'Wood, Charles, First Viscount Halifax (1800–1885)'. *Oxford Dictionary of National Biography*, Oxford University Press, 2004: doi:10.1093/ref:odnb/29865.

Stephen, Frank H. *The Economics of the Law*. Hemel Hempstead: Wheatsheaf, 1988.

Stephens, W. B. (editor). 'The City of Birmingham'. In *Victoria History of the County of Warwick*, 7, 318–53. Oxford: Oxford University Press, 1964.

Stigler, George. *The Theory of Price*, 3rd edn. New York: Macmillan, 1966.

Swanson, Timothy and Andreas Kontoleon. 'Nuisance'. In *Encyclopedia of Law and Economics*, edited by Boudewijn Bouckaert and Gerrit de Geest, 380–402. Cheltenham: Edward Elgar, 2000.

Taggart, Michael. *Private Property and Abuse of Rights in Victorian England: The Story of Edward Pickles and the Bradford Water Supply*. Oxford: Oxford University Press, 2002.

Taylor, Henry J. *New Sewage Purification Works*. Barnsley: Barnsley Corporation, 1909. Barnsley Archive and Local Studies, Barnsley Library, B628.3.

Thornburg, Elizabeth G. 'The Managerial Judge goes to Trial'. *University of Richmond Law Review*, 44 (2010): 1261–325.

Thorne, Robert. 'Fox, Sir Charles (1810–1874)'. *Oxford Dictionary of National Biography*, Oxford University Press, 2004: doi:10.1093/ref:odnb/10022.

Tromans, Stephen. 'Nuisance – Prevention or Payment'. *Cambridge Law Journal*, 41 (1982): 87–109.

Tyack, Geoffrey. *Warwickshire Country Houses*. Chichester: Phillimore & Co, 1994.

Vince, Charles Anthony. *History of the Corporation of Birmingham IV*. Birmingham: Birmingham Corporation, 1923.

Walker, Harold Hyde. *History of Harrogate under the Improvement Commissioners 1841–1884*. Harrogate: Manor Place Press, 1986.

Ward, John T. 'The Earls Fitzwilliam and the Wentworth Woodhouse Estate in the Nineteenth Century'. *Bulletin of Economic Research*, 12 (1960): 19–27.

Wohl, Anthony S. *Endangered Lives: Public Health in Victorian Britain*. London: J.M. Dent, 1983.

Yalcintas, Altug. *The 'Coase Theorem' vs. Coase Theorem Proper: How an error emerged and why it remained uncorrected so long*. 2010, available at: http://dx.doi.org/10.2139/ssrn.1628163.

Zywicki, Todd J. and Edward Peter Stringham. 'Common Law and Economic Efficiency'. *George Mason Law & Economics Research Paper*, 10–43 (2010), available at SSRN: http://ssrn.com/abstract=1673968.

Index

Modern Economic and Social History Series

General Editor
Derek H. Aldcroft, University Fellow, Department of Economic and
Social History, University of Leicester, UK

Derek H. Aldcroft
Studies in the Interwar European Economy
1 85928 360 8 (1997)

Michael J. Oliver
Whatever Happened to Monetarism?
Economic Policy Making and Social Learning in the United Kingdom
Since 1979
1 85928 433 7 (1997)

R. Guerriero Wilson
Disillusionment or New Opportunities?
The Changing Nature of Work in Offices,Glasgow 1880–1914
1 84014 276 6 (1998)

Roger Lloyd-Jones and M.J. Lewis with the assistance of M. Eason
Raleigh and the British Bicycle Industry
An Economic and Business History, 1870–1960
1 85928 457 4 (2000)

Barry Stapleton and James H. Thomas
Gales
A Study in Brewing, Business and Family History
0 7546 0146 3 (2000)

Derek H. Aldcroft and Michael J. Oliver
Trade Unions and the Economy: 1870–2000
1 85928 370 5 (2000)

Ted Wilson
Battles for the Standard
Bimetallism and the Spread of the Gold Standard in the Nineteenth Century
1 85928 436 1 (2000)

Patrick Duffy
The Skilled Compositor, 1850–1914
An Aristocrat Among Working Men
0 7546 0255 9 (2000)

Robert Conlon and John Perkins
Wheels and Deals
The Automotive Industry in Twentieth-Century Australia
0 7546 0405 5 (2001)

Sam Mustafa
Merchants and Migrations
Germans and Americans in Connection, 1776–1835
0 7546 0590 6 (2001)

Bernard Cronin
Technology, Industrial Conflict and the Development of Technical
Education in 19th-Century England
0 7546 0313 X (2001)

Andrew Popp
Business Structure, Business Culture and the Industrial District
The Potteries, c. 1850–1914
0 7546 0176 5 (2001)

Scott Kelly
The Myth of Mr Butskell
The Politics of British Economic Policy, 1950–55
0 7546 0604 X (2002)

Michael Ferguson
The Rise of Management Consulting in Britain
0 7546 0561 2 (2002)

Alan Fowler
Lancashire Cotton Operatives and Work, 1900–1950
A Social History of Lancashire Cotton Operatives in the Twentieth Century
0 7546 0116 1 (2003)

John F. Wilson and Andrew Popp (eds)
Industrial Clusters and Regional Business Networks in England, 1750–1970
0 7546 0761 5 (2003)

John Hassan
The Seaside, Health and the Environment in England and Wales since 1800
1 84014 265 0 (2003)

Marshall J. Bastable
Arms and the State
Sir William Armstrong and the Remaking of British Naval Power, 1854–1914
0 7546 3404 3 (2004)

Robin Pearson
Insuring the Industrial Revolution
Fire Insurance in Great Britain, 1700–1850
0 7546 3363 2 (2004)

Andrew Dawson
Lives of the Philadelphia Engineers
Capital, Class and Revolution, 1830–1890
0 7546 3396 9 (2004)

Lawrence Black and Hugh Pemberton (eds)
An Affluent Society?
Britain's Post-War 'Golden Age' Revisited
0 7546 3528 7 (2004)

Joseph Harrison and David Corkill
Spain
A Modern European Economy
0 7546 0145 5 (2004)

Ross E. Catterall and Derek H. Aldcroft (eds)
Exchange Rates and Economic Policy in the 20th Century
1 84014 264 2 (2004)

Armin Grünbacher
Reconstruction and Cold War in Germany
The Kreditanstalt für Wiederaufbau (1948–1961)
0 7546 3806 5 (2004)

Till Geiger
Britain and the Economic Problem of the Cold War
The Political Economy and the Economic Impact of the
British Defence Effort, 1945–1955
0 7546 0287 7 (2004)

Anne Clendinning
Demons of Domesticity
Women and the English Gas Industry, 1889–1939
0 7546 0692 9 (2004)

Timothy Cuff
The Hidden Cost of Economic Development
The Biological Standard of Living in Antebellum Pennsylvania
0 7546 4119 8 (2005)

Julian Greaves
Industrial Reorganization and Government Policy in Interwar Britain
0 7546 0355 5 (2005)

Derek H. Aldcroft
Europe's Third World
The European Periphery in the Interwar Years
0 7546 0599 X (2006)

James P. Huzel
The Popularization of Malthus in Early Nineteenth-Century England
Martineau, Cobbett and the Pauper Press
0 7546 5427 3 (2006)

Richard Perren
Taste, Trade and Technology
The Development of the International Meat Industry since 1840
978 0 7546 3648 9 (2006)

Roger Lloyd-Jones and M.J. Lewis
Alfred Herbert Ltd and the British Machine Tool Industry,
1887–1983
978 0 7546 0523 2 (2006)

Anthony Howe and Simon Morgan (eds)
Rethinking Nineteenth-Century Liberalism
Richard Cobden Bicentenary Essays
978 0 7546 5572 5 (2006)

Espen Moe
Governance, Growth and Global Leadership
The Role of the State in Technological Progress, 1750–2000
978 0 7546 5743 9 (2007)

Peter Scott
Triumph of the South
A Regional Economic History of Early Twentieth Century Britain
978 1 84014 613 4 (2007)

David Turnock
Aspects of Independent Romania's Economic History with
Particular Reference to Transition for EU Accession
978 0 7546 5892 4 (2007)

David Oldroyd
Estates, Enterprise and Investment at the Dawn of the Industrial Revolution
Estate Management and Accounting in the North-East of England, c.1700–1780
978 0 7546 3455 3 (2007)

Ralf Roth and Günter Dinhobl (eds)
Across the Borders
Financing the World's Railways in the Nineteenth and Twentieth Centuries
978 0 7546 6029 3 (2008)

Vincent Barnett and Joachim Zweynert (eds)
Economics in Russia
Studies in Intellectual History
978 0 7546 6149 8 (2008)

Raymond E. Dumett (ed.)
Mining Tycoons in the Age of Empire, 1870–1945
Entrepreneurship, High Finance, Politics and Territorial Expansion
978 0 7546 6303 4 (2009)

Peter Dorey
British Conservatism and Trade Unionism, 1945–1964
978 0 7546 6659 2 (2009)

Shigeru Akita and Nicholas J. White (eds)
The International Order of Asia in the 1930s and 1950s
978 0 7546 5341 7 (2010)

Myrddin John Lewis, Roger Lloyd-Jones, Josephine Maltby
and Mark David Matthews
Personal Capitalism and Corporate Governance
British Manufacturing in the First Half of the Twentieth Century
978 0 7546 5587 9 (2010)